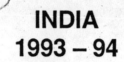

# INDIA
# 1993 – 94

INDIA
1993 - 94

# INDIA
## 1993 – 94

## INDIAN EXPRESS – VANS

**FOCUS**
**POPULAR PRAKASHAN**
**BOMBAY**

**POPULAR PRAKASHAN PVT. LTD.**
35-C, PANDIT MADAN MOHAN MALAVIYA MARG,
OPP. 'ROCHE', TARDEO, BOMBAY - 400 034

First Published October 1993

(4033)
ISBN 81-7154-773-7

PRINTED IN INDIA
Typeset by Pro Computer Services, 45, Rameshwar Prasad,
Veer Savarkar Marg, Prabhadevi, Bombay- 400 025 , Printed
by Gopsons Papers Pvt. Ltd., A-28, Sector IX, Noida and
Published by Ramdas Bhatkal for Popular Prakashan Pvt. Ltd.
35-C, Pandit Madan Mohan Malaviya Marg, Opp. 'Roche',
Tardeo, Bombay - 400 034

# CONTENTS

## LIST OF TABLES

**1. Population** 1

1.1 Growth of Population of India: 1901 to 1991 1

1.2 States of India : Population, Area and Density : 1991 3

1.3 Population Dependency Ratio : 1961, 1971 and 1981 6

1.4 Female Population and Related Indicators : 1951 – 1991 8

1.5 Trends in Urbanisation : 1901 – 1991 10

1.6 Number and Population of Villages by Population size-groups : 1971 and 1981 12

**2. Health Education & Housing** 14

2.1 Trends in Birth Rate, Death Rate and Natural Growth Rate : 1901 – 1990 14

2.2 Infant Mortality Rates : 1911 to 1990 16

2.3 Public Health Services : 1950 – 1989 18

2.4 Educational Facilities : 1950-51 – 1988-89 20

2.5 Literacy and Levels of Education
A : Literacy Rates : 1951-1991 22
B : Literates and Illiterates : 1981 and 1991 22
C : Educational Levels : 1981 23

2.6 Housing Conditions: 1981
A : Census of Houses by Types of Uses 25
B : Census of Houses by Types of Construction 26

**3. Natural Resources** 28

3.1 Land Utilisation Statistics : 1950-51 and 1987-88 28

3.2 Surface Water Resources : 1974 30

3.3 Pattern of Present Utilisation and Future Requirement of Water : 1985 and 2025 32

3.4 Reserves, Production and Balance Life of Major Minerals 33

# CONTENTS

| | | |
|---|---|---|
| 3.5 | Index Numbers of Mineral Production : 1951-1990 | 35 |
| 3.6 | Production of Fuel Minerals : 1950-1990 : | 37 |
| 3.7 | Production of Fuel Minerals : 1950-1990 : | 39 |
| 3.8 | Production of Select Metallic Minerals : 1950-1990 : | 41 |
| 3.9 | Production of Select Metallic Minerals : 1950-1990 : | 43 |
| **4.** | **Energy** | **45** |
| 4.1 | Commercial and Non-commercial Energy Consumption and Demand Projections | 45 |
| 4.2 | Relative Shares of Primary Sources of Energy : 1970-71 – 1991-92 | 47 |
| 4.3 | Sectorwise Consumption of Commercial Energy : 1953-54 – 1984-85 | 48 |
| 4.4 | Sectorwise Shares by Sources of Commercial Energy Consumption : 1953-54 – 1984-85 | 49 |
| 4.5 | Sectorwise Relative Shares of Sources of Commercial Energy Consumption : 1953-54 – 1978-79 | 51 |
| 4.6 | Trends in Production and Supply of Primary Sources of Energy : 1970-71 – 1991-92 | 53 |
| 4.7 | Crude Oil Reserves : 1966 – 1991 | 55 |
| 4.8 | Natural Gas Reserves : 1966 – 1991 | 57 |
| 4.9 | Trend in Production of Crude Oil and Natural Gas : 1970-71 – 1991-92 | 59 |
| 4.10 | Refining Capacities and Crude Throughput of Petroleum Companies | 61 |
| 4.11 | Supply Balance of Petroleum Crude and Products : 1980-81 – 1990-91 | 62 |
| 4.12 | Electricity : Installed capacity : 1950-51 – 1991-92 | 65 |
| 4.13 | Electricity Generation : 1950-51 – 1990-91 | 67 |

# CONTENTS

| | | |
|---|---|---|
| 4.14 | Plant Load Factor of Thermal Power Plants 1973-74 to 1990-91 | 69 |
| 4.15 | Electricity – Planwise Slippages in Installation of Additional Capacity | 71 |
| 4.16 | Rural Electrification : Villages Electrified : 1947 – 1990-91 | 73 |
| **5.** | **Transport** | **75** |
| 5.1 | Growth in Traffic on Indian Railways 1950-51 – 1992-93 | 75 |
| 5.2 | Growth of Road Length : 1950-51 – 1990-91 | 77 |
| 5.3 | Population of Registered Motor vehicles : 1950-51 – 1989-90 | 79 |
| 5.4 | Shares of Rail and Road Transport in goods and passenger Traffic : 1950-51 – 1988-1989 | 81 |
| 5.5 | Growth of India's Merchant Shipping Tonnage : 1951 – 1992 | 83 |
| 5.6 | Growth of Air Traffic Handled by Indian Carriers : 1960-61 – 1989-90 | 85 |
| **6.** | **Employment** | **87** |
| 6.1 | Work-force by Population Census : 1901 to 1991 | 87 |
| 6.2 | Occupational Classification of Workers : 1901 to 1981 | 88 |
| 6.3 | Distribution of Working Population by Occupation in Organised and Unorganised Sectors : 1981 | 90 |
| 6.4 | Trends In Employment in Organised Sector : 1956 to 1991 | 92 |
| 6.5 | Industry-wise Distribution of Organised Sector Employment 1961 and 1989 | 94 |
| 6.6 | Distribution of workers by Category of Employment | 96 |
| 6.7 | Industry- wise Pattern of Factory Employment 1961, 1981, 1985 and 1988. | 97 |
| 6.8 | Number of Job Seekers Registered with Employment Exchanges : 1951 – 1991 | 99 |

# CONTENTS

6.9     Estimated Backlog of Unemployment at the end of
Sixth and Seventh Plans     101

6.10    Mandays lost through Industrial Disputes : 1961-1991     102

**7.     Wages and Salaries**     **103**

7.1     Value Added per Rural and Urban Worker :
1970-71 and 1980-81     103

7.2     Ratio of per worker emoluments to Average Per Family
National Income : 1960-61 tq 1990-91     105

**8.     Agriculture : Inputs**     **107**

8.1     Pattern of Agricultural Land Holding :
1960-61 – 1985-86     107

8.2     Rainfall : Seasons and Performance     109

8.3     Trends in Area Sown and Irrigated 1950-51 – 1987-88     111

8.4     Net irrigated Area by sources of Irrigation :
1950-51 – 1987-88     113

8.5     Production and Distribution of Certified Quality Seeds :
1983-84 and 1989-90.     115

8.6     Fertilisers : Trends in Production, Imports and
Consumption 1951-52 – 1991-92     116

8.7     Pesticides : Trends in Consumption: 1950-51 – 1990-91     118

8.8     Trends in Progress of Farm Mechanisation : 1951 – 1990     119

8.9     Flow of Institutional Credit for Agriculture :
1950-51 – 1990-91     121

8.10    Estimated Gross Value of Inputs in Agriculture :
1980-81 – 1988-89     123

8.11    Productivity of Major Inputs in Agriculture :
1950-81 – 1988-89     125

# CONTENTS

**9. Agriculture : Output**      **126**

9.1   Trends in Area, Production and Productivity ; All crops : 1950-51 – 1990-91    126

9.2   Trends in Area, Production and Productivity : Foodgrains : 1950-51 – 1990-91    129

9.3   Trends in Area Production and Productivity : Non-foodgrain Crops : 1950-51 to 1990-91    132

9.4   Changes in Share of Kharif and Rabi Foodgrains Output, 1969-70– 1992-93    135

9.5   Rates of Changes in Area, Production and Yields of Major Crops 1969-70 – 1989-90    137

9.6   Trends in Yield Rates of Major Crops : 1950-51 – 1989-90    139

9.7   Yield Potentials of High Yield Seeds : 1989-90    140

9.8   Production Imports and Availability of Foodgrains : 1951-1992    141

9.9   Public Distribution System : 1971-1990.    142

9.10   Trends in Procurement Prices and Open Market Prices of Foodgrains : 1965-66 – 1991-92    143

9.11   Trends in Production of Milk, Eggs and Fish 1950-51 to 1990-91    145

9.12   Estimates of Value of Output of Agricultural Commodities 1988-89    147

**10. Industrial Sector**      **148**

10.1   Trends in Industrial Production by Major Segments (Organised Sector) 1951-1992    148

10.2   Relative growth of Factory and Non-factory Manufacturing in Real Terms Net Value Added : 1950-51 – 1990-91 (1980-81 Prices)    151

# CONTENTS

10.3  Net Value Added in Manufacturing by Factory and
      Non-factory Sectors : 1950-51 – 1990-91
      (At Current Prices).                                                    153

10.4  Structure of Industrial Sector : 1986-87 (Covered by ASI)              155

10.5  Key Parameters of Manufacturing (Factory) Sector :
      1980-81 and 1986-87                                                    157

10.6  Ownership Pattern of Industrial units :
      1986-87 (Covered by ASI)                                               160

10.7  Small Scale Industries : Key Indicators :
      1973-74 to 1991-92                                                     161

10.8  Growth of Small Scale Industries in Factory Sector :
      1973-74 to 1986-87 (Covered by ASI)                                   163

10.9  Industrial Sickness : 1979 to 1988                                     165

10.10 Index of Industrial Production by Major Groups
      1985-86 – 1991-92                                                      167

10.11 Value of output in Manufacturing (Factory) Sector :
      1970-71, 1980-81 and 1988-89                                          169

10.12 Gross Value Added in Manufacturing (Factory) Sector :
      1970-71, 1980-81 and 1988-89                                          171

10.13 Production Trends in Khadi and Village Industry :
      1980-81, 1985-86 and 1989-90                                          173

**11.  Corporate Sector**                                                    **175**

11.1  Number of companies at work and their paid-up capital :
      1950-51 – 1990-91                                                      175

11.2  Profile of Corporate Sector in Terms of Tax-paying
      Companies : 1966-67 – 1988-89                                         177

11.3  Financial Performance Indicators of RBI Samples of
      Medium and Large Public Limited Companies :
      1960-61 – 1988-89                                                      179

11.4  Financial performance Indicators of RBI Samples of
      Medium and Large Private Limited Companies :
      1960-61 – 1986-87                                                      181

# CONTENTS

11.5    Savings and Capital Formation in Private Corporate
        Sector : 1960-61 – 1991-92                              182

11.6    Financial Flows in Private Corporate Sector :
        1951-52 to 1989-90                                      184

11.7    Trends in Capital Issues : 1957 – 1991-92               186

11.8    Trends in Growth of Number of Listed companies and
        Their Stock Values : 1961-1991                          188

11.9    Stock Exchangewise Listed Companies and their paid-up
        capital : 1961-1991                                     190

11.10   Scrips Turnover on Bombay Stock Exchange :
        1985 to 1991                                            192

11.11   Share-holding pattern of Private Sector Companies :
        1989-90                                                 194

11.12   Key Financial indicators of All Non-financial Public
        Sector Enterprises 1960-61 – 1989-90                    196

11.13   Key Performance Indicators of Central
        Government-owned Non-departmental
        Running Enterprises ; 1968-69 to 1990-91                197

11.14   Additional Capital Funds Raised by Financial and
        Non-financial Public Sector Enterprises owned
        by Central Government : 1985-86 to 1992-93              199

**12      National Income                                       201**

12.1    Trends in Gross National Product and Gross
        Domestic Product : 1950-51 – 1991-92                    201

12.2    Trends in Real National Income and Per
        capita income : 1950-51 – 1991-92                       203

12.3    Sectorwise shares in Gross Domestic Product :
        1950-51 – 1990-91                                       205

12.4    Sectorwise Growth Rates of Gross Domestic
        Product : 1950-51 – 1990-91                             207

# CONTENTS

12.5 Net Domestic Product by Industry of Origin : 1950-51 – 1990-91 .......... 209

12.6 Growth Rates of Real Net Domestic Product by Industry of Origin : 1950-51 – 1990-91. .......... 212

12.7 Supply and Disposal of Nation's Economic Resources : 1960-61 – 1990-91 .......... 215

12.8 Composition and Growth of Private Consumption Expenditure : 1960-61 & 1990-91 .......... 217

**13 Saving and Investment** .......... **219**

13.1 Gross Domestic Saving and Gross Domestic Capital Formation : 1950-51 – 1991-92 .......... 219

13.2 Shares of Public and Private Sectors in Gross Domestic Savings and Gross Capital Formation : Annual Averages .......... 221

13.3 Shares of Public and Private Sectors in Real Gross Domestic Capital Formation : 1960-61 – 1991-92 .......... 224

13.4 Gross Domestic Capital Formation by Types of Assets : 1950-51 – 1990-91 .......... 226

13.5 Gross Domestic Capital Formation by Industry of use 1960-61 and 1990-91 .......... 228

13.6 Gross Financial Savings and Liabilities of Household Sector : 1970-71, 1980-81 & 1989-90. .......... 230

13.7 Price Deflectors of Gross Domestic Product and Gross Domestic Capital Formation : 1960-61 – 1990-91 .......... 232

**14 Public Finance** .......... **234**

14.1 Trends in structure of Government Expenditure – Centre, States & Union Territories : 1960-61 – 1992-93. .......... 234

14.2 Structure of Government Incomes – Centre, States & Union Territories : 1960-61 & 1992-93 .......... 236

# CONTENTS

14.3 Pattern of Central Government Income and Expenditure through Budgetary Transactions on Revenue and Capital Accounts : 1950-51 – 1993-94    238

14.4 Structure of Central Government Incomes on Revenue and Capital Accounts : 1970-71 – 1992-93    240

14.5 Structure of Central Government Development Expenditure on Revenue and Capital Accounts : 1970-71 – 1992-93    242

14.6 Structure of Central Government Non-development Expenditure on Revenue and Capital Accounts 1970-71 – 1992-93    244

14.7 Economic Classification of Central, Government Budget Expenditure 1980-81 – 1992-93    246

14.8 Trends in Tax Revenue of Centre, States & Union Territory Governments : 1950-51 – 1990-91.    247

14.9 Revenue from Major Taxes of Central Government : 1950-51 – 1992-93    249

14.10 Transfer of Resources from Centre to State and Union Territory Governments : 1951-52 –1992-93    251

14.11 Expenditure on Subsidies by Governments : 1950-51 – 1990-91    252

14.12 Expenditure on Major Explicit Subsidies by Central Government : 1980-81 – 1992-93    254

14.13 India's Defence Expenditure : 1975-76 to 1992-93    255

14.14 Outstanding Debt and Interest Burden of Central Government : 1980-81 – 1992-93    257

15    Five Year Plans    259

15.1 Overall Growth Targets and Achievements during Plan Periods    259

15.2 Key Macro indicators of Economic Performance    260

# CONTENTS

15.3    A : Sectoral growth rates and shares of Gross Value
        Added: Sixth, Seventh and Eighth Plan Periods
        B : Sectoral shares : Targets and Actuals :
        Sixth, Seventh and Eighth Plan Periods.                    261

15.4    Planwise Public Sector Plan Outlays and Actual
        Expenditures                                               263

15.5    Aggregate Resources for Sixth and Seventh Plans;
        Public and Private Sectors                                 264

15.6    Public Sector Plan Outlays and Expenditures by
        Broad Economic Sectors : First Plan to Fifth Plan
        and 1979-80                                                266

15.7    Public sector Plan Outlays and Expenditures by
        Broad Economic Sectors : Sixth and Seventh Plans           268

15.8    Sectoral Distribution of Seventh Plan Outlays for
        Centre, States & Union Territories.                        270

15.9    Inter-sectoral capital flows for plan investments :
        Sixth, Seventh and Eighth Plans.                           271

**16      Banking and Finance                                      273**

16.1    Financial Flows in the Indian Economy-Sectorwise :
        1968-69 and 1989-90                                        273

16.2    Financial Flow in the Indian Economy by Instruments :
        1968-69 and 1989-90                                        276

16.3    Assistance Sanctioned and Disbursed by All Financial
        Institutions : 1964-65 and 1970-71 to 1990-91              279

16.4    Institutionwise Cumulative Assistance Sanctioned
        and Disbursed upto March 1991                              281

16.5    Industrywise Shares of Cumulative Assistance
        Sanctioned and Disbursed by All Financial Institutions
        upto March 1991.                                           282

16.6    Growth of Deposits and Credit of Scheduled
        Commercial Banks : 1950-51 to 1991-92                      283

# CONTENTS

16.7 Sectoral Shares of Gross Bank Credit :
March 1977 and March 1991                                285

16.8 Industrywise Deployment of Gross Bank Credit :
March 1981 and March 1991                                286

16.9 Ownership and Spatial Distribution of Deposits of
Scheduled Commercial Banks : 1971 & 1988                 288

16.10 Distribution of Scheduled Commercial Bank Branches :
1969 – 1991                                               290

16.11 Progress of Regional Rural Banks : 1975-1990         292

16.12 Liquidity and Reserves Ratios Prescribed for
Commercial Banks                                         293

**17    Money and Prices                                   295**

17.1 Components of Money Supply with Public :
1950-51 – 1992-93                                         295

17.2 Sources of Expansion of Money Supply
1956-57 – 1991-92                                         297

17.3 Mechanics of Price Inflation : 1960-61 – 1990-91      299

17.4 Index Numbers of Wholesale Prices : 1950-1991         300

17.5 Index Numbers of Consumer Prices : 1960-1993          302

17.6 Inflation and Erosion of Purchasing Power of Rupee :
1950-1993                                                304

**18    Foreign Trade                                      306**

18.1 Trends in India's Imports, Exports and Trade Balance :
1950-51 – 1991-92                                         306

18.2 India's Export Earnings by Major Commodities for
Select years : 1950-51 – 1991-92                         308

18.3 India's Import Bill by Major commodities for select
years : 1950-51 – 1991-92                                310

# CONTENTS

18.4    Top 20 Destinations of India's Exports in 1990-91       311

18.5    Top 20 sources of India's Imports in 1990-91            313

18.6    India's share in World Exports of Engineering
        Goods : 1956-57 – 1989-90.                              315

**19    Balance of Payments                                     316**

19.1    Balance of Payments
        1989-90 – 1993-94                                       316

19.2    Balance of Payments
        April - September 1991-1992                             317

19.3    Ratio of External Trade and Net Current and
        Capital Accounts Balances to GDP : 1955-56 to 1990-91   319

19.4    A: Foreign Exchange Reserves of India : 1950-1991       321
        B: Foreign Currency Reserves 1991 and 1992-93           323

19.5    Remittances of Profits, Interests etc. from India :
        1956-57 – 1986-87                                       324

19.6    A comparison with other Asian Countries                 325

**20    External Assistance                                     327**

20.1    Inflow of External Assistance : 1960-61 to 1992-93      327

20.2    External Assistance Authorised and Utilised :
        1974-75 to 1990-91                                      329

20.3    Shares of IDA and IBRD in Aid to India :
        1980 to 1991-92                                         331

20.4    Commercial Borrowings from Abroad :
        Approved and Utilised : 1980-81 to 1991-92              332

20.5    External Debt Outstanding and Debt-Servicing :
        1984-85 to 1990-91                                      333

20.6    External Debt-Service Ratios 1984-85 to 1990-91         335

## 1.1 Growth of Population of India : 1901 to 1991

| Census Year | Population Million 1 March | Population Increase | | |
|---|---|---|---|---|
| | | Million | Percent | |
| | | | Decenial | Annual |
| 1901 | 238.4 | | | |
| 1911 | 252.1 | 13.7 | 5.75 | 0.56 |
| 1921 | 251.3 | - 0.8 | - 0.32 | - 0.03 |
| 1931 | 279.0 | 27.7 | 11.02 | 1.05 |
| 1941 | 318.7 | 39.7 | 14.23 | 1.34 |
| 1951 | 361.1 | 42.4 | 13.30 | 1.26 |
| 1961 | 439.2 | 78.1 | 21.63 | 1.98 |
| 1971 | 548.2 (c) | 109.0 | 24.82 | 2.24 |
| 1981 (a) | 685.3 | 135.1 | 24.64 | 2.23 |
| 1991 (b) | 843.9 | 160.6 | 23.50 | 2.13 |

Notes : (a) The 1981 census was not conducted in Assam. The figure here includes revised estimate of Assam populations : 18.0 million instead of
the earlier 19.9 million.
(b) The 1991 census was not conducted in Jammu & Kashmir; the figure
here includes projected population estimate of 7.7 million for J&K.
(c) As on 1 April 1971.

❏ In terms of population, India is the second largest country in the world next
only to China. It accounts for 15.6% of the world population : every sixth per-
son is an Indian.

❏ During the 1981-91 decade, our population increased by 160.6 million i.e.
equivalent to the total population of Brazil which ranks sixth in the world.

❏ Although the annual population growth rate during 1981-91 declined as compared to that during the preceding two decades, in absolute number our population increased by a compound rate of 14.6 million annually. In other words,
we included in our fold every year the total population of countries like Neth-
erlands or Saudi Arabia. Or say, more than the 1981 population of Haryana —

the smallest among our major states – was added every year thereafter during the last decade.

❏ During the four decades of planned development since 1951 our population has increased 2.33 times. Mounting burden of population, growing at a high rate, is at the root of our general level of poverty. Development resources have been found inadequate for providing the minimum basic necessities and social welfare of the masses. In short, this has negated the gains of economic growth even at the improved levels during the 1980s.

## Mounting Burden of Population on Nation's Resources

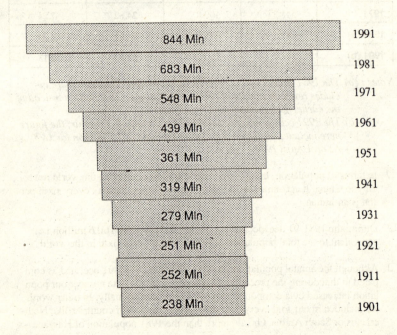

| | |
|---|---|
| 844 Mln | 1991 |
| 683 Mln | 1981 |
| 548 Mln | 1971 |
| 439 Mln | 1961 |
| 361 Mln | 1951 |
| 319 Mln | 1941 |
| 279 Mln | 1931 |
| 251 Mln | 1921 |
| 252 Mln | 1911 |
| 238 Mln | 1901 |

## 1.2.    States of India : Population, Area and Density : 1991

| States (Ranked by population) | Population : 1991 | | | Area | | | Density | |
|---|---|---|---|---|---|---|---|---|
| | Million | % to Total | Rank | '000 sq. km | % to Total | Rank | No. per sq.km | Rank |
| Major States | 809.0 | 95.8 | | 2,811 | 85.5 | | 288 | |
| Uttar Pradesh | 138.8 | 16.5 | 1 | 294 | 9.0 | 4 | 471 | 4 |
| Bihar | 86.3 | 10.2 | 2 | 174 | 5.3 | 8 | 497 | 3 |
| Maharashtra | 78.7 | 9.3 | 3 | 308 | 9.4 | 3 | 256 | 9 |
| West-Bengal | 68.0 | 8.1 | 4 | 89 | 2.7 | 11 | 766 | 1 |
| Andhra Pradesh | 66.3 | 7.9 | 5 | 275 | 8.4 | 5 | 241 | 10 |
| Madhya Pradesh | 66.1 | 7.8 | 6 | 443 | 13.5 | 1 | 149 | 14 |
| Tamil Nadu | 55.6 | 6.6 | 7 | 130 | 4.0 | 10 | 428 | 5 |
| Karnataka | 44.8 | 5.3 | 8 | 192 | 5.8 | 7 | 234 | 11 |
| Rajasthan | 43.9 | 5.2 | 9 | 342 | 10.4 | 2 | 128 | 15 |
| Gujarat | 41.2 | 4.9 | 10 | 196 | 6.1 | 6 | 210 | 12 |
| Orissa | 31.5 | 3.7 | 11 | 156 | 4.7 | 9 | 202 | 13 |
| Kerala | 29.0 | 3.4 | 12 | 39 | 1.1 | 15 | 747 | 2 |
| Assam | 22.3 | 2.6 | 13 | 79 | 2.4 | 12 | 284 | 8 |
| Punjab | 20.2 | 2.4 | 14 | 50 | 1.5 | 13 | 401 | 6 |
| Haryana | 16.3 | 1.9 | 15 | 44 | 1.4 | 14 | 369 | 7 |
| Other States | 23.5 | 2.8 | | 465 | 14.2 | | 51 | |
| Jammu & Kashmir | 7.7 | 0.9 | 1 | 222 | 6.8 | 1 | 76 | 6 |
| Himachal Pradesh | 5.1 | 0.6 | 2 | 56 | 1.7 | 3 | 92 | 3 |
| Tripura | 2.7 | 0.3 | 3 | 10 | 0.3 | 8 | 262 | 2 |

contd.......

| States (Ranked by population) | Population : 1991 | | | Area | | | Density | |
|---|---|---|---|---|---|---|---|---|
| | Million | % to Total | Rank | '000 sq. km | % to Total | Rank | No. per sq.km | Rank |
| Manipur | 1.8 | 0.2 | 4 | 22 | 0.7 | 5 | 82 | 4 |
| Meghalaya | 1.8 | 0.2 | 5 | 22 | 0.7 | 4 | 78 | 5 |
| Nagaland | 1.2 | 0.1 | 6 | 17 | 0.5 | 7 | 73 | 7 |
| Goa | 1.2 | 0.1 | 7 | 4 | 0.1 | 10 | 316 | 1 |
| Arunachal Pradesh | 0.9 | 0.1 | 8 | 84 | 2.6 | 2 | 10 | 10 |
| Mizoram | 0.7 | 0.1 | 9 | 21 | 0.6 | 6 | 33 | 9 |
| Sikkim | 0.4 | 0.1 | 10 | 7 | 0.2 | 9 | 57 | 8 |
| Union Territories | 11.4 | 1.4 | | 11 | 0.3 | | 1,036 | |
| Delhi | 9.4 | 1.1 | 1 | 2 | - | 2 | 6,319 | 1 |
| Pondicherry | 0.8 | 0.1 | 2 | 0.5 | - | 3 | 1,605 | 4 |
| Chandigarh | 0.6 | 0.1 | 3 | 0.1 | - | 5 | 5,620 | 2 |
| Andaman & Nicobar | 0.3 | - | 4 | 8 | 0.3 | 1 | 34 | 7 |
| Dadra & Nagar Haveli | 0.1 | - | 5 | 0.5 | - | 4 | 282 | 6 |
| Daman & Diu | 0.1 | - | 6 | 0.1 | - | 6 | 906 | 5 |
| Lakshad-weep | 0.05 | - | 7 | 0.03 | - | 7 | 1,615 | 3 |
| India : Total | 843.9 | 100.0 | | 3,287 | 100.0 | | 267 | |

*Notes : (a) Totals may not add due to rounding off population projected for Jammu & Kashmir.*

❑   India has the second largest population in the world, next only to China.

❏ Uttar Pradesh which is the most populous state of India has higher population than all other countries of the world except the five most populous namely, China, USSR, USA, Indonesia and Brazil.

❏ Each one of the major states of India has population exceeding 15 million. Therefore each is larger than many other countries in terms of population. Population of Haryana, the smallest among the major states was 16.3 million by 1991 census count.

❏ The fifteen major states account for 96% of the country's population. The seven most populous among them accommodate two-thirds of total population.

❏ In terms of land area, the fifteen major states occupy 86% of total area and the seven populatious states account for 52% area. Madhya Pradesh is the largest state in terms of area.

❏ Density of population in any state would depend on several factors such as the type of terrain, climatic conditions soil fertility, infrastructual facility, and the overall economic activity, to attract and support people with means of livelihood.

## Population (Statewise %)

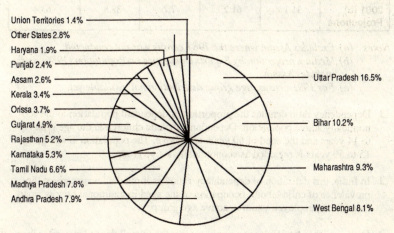

Union Territories 1.4%
Other States 2.8%
Haryana 1.9%
Punjab 2.4%
Assam 2.6%
Kerala 3.4%
Orissa 3.7%
Gujarat 4.9%
Rajasthan 5.2%
Karnataka 5.3%
Tamil Nadu 6.6%
Madhya Pradesh 7.8%
Andhra Pradesh 7.9%

Uttar Pradesh 16.5%
Bihar 10.2%
Maharashtra 9.3%
West Bengal 8.1%

## 1.3 Population Dependency Ratio : 1961, 1971 & 1981

*(Percent)*

| Census | Age Group Distribution | | | Dependents | |
|---|---|---|---|---|---|
| | 0-14 Yrs | 15-59 Yrs | 60 Yrs. & above | 0 to 14 Yrs. Plus 60 & Above Yrs. | Dependency Ratio To Active Group |
| 1961 | 41.0 | 53.3 | 5.7 | 46.7 | 87.6 |
| 1971 | 42.0 | 52.0 | 6.0 | 48.0 | 92.3 |
| 1981 (a) | | | | | |
| Nos. Million | 263.1 | 358.7 | 43.5 | 306.6 | |
| Percent | 39.6 | 53.9 | 6.5 | 46.1 | 85.5 |
| Males | 39.4 | 54.2 | 6.4 | 45.8 | 43.9 |
| Females | 39.6 | 53.8 | 6.6 | 46.2 | 41.4 |
| Rural | 40.5 | 52.7 | 6.8 | 47.3 | 67.3 |
| Urban | 36.6 | 58.0 | 5.4 | 42.0 | 18.1 |
| 1991 (c) | | | | | |
| 2001 (b) Projections | 31.1 | 61.2 | 7.7 | 38.8 | 63.4 |

*Notes : (a) Excludes Assam where the 1981 census was not conducted*
*(b) Medium projection by Experts Committee on Population (1986) and includes Assam*
*(c) For 1991 census, age group distribution not available yet.*

❑ Dependency ratio denotes the proportion of dependent population to the economically active population. Dependents include children in the age group 0 to 14 years and the aged of 60 years and above. The population in age-group 15 to 59 years is regarded as economically active group.

❑ In India, this definition of dependency ratio has limited relevance given the prevalence of child labour, occupation of the aged in traditional sectors, apart from the unemployed youth in active age group.

❑ Data available for 1981 census suggest that the overall dependency ratio then was around 85%. Of this, male dependence was 44% and female about 41%.

Similarly dependency in rural areas constituted a high proportion of 67% of the total economically active population (15-59 years group) while for the urban areas it was only about 18%.

❏ For 1991 census, the distribution of population by age group was not available. However, with the decline in growth rate of population, the proportion of children upto 4 years would decline whereas with the decline in mortality the proportion of the aged 60 plus group would rise. The population of the economically age group would increase and so the dependency ratio would decline. This is illustrated by the data projected by the experts committee for 2001 which assumed a medium population growth rate of 1.8% per annum.

|      | No. of Youths | No. of old man | No. of Children |
|------|---------------|----------------|-----------------|
| 1961 | 5.33          | 0.57           | 4.10            |
| 1971 | 5.20          | 0.60           | 4.20            |
| 1981 | 5.40          | 0.60           | 4.00            |
| 2001 | 6.10          | 0.80           | 3.10            |

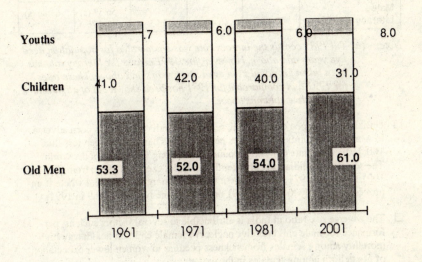

## 1.4 Female Population and Related Indicators : 1951-1991

| Census<br>Indicators | 1951 | 1961 | 1971 | 1981 | 1991<br>(Provisional) |
|---|---|---|---|---|---|
| **TOTAL POPULATION** | | | | | |
| Million | 361 | 439 | 548 | 683 | 844 |
| Annual growth % | 1.26 | 1.98 | 2.24 | 2.23 | 2.13 |
| **FEMALE POPULATION** | | | | | |
| Million | 176 | 213 | 264 | 330 | 406 |
| Annual growth % | 1.28 | 1.93 | 2.17 | 2.26 | 2.09 |
| Proportion to total population % | 48.5 | 48.5 | 48.2 | 48.3 | 48.1 |
| No. per 100 males | 94.6 | 94.1 | 93.0 | 93.4 | 92.9 |
| Female Literacy rate % | 8.86 | 15.34 | 21.97 | 29.75 (a)<br>28.46 | 39.42 (a) |
| Male Literacy rate % | 27.16 | 40.40 | 45.95 | 56.37 (a)<br>53.45 | 63.86 (a) |

*Note : (a) Till 1981 census the literacy rate was enumerated for population aged five years and above. However, for 1991 census the literacy rate has been taken for population aged seven years and above. These rates for 1991 and comparable for 1981 has been shown out of alignment in respective columns above.*

❑ Unlike in developed countries the sex ratio in India has always been adverse to women; the number of females per 100 males has always been less than 100. India's sex rate currently around 93 is among the lowest in the world. The sex ratio in India has consistently declined, except in 1981, from 97.2 in 1901 to 93.0 in 1971, from where it improved marginally to 93.4 where it improved marginally to 93.4 in 1991 only to decline further to 92.9 in 1991.

❑ The adverse sex-ratio in India is attributable to several factors such as, performance for male child relative neglect of female child on health care high mortality among females from sickness peculiar to women lower expectation of life at birth among females in the past etc.

- Literacy rate among females has greatly lagged behind that among males, due to socio-economic constrained and unfavorable attitude towards female education in the past.

- During the past four decades however, female literacy has improved 4.3 times between 1951 and 1991, whereas the male literacy rate improved at a slaver pace by 2.2 items over the period. As a result, the male literacy rate which was three-times that for females in 1951, declined to less than 1.6 times by 1991.

- Still however, by provisional 1991 census data, 61 out of 100 females were still illiterate against 36 illiterates among 100 males.

- According to 1991 census, Kerala has the highest female literacy rate of 80.93%, improving from 75.65% of 1981 population aged seven years and above. Rajasthan continues to have the lowest literacy rate among females – 20.84% in 1991 against 13.99% in 1981.

## 1.5 Trends in Urbanisation : 1901 to 1991

| Census Year | Population (million) | | | Annual Rate of Growth (%) | | | Percentage to Total Population | |
|---|---|---|---|---|---|---|---|---|
| | Total | Rural | Urban | Total | Rural | Urban | Rural | Urban |
| 1901 | 238.4 | 212.6 | 25.8 | .. | .. | .. | 89.2 | 10.8 |
| 1911 | 252.1 | 226.2 | 25.9 | 0.56 | 0.62 | 0.03 | 89.7 | 10.3 |
| 1921 | 251.3 | 223.2 | 28.1 | -0.03 | -0.13 | 0.80 | 88.8 | 11.2 |
| 1931 | 279.0 | 245.5 | 33.5 | 1.05 | 0.96 | 1.76 | 88.0 | 12.0 |
| 1941 | 318.7 | 274.5 | 44.2 | 1.34 | 1.12 | 2.81 | 86.1 | 13.9 |
| 1951 | 361.1 | 298.7 | 62.4 | 1.26 | 0.85 | 3.53 | 82.7 | 17.3 |
| 1961 | 439.2 | 360.3 | 78.9 | 1.98 | 1.89 | 2.37 | 82.0 | 18.0 |
| 1971 | 548.2 | 439.1 | 109.1 | 2.24 | 2.00 | 3.29 | 80.1 | 19.9 |
| 1981 | 683.3 (a) | 524.0 (b) | 159.3 (b) | 2.23 | 1.79 | 3.88 | 76.7 | 23.3 |
| 1991 | 843.9 | 626.9 (b) | 217.0 (c) | 2.13 | 1.78 | 3.14 | 74.3 | 25.7 |

*Notes : All percentages calculated before rounding of the figures.*
*(a) Revised estimate including Assam*
*(b) Derived by proportions in unrevised data*
*(c) Provisionally reported figure.*

❑ Over the past nine decades singe 1911-21 the urban population of India has been rising faster than the rural population and the total population. Particularly during the last three decades the urban population growth rate has been more than 3% per annum. Consequently, the proportion of urbanised population has increased from 11% in 1921 to almost 26% in 1991.

❑ For 1991 census, though rural-urban break-up was not directly given in the first provisional results, it was reported that the urban population was estimated at 217 million persons in 4,689 towns and cities. The urbanisation of population had thus reached 25.7%. The number of urban centres with population of one lakh and above had reached 291 (excluding J&K) which together accounted for about 65% of the total urban population in 1991.

❑ Going by the data in the **World Development Report 1991** of the World Bank India's urbanisation ratio in 1989 was placed at 27%, which was the seventh lowest ahead of countries like Kenya, Thailand, Sri Lanka, Bangladesh, Uganda and Nepal.

❑ The number of "million-plus" cities by 1991 census was 23. According to World Bank data for 1990, such cities in India accounted for 32% of urban population and 9% of the total population.

❑ Compared to Mexico-the largest city in the world with its population of 20.2 million, our largest metropolitan city of Greater Bombay (12.6 million) is listed sixth, Calcutta (10.6 million) at tenth and Delhi (8.4 million) the twenteeth in the World.

❑ Despite the relatively low urbanisation ratio, the economic and social strains of urban life in our country have reached unbearable limits due to the inadequacy of infrastructural facilities like housing, water supply, sanitation, education, transportation etc.

## Urbanisation Ratio

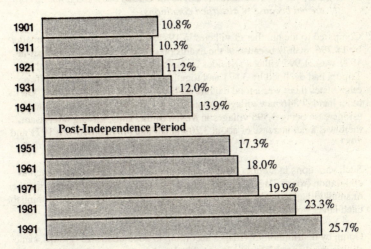

| Year | Ratio |
|------|-------|
| 1901 | 10.8% |
| 1911 | 10.3% |
| 1921 | 11.2% |
| 1931 | 12.0% |
| 1941 | 13.9% |

Post-Independence Period

| Year | Ratio |
|------|-------|
| 1951 | 17.3% |
| 1961 | 18.0% |
| 1971 | 19.9% |
| 1981 | 23.3% |
| 1991 | 25.7% |

## 1.6    Number and Population of Villages by Population Size-groups : 1971 and 1981

| Population Size-Group | Number of Villages | | | | Percentage to Total Village Population | |
|---|---|---|---|---|---|---|
| | Number | | Percent | | | |
| | 1971 (a) | 1981 (a) | 1971 (a) | 1981 (a) | 1971 (a) | 1981 (a) |
| Less than 500 | 318,633 | 270,795 | 55.3 | 48.6 | 16.4 | 12.5 |
| 500 - 999 | 132,990 | 135,928 | 23.1 | 24.4 | 21.5 | 19.1 |
| 1000 - 1999 | 81,973 | 94,486 | 14.2 | 17.0 | 25.8 | 25.9 |
| 2000 - 4999 | 36,005 | 46,892 | 6.3 | 8.4 | 23.8 | 27.1 |
| 5000 - 9999 | 4,974 | 7,202 | 0.9 | 1.3 | 7.4 | 9.3 |
| 10,000 & above | 1,358 | 1,834 | 0.2 | 0.3 | 5.1 | 6.1 |
| Total | 575,933 | 557,137 | 100.0 | 100.0 | 100.0 | 100.0 |

*Note :   (a) Data for 1981 exclude Assam as the census there could not be con-
ducted because of disturbed conditions.*

❑ Compared to the number of villages in 1971, the number for 1981 is smaller by 18,796, mainly because of the exclusion of Assam where the number in 1971 was 21,995 villages. Besides however, the number of villages for Tripura had declined by 3,871 and together with smaller declines in a few other states there was a total decline of 4,747 villages over the decade. On the other hand, 7,846 new villages got added by the 1981 census count, the largest increase being 3,596 villages in Maharashtra. Thus, leaving out Assam, there was a net increase of about 3,200 inhabitate villages between 1971 and 1981.

❑ Such variations in number of villages occurs due to several reasons such as emigration from villages, while their resettlement elsewhere in larger number of small villages, as also newer settlements coming up in previously uninhabitated lands would add to the number of villages.

❑ Going by distribution of villages according to population size- groups, same shift in number to higher group would take place because of population growth over the decade. Thus, in 1971, over 78% of the total number of villages had population of less than 1000 persons, and 38% of the total rural population lived in such small size villages. By 1981 census, such smaller villages declined to 73% of the total number and accounted for 32% of the rural population.

- ❏ From 1971 to 1981, there was distinct increase in the of number of rural settlements of 1000 and above. Concentration of population is observed in size-group of 1000 to 5000 where almost half the rural population lives.

- ❏ The average population of a village in 1981 in the country was 911. Kerala had the highest average of almost 17,000 persons per village. The lowest average was in Arunachal Pradesh, but Himachal Pradesh, Meghalaya and Andaman had significantly low averages.

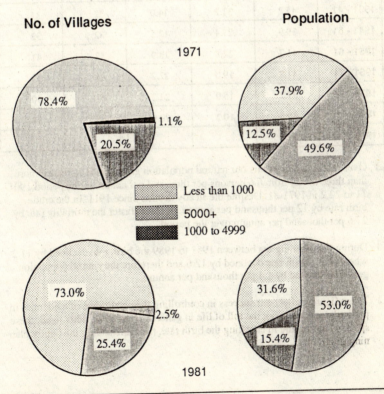

**No. of Villages**                **Population**

1971

78.4%      1.1%          37.9%
20.5%                     12.5%      49.6%

▦ Less than 1000
▦ 5000+
▦ 1000 to 4999

73.0%      2.5%          31.6%      53.0%
25.4%                     15.4%

1981

# HEALTH, EDUCATION & HOUSING

## 2.1 Trends in Birth Rate, Death Rate and Natural Growth Rate : 1901 - 1990

| Period | Rate per '000 Population per annum | | | Expectation of Life at Birth (years) | |
|---|---|---|---|---|---|
| | Birth Rate | Death Rate | Natural Growth Rate | Male | Female |
| 1901 - 11 | 49.2 | 42.6 | 6.6 | 23 | 23 |
| 1911 - 21 | 48.1 | 47.2 | 0.9 | 19 | 21 |
| 1921 - 31 | 46.4 | 36.3 | 10.1 | 27 | 27 |
| 1931 - 41 | 45.2 | 31.2 | 14.0 | 32 | 31 |
| 1941 - 51 | 39.9 | 27.4 | 12.5 | 32 | 32 |
| 1951 - 61 | 41.7 | 22.8 | 18.9 | 42 | 41 |
| 1961 - 71 | 41.2 | 19.0 | 22.2 | 46 | 45 |
| 1971 - 81 | 37.2 | 15.0 | 22.2 | 51 | 50 |
| 1989 | 30.5 | 10.2 | 20.3 | 58 | 59 |
| 1990 | 29.9 | | | | |

❑ Over the last eighty years our natural population growth rate increased more than three times, from 6.6 persons per thousand per annum in the period 1901-11 to 22.2 in 1971-81. Despite the steady decline since 1911, in the crude birth rate by 12 per thousand per annum, declined faster the mortality rate by 27.6 per thousand per annum over the period.

❑ During the planning era between 1951 to 1989 the birth rate declined by 11.2 whereas the death rate declined by 12.6 and therefore the natural population growth increased by 1.4 per thousand per annum.

❑ These figures reflect our success in controlling the occurrence of epidemics in particular and reducing the toll of life in general. But, on the other hand, these speak of our failure in checking the birth rate, notwithstanding the family planning programme.

- Birth and death rates continue to be higher in rural than in urban areas, indicating the poor reach of the health facilities in villages.

- Our birth rate of 31 for 1989 was the fourth lowest in the world whereas our crude death rate of 11 was the fifth lowest. Sri Lanka, China and Indonesia have lower birth rates and death rates than ours.

- Our relatively better performance in reducing the death rate showed up in improving the average expectancy of life at birth from 23 years to 50 years over the eight decades till 1981, and further to 59 years by 1989. However, we are behind Sri Lanka (71 years), China (70) and Indonesia (61) and are on par with Kenya. Sri Lanka and China compare well on this score with some of the countries in the high income group, and most of the countries in the middle income group. We have yet a long way to go.

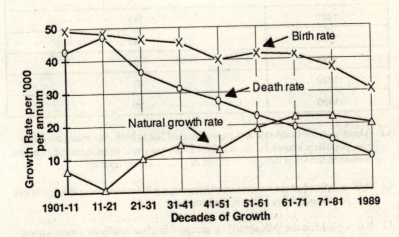

## 2.2   Infant Mortality Rates : 1911 to 1990

| Period/Year | Infant mortality Rate (per '000 live birth/per annum) |
|:---:|:---:|
| 1911 - 15 | 204 |
| 1916 - 20 | 219 |
| 1921 - 25 | 174 |
| 1926 - 30 | 178 |
| 1931 - 35 | 174 |
| 1936 - 40 | 161 |
| 1941 - 45 | 161 |
| 1946 - 50 | 134 |
| 1951 - 61 | 146 |
| 1961 - 71 | 129 |
| 1980 | 114 |
| 1985 | 97 |
| 1988 | 94 |
| 1989 | 91 |
| 1990 | 80 |

❑ Along with the death rate and expectation of life at birth, the infant mortality rate, popularly known by the acronym IMR, has come to be regarded as an important indicator of the quality of life of people in any country.

❑ IMR is defined as the number of children dying before reaching the age of one year per thousand live births in the same year.

❑ It is argued that the IMR should be accepted internationally as a more important index of the socio-economic well-being of a country than conventional indicators like GNP growth rate or per capita income level, on the grounds that economic growth is only a means to providing a better quality of life (QOL) and not an end in itself. Protagonists of such a shift argue that while high economic growth rate may not necessarily improve the QOL, it is possible to ensure a better QOL even under modest economic growth rates. Environmental hazards, often a concomitant of modern high growth process, endanger the survival of new-borns and vulnerable infants. Instead, investment for providing better facilities for child delivery and health, female education and awareness about child care, is important for improving the quality of life and infant-mortality rate.

❑ From an average of 204 during 1911-15 the Indian IMR declined to 129 by 1961-71 to 94 by 1988. However, there are considerable variations of IMR within the country with the lowest of 25 in Kerala and the highest of 123 in Uttar Pradesh and Orissa. The differential is still large in backward districts and remote rural areas.

❑ Again, by International Standards, our current IMR level is quite high, and among the low-income economies Sri Lanka, China, Indonesia and Kenya have better records.

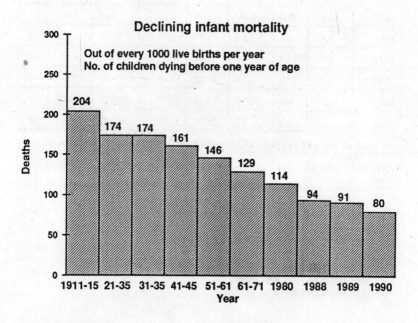

**Declining infant mortality**

Out of every 1000 live births per year
No. of children dying before one year of age

## 2.3   Public Health Services : 1950 – 1989

| Year | Registered Doctors | | Hosp-itals | Dispen-saries | Primary Health Centres (b) | Health Sub Centres (b) | Beds (a) | |
|---|---|---|---|---|---|---|---|---|
| | No. in Lakhs | Per Lakh People | No. in '000 | No. in '000 | No. in '000 | No. in '000 | No. in '000 | Per Lakh Peop le |
| 1950 | 0.59 | 16.5 | 2.72 | 6.89 | n.a. | n.a | 112 | 31 |
| 1955 | 0.70 | 18.0 | 3.09 | 7.10 | 0.73 | n.a | 146 | 36 |
| 1960 | 0.76 | 17.6 | 4.01 | 9.87 | 2.80 | n.a | 200 | 46 |
| 1965 | 1.00 | 20.7 | 3.90 | 9.49 | 4.48 | n.a. | 295 | 61 |
| 1970 | 1.39 | 25.8 | 4.24 | 10.51 | 5.11 | 28.49 | 326 | 60 |
| 1975 | 1.98 | 33.0 | 4.02 | 11.30 | 5.33 | 34.09 | 404 | 66 |
| 1980 | 2.55 | 37.2 | 6.67 | 15.97 | 5.74 | 51.41 | 561 | 82 |
| 1985 | 3.08 | 44.8 | 7.47 | 25.58 | 12.93 (c) | 92.48 | 657 | 86 |
| 1987 | 3.31 | 48.2 | 9.83 | 27.73 | 16.45 | 109.64 | 719 | 93 |
| 1988 | n.a | n.a | 10.15 | 29.19 | 16.54 | 110.28 | 623 (d) | 79 |
| 1989 | n.a | n.a | 10.17 | 28.30 | 20.53 | 130.39 | 625 | 78 |
| Annual ratio of increase (%) between 1950 and latest year available | | | | | | | | |
| 1987 or 1988 | 4.8 (e) | 2.9 | 3.5 | 3.9 | 9.9 (e) | 7.8 (f) | 5.2 | 3.0 |

Notes : (a) Covers all beds in hospitals, dispensaries, PHCs and voluntary organi
sations
(b) Relates to financial years e.g. 1970=1970-71
(c) Includes sub-centres
(d) Includes beds in hospitals and dispensaries only
(e) Between 1955 and 1988
(f) Between 1970 and 1988

❑ Latest available information as of 1 January 1989 indicates that nearly 56% of hospitals accounting for 30% of beds were under the ownership of private or voluntary organisations, while 41% of hospitals with 67% of beds were under government–run facilities and only a small proportion were looked after by the local bodies. Thus, hospitals run by government were fewer in number and much-too-overcrowded in terms of beds. In contrast the proportion of privately-owned hospitals was large with low density of beds to be looked after. Besides, only one-third of the number of hospitals (31%) with only 16% of the number of beds in the country are located in rural areas while urban areas have very much larger shares.

❑ These lower proportions of the government-managed public health facilities and locations in rural areas speak about the scarce attention given to the provision of public health facilities for the masses, resulting in its lop-sided availability for the poor as against the urban affluent classes of population in the country.

❑ In the opinion of those concerned among the medical profession, what needs urgent attention is expansion of facilities providing simple and cheap but effective preventive health care rather than the prevalent emphasis on sophisticated, personalised, expensive and urban-based medical services.

## 2.4   Educational Facilities : 1950-51 – 1988-89

| | 1950-51 | 1960-61 | 1970-71 | 1980-81 | 1987-88 | 1988-89 | Annual Rate of Increase (%) |
|---|---|---|---|---|---|---|---|
| Students Enrolled ('00,000) | | | | | | | |
| In Classes I-V | 192 | 350 | 570 | 738 | 929 | 957 | 4.35 |
| % to popul. 6-11 age | 43.1 | 62.4 | 72.6 | 80.5 | 97.9 | 99.6 | |
| In Classes VI-VIII | 31 | 67 | 133 | 207 | 299 | 309 | 6.32 |
| % to popul. 11-14 age | 12.9 | 22.6 | 34.2 | 41.9 | 55.1 | 57.0 | |
| In Classes IX-XII | 12 | 29 | n.a | 95 | 179 | 185 | 7.58 |
| % to popul. 14-17 age | 5.3 | 11.4 | n.a. | 20.5 | 25 | 25.3 | |
| In Degree Level & Above | 2 | 6 | 25 | 30 | 35 | n.a | 8.04 |
| Educational Institutions ('000) | | | | | | | |
| Primary/Junior | 210 | 330 | 408 | 494 | 544 | 548 | 2.61 |
| Middle/Senior | 14 | 50 | 91 | 119 | 141 | 144 | 6.44 |
| High/Higher Secondary | 7 | 17 | 37 | 51 | 71 | 73 | 6.46 |
| Colleges for general education | 542 | 1,082 | 2,285 | 3,421 | 4,329 | 4,718 | 5.78 |
| No. of universities | 27 | 45 | 100 (a) | 123 (a) | 176 (a) | 181 | 5.20 |
| Teaching Staff ('000) | | | | | | | |
| Primary Schools | 538 | 742 | 1,060 | 1,363 | 1,617 | 1603 | 3.02 |
| Middle Schools | 85 | 345 | 638 | 852 | 1,014 | 1033 | 6.93 |
| Higher Secondary Schools | 127 | 296 | 629 | 912 | 1,243 | 1236 | 6.36 |

*Note :  (a) Includes deemed universities and institutions of national importance.*

- ❏ Human resource development is an integral part of the programmes aiming at improving the quality of life, and extension of educational facilities is an essential effort in that direction.

- ❏ Inspite of the constitutional provision for ensuring free and compulsory education for children upto the age of 14 years by 1960, and subsequent commitments to attain universal elementary education the progress has fallen short of the target.

- ❏ While enrollment of 98% of children in the age-group 6-11, by 1987-88 looks impressive, the figure conceals the facts of irregular attendance and large-scale dropouts. Poverty, lack of awareness and sincere appreciation among parents about the importance of children's education, family compulsion to engage children for seasonal manual work on the farms are among the factors responsible for irregular attendance and dropouts. Reportedly, in 1985-88 the dropout rate in I to V classes was 48% and in I to VIII it was 64%.

## Educational Facilities 1950 - 51 & 1988 - 89

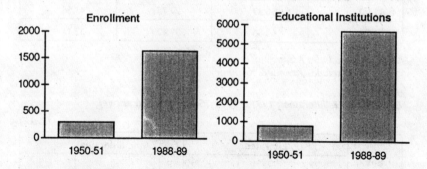

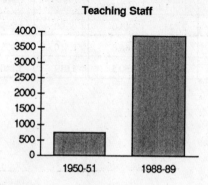

## 2.5   Literacy and Levels of Education :

*A: Literacy Rates : 1951 - 1991*

*(Per cent)*

| Census | Males | Females | Combined |
|---|---|---|---|
| **Population Aged Five Years and Above (census norm till 1981)** | | | |
| 1951 | 27.16 | 8.86 | 18.33 |
| 1961 | 40.40 | 15.34 | 28.31 |
| 1971 | 45.95 | 21.97 | 34.45 |
| 1981 (a) | 53.45 | 28.46 | 41.42 |
| **Population Aged Seven Years and Above (census norm since 1981)** | | | |
| 1981 (a) | 56.37 | 29.75 | 43.56 |
| 1991 (b) | 63.86 | 39.42 | 52.11 |

*Notes : (a) Excludes Assam*
*(b) Excludes Jammu & Kashmir*

*B : Literates & Illiterates : 1981 & 1991  (Seven Years & above)*

*(Lakh)*

| Sex | Literates | | | Illiterates | | |
|---|---|---|---|---|---|---|
| | 1981 | 1991 | % Change | 1981 | 1991 | % Change |
| **Males** | 1,569 | 2,243 | 43.0 | 1209 | 1,267 | 4.8 |
| **Females** | 770 | 1,278 | 66.0 | 1,810 | 1,973 | 9.0 |
| **Total** | 2,339 | 3,521 | 50.5 | 3,019 | 3,240 | 7.3 |

### C : Educational Levels : 1981 (Students aged five years and above)

| | Males | | Females | | Total | | Literates as % of Population of 5 Years & above |
|---|---|---|---|---|---|---|---|
| | Lakh | % | Lakh | % | Lakh | % | |
| 1. Literates with Education level | 1,139 | 70.6 | 531 | 66.6 | 1,670 | 69.3 | 28.7 |
| Primary | 489 | 30.3 | 271 | 34.0 | 760 | 31.5 | 13.1 |
| Middle | 290 | 18.0 | 134 | 16.8 | 424 | 17.6 | 7.3 |
| Matric / Higher Secondary | 279 | 17.3 | 100 | 12.5 | 379 | 15.7 | 6.5 |
| Non-Technical Diploma not Equal to a Degree (a) | 2 | 0.1 | 1 | 0.1 | 3 | 0.1 | 0.1 |
| Technical Diploma not Equal to a Degree | 8 | 0.5 | 2 | 0.3 | 10 | 0.4 | 0.2 |
| Graduate and Above | 71 | 4.4 | 23 | 2.9 | 94 | 3.9 | 1.6 |
| 2. Literates without Education | 474 | 29.4 | 26.6 | 33.4 | 740 | 30.7 | 12.7 |
| Total | 1,613 | 100.0 | 797 | 100.0 | 2,410 | 100.0 | 41.4 |

Note : (a) Includes certificate courses not equal to degree

❑ Since Independence our literacy rate has increased almost threefold to 52% by 1991.

❑ During the last decade number of literates increased by almost 12 crores or by over 50% but at the same time increase in number of illiterates by over 2 crores or 7.3% in the specified age-group is significant and indicates the increasing parasitic burden on the society.

❑ Even as the literacy rate among females in the specified age group has been rising and their number increased by 66% in 1981-91, they are much less than the number of male literates, and illiteracy among females have been increasing rapidly.

❑ Even though by 1981 data, one-third among the literate people had no formal education; only 8.4% of people aged five years or above had education of matriculation or above, and among them only 1.6% graduated. If the education were to be defined as completion of primary or middle school levels or as literacy even without any formal education, the estimates of so called literates in the country would probably diminish.

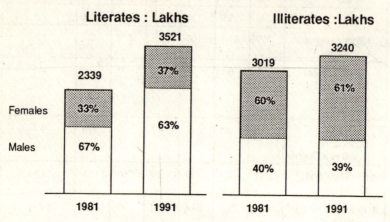

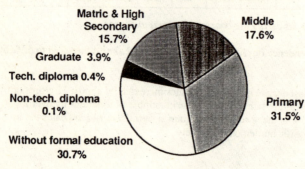

## 2.6　Housing Conditions : 1981

### A: Census of Houses by Types of Uses

| Use Pattern | Houses ('000 nos.) | As % of | |
|---|---|---|---|
| | | Occupied Houses | Total Number of Houses |
| I　Occupied Houses | 142,954 | 100.0 | 94.7 |
| 1.　Residence | 107,202 | 75.0 | 71.0 |
| 2.　Shop-cum-Residence | 1,428 | 1.0 | 0.9 |
| 3.　Workshop-cum-residence Households | 3,002 | 2.1 | 2.0 |
| 4.　Hotels, Tourist Houses, Sarais, Dharamshalas, Inspection Houses | 210 | 0.1 | 0.1 |
| 5.　Shops Excluding Eating Houses | 3,699 | 2.6 | 2.5 |
| 6.　Business Premises and Offices | 714 | 0.5 | 0.5 |
| 7.　Factories, Workshops, Worksheds | 2,293 | 1.6 | 1.5 |
| 8.　Restaurants, Eating Places and Sweetmeat Shops | 593 | 0.4 | 0.4 |
| 9.　Places for Entertainment and Community Gathering, Panchayats | 191 | 0.1 | 0.1 |
| 10. Places of worship | 1,526 | 1.1 | 1.0 |
| 11. Others | 22,096 | 15.5 | 14.7 |
| II　Unoccupied Houses | 8,047 | - | 5.3 |
| 　Total I + II | 151,001 | | 100.0 |

## B: Census of Houses by Types of Construction

| Types of House Structure by Material Used for Walls | As % of Total Number of Houses |
|---|---|
| I　Houses of Inferior Material | 61.3 |
| 1.　Grass, Leaves, Reeds, Bamboo | 11.1 |
| 2.　Mud | 41.1 |
| 3.　Unburnt Bricks | 7.6 |
| 4.　Wood | 1.0 |
| 5.　G.I. Sheets or other Metal Sheets | 0.5 |
| II　Houses of Reasonably Good Material | 38.7 |
| 6.　Burnt Bricks | 26.4 |
| 7.　Stone | 10.1 |
| 8.　Cement Concrete | 1.6 |
| 9.　Other Materials not Specified Above | 0.6 |
| Total (I + II) | 100.0 |

❏　According to 1981 census listing of houses, the bulk of them accounting for 71% were used for residential purposes and only 8% were utilised for economic activity. Of these 8%, 2.9% were used for dual purposes such as residence-cum-shop or household industry. The specific distribution is however insufficient as details for 20% were not available – classified as "others" and "unoccupied", at the time of listing.

❏　The pattern by material used as shown here for 1981 was not significantly different from that for 1971 census when 61.6% were made of inferior material then. Of the pucca houses the proportion of those showing improvement in 1981 were of burnt bricks (24.2%) and cement concrete (0.3%).

❏

## Houses by Types of Uses

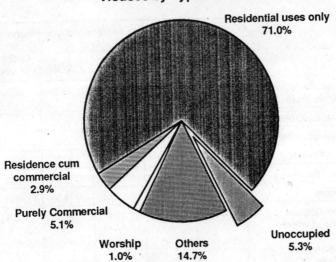

Residential uses only
71.0%

Residence cum
commercial
2.9%

Purely Commercial
5.1%

Worship
1.0%

Others
14.7%

Unoccupied
5.3%

## Houses by Types of Material Used

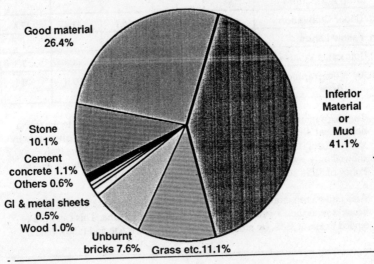

Good material
26.4%

Stone
10.1%

Cement
concrete 1.1%
Others 0.6%

GI & metal sheets
0.5%
Wood 1.0%

Unburnt
bricks 7.6%

Grass etc.11.1%

Inferior
Material
or
Mud
41.1%

India 1993-94

# NATURAL RESOURCES

## 3.1 Land Utilisation Statistics : 1950-51 and 1987-88

| Land Use | Million Hectares | | % to Geographical Area | | Increase in Area Million Hectares |
|---|---|---|---|---|---|
| | 1950-51 | 1987-88 | 1950-51 | 1987-88 | |
| A. Not Available for Crop Agriculture | 159.1 | 147.1 | 48.3 | 44.8 | -12.0 |
| a. Non-agricultural Uses | 9.4 | 20.8 | 2.9 | 6.3 | +11.4 |
| b. Barren Unculturable | 38.2 | 20.4 | 11.6 | 6.2 | -17.9 |
| c. Under Forests | 40.5 | 66.9 | 12.3 | 20.3 | +26.4 |
| d. Under Misc-trees | 19.8 | 3.5 | 6.0 | 1.1 | -16.3 |
| e. Pastures | 6.7 | 11.8 | 2.0 | 3.6 | +5.2 |
| f. Information not Available of which : Under Illegal Occupation of (i) Pakistan (ii) China | 44.5 - - | 23.7 7.9 4.3 | 13.5 - - | 7.2 2.4 1.3 | -20.8 - - |
| B. Available for Crop Agriculture | 169.7 | 165.8 | 51.7 | 50.4 | +18.9 |
| g. Under Cultivation | 118.7 | 136.2 | 36.1 | 41.4 | +17.4 |
| h. Fallow Lands | 28.1 | 29.6 | 8.6 | 9.0 | 1.5 |
| i) Culturable Wastes | 22.9 | 15.6 | 7.0 | 4.8 | -7.3 |
| Total : Geographical Area | 328.8 | 328.7 | 100.0 | 100.0 | -0.1 |

❑ The sharp increase in area under forests means transfer of lands to the forest department. Sizable segments are sparsely covered by trees and often only by shrubs. Satellite pictures of 1980-82 when subjected to expert analysis showed only about 14% of area actually under forests. The National Forest Policy of 1988 stipulates 33% of area under forest cover.

❑ Area under crop cultivation (net) shows next larger increase of 17.4 million hectares over the 37-years period or 5.7% of the total area. This can be extended to about 50%, by reclamation of culturable waste and fallow lands.

However, this would take a long time because of the prohibitive costs. The short run solution to increasing agricultural production would lie in improving land productivity and intensive activation rather than extension of area for cropping. It would be equally important to prevent soil degradation resulting on account of erosion by water, wind, heat and salinity and alkalinity due to water-logging etc.

## Pattern of Land Use

### 1950-51

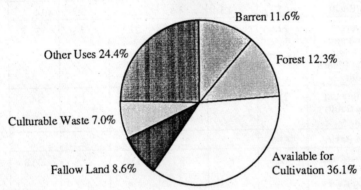

Barren 11.6%

Other Uses 24.4%

Forest 12.3%

Culturable Waste 7.0%

Fallow Land 8.6%

Available for Cultivation 36.1%

### 1986-87

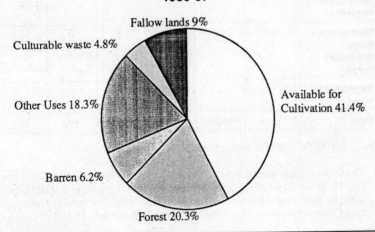

Fallow lands 9%

Culturable waste 4.8%

Other Uses 18.3%

Available for Cultivation 41.4%

Barren 6.2%

Forest 20.3%

## 3.2 Surface Water Resources : 1974

| River basins | Average Annual Flow | | Utilisable Annual Flow | | Approximate Annual Utilisation | |
|---|---|---|---|---|---|---|
| | MHM | % | MHM | % | MHM | Col. 5 as % of Col 3 |
| | (1) | (2) | (3) | (4) | (5) | (6) |
| Indus Basin | 7.7 | 4.3 | 4.6 | 6.8 | 3.7 | 80.4 |
| Godavari, Krishna and Other East-flowing Rivers of South | 22.5 | 12.6 | 19.0 | 27.1 | 7.3 | 38.4 |
| West-flowing Rivers South of Tapi | 21.8 | 12.3 | 3.0 | 4.3 | 1.1 | 36.7 |
| Ganga Basin | 51.0 | 28.7 | 25.0 | 35.7 | 8.5 | 34.0 |
| Mahanadi and Other East-flowing rivers upto Godavari | 12.3 | 6.9 | 9.1 | 13.0 | 2.8 | 30.8 |
| West-flowing Rivers North of Narmada | 2.5 | 1.4 | 2.0 | 2.9 | 0.5 | 25.0 |
| Brahmaputra Basin (including Barak) | 54.0 | 30.3 | 2.4 | 3.4 | 0.5 | 20.8 |
| Narmada and Tapi | 6.2 | 3.5 | 4.9 | 7.9 | 0.6 | 12.2 |
| Total | 178.0 | 100.0 | 70.0 | 100.0 | 25.0 | 35.7 |

*Notes : (a) MHM = Million hectare metres*

❑ Out of the average annual flow of 178 million hectare metres (MHM) of water flowing in our major river basins the utilisable flow is placed at 70 MHM, or 40%, by the National Commission on Agriculture. This is considered adequate for most purposes. The actual utilisation is so far only 25 MHM. Ganga and Godavari- Krishna hold the highest utilisable potential. Their aggregate utilisation is 63% of their potential.

❑ In our country, the task of water management – to slow down the speed as it flows into the streams or to sea – is rendered most difficult because of the denundation of forests, drying of grasslands and soil erosion.

❑ Consequently we sometimes have the dual problem of flash floods and drought.

❑ In most of our irrigation and flood control programmes we have adopted the high-cost civil engineering methods, often for variety of avoidable reasons, rather than the more preferable and less costly measures like afforestation, conversion of wasteland into grassland and soil conservation. This latter route could improve the availability and utilisation of our water resources and also offer other advantages of economic balance.

## 3.3 : Pattern of Present utilisation and Future Requirement of Water : 1985 and 2025

*(Million hectare metres)*

| Water Use by Purpose | Utilisation : 1985 | | | Future estimated requirement : 2025 | | |
|---|---|---|---|---|---|---|
| | Surface Water | Ground Water | Total | Surface Water | Ground Water | Total |
| 1. Irrigation | 33.14 | 17.34 | 50.48 | 61.17 | 24.37 | 65.54 |
| 2. Net Consumption for | 0.79 | 0.06 | 0.85 | 3.53 | 0.43 | 3.96 |
| (a) Domestic and Municipal Supply | 0.22 | 0.08 | 0.28 | 1.21 | 0.43 | 1.64 |
| (b) Industrial Use | 0.14 | - | 0.14 | 0.82 | - | 0.82 |
| (c) Thermal Power Generation | 0.43 | - | 0.43 | 1.50 | - | 1.50 |
| 3. Pisciculture | - | - | - | 2.79 | - | 2.79 |
| 4. Forestry | - | - | - | 2.21 | - | 2.21 |
| 5. Livestock Need | 0.49 | - | 0.49 | 1.18 | - | 1.18 |
| Total Demand | 32.42 | 17.40 | 51.82 | 70.88 | 24.80 | 95.68 |
| Total Utilisable Flow | 68.41 | 35.58 | 103.99 | 68.41 | 35.58 | 103.99 |
| Demand as Percent of Utilisable Flow | 50.3 | 48.9 | 49.8 | 103.6 | 69.7 | 92.0 |

❏ In 1985, irrigation alone accounted for 97% of the total demand for water, two-thirds of which was met from surface water resources. Including other uses, total demand for water was about half of the utilisable flow.

❏ By projections for 2025 AD, almost 92% of the utilisable flow of water is likely to be consumed. Share of irrigation in total demand is likely to diminish to 68%. But three-fourths of the irrigation needs would be drawn from surface resources. Therefore, including increased claims of other users, the total demand for surface water may exceed the total utilisable flow, as estimated way back in 1974 (Table 3.2)

❏ Even for ground water, a large claim would be for minor irrigation purposes.

## 3.4. Reserves, Production and Balance Life & Major Minerals

*(Million tonnes)*

| Minerals (Ranked by Value of Output in 1988) | Reserves as on 1.1.1985 | Production 1988 (Provisional) | Balance Life at Current Rate of Production : No. of Years (c) |
|---|---|---|---|
| Fuels | | | |
| Crude Oil | 757 (a) | 33.3 (a) | 23 |
| Coal | 192,359 (a) | 213.4 (a) | 901 |
| Natural gas (bln. cu. mt.) | 686 (a) | 10,245.0 (a) | 67 |
| Lignite | 6,210 (b) | 13.9 (a) | 447 |
| Metallic Minerals | | | |
| Iron Ore | 11,977 | 50.00 | 240 |
| Copper Ore | 325 | 5.06 | 64 |
| Chromite | 54 | 0.82 | 66 |
| Zinc & lead concentrates | 160 | 0.16 | 1,000 |
| Gold Ore | 11 | 0.42 | 26 |
| Bauxite | 2333 | 3.96 | 589 |
| Manganese Ore | 154 | 1.30 | 118 |
| Non-Metallic Minerals | | | |
| Limestone | 69,354 | 63.00 | 1,101 |
| Magnesite | 222 | 0.51 | 438 |
| Dolomite | 4608 | 2.21 | 2,085 |
| Kaolin (Chinaclay) | 872 | 0.58 | 1,503 |
| Gypsum | 319 | 1.43 | 223 |
| Fluorite (graded & cons) | 2 | 0.02 | 100 |
| Barytes | 71 | 0.45 | 158 |
| Diamond | 1,001 | 14.20 | 70 |
| Fireclay | 703 | 0.60 | 1,172 |
| Kyanite (raw) | 2 | 0.04 | 50 |
| Asbestos | 1 | 0.03 | 33 |

*Notes : (a) 1990*
      *(b) 1989*
      *(c) At annual rate of production shown in previous column.*

❑   Coal and lignite are our important fuel resources, and iron ore and bauxite are the important metallic mineral reserves of the country.

❑   In terms of our share in the world reserves of various minerals. India ranks 9th with its coal reserves accounting for 5.7% share, but with regard to crude oil and natural gas its position is 16th and 20th respectively with shares being little less than one percent each. India's bauxite reserves are the 5th largest with the World share of 4.6% and for iron ore it ranks 7th with a share of 5.1% of world reserves.

## India 's Share in world reserves

| Mineral | World reserves | India's Share & rank | To last |
|---|---|---|---|
| Crude oil 136.5 tns billion tns | | 0.8% 15th | 23 yrs. |
| Natural gas 119.4 trillion Cu. mt. | | 0.85% 20th | 67 yrs. |
| Coal 1,079 billion tns. | | 5.7% 9th | 901 yrs. |
| Iron Ore 64.6 billion tns | | 5.1% 7th | 240 yrs. |
| Bauxite 21.8 billion tns. | | 4.6% 5th | 589 yrs. |

## 3.5    Index Numbers of Mineral Production : 1951 to 1990

*(Base : 1980-81 = 100)*

| Year<br>Weights  % | Fuels<br>81.3 | Metallic<br>Minerals<br>11.2 | Non-Metallic<br>Minerals<br>7.5 | All<br>Minerals<br>100.0 |
|---|---|---|---|---|
| 1951 | 24.00 | 17.21 | n.a | 24.26 |
| 1956 | 27.57 | 19.99 | n.a | 27.90 |
| 1961 | 38.80 | 49.71 | 46.14 | 41.09 |
| 1966 | 56.83 | 60.54 | 60.82 | 57.76 |
| 1971 | 64.04 | 73.09 | 75.73 | 66.17 |
| 1976 | 87.38 | 107.64 | 98.00 | 90.41 |
| 1981 | 117.24 | 100.00 | 106.00 | 114.00 |
| 1986 | 186.77 | 134.00 | 141.00 | 178.00 |
| 1991 | 236.09 | 163.75 | 177.66 | 223.82 |
| **Compound annual rates of increase (%)** | | | | |
| 1951-61 | 4.92 | 11.19 | n.a | 5.41 |
| 1961-71 | 5.14 | 3.93 | 5.08 | 4.88 |
| 1971-81 | 6.23 | 3.18 | 3.42 | 5.59 |
| 1981-91 | 7.3 | 5.1 | 5.3 | 7.0 |
| 1951-90 | 5.96 | 5.83 | 4.59 (a) | 5.78 |

*Notes : a.    For the period 1961 to 1990.*

❑  Our overall minerals production has been accelerating since 1961, and the highest rate of increase was recorded during the latest decade of 1981 to 1991.

❑  We have been depleting our fuel mineral reserves more rapidly decade after decade. Average annual rate of increase in fuel output over the four decades was the highest among the three classes of mineral resources.

❑  The output growth for metallic minerals during the first decade was excessively high — over 11% per annum, but thereafter it came down considerably in the next two decades.

❑ Non-metallic minerals' rate of output growth was also subdued during 1971-81. Thereafter, it picked up rapidly, reflecting to an extent the exploitation of limestone for the many large cement plants that came up during the last decade.

**All Minerals Production Index**

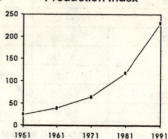

**Fuel Minerals Production Index**

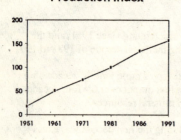

**Metallic Minerals Production Index**

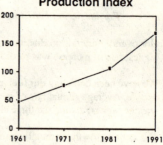

**Non-Metallic Minerals Production Index**

## 3.6    Production of Fuel Minerals

| Years | Coal Million tonnes | Lignite Million tonnes | Crude petroleum Million tonnes | Natural Gas : Utilised ( Million Cubic Metres) |
|---|---|---|---|---|
| 1950 | 32.8 | - | 0.3 | - |
| 1955 | 38.8 | - | - | - |
| 1960 | 92.6 | Neg 1 | 0.5 | 147 |
| 1965 | 67.2 | 2.3 | 3.0 | 325 |
| 1970 | 73.7 | 3.5 | 6.8 | 676 |
| 1975 | 95.9 | 2.8 | 8.3 | 1,252 |
| 1980 | 109.2 | 4.5 | 9.4 | 1,462 |
| 1985 | 149.2 | 7.8 | 29.9 | 4,688 |
| 1990 | 213.4 | 13.9 | 33.3 | 10,245 |
| **Compound annual rates of increase (%)** | | | | |
| 1950-60 | 4.8 | - | 5.2 | - |
| 1960-70 | 3.4 | 8.8 (a) | 29.8 | 16.5 |
| 1970-80 | 4.0 | 2.5 | 3.3 | 8.0 |
| 1980-90 | 6.9 | 11.9 | . 13.5 | 21.5 |
| 1950-90 | 4.8 | 7.5 (b) | 12.5 | 15.2 (c) |

*Notes : (a) Refers to 1965 & 1970,*
*(b) Refers to 1965 & 1990*
*(c) Refers to 1960 & 1990*

❏ Where the quantitative production of all the fuel minerals was sharply stepped up during the last decade, the annual rate of increase in output was more rapid in the case of crude oil and natural gas as compared to those for coal and lignite.

❏ The production of crude oil and natural gas during the last decade was so rapidly enhanced that their annual rates of increases over the four decades turned out to be much higher than those for coal and lignite.

❏ Large quantities of natural gas are being flared for want of infrastructure for transportation but more so because of the delay in putting up user industries.

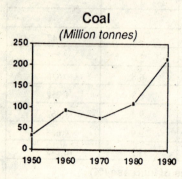

Coal
*(Million tonnes)*

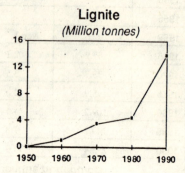

Lignite
*(Million tonnes)*

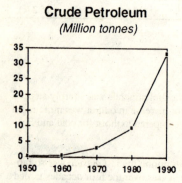

Crude Petroleum
*(Million tonnes)*

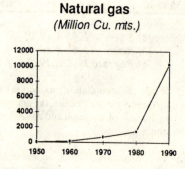

Natural gas
*(Million Cu. mts.)*

## 3.7    Production of Fuel Minerals : 1950-1990

*(In Rs. Crores)*

| Years | Coal | Lignite | Crude Petroleum | Natural Gas | Total |
|-------|------|---------|-----------------|-------------|-------|
| 1950 | 46.7 | - | 0.1 | - | 46.8 |
| 1955 | 60.0 | - | 0.2 | - | 60.2 |
| 1960 | 108.8 | 0.1 | 2.3 | 0.3 | 111.5 |
| 1965 | 169.9 | 4.7 | 20.5 | 1.0 | 196.1 |
| 1970 | 263.0 | 9.0 | 73.5 | 3.2 | 348.7 |
| 1975 | 559.6 | 14.9 | 227.6 | 4.6 | 806.7 |
| 1980 | 1,299.6 | 42.8 | 366.5 | 5.7 | 1714.6 |
| 1985 | 3,070.8 | 131.2 | 4517.8 | 16.6 | 7736.4 |
| 1990 | 6,010.8 | 343.9 | 7,044.3 | 1475.6 | 14,874.6 |
| Compound annual rates of increase (%) | | | | | |
| 1950-60 | 8.8 | - | 36.8 | - | 9.1 |
| 1960-70 | 9.2 | 56.8 | 41.4 | 26.7 | 12.1 |
| 1970-80 | 17.3 | 16.9 | 17.4 | 5.9 | 17.3 |
| 1980-90 | 16.6 | 23.2 | 34.4 | 74.3 | 24.1 |
| 1950-90 | 12.9 | 31.2 (a) | 32.1 | 32.8 (a) | 15.5 |

*Notes : (a)  Refers to 1960 & 1990.*

❑  Rate of increase in value of output is the combined result of the quantitative output growth and price increases.

❑  All the mineral fuels are under the administered price regime, and increases are expected mostly to compensate for the increase in cost of production, though often with some time-lag as in the case of coal, but rarely to curb the excessive growth in consumption as in the case of petroleum products.

❑  Rate of increase in prices during the last decade was much more for crude oil and natural gas as compared to that for coal and lignite. Price of natural gas recorded a sharp increase at the rate of 43% per annum during the last decade.

Highest rate of 12.8% per annum in coal prices was noted during the decade of 1970-80.

### Coal *(Rs. Crores)*

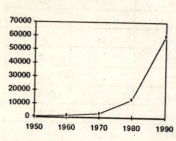

### Lignite *(Rs. Crores)*

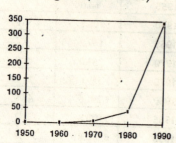

### Crude Petroleum *(Rs. Crores)*

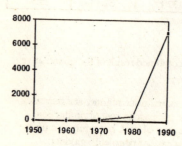

### Natural Gas *(Rs. Crores)*

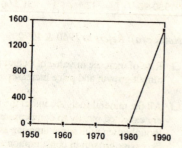

## 3.8   Production of Select Metallic Minerals 1950-1990

*(In Quantity terms)*

| Years | Iron Ore Million tonnes | Manganese Ore Million tonnes | Copper Ore Million tonnes | Lead Concentrates '000 tonnes | Zinc Concentrates '000 tonnes |
|---|---|---|---|---|---|
| 1950 | 3.0 | 0.9 | 0.37 | 2.0 | 0.7 |
| 1955 | 7.0 | 1.7 | 0.36 | 3.1 | 4.8 |
| 1960 | 16.6 | 1.5 | 0.45 | 6.2 | 9.8 |
| 1965 | 23.9 | 1.6 | 0.47 | 5.5 | 9.6 |
| 1970 | 31.4 | 1.7 | 0.52 | 3.9 | 15.9 |
| 1975 | 41.8 | 1.6 | 1.84 | 15.1 | 39.2 |
| 1980 | 41.9 | 1.7 | 2.01 | 16.8 | 46.5 |
| 1985 | 44.2 | 1.3 | 4.21 | 35.4 | 87.1 |
| 1990 | 53.7 | 1.4 | 5.29 | 43.4 | 137.6 |
| **Compound Annual Rates of Increase (%)** | | | | | |
| 1950-60 | 18.7 | 5.2 | 2.0 | 12.0 | 30.2 |
| 1960-70 | 6.6 | 1.3 | 1.5 | -4.5 | 5.0 |
| 1970-80 | 2.9 | - | 14.5 | 15.7 | 11.3 |
| 1980-90 | 2.5 | -1.9 | 10.2 | 10.0 | 11.5 |
| 1950-90 | 7.5 | 1.1 | 6.9 | 8.0 | 14.1 |

❑ Production of iron ore, of which we have abundant reserves, increased noticably between 1970 and 1975 but thereafter it stagnated around 42 million tonnes for over a decade, only to further increase rapidly during the next-five years till 1990.

❑ Manganese ore which is an essential input in steel making has on the other hand however around 1.5 million tonnes all through the four decades almost.

❑ Production of ores of other important metals like copper, lead and zinc, has shown a consistently rising trend since 1975.

### Iron Ore
*(Million tonnes)*

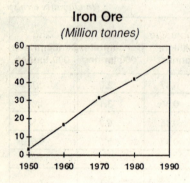

### Manganese Ore
*(Million tonnes)*

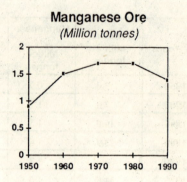

### Copper Ore
*(Million tonnes)*

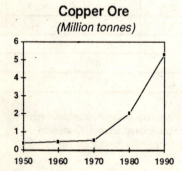

### Lead Concentrates
*('000 tonnes)*

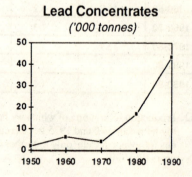

## 3.9 Production of Select Metallic Minerals 1950-1990

*(Rs. crores)*

| Years | Iron Ore | Manganese Ore | Copper Ore | Lead Concentrates | Zinc Concentrates | Total (Including others minerals) |
|---|---|---|---|---|---|---|
| 1950 | 1.5 | 4.7 | 1.2 | Negl | Negl | 13.5 |
| 1955 | 4.7 | 11.7 | 2.6 | 0.1 | 0.2 | 25.1 |
| 1960 | 14.0 | 8.9 | 2.4 | 0.2 | 0.3 | 32.6 |
| 1965 | 20.6 | 8.9 | 2.5 | 0.3 | 0.4 | 38.3 |
| 1970 | 36.9 | 7.8 | 4.4 | 0.5 | 1.6 | 62.0 |
| 1975 | 76.7 | 13.4 | 19.6 | 2.5 | 5.9 | 150.7 |
| 1980 | 124.5 | 25.8 | 32.9 | 4.7 | 12.0 | 251.8 |
| 1985 | 254.1 | 33.0 | 89.9 | 23.4 | 44.7 | 573.8 |
| 1990 | 484.0 | 54.1 | 138.6 | 31.5 | 77.7 | 1,063.2 |
| Compound annual rates of increase (%) | | | | | | |
| 1950-60 | 25.0 | 6.6 | 7.2 | 14.9 (a) | 8.5 (a) | 9.2 |
| 1960-70 | 10.2 | -1.3 | 6.3 | 9.6 | 18.2 | 6.6 |
| 1970-80 | 12.9 | 12.7 | 22.3 | 25.1 | 22.3 | 15.0 |
| 1980-90 | 14.5 | 7.9 | 15.5 | 21.0 | 20.5 | 15.6 |
| 1950-91 | 15.5 | 6.3 | 12.6 | 17.9 (b) | 18.6 (b) | 11.5 |

*Notes* (a) *Refers to 1955 to 1960*
(b) *Refers to 1955 to 1990*

❑ Entire mining of copper, lead and zinc is under the public sector and so are the plants producing these important metals. Those ores are therefore more or less for captive consumption.

❑ More than half of iron ore and manganese ore production comes from the mines in the public sector. Likewise, major steel producing plants, except of TISCO, are also owned by the public sector undertakings.

❑ Price element in the value of production of these important minerals would essentially reflect the increases in the cost of mining of ores.

### Zinc Concentrates Ore
*(Rs. Crores)*

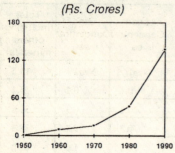

### Iron Ore *(Rs. Crores)*

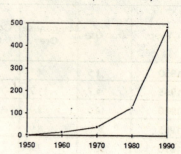

### Manganese Ore *(Rs. Crores)*

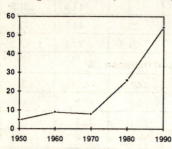

### Copper Ore *(Rs. Crores)*

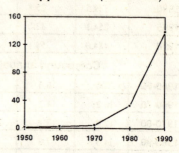

### Lead Concentrates Ore
*(Rs. Crores)*

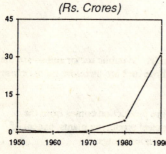

### Zinc Concentrates Ore
*(Rs. Crores)*

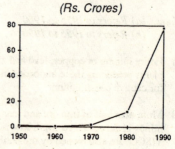

4

## 4.1 Commercial and Non-commercial Energy Consumption and Demand Projections

*(Million tonnes of coal replacement)*

| Year | Commercial | Non-commercial | Total |
|---|---|---|---|
| I : N.B. Prasad Working Group - 1979 (Consumption) | | | |
| 1953 - 54 | 60 | 126 | 186 |
| 1960 - 61 | 101 | 146 | 247 |
| 1965 - 66 | 147 | 160 | 307 |
| 1970 - 71 | 197 | 172 | 370 |
| 1975 - 76 | 253 | 195 | 448 |
| II : Energy Demand Screening Group - 1986 (Projections) | | | |
| 1984 - 85 | 428 | 313 | 741 |
| 1989 - 90 | 682 | 343 | 1,025 |
| 1994 - 95 | 907 | 369 | 1,276 |
| 1999 - 2000 | 1,224 | 407 | 1,631 |
| 2004 - 05 | 1,637 | 411 | 2,048 |
| Annual Rates of Increase (%) | | | |
| 1953 - 76 | 6.8 | 2.0 | 4.1 |
| 1984 - 90 | 9.8 | 1.8 | 6.7 |
| 1989 - 95 | 5.9 | 1.5 | 4.5 |
| 1994 - 2000 | 6.2 | 2.0 | 5.7 |
| 1999 - 2005 | 6.0 | 0.2 | 4.7 |

❏ Promotion of lift irrigation schemes enhanced pace of industrialisation. Expansion of rail and road transport under the development plans have shown up in rapid increase of commercial energy consumption. Particularly from 1968-69 the proportion of commercial energy in total energy consumption exceeded that of non-commercial energy. While total energy consumption rose 2.5 times between 1953 - 54 and 1975 - 76, consumption of commercial energy

rose four-fold, increasing at the rate of 7% per annum. Its share of the total by
the end of this period was 56%.

❑ According to projections made in 1986. consumption of commercial energy
was to increase at about 10% per annum during 1984-89 period with its share
rise from 58% on 1984-85 to 67% in 1988-89. It was assumed that thereafter,
the growth rate of commercial energy consumption would to taper off to 6%
per annum during the 1999-2005 period, but its share in total energy consumption would reach 80%, as the growth rate of non-commercial energy consumption would diminish to barely 0.2% per annum.

## Total energy consumption/demand

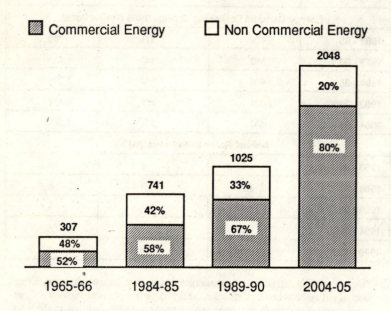

## 4.2 Relative Shares of Primary Sources of Energy : 1970 -71 — 1991 - 92

*(Per cent)*

| Year | Lignite | Coal | Oil | Natural Gas | Hydro Power | Nuclear Power |
|---|---|---|---|---|---|---|
| 1970 - 71 | 2.8 | 60.1 | 31.1 | 2.1 | 3.5 | 0.3 |
| 1975 - 76 | 1.9 | 63.1 | 28.5 | 2.6 | 3.6 | 0.3 |
| 1980 - 81 | 2.7 | 61.2 | 29.3 | 2.2 | 4.2 | 0.3 |
| 1984 - 85 | 3.1 | 58.7 | 29.3 | 5.0 | 3.6 | 0.3 |
| 1985 - 86 | 2.9 | 56.0 | 32.7 | 5.1 | 3.1 | 0.3 |
| 1989 - 90 | 3.5 | 55.8 | 29.7 | 8.1 | 2.9 | 0.2 |
| 1990 - 91 | 3.5 | 56.5 | 28.5 | 8.1 | 3.2 | 0.3 |
| 1991 - 92 | 3.7 | 57.7 | 27.2 | 8.1 | 3.0 | 0.2 |

*Note : Raw totals may not add up to 100 due to rounding up of the percentage shares*

❑ Coal, of which we have abundant reserves, constitutes by far the largest sources of primary energy in our country.

❑ From 60% in 1970-71, its share in total supplies of primary energy sources increased to 63% in 1975 - 76 but the share declined steadily and remained low 60% since 1978 - 79. It has gone down to about 56% in recent years.

❑ During 1989 - 90 and 1990 - 91, there were reports of considerable shortages and irregular supplies of coal to consumers. Also, complaints about inferior quality, high ash content and presence of useless foreign material have been on the rise. On the other hand, because of the increases in rail freights, the relative cost of coal to the consumers has increased. These factors have induced some of the consumers to switch over to fuel oil where possible.

❑ The share of fuel oil in total availability of primary energy sources has fluctuated around 30%.

❑ The impressive rise in the share of natural gas is noteworthy as it reflects the lowering of the proportion of gas flared from 50% in the early seventies to less than 30% in 1990-91.

❑ The combined share of oil and natural gas has been on the rise implying a marked shift in preference for hydrocarbons, notwithstanding our dependence on imports to meet the demand.

## 4.3   Sectorwise Consumption of Commercial Energy : 1953 - 54 — 1984 - 85

| Year | House-hold | Agri-culture | Industry | Trans-port | Others | Total |
|---|---|---|---|---|---|---|
| Consumption in Million tonnes of coal replacement | | | | | | |
| 1953 - 54 | 12.7 | 1.8 | 22.4 | 21.5 | 1.7 | 60.1 |
| 1960 - 61 | 20.8 | 3.6 | 39.7 | 34.2 | 2.9 | 101.2 |
| 1970 - 71 | 35.5 | 9.1 | 76.3 | 64.6 | 11.8 | 197.2 |
| 1978 - 79 | 40.3 | 31.3 | 113.4 | 93.2 | 16.1 | 294.3 |
| 1979 - 80 (a) | 64.1 | 38.4 | 156.0 | 134.0 | 17.2 | 409.7 |
| 1984 - 85 (a) | 98.9 | 52.6 | 220.5 | 169.5 | 22.9 | 564.4 |
| Percent Shares in Consumption | | | | | | |
| 1953 - 54 | 21.1 | 3.0 | 37.3 | 35.8 | 2.8 | 100 |
| 1960 - 61 | 20.6 | 3.6 | 39.2 | 33.8 | 2.8 | 100 |
| 1970 - 71 | 18.0 | 4.3 | 38.7 | 32.7 | 6.0 | 100 |
| 1978 - 79 | 13.7 | 10.6 | 38.5 | 31.7 | 5.5 | 100 |
| 1979 - 80 | 15.7 | 9.4 | 38.2 | 32.8 | 3.9 | 100 |
| 1984 - 85 | 18.2 | 9.8 | 36.4 | 31.4 | 4.2 | 100 |

*Note : (a) Estimated by CMIE*

❑ Industry and transport sectors happen to be the two largest claimants in commercial energy consumption in the country, together accounting for nearly 70% of the total. Although the share of each of these sectors had decline, particularly between 1979-80 and 1984-85, projection exercises suggest that their respective shares would continue to improve steadily till the year 2000 and the share of transport sector even beyond that year.

❑ While the share of agriculture in consumption of commercial energy improved particularly rapidly after 1970-71 to about 10% between 1978-79 and 1984-85, its share in future is expected to diminish.

❑ On the other hand, consumption share of the household sector after reaching a low 1978-79, started picking up once again. It is expected to increase more rapidly, almost doubling its claim by 2005.

## 4.4 Sectorwise Shares by Sources of Commercial Energy Consumption : 1953 - 54 — 1984 - 85

*(Per cent)*

| Year | House-hold | Agri-culture | Industry | Transport | Others | Total |
|---|---|---|---|---|---|---|
| **Coal** | | | | | | |
| 1953 - 54 | 7.6 | - | 48.1 | 42.2 | 2.1 | 100 |
| 1960 - 61 | 8.4 | - | 47.1 | 42.5 | 2.0 | 100 |
| 1970 - 71 | 7.9 | - | 60.5 | 31.0 | 0.6 | 100 |
| 1978 - 79 | 5.8 | - | 73.4 | 18.0 | 2.8 | 100 |
| 1984 - 85 | 3.0 | - | 78.0 | 13.0 | 6.0 | 100 |
| **Oil** | | | | | | |
| 1953 - 54 | 41.1 | 6.8 | 15.3 | 36.8 | - | 100 |
| 1960 - 61 | 37.7 | 6.2 | 16.5 | 39.6 | - | 100 |
| 1970 - 71 | 28.4 | 4.6(a) | 11.2 | 48.6 | 7.2 | 100 |
| 1978 - 79 | 20.3 | 13.7 (a) | 6.4 | 55.4 (b) | 4.2 | 100 |
| 1984 - 85 | 29.0 | 10.0 | 5.0 | 56.0 | - | 100 |
| **Electricity** | | | | | | |
| 1953-54 | 9.2 | 2.6 | 65.8 | 7.9 | 1.5 | 100 |
| 1960-61 | 8.9 | 4.7 | 68.7 | 4.7 | 13.0 | 100 |
| 1970-71 | 7.9 | 9.3 | 70.7 | 2.7 | 9.2 | 100 |
| 1978-79 | 9.1 | 14.2 | 63.8 | 3.1 | 9.8 | 100 |
| 1984-85 | 11.0 | 16.0 | 62.0 | 2.0 | 9.0 | 100 |

*Notes : (a) Includes consumption for tractors used in farming-cum-transportation in rural areas.*
*(b) Estimated by CMIE.*

❑ Industry and transport are to be the largest users of coal. The share of industry increased rapidly while that of transport has dwindled because of the shift from coal to diesel by railways.

❑ The change over to diesel by the railways has increased the share of the transport sector in oil consumption. Besides, the rapid increase of road transport has placed the transport sector as the largest user of oil. Interestingly, in early years the top position was claimed by the household sector, and in the subsequent years also its share in oil consumption, though declining, continues to be more that of industry which is also declining the share of agriculture has also increased in recent years, partly due to increased use of tractors for farming-cum-transport uses.

❑ Electricity is largely consumed by the industries; agriculture has taken the second place since 1970-71 largely because of rural electrification and increasing use of pump-sets for lift irrigation.

## 4.5    Sectorwise Relative Shares of Sources of Commercial Energy Consumption :1953-54 - 1978-79

*(Per cent)*

| Year | Coal | Oil | Electricity | Total |
|------|------|-----|-------------|-------|
| **Household** | | | | |
| 1953 - 54 | 17.3 | 77.2 | 5.5 | 100 |
| 1960 - 61 | 13.5 | 79.3 | 7.2 | 100 |
| 1970 - 71 | 11.5 | 77.7 | 10.8 | 100 |
| 1978 - 79 | 10.0 | 71.2 | 18.8 | 100 |
| **Agriculture** | | | | |
| 1953 - 54 | - | 89.0 | 11.0 | 100 |
| 1960 - 61 | - | 77.4 | 22.6 | 100 |
| 1970 - 71 | - | 49.8 | 50.2 | 100 |
| 1978 - 79 | - | 61.8 (a) | 38.2 | 100 |
| **Industry** | | | | |
| 1953 - 54 | 61.5 | 16.2 | 22.3 | 100 |
| 1960 - 61 | 52.6 | 18.2 | 29.2 | 100 |
| 1970 - 71 | 40.7 | 14.3 | 45.0 | 100 |
| 1978 - 79 | 44.5 | 7.9 | 47.6 | 100 |
| **Transport** | | | | |
| 1953 - 54 | 56.4 | 40.8 | 2.8 | 100 |
| 1960 - 61 | 46.8 | 50.8 | 2.4 | 100 |
| 1970 - 71 | 24.6 | 73.2 | 2.2 | 100 |
| 1978 - 79 | 13.3 | 83.9 | 2.8 | 100 |
| **Others** | | | | |
| 1953 - 54 | 35.3 | - | 64.7 | 100 |
| 1960 - 61 | 24.1 | - | 75.9 | 100 |
| 1970 - 71 | 2.6 | 59.2 | 38.2 | 100 |
| 1978 - 79 | 11.9 | 36.2 | 57.9 | 100 |

*Note : (a) Includes consumption for tractors used in farming-cum- transportation in rural areas.*

❑ Household sector meets three-fourths of its energy needs from oil though dependence on electricity is on the rise.

❑ Agriculture depends largely on oil though share of electricity as the source is seen to be rising.

❑ Industry seems to be shifting over from coal and oil to electricity.

❑ Transport switched over from coal to oil rather rapidly, and the share is likely to shift somewhat from oil to electricity where rail traffic is concerned.

## 4.6 Trends in Production and Supply of Primary sources of Energy : 1970 - 71 – 1991 - 92

| | 1970-71 | 1975-76 | 1980-81 | 1985-86 | 1990-91 | 1991-92 |
|---|---|---|---|---|---|---|
| **IN ABSOLUTE QUANTITIES** | | | | | | |
| **Lignite** (million tonnes) | 3.39 | 3.03 | 5.11 | 8.05 | 13.44 | 14.99 |
| **COAL (MILLION TONNES)** | | | | | | |
| Production | 72.95 | 99.68 | 113.91 | 154.20 | 211.73 | 229.28 |
| Supply | 72.95 | 99.68 | 114.22 | 156.65 | 217.61 | 235.28 |
| **OIL (MILLION TONNES)** | | | | | | |
| Production | 6.82 | 8.45 | 10.51 | 30.17 | 33.03 | 30.34 |
| Supply | 18.51 | 2.07 | 26.76 | 44.79 | 53.73 | 54.37 |
| **Natural Gas (mln. cu.mtrs)** | 1,445.00 | 2,368.00 | 2,358.00 | 8,134.00 | 17,998.00 | 18,885.00 |
| **Hydro Power (Mln. Kwh)** | 25,248.00 | 33,302.00 | 46,542.00 | 50,933.00 | 71,535.00 | 72,615.00 |
| **Nuclear Power** | 2,417.00 | 2,626.00 | 3,001.00 | 4,985.00 | 6,244.00 | 5,644.00 |
| **OIL EQUIVALENT (MILLION TONNES)** | | | | | | |
| **Lignite** | 1.66 | 1.48 | 2.50 | 3.94 | 6.75 | 7.35 |
| **COAL** | | | | | | |
| Production | 33.75 | 48.84 | 55.82 | 75.56 | 103.75 | 112.35 |
| Supply | 33.75 | 48.84 | 55.97 | 76.76 | 106.63 | 115.29 |

|  | 1970-71 | 1975-76 | 1980-81 | 1985-86 | 1990-91 | 1991-92 |
|---|---|---|---|---|---|---|
| **OIL** |  |  |  |  |  |  |
| Production | 6.82 | 8.55 | 10.51 | 30.17 | 33.03 | 30.34 |
| Supply | 18.51 | 22.07 | 26.76 | 44.79 | 53.73 | 54.37 |
| Natural Gas | 1.24 | 2.03 | 2.02 | 6.97 | 15.33 | 16.18 |
| Hydro Power | 2.10 | 2.78 | 3.88 | 4.24 | 5.96 | 6.05 |
| Nuclear Power | 0.20 | 0.22 | 0.25 | 0.42 | 0.52 | 0.47 |
| Total | 59.46 | 77.42 | 91.38 | 137.12 | 188.85 | 199.69 |

❑ Lignite deposits are largely located in Tamil Nadu which accounts for 78% of total reserves in the country. Although its production has been increasing, lignite contributes 3.5% of our total energy supplies. A small quantity of superior coking coal is imported for blending with indigenous quality for use in steel plants. As for crude petroleum oil our import dependence has declined from 64% in 1970-71 to 38% in 1990-91, but it is still high due to slow- down in indigenous production as against rising demand for petroleum products. Overall, our dependence on imports for our energy needs declined from 19.5% in 1970-71 to 13.5% in 1990-91.

❑ Supplies of all energy sources except hydro power increased at a faster rates during the eighties as compared to the seventies. Annual growth rate of total energy supply increased from 4.4% during the seventies to 7.5% per annum during the eighties giving an average rate of 6% over the two decades.

❑ These annual rates of increase in total energy supplies could be meaning fully compared with those of our real GDP which averaged 3.1% during the seventies and 5.5% per annum during the eighties. These suggest an average energy intensity of 1.4 in our economic growth process.

## 4.7 Crude Oil Reserves : 1966 to 1991

*(million tonnes)*

| As on 1 January | On-shore fields | | | Off-shore : Bombay High | Total Reserves |
|---|---|---|---|---|---|
| | Gujarat | Assam | Total | | |
| 1966 | 62.73 | 90.27 | 153.00 | – | 153.00 |
| 1967 | 65.88 | 88.96 | 154.84 | – | 154.84 |
| 1968 | 64.92 | 76.08 | 141.00 | – | 141.00 |
| 1969 | 59.80 | 72.51 | 132.31 | – | 132.31 |
| 1970 | 56.38 | 71.46 | 127.84 | – | 127.84 |
| 1971 | 51.08 | 62.70 | 113.78 | – | 113.78 |
| 1972 | 52.28 | 72.90 | 125.18 | – | 125.18 |
| 1973 | 49.45 | 77.87 | 127.32 | – | 127.32 |
| 1974 | 48.45 | 76.05 | 124.50 | – | 124.50 |
| 1975 | 45.72 | 84.41 | 130.13 | 13.77 | 143.90 |
| 1976 | 45.79 | 81.99 | 127.78 | 147.68 | 275.46 |
| 1977 | 45.62 | 82.28 | 127.90 | 175.28 | 303.18 |
| 1978 | 47.49 | 78.50 | 125.99 | 221.04 | 347.03 |
| 1979 | 45.34 | 82.81 | 128.15 | 226.29 | 354.44 |
| 1980 | 52.73 | 82.65 | 135.38 | 230.95 | 366.33 |
| 1981 | 51.48 | 89.00 | 140.48 | 328.29 | 468.77 |
| 1982 | 53.18 | 91.52 | 144.70 | 325.18 | 469.88 |
| 1983 | 90.58 | 97.03 | 187.61 | 338.70 | 526.31 |
| 1984 | 88.00 | 99.01 | 187.01 | 323.81 | 510.82 |
| 1985 | 88.61 | 101.80 | 188.41 | 311.10 | 499.51 |
| 1986 | 98.64 | 113.83 | 212.47 | 345.54 | 558.01 |

*contd. . .*

| As on 1 January | On-shore fields | | | Off-shore : Bombay High | Total Reserves |
|---|---|---|---|---|---|
| | Gujarat | Assam | Total | | |
| 1987 | 132.05 | 119.03 | 251.08 | 330.35 | 581.43 |
| 1988 | 143.02 | 124.38 | 267.40 | 371.04 | 638.44 |
| 1989 | 155.12 | 140.24 | 295.36 | 430.86 | 426.22 |
| 1990 | 161.71 | 144.95 | 306.66 | 450.74 | 757.40 |
| 1991 | 158.26 | 156.22 | 314.48 | 491.67 | 806.15 |
| **Compound Annual Rates of Increase (%)** | | | | | |
| 1966 - 74 | -3.2 | -2.1 | -2.5 | | -2.5 |
| 1974 - 83 | 7.2 | 2.7 | 4.7 | 12.6 (a) | 17.4 |
| 1983 - 86 | 2.9 | 5.5 | 4.2 | 0.7 | 2.0 |
| 1986 - 90 | 13.2 | 6.2 | 9.6 | 6.9 | 7.9 |
| 1966 - 90 | 4.0 | 2.0 | 2.9 | 8.3 (b) | 6.9 |

*Notes : (a) 1976 to 1983*
*(b) 1976 to 1990*

❑ Discovery of crude oil reserves in Bombay High Off-shore in 1975 marked a significant turning point in the oil economy of India, as by that time the reserves in Gujarat and Assam had steadily dwindled and continued to stagnate thereafter till 1982 and 1980 respectively.

❑ Massive addition from Bombay High from 1976 onwards meant doubling of oil reserves. However, during the mid-eighties reserves in Bombay High stagnated and even showed some decline. But the reserves position thereafter again started increasing after 1986 due to the new discovery of Neelam oil field.

❑ Gujarat reserves again stated improving during the eighties but more notably during the second half due to the additional reserves located in Gandhar Dahej fields in the Gulf of Cambay.

❑ Assam reserves also improved during the late eighties but this one time largest reserves of the country became the smallest after 1981 when Gujarat surpassed the position and Bombay High continued at the top.

❑ If no new discoveries are added in the coming years then the total recoverable reserves could last for no more than 22 years from 1990 at the current rate of production.

## 4.8 Natural Gas Reserves : 1966 to 1991

*(billion cubic metres)*

| As on 1 January | On-shore Fields | | | | Off-shore Bombay High | Total Reserves |
|---|---|---|---|---|---|---|
| | Gujarat | Assam | Rajasthan | Total | | |
| 1966 | 23.09 | 40.06 | | 63.15 | – | 63.15 |
| 1967 | 24.65 | 42.60 | | 67.25 | – | 67.25 |
| 1968 | 21.80 | 41.54 | | 63.34 | – | 63.34 |
| 1969 | 22.90 | 42.10 | | 65.60 | – | 65.60 |
| 1970 | 19.66 | 42.82 | | 62.48 | – | 62.48 |
| 1971 | 18.84 | 43.45 | | 62.29 | – | 62.29 |
| 1972 | 16.88 | 45.25 | 0.38 | 62.51 | – | 62.51 |
| 1973 | 16.35 | 49.71 | 0.38 | 66.44 | – | 66.44 |
| 1974 | 16.18 | 51.30 | 0.38 | 67.86 | – | 67.86 |
| 1975 | 15.72 | 65.24 | 0.43 | 81.39 | 6.28 | 87.67 |
| 1976 | 15.41 | 61.42 | 0.43 | 78.26 | 106.62 | 184.88 |
| 1977 | 16.20 | 63.76 | 0.43 | 80.39 | 148.08 | 228.47 |
| 1978 | 15.66 | 63.62 | 0.43 | 79.71 | 186.15 | 265.86 |
| 1979 | 15.80 | 63.35 | 0.43 | 79.58 | 264.64 | 344.22 |
| 1980 | 16.39 | 63.53 | 0.43 | 80.35 | 270.96 | 351.31 |
| 1981 | 15.99 | 65.19 | 0.43 | 80.61 | 329.04 | 410.65 |
| 1982 | 18.18 | 70.66 | 0.43 | 89.27 | 330.62 | 419.89 |
| 1983 | 18.95 | 78.67 | 0.43 | 98.05 | 377.21 | 475.26 |
| 1984 | 18.60 | 81.31 | 0.54 | 100.45 | 377.80 | 478.25 |
| 1985 | 21.87 | 87.67 | 0.54 | 110.08 | 368.55 | 478.63 |
| 1986 | 26.99 | 91.83 | 0.54 | 119.36 | 377.69 | 497.05 |
| 1987 | 41.26 | 97.82 | 0.74 | 139.82 | 400.99 | 540.81 |

*contd. . .*

| As on 1 January | On-shore Fields | | | | Off-shore Bombay High | Total Reserves |
|---|---|---|---|---|---|---|
| | Gujarat | Assam | Rajasthan | Total | | |
| 1988 | 62.11 | 105.49 | 0.78 | 168.38 | 411.09 | 579.47 |
| 1989 | 85.59 | 120.49 | 1.00 | 207.08 | 447.47 | 654.55 |
| 1990 | 92.58 | 135.47 | 1.04 | 229.09 | 457.36 | 686.45 |
| 1991 | 93.39 | 151.68 | 1.22 | 246.29 | 483.50 | 729.79 |
| Compound Annual Rates of Interest (%) | | | | | | |
| 1966 - 74 | -4.3 | 3.1 | | 0.9 | | 0.9 |
| 1974 - 83 | 1.8 | 4.9 | 1.4 | 4.2 | 19.8 (a) | 24.1 |
| 1983 - 86 | 12.5 | 5.3 | 7.9 | 6.8 | -1.0 | 1.5 |
| 1986 - 90 | 33.4 | 7.0 | 16.7 | 17.7 | 4.9 | 8.4 |
| 1966 - 90 | 5.6 | 4.7 | 6.9 | 5.5 | 11.0 (b) | 10.5 |

Notes : (a) 1976 to 1983
        (b) 1976 to 1990

❑ Natural gas has gained in importance as a supplementary source of energy and as an alternative feedstock for fertiliser and petrochemicals industries.

❑ Total reserves of natural gas have increased at the average rate of over 10% per annum, though in late eighties the pace increased. Bombay High accounts for as much as two-thirds of the total gas reserves.

❑ At the present rate of production of 16 billion cubic metres, the existing reserves could last for about 40 years.

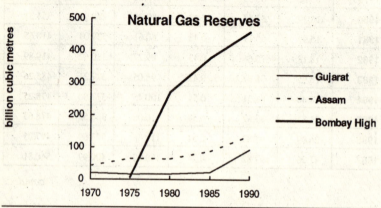

## 4.9 : Trend in Production of Crude Oil and Natural gas : 1970 - 71 — 1991 - 92

| Year | Crude Oil Prodn. (million tonnes) | Natural Gas (million cubic metres) | | | | | Total Crude Oil & Natural Gas in Mtoe |
|---|---|---|---|---|---|---|---|
| | | Gross Output | Flared | | Net Output | Net Output in Mtoe (b) | |
| | | | Volume | % of Gross Output | | | |
| | 1 | 2 | 3 | 4 | 5 | 6 | 7 |
| 1970 - 71 | 6.822 | 1,445 | 762 | 52.7 | 647 | 0.55 | 7.372 |
| 1975 - 76 | 8.448 | 2,368 | 1,082 | 45.7 | 1,124 | 0.96 | 9.408 |
| 1980 - 81 | 10,507 | 2,358 | 769 | 32.6 | 1,522 | 1.30 | 11.807 |
| 1981 - 82 | 16.194 | 3,851 | 1,519 | 39.4 | 2,222 | 1.90 | 18.094 |
| 1982 - 83 | 21.063 | 4,936 | 1,888 | 38.2 | 2,957 | 2.53 | 23.593 |
| 1983 - 84 | 26.020 | 5,961 | 2,517 | 42.2 | 3,399 | 2.91 | 28.930 |
| 1984 - 85 | 28.990 | 7,241 | 3,052 | 42.1 | 4,141 | 3.55 | 32.540 |
| 1985 - 86 | 30.168 | 8,134 | 3,118 | 38.3 | 4,950 | 4.24 | 34.408 |
| 1986 - 87 | 30.480 | 9,853 | 2,718 | 27.6 | 7,072 | 6.06 | 36.540 |
| 1987 - 88 | 30.357 | 11,467 | 3,445 | 30.0 | 7,968 | 6.83 | 37.187 |
| 1988 - 89 | 32.040 | 12,217 | 3,883 | 29.4 | 9,250 | 7.93 | 39.970 |
| 1989 - 90 | 34.087 | 16,989 | 5,721 | 33.7 | 11,172 | 9.57 | 43.657 |
| 1990 - 91 | 33.030 | 17,998 | 5,161 | 28.7 | 12,743 | 10.92 | 43.950 |
| 1991 - 92 | 30.342 | 20,805 | - | - | - | - | - |
| Compound annual rate of increase (%) | | | | | | | |
| 1970 - 71 & 1980 - 81 | 4.41 | 5.02 | 0.09 | | 8.93 | 8.93 | 4.82 |
| 1980 - 81 & 1990 - 91 | 12.14 | 22.54 | 20.97 | | 23.68 | 23.72 | 14.05 |
| 1970 - 71 & 1990 - 91 | 8.21 | 13.44 | 10.04 | | 16.07 | 16.12 | 9.34 |

Notes : (a) *Col.5 is netted for gas re-injected into the wells not separately shown here as the quantity is small and proportion to gross output is declining over the years.*

(b) *Col. 6 : Mtoe = Million tonnes of oil equivalent. One million cubic metres of gas is equivalent to 856.8 tonnes of oil.*

❑ Production of crude oil and natural gas increased at a rapid rate during the eighties, thanks to the discoveries in Bombay High Off-shore fields in 1975 from which output picked up from 1979 onwards.

❑ During the early seventies, between 45 to 50% of the natural gas output was flared. Thereafter the proportion of flared gas remained consistently below 40% between 1978 - 79 and 1982 - 83. Since 1985-86, there has been a rapid decline in the proportion though absolute volume of gas flared has increased.

❑ The volume of 5,161 million cubic metres of gas flared during 1990-91 would be valued at about Rs 720 crores. But more importantly it was equivalent to 4.42 million tonnes of crude oil, which is about a fifth of our imports of crude oil in 1990 - 91. At international prices, this would mean about Rs 1,300 crores worth of foreign exchange in 1990 - 91.

❑ This in itself amply explains the urgency to reduce the gas flared up and expedite steps for its alternative uses, like feedstock for fertiliser and petrochemical plants, power generation and for transport vehicles in its compressed form.

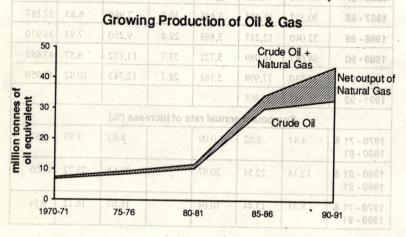

Growing Production of Oil & Gas

## 4.10 Refining Capacities and Crude Throughput of Petroleum Companies

*(million tonnes per annum)*

| Petroleum Refining Companies | Refining capacity | | | Crude Throughput | | |
|---|---|---|---|---|---|---|
| | | | | 1989-90 | | 1990-91 Estimate |
| | 1970-71 | 1980-81 | 1990-91 | Actual | % | |
| Indian Oil Corpn. | 6.82 | 10.92 | 24.40 | 23.53 | 45.3 | 23.53 |
| Bharat Petroleum Corpn. | 3.54 | 4.90 | 6.00 | 7.04 | 13.6 | 6.40 |
| Hindustan Petroleum Corpn. | 3.55 | 4.43 | 8.00 (a) | 10.03 | 19.3 | 9.80 |
| Cochin Refineries | 2.50 | 2.91 | 4.50 | 4.62 | 8.9 | 4.75 |
| Madras Refineries | 1.98 | 2.61 | 5.60 | 5.51 | 10.6 | 5.43 |
| Bongaigaon Refinery | - | 0.05 | 1.35 | 1.21 | 2.3 | 1.28 |
| Total | 18.39 | 25.82 | 49.85 (a) | 51.94 | 100.0 | 51.19 |

*Note : (a) Excludes 2 millions tonnes of swing refining capacity.*

❑ Ever since the nationalisation of foreign oil companies during 1974 - 76, the crude oil and natural gas exploration/refining in India has so far been entirely under the public sector. The change in policy to allow private sector participation has been only recently initiated.

❑ Indian Oil Corporation is today the largest organisation in the industry with 47% of the total refining capacity in the country and almost 57% product marketing share. Among its six refineries the one at Digboi in Assam is the oldest, set up in 1901 and the smallest in the country, whereas the 25 year old Koyali refinery in Gujarat is the largest, having in terms of nearly 20% share in refining capacity.

❑ As against the aggregate crude oil refining capacity of about 52 million tonnes per annum and near 100% capacity utilisation, the indigenous crude production throughput is around 33-34 million tonnes in recent years and the balance one-third of the total refinery throughout is imported crude. On top of this about 13% of the domestic consumption of petroleum products is met through imports. It is a long way to self-sufficiency in every respect, except through curtailing the consumption growth.

## 4.11 Supply Balance of Petroleum Crude and Products : 1980-81 - 1990-91

*(million tonnes)*

|  | 1980-81 | 1985-86 | 1986-87 | 1987-88 | 1988-89 | 1989-90 | 1990-91 |
|---|---|---|---|---|---|---|---|
| **Crude Oil** | | | | | | | |
| Domestic Output | 10.51 | 30.17 | 30.48 | 30.35 | 32.04 | 34.09 | 33.03 |
| Net Imports | 16.22 | 14.61 | 15.48 | 17.93 | 17.81 | 19.49 | 20.70 |
| Change in Stocks & Discrepancy | -0.89 | -1.87 | -0.26 | -0.53 | -1.05 | -1.64 | -1.96 |
| Refinery Throughput | 29.84 | 42.91 | 45.70 | 47.75 | 48.80 | 51.94 | 51.77 |
| Refinery Boiler Fuel & Losses (Excl. RBF) | -1.72 | -3.03 | -2.94 | -3.02 | -3.10 | -3.64 | -3.60 |
| **Petroleum Products** | | | | | | | |
| Domestic Output | 24.12 | 39.88 | 42.76 | 44.73 | 45.70 | 48.30 | 48.17 |
| Net Imports | 7.25 | 1.91 | 0.56 | 0.54 | 3.96 | 3.97 | 7.00 |
| Change in Stocks & Discrepancy | -0.47 | -0.92 | 0.34 | 1.15 | 0.43 | 1.83 | -0.40 |
| **Imports of Crude** | | | | | | | |
| Quantity | 16.22 | 15.14 | 15.48 | 17.93 | 17.81 | 19.49 | 20.70 |
| Value Rs. crore | 3,349 | 3,687 | 2,120 | 2,986 | 2,863 | 4,089 | 6,118 |
| **Imports of Petroleum Products** | | | | | | | |
| Quantity | 7.29 | 3.87 | 3.05 | 3.95 | 6.26 | 6.56 | 8.66 |
| Value (Rs. crore) | 1,918 | 1,273 | 653 | 979 | 1,516 | 2,255 | 4,660 |

*contd...*

| | 1980-81 | 1985-86 | 1986-87 | 1987-88 | 1988-89 | 1989-90 | 1990-91 |
|---|---|---|---|---|---|---|---|
| **Gross Import (Rs. crore)** <br> **Crude and Petroleum Products** | | | | | | | |
| Import bill | 5,267 | 4,960 | 2,773 | 3,965 | 4,379 | 6,344 | 10,778 |
| As % of Total Exports | 78.48 | 45.53 | 22.27 | 25.30 | 21.57 | 22.92 | 33.14 |
| Import Bill (Rs. crore) | 5,259 | 4,315 | 2,362 | 3,316 | · 3,855 | 5,648 | 9,861 |
| RBF = Consumptions as Refinery boiler fuel | 0.2 | 13% | 15 | 16% | 12 | 11 | 8.5 |

❑ During the eighties, domestic production of crude oil increased 12% per annum as against refinery throughput at 7%. But the quantity produced was insufficient and necessitated crude import growth at 2.5% per annum. Although dependence on imports for refinery throughput was reduced from 67% in 1980-81 to 43% in 1990-91, it was still high as cost of our crude imports increased at the rate of 6.2% per annum.

❑ During the eighties, the consumption of petroleum products increased at 6% per annum as compared to the 7% annual rate of increase in domestic production. This enabled us to drastically curtail dependence on product imports from 23.5% of consumption in 1980-81 to little over 1% during 1986-87 and 1987-88. But thereafter it increased to 7% in the next five years and about 13% in 1990-91. Even though quantity in 1990-91 was down to about 7 million tonnes, the same as in 1980-81, our import bill for petroleum products increased 9.3% per annum during the decade, reflecting almost entirely the increase in international prices.

❑ We have been exporting some petroleum products, the earnings from which finance about 10% of our gross import bill for crude and petroleum products.

## Crude Oil

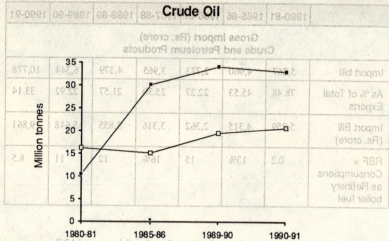

□ During the eighties, domestic production of crude oil increased 12% per annum as against refinery throughput at 7%. But the quantity produced was insufficient and necessitated crude import growth at 2.5% per annum. Although dependence on imports for refinery throughput was reduced from 67% in 1980-81 to 43% in 1990-91, it was still high as most of our crude imports increased at the rate of 0.2% per annum.

## Petroleum Products

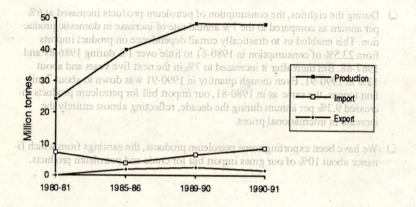

## 4.12 : Electricity Installed Capacity : 1950-51 - 1991-92

*(million watts)*

| Year | Public Utilities | | | | Non-Utilities | Total |
|------|-------|---------|---------|-------|-----------|-------|
|      | Hydel | Thermal | Nuclear | Total | | |
| 1950 | 559 | 1,153 | - | 1,712 | 588 | 2,300 |
| 1955 | 939 | 1,756 | - | 2,695 | 723 | 3,418 |
| 1960 - 61 | 1,917 | 2,736 | - | 4,657 | 1,001 | 5,654 |
| 1965 - 66 | 4,124 | 4,903 | - | 9,027 | 1,146 | 10,171 |
| 1970 - 71 | 6,383 | 7,906 | 420 | 14,709 | 1,562 | 16,271 |
| 1975 - 76 | 8,464 | 11,013 | 640 | 20,117 | 2,132 | 22,249 |
| 1980 - 81 | 11,791 | 17,563 | 860 | 30,214 | 3,102 | 33,316 |
| 1985 - 86 | 15,472 | 29,967 | 1,230 | 46,669 | 5,504 | 52,173 |
| 1986 - 87 | 16,196 | 31,740 | 1,230 | 49,166 | 5,714 | 54,880 |
| 1987 - 88 | 17,265 | 35,560 | 1,230 | 54,055 | 6,345 | 60,400 |
| 1988 - 89 | 17,798 | 39,677 | 1,230 | 58,705 | 6,520 | 65,202 |
| 1989 - 90 | 18,308 | 43,754 | 1,465 | 63,527 | 6,874 | 70,401 |
| 1990 - 91 | 18,753 | 45, 737 | 1,565 | 66,055 | 8,402 | 74,457 |
| 1991 - 92 | 19,368 | 48,215 | 2,035 | 69,618 | 9,000 | 78,618 |
| Compound Annual Rate of Increase (%) | | | | | | |
| 1950-60-1960-61 | 13.1 | 9.0 | - | 10.5 | 5.5 | 9.4 |
| 1960-61 - 1970-71 | 12.8 | 11.2 | - | 12.2 | 4.6 | 11.2 |
| 1970-71 - 1980-81 | 6.3 | 8.3 | 7.4 | 7.4 | 7.1 | 7.4 |
| 1980-81 - 1985-86 | 5.6 | 11.3 | 7.4 | 9.1 | 12.2 | 9.4 |
| 1985-86 - 1990-91 | 3.6 | 8.4 | 3.6 | 6.8 | 5.7 (a) | 7.8 (a) |
| 1980-81 - 1990-91 | 4.6 | 9.8 | 5.4 | 7.9 | 9.2 (b) | 8.7 (b) |
| 1950-90 1990-91 | 9.1 | 9.6 | - | 9.5 | 6.5 (c) | 9.2 (c) |

Notes : (a) Relates to 1985-86 to 1989-90
      (b) Relates to 1980-81 to 1989-90
      (c) Relates to 1950 to 1989-90

❏ India is richly endowed with hydro power potential of about 84,000 MW, three-fourths of which is located in north and north- eastern regions. However, only a little over one-fifth of the potential has been harnessed by March 1991 partly because of natural factors such as unfavourable terrain of the regions of high potential. But these are also other factors such as inter-state political differences and financial constraints.

❏ Under Indian conditions a 40:60 proportion of hydro to thermal power capacity is considered fair and adequate.

❏ During the fifties and sixties, hydro power capacity was increased at a more rapid rate of around 13% per annum. Consequently the share of hydro installed capacity remained well above 40% during the sixties and Seventies. After 1979-80 however, this share has steadily declined, year after year, to reach 28% by 1990-91, as installation of thermal and nuclear power capacity speeded up to surpass hydel growth rates.

❏ Hydel power is cheaper and the plant life is generally longer than the thermal plants. Besides it is associated with multi-purpose irrigation projects in many cases. In view of these factors as well as the overall economics of meeting the future demand for power, it could be appropriate to take corrective measures to reach once again the ideal 40:60 ratio. Slow-down in growth of hydel capacity to as low as 4.6% during the eighties is disturbing as overall demand for electricity has been rising at over 9% annually.

## Pattern of Electricity Installed Capacity MW

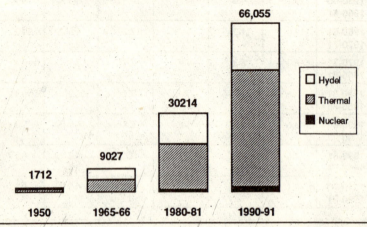

## 4.13 : Electricity Generation : 1950-51 - 1990-91

*(million units)*

| Year | Public Utilities | | | | Non-Utilities | Total |
|---|---|---|---|---|---|---|
| | Hydel | Thermal | Nuclear | Total | | |
| 1950 | 2,520 | 2,587 | - | 5,107 | n.a | 5,107 |
| 1955 | 3,742 | 4,850 | - | 8,592 | n.a. | 8,592 |
| 1960 - 61 | 7,837 | 9,100 | - | 16,937 | 3,186 | 20,123 |
| 1965 - 66 | 15,225 | 17,765 | - | 32,990 | 3,835 | 36,825 |
| 1970 - 71 | 25,248 | 28,162 | 2,417 | 55,827 | 5,384 | 61,211 |
| 1975 - 76 | 33,302 | 43,303 | 2,626 | 79,231 | 6,695 | 85,926 |
| 1980 - 81 | 46,542 | 61,301 | 3,001 | 110,844 | 8,420 | 119,264 |
| 1985 - 86 | 50,933 | 114,119 | 4,985 | 170,037 | 13,000 | 183,037 |
| 1986 - 87 | 53,764 | 128,818 | 5,023 | 187,605 | 13,600 | 201,205 |
| 1987 - 88 | 47,396 | 149,464 | 5,034 | 201,894 | 16,900 | 218,794 |
| 1988 - 89 | 57,793 | 157,510 | 5,822 | 221,125 | 19,000 | 240,125 |
| 1989 - 90 | 61,996 | 178,522 | 4,623 | 245,141 | 20,800 | 265,941 |
| 1990 - 91 | 71,535 | 186,452 | 6,244 | 264,231 | n.a. | n.a. |
| Compound Annual Rate of Increase (%) | | | | | | |
| 1950-61 1960-61 | 12.0 | 13.4 | - | 12.7 | n.a. | 14.7 |
| 1960-61 - 1970-71 | 12.4 | 12.0 | - | 12.7 | 5.4 | 11.8 |
| 1970-71 - 1980-81 | 6.3 | 8.1 | 2.2 | 7.2 | 4.6 | 6.9 |
| 1980-81 - 1985-86 | 1.8 | 13.2 | 10.7 | 8.9 | 9.1 | 8.9 |
| 1985-86- 1990-91 | 7.0 | 10.3 | 4.6 | 9.2 | 12.5 (a) | 9.8 (a) |
| 1980-81 - 1990-91 | 4.4 | 11.8 | 7.6 | 9.1 | 10.6 (b) | 9.3 (b) |
| 1950-90- 1990-91 | 8.7 | 11.3 | - | 10.4 | 6.7 (c) | 9.3 (c) |

*Notes : (a) Relates to 1985-86 to 1989-90*
*(b) Relates to 1980-81 to 1989-90*
*(c) Relates to 1950 to 1989-90*

❑ The trend in growth rates of power generation – hydel, thermal, nuclear – is broadly similar to that of respective installation of additional capacities, though in the case of thermal power the growth rate of power generation during the eighties was significantly higher than that of capacity installation. Growth in thermal generation depends upon the regularity of fuel supplies and its quality, but more particularly on the operational efficiency levels attained by thermal plants as indicated by the plant load factor.

❑ In the case of hydel power generation, year to year variations are determined by the behaviour of monsoons, which determine the flow of water into hydel reservoirs.

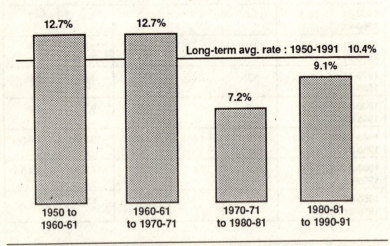

**Annual Growth Rates of Electricity Generator (Utilities)**

12.7%  12.7%  Long-term avg. rate : 1950-1991  10.4%
9.1%
7.2%

| 1950 to 1960-61 | 1960-61 to 1970-71 | 1970-71 to 1980-81 | 1980-81 to 1990-91 |

## 4.14 : Plant Load Factor (PLF) of Thermal Power Plants : 1973-74 to 1990-91

| Year | Average PLF % | Year | Average PLF % |
|---|---|---|---|
| 1973-74 | 50.4 | 1982-83 | 49.4 |
| 1974-75 | 52.7 | 1983-84 | 47.9 |
| 1975-76 | 51.9 | 1984-85 | 50.1 |
| 1976-77 | 55.3 | 1985-86 | 52.4 |
| 1977-78 | 52.7 | 1986-87 | 53.2 |
| 1978-79 | 49.5 | 1987-88 | 56.5 |
| 1979-80 | 44.3 | 1988-89 | 55.0 |
| 1980-81 | 45.0 | 1989-90 | 56.5 |
| 1981-82 | 46.8 | 1990-91 | 53.8 |

### Sectorwise PLF : 1984-85 and 1991-92

*(Percent)*

| Ownership Sector | 1984-85 | 1989-90 | 1990-91 | 1991-92 |
|---|---|---|---|---|
| State Electricity Boards | 44.9 | 53.0 | 47.70 | 46.06 |
| Central Sector | 55.4 | 62.2 | 58.10 | 64.7 |
| Private Sector | 63.0 | 69.5 | 58.4 | 56.7 |

❏ Plant load factor (PLF) is the percentage of actual electricity generated in a power plant to the maximum producible by the plant operating at full capacity during the period. The PLF is therefore a measure of operational efficiency.

❏ The average PLF of thermal power plants in the country deteriorated from the peak level of 55.3% in 1976-77 to a low point of 44.3% in 1979-80 and remained below 50% during the Sixth Plan period. During the Seventh Plan, the average PLF gradually rose to a new peak of 56.5% in 1987-88 and 1989-90 against a desireable norm of 58%.

❑ The average PLF is generally at satisfactory levels in Central Government owned plants and private sector thermal plants, but it is generally poor in those under the State Electricity Boards. However, during the Seventh Plan, between 1984-85 and 1989-90 the average PLF of SEBs improved sharply by 18%, while that of the central and private sector plants, already operating at higher PLF levels, showed obviously smaller increment of 12% and 10% respectively on PLF.

### Trend in Average PLF of Thermal Power Plants 1973-74 to 1990-91

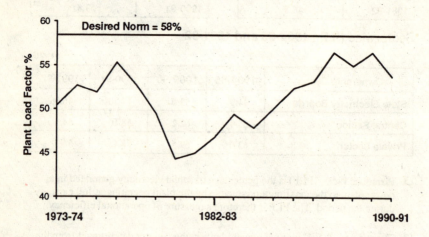

## 4.15 Electricity - Planwise Slippages in Installation of Additional Capacity

*(Mega Watts)*

| Plan Periods/Years | Target | Achieve-ments | Slippage (-)/Excess (+) | |
|---|---|---|---|---|
| | | | MW | % |
| First Plan : 1951-56 | 1,300 | 1,100 | -200 | -15.4 |
| Second Plan : 1956-61 | 3,500 | 2,250 | -1,250 | -35.7 |
| Third Plan : 1961-66 | 7,040 | 4,520 | -2,520 | -35.8 |
| Annual Plan : 1966-69 | 5,430 | 4,120 | -1,310 | -24.1 |
| Fourth Plan : 1969-74 | 9,264 | 4,579 | -4,685 | -50.5 |
| Fifth Plan : 1974-79 | 12,499 | 10,202 | -2,297 | -18.4 |
| Annual Plan : 1979-80 | 2,945 | 1,799 | -1,146 | -38.9 |
| Sixth Plan : 1980-85 | 19,666 | 14,226 | -5,440 | -27.7 |
| 1980 - 81 | 2,687 | 1,823 | -864 | -32.2 |
| 1981 - 82 | 4,087 | 2,175 | -1,912 | -46.8 |
| 1982 - 83 | 4,354 | 3,060 | -1,294 | -29.7 |
| 1983 - 84 | 4,236 | 4,088 | -148 | -3.5 |
| 1984 - 85 | 4,302 | 3,080 | -1,222 | -28.4 |
| Seventh Plan : 1985 - 90 | 22,245 | 21,402 | -843 | -3.8 |
| 1985 - 86 | 4,460 | 4,223 | -237 | -5.3 |
| 1986 - 87 | 3,396 | 2,625 | -771 | -22.7 |
| 1987 - 88 | 4,916 | 4,981 | +65 | +1.3 |
| 1988 - 89 | 4,497 | 4,885 | +388 | +8.6 |
| 1989 - 90 | 4,892 | 4,688 | -204 | -4.2 |
| Annual Plan : 1990 - 91 | 4,212 | 2,777 | -1,435 | -34.1 |
| Annual Plan : 1991 - 92 | 3,811 | 3,027 | -784 | -20.6 |

❑ Although for each successive Five Year Plan we planned for a higher target of capacity installation, the record of actual achievements has been one of slippages ranging between 50.5% in the Fourth Plan to 3.8% in the Seventh Plan.

❑ Several factors are responsible for the slippages, such as delay in project completion due to paucity of funds, delays in supply of equipment, midway change in scope of projects, unforeseen geological problems, labour unrest etc., and often surprisingly weak project management.

❑ Planning essentially means assuming and accounting for such factors, including monitoring the progress at every stage and timely resolution of problems through effective management, so as to attain the physical targets within the limits of funds. Slippages in the essential infrastructural sector rather reflects more the weakness of planning itself than of project management.

### Target vs Achievement in establishing generation capacity (MW)

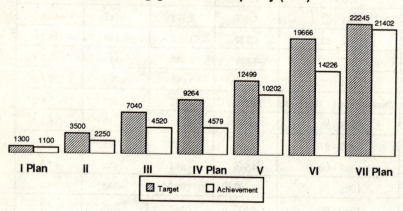

## 4.16 Villages Electrified Between 1947 and 1990-91

| At the end of | Villages electrified | |
|---|---|---|
| | Cumulative Number | As % of total No. of Villages |
| 1947 | 1,500 | 0.3 |
| 1950 - 51 | 3,061 | 0.5 |
| 1955 - 56 | 7,296 | 1.3 |
| 1960 - 61 | 21,754 | 3.8 |
| 1965 - 66 | 45,148 | 7.8 |
| 1970 - 71 | 106,774 | 18.5 |
| 1974 - 75 | 173,533 | 27.2 |
| 1975 - 76 | 185,806 | 32.3 |
| 1976 - 77 | 202,843 | 35.2 |
| 1977 - 79 | 216,863 | 37.6 |
| 1978 - 79 | 232,770 | 40.4 |
| 1979 - 80 | 249,795 | 43.4 |
| 1980 - 81 | 272,625 | 47.3 |
| 1981 - 82 | 296,511 | 51.5 |
| 1982 - 83 | 323,881 | 56.2 |
| 1983 - 84 | 347,561 | 60.3 |
| 1984 - 85 | 370,332 | 64.3 |
| 1985 - 86 | 390,294 | 67.7 |
| 1986 - 87 | 414,895 | 71.2 |
| 1987 - 88 | 435,653 | 75.2 |
| 1988 - 89 | 455,491 | 78.7 |
| 1989 - 90 | 470,580 | 81.3 |
| 1990 - 91 | 481,124 | 83.1 |
| 1991 - 92 | 485,813 | 83.9 |

❏ A village is regarded to have been electrified even it a single electricity connection is provided in that village.

❏ In spite of the cost involved in satisfying this limit of definition, the progress of rural electrification in our country is highly commendable. From just 3,061 villages or 0.5% of their total number electrified before the commencement of planning, the figure reached to 481,124 villages electrified or 83.1% of the total by March 1991.

❏ The point of thrust in rural electrification needs to be aimed at extending connections to households for operating cottage units as also to ensuring regularity in power supply for pump sets for watering the fields at the right time.

## Villages Electrified (%)

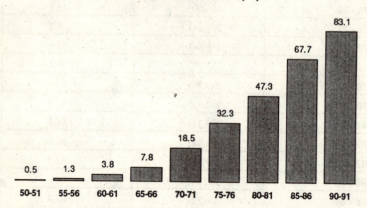

# TRANSPORT 5

## 5.1 Growth in Traffic on Indian Railways 1950-51 - 1992-93

| Year | No. of Passengers (million) | | | Revenue - Earning Goods Traffic (Mln. tonnes) |
|---|---|---|---|---|
| | Suburban | Non-Suburban | Total | |
| 1950 - 51 | 412 | 812 | 1,284 | 73.2 |
| 1955 - 56 | 495 | 780 | 1,275 | 92.2 |
| 1960 - 61 | 680 | 914 | 1,594 | 169.8 |
| 1965 - 66 | 1,018 | 1,064 | 2,082 | 162.0 |
| 1970 - 71 | 1,219 | 1,212 | 2,431 | 167.9 |
| 1975 - 76 | 1,639 | 1,306 | 2,945 | 196.8 |
| 1980 - 81 | 2,000 | 1,613 | 3,613 | 195.9 |
| 1985 - 86 | 1,884 | 1,549 | 3,433 | 258.5 |
| 1986 - 87 | 2,017 | 1,577 | 3,594 | 277.8 |
| 1987 - 88 | 2,155 | 1,637 | 3,792 | 290.2 |
| 1988 - 89 | 2,005 | 1,495 | 3,500 | 302.1 |
| 1989 - 90 | 2,129 | 1,544 | 3,673 | 310.0 |
| 1990 - 91 | 2,344 | 1,609 | 3,953 | 318.0 |
| 1991 - 92 (RE) | 2,411 | 1,662 | 4,073 | 337.4 |
| 1992-93 (BE) | 2,540 | 1,741 | 4,281 | 354.0 |
| Compound Annual Rate of Increase (%) | | | | |
| 1950 - 51 to 1960 - 61 | 5.1 | 0.5 | 2.2 | 5.1 |
| 1960 - 61 to 1970 - 71 | 6.0 | 2.9 | 4.3 | 3.4 |
| 1970 - 71 to 1980 - 81 | 5.1 | 2.9 | 4.0 | 1.6 |
| 1980 - 81 to 1990 - 91 | 1.6 | -0.02 | 0.9 | 5.0 |
| 1950 - 51 to 1990 - 91 | 4.4 | 1.5 | 2.9 | 3.7 |

❑ The development of railway network upto the pre-Independence years was quite extensive, though track gauges varied in different regions depending upon the load potential envisaged then. In the post-Independence period, there-fore, route length has been extended just by 16% in four decades, from 53,596 kms in 1950-51 to 62,367 kms by the end of 1990-91. No doubt considerable attention and resources were devoted to the modification of gauges and strengthening of tracks. Thus, for instance, track electrification increased from 388 kms in 1950-51 (less than one per cent) to 9,968 kms or 16% of the total route length by 1990-91. The network touched 7,100 stations in 1990-91 against 5,976 in 1950-51.

❑ After the 1960's the growth rate of passenger traffic tapered off. But here the suburban traffic which serves as mass-rapid- transit mode and accounts for about two thirds of the total passenger traffic, has grown at a relatively faster rate. This segment plying in urban areas, also strains the finances of the rail-ways because of heavily subsidised fare structure. All the same, the slow-down in growth rates does not imply saturation of the potential, considering the over-crowding and non-availability of tickets most of the time. At the same time there has been a massive shift towards road transport which also of-fers an added advantage of reaching remote places not touched by the railway network.

❑ As for the goods traffic on the railways, the growth rate of haulage, after slowly down during the 1960's and 1970s, surged forward in the 1980s. The complaints of non-availability of wagons have been fewer. Here too growth of road transport has provided noteworthy relief.

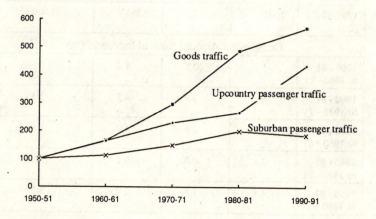

## 5.2    Growth of Road Length 1950-51 - 1990-91

| Year | Road Length ('000 km) | | | | As % of Total Road Length | |
|---|---|---|---|---|---|---|
| | Surfaced Roads | Unsurfaced Roads | Total | Of which National Highways | National Highways | Surfaced Roads |
| 1950 - 51 | 157 | 243 | 400 | 20 | 5.0 | 39.3 |
| 1955 - 56 | 209 | 270 | 479 | 21 | 4.4 | 43.6 |
| 1960 - 61 | 263 | 261 | 524 | 24 | 4.6 | 50.2 |
| 1965 - 66 | 343 | 427 | 770 | 24 | 3.1 | 44.5 |
| 1970 - 71 | 398 | 520 | 918 | 24 | 2.6 | 43.4 |
| 1975 - 76 | 551 | 698 | 1,249 | 29 | 2.3 | 44.1 |
| 1980 - 81 | 683 | 807 | 1,490 | 32 | 2.1 | 45.8 |
| 1985 - 86 | 825 | 901 | 1,726 | 32 | 1.9 | 47.8 |
| 1986 - 87 | 858 | 922 | 1,780 | 32 | 1.8 | 48.2 |
| 1987 - 88 | 888 | 955 | 1,843 | 32 | 1.7 | 48.2 |
| 1988 - 89 | 920 | 985 | 1,905 | 33 | 1.7 | 48.3 |
| 1989 - 90 | 960 | 1,010 | 1,970 | 34 | 1.7 | 48.7 |
| 1990 - 91 | 1,001 | 1,036 | 2,037 | 34 | 1.7 | 49.1 |
| Compound Annual Rate of Increase (%) | | | | | | |
| 1950 - 51 to 1960 - 61 | 5.3 | 0.7 | 2.7 | 1.8 | | |
| 1960 - 61 to 1970 - 71 | 4.2 | 7.1 | 5.8 | - | | |
| 1970 - 71 to 1980 - 81 | 5.5 | 4.5 | 5.0 | 2.9 | | |
| 1980 - 81 to 1990 - 91 | 3.9 | 2.5 | 3.2 | 0.6 | | |
| 1950 - 51 to 1989 - 90 | 4.8 | 3.7 | 4.2 | 1.4 | | |

❑ The road network in the country is much more extensive than the railways, having increased five folds in length from 4 lakh kms in 1950-51 to 20.4 lakh kms by 1990-91. Thereby an estimated 90% of the villages with population of over 1,500 were linked to roads by the end of the Seventh Plan.

❑ The growth of all - weather surfaced roads has been faster than that of the unsurfaced roads during these few decades : 4.8% per annum against 3.7%. Hence, the ratio of surfaced roads has increased from 39% in 1950-51 to 49.1 by 1990-91. However, by the end of the Seventh Plan, 62% of the smaller villages with population of less than 1,000 still remained inaccessible by all weather roads.

❑ The national highways constitute less than 2% of the total road length, and most of it remains congested with heavy-load long- distance traffic, and where these are of single-lane, they cause traffic jams, fuel and time losses. Their effective utilisation as supplement to railways gets affected.

## Growth of Road Length

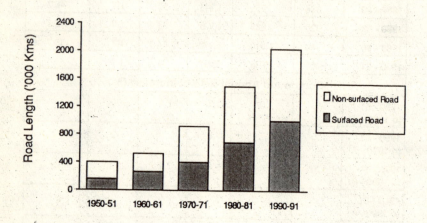

## 5.3 Population of Registered Motor Vehicles 1950-51 - 1989-90

*('000 Nos)*

| Year | Two-Wheelers | Cars Jeeps & Taxis | Buses | Trucks | Other Vehicles | Total |
|------|------|------|------|------|------|------|
| 1950 - 51 | 27 | 159 | 34 | 82 | 4 | 306 |
| 1955 - 56 | 41 | 203 | 47 | 119 | 16 | 426 |
| 1960 - 61 | 88 | 310 | 57 | 168 | 42 | 665 |
| 1965 - 66 | 226 | 456 | 73 | 259 | 85 | 1,099 |
| 1970 - 71 | 576 | 682 | 94 | 343 | 170 | 1,865 |
| 1975 - 76 | 1,045 | 776 | 114 | 365 | 379 | 3,679 |
| 1980 - 81 | 2,528 | 1,117 | 154 | 527 | 847 | 5,173 |
| 1885 - 86 | 6,264 | 1,710 | 228 | 878 | 1,401 | 10,481 |
| 1986 - 87 | 7,658 | 1,895 | 247 | 967 | 1,580 | 12,347 |
| 1987 - 88 | 9,155 | 2,219 | 260 | 1,177 | 1,747 | 14,558 |
| 1988 - 89 | 10,685 | 2,284 | 293 | 1,140 | 2,086 | 16,488 |
| 1989 - 90 | 12,394 | 2,797 | 312 | 1,324 | 2,505 | 19,332 |
| **Compound Annual Rates of Increase (%)** | | | | | | |
| 1950 - 51 to 1960 - 61 | 12.5 | 6.9 | 5.3 | 7.4 | 26.5 | 8.1 |
| 1960 - 61 to 1970 - 71 | 20.7 | 8.2 | 5.1 | 7.4 | 15.0 | 10.9 |
| 1970 - 71 to 1980 - 81 | 15.9 | 5.1 | 5.1 | 4.4 | 17.4 | 10.7 |
| 1980 - 81 to 1989 - 90 | 19.3 | 10.7 | 8.2 | 10.8 | 12.8 | 15.8 |
| 1950 - 51 to 1988 - 89 | 17.1 | 7.3 | 5.8 | 7.2 | 17.9 | 11.1 |

❑ The population of all types of motor vehicles has increased impressively since 1950-51, but more particularly during the 1980s.

❑ The number of two-wheelers during the eighties increased at the rate of almost 20% annually, as it come to be regarded as a necessary and most convenient personalised mode of transport. Its growth was aided by loans/hire purchase facilities offered by banks and leasing agencies. Their number crossed the 10 million mark by the end of 1988-89. It is only during 1991-92 that their production and sales have been adversely affected because of the curbs on financing the purchases as also the high cost of fuel and maintenance for middle class urbanites.

❑ In recent years the growth of trucks population was impressive during the seventies (17.4%) when rail transport became inadequate to cope with the rising volume of goods haulage. On the other hand, the growth of buses has remained moderate even as the alternative mass passenger transport vehicle. Here the continuing over-use of old and fuel inefficient vehicles has been partly responsible.

❑ As against this, growth of personalised four-wheeler vehicles has been relatively high, notwithstanding the frequent hikes in their prices. Increased fuel and maintenance costs have not proved as deterrents to their purchases, though late 1991 showed a sharp fall in sales.

## Changing Pattern of Vehicle Population : 1950-51 & 1989-90

### 1950-51                                   1989-90

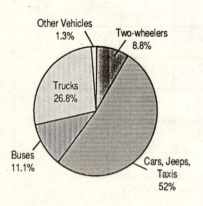
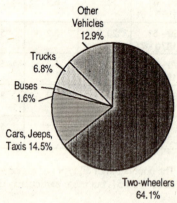

## 5.4 Shares of Rail and Road transport in Goods and passengers Traffic : 1950-51 - 1988-89

| Year | Rail | Road | Total | % Shares by | |
|---|---|---|---|---|---|
| | | | | Rail | Road |
| Goods Traffic : Billion tonne-kms | | | | | |
| 1950-51 | 44 | 6 | 50 | 89 | 11 |
| 1955-56 | 60 | 9 | 69 | 87 | 13 |
| 1960-61 | 88 | 35 | 123 | 71 | 29 |
| 1965-66 | 117 | 55 | 172 | 68 | 32 |
| 1970-71 | 127 | 67 | 194 | 66 | 34 |
| 1975-76 | | | | | |
| 1980-81 | 159 | 98 | 257 | 62 | 38 |
| 1985-86 | 206 | 193 | 399 | 52 | 48 |
| 1986-87 | 223 | 210 | 433 | 51 | 49 |
| 1987-88 | 231 | 238 | 469 | 49 | 51 |
| 1988-89 | 230 | 275 | 505 | 46 | 54 |
| Passenger Traffic : Billion passenger kms | | | | | |
| 1950-51 | 66 | 23 | 89 | 74 | 26 |
| 1955-56 | 62 | 31 | 93 | 67 | 33 |
| 1960-61 | 78 | 57 | 135 | 58 | 42 |
| 1965-66 | 96 | 95 | 191 | 50 | 50 |
| 1970-71 | 118 | 169 | 287 | 41 | 59 |
| 1975-76 | 149 | 225 | 374 | 40 | 60 |
| 1980-81 | 209 | 353 | 562 | 37 | 63 |
| 1985-86 | 241 | 850 | 1,091 | 22 | 78 |
| 1986-87 | 257 | 893 | 1,150 | 22 | 78 |
| 1987-88 | 269 | 980 | 1,249 | 22 | 78 |
| 1988-89 | 264 | 905 | 1,169 | 23 | 77 |

❑ Road transport in the movement of goods and passengers has come to command a growing share over the years. This on one hand reflects the rapid extension of surfaced road network whereby preference has shifted in favour of motor vehicles for door-to-door delivery of goods as also for reaching remote places which are not covered by the railway network. On the other hand, it also indicates the inability of railway to cope up with the growing demands. This was caused by the shortages of wagons, lack of punctuality, and longer turnaround time.

❑ The share of passenger transport by roads increased from 26% in 1950-51 to 77% by 1988-89. Railways, on the other hand, lost their share of growing goods transport from 89% in 1950-51 to 46% by 1988-89.

## Rising Preference for Road Transport

### Shares in Goods Traffic

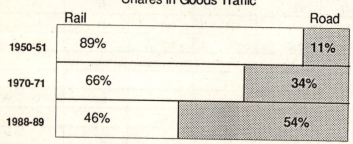

### Shares in Passenger Traffic

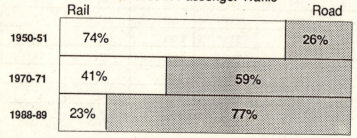

## 5.5    Growth of India's Merchant Shipping Tonnage : 1951-1992

| Growth of Tonnage | | | Share in Overseas Cargo Carried | |
|---|---|---|---|---|
| Year December End | Coastal & Overseas Trade | | Year | Percent |
| | No. of Ships | Gross Registered Tonnage ('000 GRT) | | |
| 1951 | 103 | 391 | 1955 - 56 | 6.5 |
| 1956 | 124 | 517 | 1960 - 61 | 9.0 |
| 1961 | 174 | 901 | 1965 - 66 | 12.9 |
| 1966 | 231 | 1.792 | 1970 - 71 | 19.8 |
| 1971 | 255 | 2,500 | 1975 - 76 | 35.1 |
| 1975 | 330 | 4,464 | 1980 - 81 | 32.3 |
| 1980 | 383 | 5,679 | 1985 - 86 | 34.7 |
| 1985 | 368 | 5,950 | 1986 - 87 | 37.0 |
| 1986 | 359 | 5,478 | 1987 - 88 | 38.9 |
| 1987 | 362 | 5,469 | 1988 - 89 | 34.2 |
| 1988 | 378 | 5,593 | 1989 - 90 | 36.0 |
| 1989 | 402 | 5,906 | 1990 - 91 | 37.0 |
| 1990 (March) | 408 | 5,980 | | |
| 1991 (March) | 418 | 6,030 | | |
| 1992 (March) | 415 | 5,939 | | |

❑   From a base of 3.9 lakh gross registered tonnage (GRT) in 1951 to 59.4 lakh GRT by 1992 makes an impressive 15-fold increase in the carrying capacity of a merchant shipping fleet. However, its share in world GRT is a meagre 1.5% which puts it at 17th place despite having a vast coast-line with 12 major ports.

❑ The share of Indian bottoms in carrying the country's overseas cargo trade has increased from 6.5% to 37%, over the years. Ideally this share should be 50% considering the low volume and growth of our sea-borne export trade. A large number of old and outmoded ships, and shortage of specialised vessels, lack of containerisation and handling facilities at major ports put us at a disadvantage in attaining a higher share.

❑ These deficiencies of our merchant fleet are on account of our excessive dependence on foreign shipyards for acquisition of new ships. Foreign exchange restrictions are a great impediment to modernisation of the fleet.

## Growth of Gross Registered Tonnage

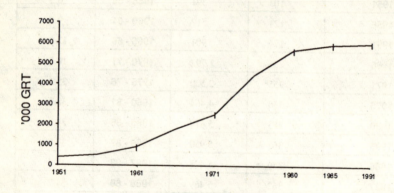

## Share of Overseas Cargo Carried

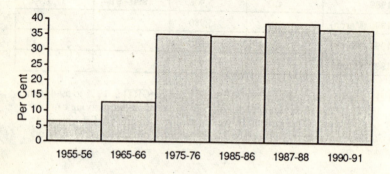

## 5.6 Growth of Air Traffic Handled by Indian Carriers 1960-61 - 1989-90

| Year | Revenue Passengers Carried ('000 nos) | | | Total Revenue Tonne kms (Million) | | |
|---|---|---|---|---|---|---|
| | Air-India | Indian Airlines | Vayudoot | Air-India | Indian Airlines | Vayudoot |
| 1960-61 | 123 | 790 | | 76.0 | 83.2 | |
| 1965-66 | 218 | 1,205 | | 149.0 | 108.2 | |
| 1970-71 | 487 | 2,161 | | 275.2 | 161.5 | |
| 1975-76 | 721 | 3,359 | | 582.0 | 248.9 | |
| 1980-81 | 1,418 | 5,408 | 19(a) | 980.1 | 420.2 | 0.3 (a) |
| 1985-86 | 1,730 | 9,130 | 232 | 1,11.0 | 720.0 | 7.0 |
| 1986-87 | 1,830 | 9,875 | 325 | 1,206.3 | 776.1 | 11.1 |
| 1987-88 | 2,133 | 10,440 | 449 | 1,386.1 | 840.2 | 14.6 |
| 1988-89 | 2,123 | 10,110 | 523 | 1,372.3 | 841.3 | 17.0 |
| 1989-90 | 2,246 | 9,850 | 561 | 1,441.6 | 825.8 | 19.3 |
| **Compound Annual Rates of Increases (%)** | | | | | | |
| 1960-61 to 1970-71 | 14.8 | 10.6 | - | 13.7 | 6.9 | - |
| 1970-71 to 1980-81 | 11.3 | 9.6 | - | 13.5 | 10.0 | - |
| 1980-81 to 1989-90 | 5.2 | 6.9 | 52.7 (b) | 4.4 | 7.8 | 68.3 (b) |
| 1960-61 to 1989-90 | 10.5 | 9.1 | - | 10.7 | 8.2 | - |

*Notes : a. Relates to 1981-82, the first year of operation*
*b. Relates to 1981-82 to 1989-90*

❑ Indian Airlines handles the domestic air traffic, including some places in neighboring countries. Vayudoot, set up in 1981 connects small business centres and tourist spots. Air-India on the other hand, shares the overseas air traffic both inward and outward with other world airlines.

❑ The spectacular growth of air-traffic over the past three decades reflects the change in style of operations by business organisations which account for nearly 70% of the passenger traffic, largely because of the need for rapid transit between important destinations and saving on time of executives on business trips.

❑ It is from these considerations basically that the scheme of granting licences for plying air-taxis has been mooted recently.

❑ Air travel is also increasingly preferred by international tourists coming to India to see places of interest. Air travel thus plays an important role in promotion of tourism.

### Revenue Passengers Carried ('000 nos)

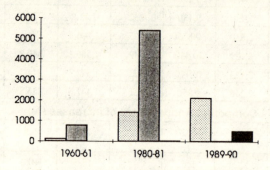

### Total Revenue Tonne kms

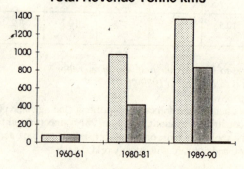

# EMPLOYMENT

## 6.1   Workforce by Population Census : 1901 to 1991

| Census year | Workers (a) | Non-Workers | Total | Workers | Non-Workers |
|---|---|---|---|---|---|
| | Million | | | Percentage of total | |
| 1901 | 111 | 128 | 239 | 47 | 53 |
| 1911 | 121 | 131 | 252 | 48 | 52 |
| 1921 | 118 | 133 | 251 | 47 | 53 |
| 1931 | 121 | 158 | 279 | 43 | 57 |
| 1951 | 140 | 217 | 357 | 39 | 61 |
| 1961 | 189 | 250 | 439 | 43 | 57 |
| 1971 | 180 | 368 | 548 | 33 | 67 |
| 1981 (b) | 223 | 442 | 665 | 34 | 66 |
| 1991 (c) | 315 | 522 | 837 | 38 | 62 |

Notes : (a) *Workers include all those doing some economic activity*
      (b) *1981 census excludes Assam where population census was not carried out.*
      (c) *Excludes J&K where census was not held.*

❑ Even after Independence our Census organisation has been largely run by demographers, mainly for the demographers. As a result the requirements of adequate data for those formulating economic policies and programmes remains neglected.

❑ The definitions of workers and non-workers have changed in almost every Census. Therefore, the figures tabulated here are non-comparable from one Census to the next one. Because of these limitations, there is hardly any scope for a worthwhile comment. The figures could be used for any analysis with extreme care and caution.

## 6.2 Occupational Classification of Workers : 1901 to 1981

*(per cent)*

| Occupations by Economic Activity | Census years | | | | | | | |
|---|---|---|---|---|---|---|---|---|
| | 1901 | 1911 | 1921 | 1931 | 1951 | 1961 | 1971 | 1981(d) |
| **A. Agriculture & Allied Activities** | 71.7 | 74.9 | 76.0 | 74.8 | 72.1 | 71.8 | 72.1 | 68.8 |
| 1. Cultivators | 50.6 | 49.8 | 54.4 | 45.1 | 50.0 | 52.8 | 43.4 | 41.6 |
| 2. Agricultural Labourers | 16.9 | 20.6 | 17.4 | 24.8 | 19.7 | 16.7 | 26.3 | 24.9 |
| 3. Engaged in livestock, fishing, forestry, plantations etc. | 4.2 | 4.5 | 4.2 | 4.9 | 2.4 | 2.3 | 2.4 | 2.3 |
| **B. Non- agricultural Activities** | 28.3 | 25.1 | 24.0 | 25.2 | 27.9 | 28.2 | 27.9 | 31.2 |
| 4. Mining & Quarrying | 0.1 | 0.2 | 0.3 | 0.3 | 0.6 | 0.5 | 0.5 | 0.6 |
| 5. Manufacturing | 11.7 | 9.9 | 9.3 | 8.9 | 9.0 | 10.6 | 9.5 | 11.3 |
| (i) Household Industry (b) | (c) | (c) | (c) | (c) | (c) | 6.4 | 3.5 | 3.5 |
| (ii) Other than Household Industry | 11.7 | 9.9 | 9.3 | 8.9 | 9.0 | 4.2 | 6.0 | 7.8 |
| 6. Construction | 0.8 | 1.0 | 0.9 | 1.0 | 1.1 | 1.1 | 1.2 | 1.6 |
| 7. Trade & Commerce | 6.1 | 5.5 | 5.7 | 5.6 | 5.2 | 4.0 | 5.6 | 6.2 |
| 8. Transport; Storage & Communications | 1.1 | 1.1 | 0.9 | 1.0 | 1.5 | 1.6 | 2.4 | 2.7 |
| 9. Other services | 8.5 | 7.4 | 6.9 | 8.4 | 10.5 | 10.4 | 8.7 | 8.8 |
| Total | 100.0 | 100.0 | 100.0 | 100.0 | 100.0 | 100.0 | 100.0 | 100.0 |

*Notes :(a) Workers include all those who participate in any type of economic activity.*

      *(b) Include persons engaged in household activities under categories 3 and 4 also.*

      *(c) Included under categories 3, 4 and 5(ii)*

      *(d) Excludes Assam where 1981 Census was not conducted.*
         *Break up for 1991 Census not available.*

❑ Because of definitional changes from one Census to another, these data suffer from limitations of non-comparability. These should be used with adequate care and caution for any broad analytical purposes.

## 6.3 Distribution of Working Population by Occupation in Organised and Unorganised sectors : 1981

| Occupation by Economic Activity | Organised | | Unorganised (a) | | Total | | As % of line totals | |
|---|---|---|---|---|---|---|---|---|
| | Lakh Nos | % | Lakh Nos | % | Lakh Nos | % | Organ- ised | Unorg- anised |
| A. Agriculture & Allied Activities | 13 | 5.7 | 1,517 | 76.0 | 1,530 | 68.8 | 1 | 99 |
| 1. Cultivators | - | - | 925 | 46.3 | 925 | 41.6 | - | 100 |
| 2. Agricultural labourers | - | - | 555 | 27.8 | 555 | 24.9 | - | 100 |
| 3. Others | 13 | 5.7 | 37 | 1.9 | 50 | 2.3 | 26 | 74 |
| B. Mining & Manufacturing | 89 | 38.9 | 211 | 10.6 | 300 | 13.5 | 30 | 70 |
| 4. Mining & quarrying | 9 | 3.9 | 4 | 0.2 | 13 | 0.6 | 69 | 31 |
| 5. Manufacture & Repairs | 68 | 29.7 | 183 | 9.2 | 251 | 11.3 | 27 | 73 |
| 6. Construction | 12 | 5.3 | 24 | 1.2 | 36 | 1.6 | 33 | 67 |
| C. Services | 127 | 55.4 | 268 | 13.4 | 395 | 17.7 | 32 | 68 |
| 7. Transport storage & economic actions | 28 | 12.2 | 33 | 1.6 | 61 | 2.7 | 46 | 54 |
| 8. Trade & Commerce | 4 | 17 | 135 | 6.8 | 139 | 6.2 | 3 | 97 |
| 9. Other Services | 95 | 41.5 | 100 | 5.0 | 195 | 8.8 | 49 | 51 |
| Total | 229 | 100.0 | 1996 | 100.0 | 2225 (b) | 100.0 | 10 | 90 |

Notes : (a) Derived by deduction of organised sector workers from the total
     (b) Excludes Assam.
     Break-up for 1991 Census not available.

❏ Although the organised sector accounts for only 10% share in total working population, it is an important part of the economic activity. Of late, it has emerged as the most powerful and exploitative class of the population whose bargaining power cannot be ignored.

## PATTERN OF EMPLOYMENT : 1981

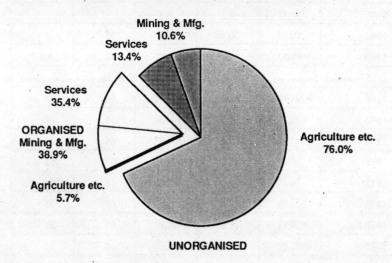

Mining & Mfg.
10.6%

Services
13.4%

Services
35.4%

ORGANISED
Mining & Mfg.
38.9%

Agriculture etc.
5.7%

Agriculture etc.
76.0%

UNORGANISED

## 6.4　Trends in Employment in Organised Sector : 1956 to 1991

| March End | Employment : '00,000 | | | % share in total employed | |
|---|---|---|---|---|---|
| | Public Sector | Private Sector | Total | Public Sector | Private Sector |
| 1956 | 52.34 | n.a | n.a | - | - |
| 1961 | 70.50 | 50.40 | 120.90 | 58 | 42 |
| 1965 | 89.57 | 60.40 | 149.97 | 60 | 40 |
| (a) Figures for following years are not comparable with those for earlier years | | | | | |
| 1966 | 93.79 | 68.13 | 161.92 | 58 | 42 |
| 1970 | 103.74 | 66.85 | 170.59 | 61 | 39 |
| 1971 | 107.31 | 67.42 | 174.73 | 61 | 39 |
| 1972 | 112.09 | 67.69 | 179.78 | 62 | 38 |
| 1973 | 119.71 | 68.49 | 180.20 | 64 | 36 |
| 1974 | 124.80 | 67.94 | 192.74 | 65 | 35 |
| 1975 (a) | 128.83 | 68.08 | 196.91 | 65 | 35 |
| 1976 | 133.22 | 68.44 | 201.66 | 66 | 34 |
| 1977 | 137.66 | 68.67 | 206.33 | 67 | 33 |
| 1978 | 142.00 | 70.43 | 212.43 | 67 | 33 |
| 1979 | 146.76 | 72.08 | 218.84 | 67 | 33 |
| 1980 | 150.78 | 72.27 | 223.05 | 68 | 32 |
| 1981 | 154.84 | 73.95 | 228.79 | 68 | 32 |
| 1982 | 159.46 | 75.47 | 234.93 | 68 | 32 |
| 1983 | 164.56 | 75.52 | 240.08 | 69 | 31 |
| 1984 | 168.69 | 73.45 | 242.14 | 70 | 30 |
| 1985 | 172.69 | 73.09 | 245.78 | 70 | 30 |

*contd . . .*

| March End | Employment : '00,000 | | | % share in total employed | |
|---|---|---|---|---|---|
| | Public Sector | Private Sector | Total | Public Sector | Private Sector |
| 1986 | 176.83 | 73.73 | 250.56 | 71 | 29 |
| 1987 | 180.25 | 73.64 | 253.89 | 71 | 29 |
| 1988 | 183.20 | 73.91 | 257.12 | 71 | 29 |
| 1989 | 185.16 | 74.70 | 259.86 | 71 | 29 |
| 1990 | 187.29 | 75.90 | 263.19 | 71 | 29 |
| 1991 | 189.65 | 78.54 | 268.19 | 71 | 29 |
| Annual rate of increase % | | | | | |
| 1961 & 1966 | 6.2 | 4.6 | 5.5 | | |
| 1966 & 1975 | 3.6 | -0.0 1 | 2.2 | | |
| 1980 & 1990 | 2.2 | 0.5 | 1.7 | | |

Notes : (a) *Organised Sector covers all the enterprises in the public sector and most agricultural establishment in the private sector employing 25 or more workers from 1961 to 1965 and 10 or more workers from 1966 onwards.*
(b) *Data from March 1976 are based on National Industrial Classification introduced from 1 April 1975; and are not comparable with those for earlier years.*

❑ Notwithstanding the diminishing annual growth rate of overall employment in the organised sector particularly during the least decade, this segment which includes the unionised employees, has emerged as the most powerful and exploitative class in the economy.

❑ The growth rate of employment in the public sector has remained higher than that in the private sector. As a result the share of public-sector in the total organised sector employment has increased to 71% since 1986. However, unfortunately, the record of relative productivity of this larger portion of workers leaves much to be desired and is best not commented upon. Even a marginal but sustained improvement can significantly improve the health of the economy, since the public sector commands a predominant position in infrastructure and key industries.

## 6.5   Industry-wise Distribution of Organised Sector Employment : 1961 & 1989

*('000 persons)*

| Industry groups | March-end 1961 | | | March-end 1989 | | |
|---|---|---|---|---|---|---|
| | Public Sector | Private Sector | Total | Public Sector | Private Sector | Total |
| Agriculture, incl. Forestry etc. | 180 (21) | 670 (79) | 850 (100) | 565 (39) | 870 (61) | 1,435 (100) |
| Industry | 1,325 (26) | 3,850 (74) | 5,175 (100) | 4,851 (51) | 4,591 (49) | 9,442 (100) |
| Mining & quarrying | 129 (19) | 550 (81) | 679 (100) | 959 (91) | 97 (9) | 1054 (100) |
| Manufacturing | 369 (11) | 3,020 (89) | 3,389 (100) | 1,848 (30) | 4,389 (70) | 6,237 (100) |
| Construction | 603 (72) | 240 (28) | 843 (100) | 1,180 (95) | 64 (5) | 1,244 (100) |
| Electricity, gas & Sanitary Services | 224 (85) | 40 (15) | 264 (100) | 866 (95) | 41 (5) | 907 (100) |
| Services | 5,545 (91) | 520 (9) | 6,065 (100) | 13,099 (87) | 2,099 (13) | 15,108 (100) |
| Trade & Commerce | 94 (37) | 160 (63) | 254 (100) | 144 (33) | 286 (67) | 430 (100) |
| Transport, Storage & Communications | 1,724 (96) | 80 (4) | 1,804 (100) | 3,026 (98) | 51 (2) | 3,077 100 |
| Finance, insurance, real estate etc. | n.a | n.a | n.a | 1,116 (52) | 243 (18) | 1,359 (100) |
| Other services incl. government administration | 3,227 (93) | 280 (7) | 4,007 (100) | 8,813 (86) | 1,429 (14) | 10,242 (100) |
| Total | 7,050 (58) | 5,040 (42) | 12,090 (100) | 18,515 (71) | 7,470 (29) | 25,985 (100) |

❑ In a certain sense, organised sector is the hub of the Indian economy and so it tends to loom large in public imagination. Nevertheless, it accounts for only 10% of our total labour force. The unorganised sector accounts for the remaining 90% covering large part of agricultural workers, and those engaged in small and cottage industry, trade, professional services etc. The entire unorganised segment falls within the private sector.

❑ Barring general services like govt. administration, organised manufacturing accounts for the largest – around one-fourth – share of employment, where share of public sector has increased almost three-folds over the years.

❑ Public Sector employment is largely in mining, construction, electricity, transport and financial services. While private sector is predominantly employing in manufacturing, trade and commerce.

## Organised Sector Employment by Broad Activity Groups
## March 1989 : 259.85 lakh persons.

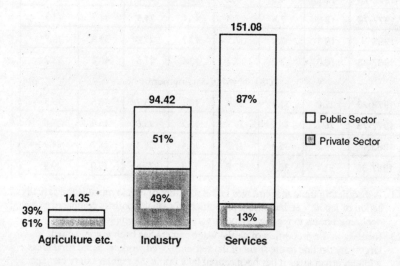

## 6.6   Distribution of Workers by Category of Employment

*(per cent)*

| Years | Rural | | | Urban | | | Combined (Rural + Urban) |
|---|---|---|---|---|---|---|---|
| | Male | Female | Total | Male | Female | Total | |
| **Self-employed** | | | | | | | |
| 1972-73 | 65.9 | 64.5 | 65.4 | 39.2 | 48.4 | 40.9 | 61.4 |
| 1977-78 | 62.8 | 62.1 | 62.5 | 40.4 | 49.5 | 42.4 | 59.3 |
| 1983 | 60.4 | 61.9 | 61.0 | 40.9 | 45.8 | 41.9 | 57.3 |
| 1987-88 | 58.6 | 60.9 | 59.4 | 41.6 | 47.1 | 42.8 | 56.3 |
| **Salaried regular employment** | | | | | | | |
| 1972-73 | 12.1 | 4.1 | 9.2 | 50.7 | 27.8 | 46.4 | 15.3 |
| 1977-78 | 10.6 | 2.8 | 7.8 | 46.4 | 24.9 | 41.7 | 13.2 |
| 1983 | 10.3 | 2.8 | 7.5 | 43.7 | 25.8 | 39.9 | 13.7 |
| 1987-88 | 10.0 | 3.6 | 7.7 | 43.4 | 27.5 | 40.2 | 13.7 |
| **Casual wage employment** | | | | | | | |
| 1972-73 | 22.0 | 31.4 | 25.4 | 10.1 | 23.7 | 12.6 | 23.3 |
| 1977-78 | 26.7 | 35.1 | 29.7 | 13.2 | 25.6 | 15.9 | 27.5 |
| 1983 | 29.2 | 35.3 | 31.5 | 15.4 | 28.4 | 18.2 | 28.9 |
| 1987-88 | 31.4 | 35.4 | 32.8 | 14.7 | 25.4 | 17.0 | 29.9 |

❑ A disquieting trend that emerges in the structure of employment is the casuali-sation of labour - an increasing proportion of casual labour as compared to the declining phases to regular salary earners and the self-employed.

❑ Increase in the proportion of casual wage earners has been accompanied largely by decline in the share of the self-employed workers in the rural areas, while in urban areas it has been caused by a fall in the regular salary earners.

❑ In recent years, in the urban areas the proportion of females has increased among the self-employed as well as salary-earners, while in casual workers it has declined. This is jointly the result of improved educational link of females and their work opportunity in urban areas, including in specialised services.

## 6.7 Industry-wise Pattern of Factory Employment : 1961, 1981, 1985 & 1988

| Industry | Average daily employment ('000) June-end | | | | CARG (%) | | |
|---|---|---|---|---|---|---|---|
| | 1961 | 1981 | 1985 | 1988 | 1961-81 | 1981-88 | 1961-88 |
| Food products | 557 | 1,000 | 1,056 | 1,081 | 3.0 | 1.1 | 2.5 |
| Beverages & tobacco products | 182 | 197 | 167 | 142 | 0.4 | -4.5 | 0.9 |
| Textiles | 1,206 | 1,787 | 1,738 | 1,677 | 2.0 | -0.9 | 1.2 |
| Wood & cork furnitures | 69 | 130 | 162 | 169 | 3.2 | 3.8 | 3.4 |
| Papers & products | 42 | 317 | 336 | 348 | 10.6 | 1.3 | 8.1 |
| Leather products (except footwear) | 20 | 55 | 64 | 79 | 5.2 | 5.3 | 5.2 |
| Rubber, plastics & petroleum products | 57 | 175 | 211 | 260 | 5.8 | 5.8 | 5.8 |
| Chemicals & chemical products | 146 | 460 | 502 | 555 | 5.9 | 2.7 | 5.1 |
| Non metallic mineral products | 193 | 363 | 455 | 520 | 3.2 | 5.3 | 3.7 |
| Basic metals | 178 | 503 | 557 | 608 | 5.3 | 2.7 | 4.7 |
| Metal products | 135 | 257 | 305 | 287 | 3.3 | 1.6 | 2.8 |
| Non-electrical machinery | 215 | 503 | 515 | 527 | 4.3 | 0.7 | 3.4 |
| Electrical machinery | 87 | 351 | 363 | 402 | 7.2 | 2.0 | 5.8 |
| Transport equipment | 358 | 417 | 480 | 487 | 0.8 | 2.2 | 1.1 |
| Misc Industrialists products | 130 | 72 | 74 | 99 | -2.9 | 4.7 | -1.0 |
| Electricity, gas & steam | 44 | 99 | 121 | 129 | 4.1 | 3.9 | 4.1 |
| Others | 285 | 425 | 459 | 504 | 2.0 | 2.5 | 2.1 |
| Total : All Industries | 3,904 | 7,111 | 7,565 | 7,874 | 3.0 | 1.5 | 2.6 |

CARG : Compound Annual Rate of Growth

❑ Between 1961 and 1988, the average daily employment in factories increased at an annual rate of 2.6% which is less than half the growth rate recorded in index of industrial production.

❑ Between 1961 and 1981, high employment growth rates ranging between 5% and 11% were recorded in industries like paper& paper products, chemicals & chemical products, petroleum products, basic metals and leather products.

❑ Between 1981 and 1988, as against the overall industrial production growth rate of about 7%, only three industries could sustain employment growth of about 5% per annum, namely petroleum products, non-metallic mineral products and leather products. On the other hand industry groups such as beverages and tobacco products and textiles recorded negative growth rates of employment over the period.

❑ Since 1985, the average daily employment in factories has hovered around 77 lakh persons. This signals induction of modern machinery which are less labour-intensive and offer higher labour productivity due to better technology in some specific industries.

## CARG (%) Total of all industries

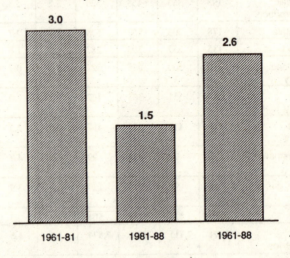

3.0      1.5      2.6

1961-81      1981-88      1961-88

## 6.8 Number of Job-seekers Registered with Employment Exchanges : 1951 - 1991

('00,000)

| December end | No. of exchanges | Educated | | | | Unskilled Manual labourers & Others | Total |
|---|---|---|---|---|---|---|---|
| | | Matriculates | Higher Secondary | Graduates & Post graduates | Total | | |
| 1961 | 325 | 4.63 | 0.71 | 0.56 | 5.90 | 12.43 | 18.33 |
| 1965 | 376 | 5.80 | 1.76 | 0.86 | 8.42 | 17.43 | 25.85 |
| 1970 | 429 | 11.01 | 4.44 | 2.77 | 18.22 | 22.47 | 40.69 |
| 1975 | 504 | 26.41 | 12.28 | 9.36 | 48.05 | 45.21 | 93.26 |
| 1980 | 638 | 45.68 | 20.71 | 15.24 | 81.64 | 80.36 | 162.00 |
| 1981 | 663 | 50.08 | 23.25 | 16.85 | 90.18 | 88.20 | 178.38 |
| 1982 | 692 | 55.60 | 24.39 | 17.69 | 97.68 | 99.85 | 197.53 |
| 1983 | 726 | 63.74 | 28.14 | 19.68 | 111.56 | 107.97 | 219.53 |
| 1984 | 745 | 73.01 | 30.76 | 21.59 | 125.56 | 110.11 | 235.47 |
| 1985 | 800 | 80.45 | 35.30 | 24.00 | 139.75 | 122.95 | 262.70 |
| 1986 | 821 | 94.46 | 41.45 | 28.61 | 164.42 | 136.79 | 301.31 |
| 1987 | 835 | 97.25 | 42.59 | 28.85 | 168.69 | 133.78 | 302.47 |
| 1988 | 840 | 101.70 | 44.20 | 29.22 | 175.12 | 125.38 | 300.50 |
| 1989 | 849 | n.a. | n.a. | n.a. | 191.36 | 136.40 | 327.76 |
| 1990 | 851 | n.a. | n.a. | n.a. | n.a. | n.a. | 346.32 |
| 1991 | 772 | n.a. | n.a. | n.a. | n.a. | n.a. | 363.00 |
| Compound annual rates of increase (%) | | | | | | | |
| 1980 - 1985 | 4.6 | 12.0 | 11.3 | 9.5 | 11.3 | 8.9 | 10.2 |
| 1985 - 1990 | 1.2 | 8.1(a) | 7.8(a) | 6.8(a) | 8.1(b) | 2.6(b) | 5.7 |

*Notes : (a) 1955 to 1988*
*(b) 1985 to 1989*

❏ The above figures cannot be taken as precise indicators of unemployment because by and large they cover the urban areas and only a small portion of rural unemployed gets registered. Besides, not all the job-seekers are registered and secondly not all those who are registered are unemployed. Many of the registered candidates are employed but are looking for change of job. According to NSS-1983, 25.6% on the live register were unemployed and 28.6% of the unemployed got themselves registered at the exchanges.

❏ Data by educational qualifications become available only when furnished in reply to parliament questions.

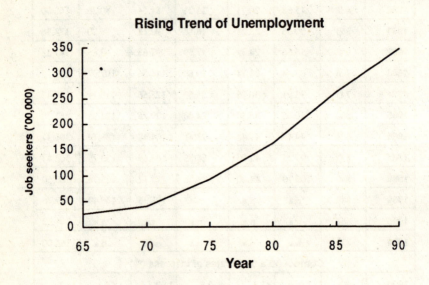

**Rising Trend of Unemployment**

## 6.9  Estimated Backlog of Unemployment at the End of Sixth and Seventh Plans

| Particulars | Sixth Plan 1980-85 | Seventh Plan 1985-90 |
|---|---|---|
| 1. Backlog of unemployment at the commencement of the plan (million) | 11.31 | 7.84 |
| 2. Backlog of unemployment as % of labour force | 4.8 | 2.9 |
| 3. Estimated increase in labour force during the plan period in age group 15-59 years (million) | 32.13 | 36.27 |
| 4. Employment to be provided to (1+3) (million) | 43.44 | 44.11 |
| 5. Projected generation of employment during the plan period (million jobs and years) | 34.28 35.60(a) | 40.36 |
| 6. Backlog of unemployment at the end of the plan (4-5) (million) | 7.84(a) | 3.75 |
| 7. Backlog of unemployment as % of labour force | 2.9 | 1.2 |

*Notes : (a) Estimated.*
*(In Age Group 15-59 years on usual status basis i.e., chronically un-employed during a period of one year or more.)*

## 6.10   Mandays lost through Industrial Disputes : 1961 - 1991

| Year | Estimated employment Organised Sector ('000) | No. of disputes | No. of workers involved ('000) | No. of mandays lost ('000) | | |
|------|------|------|------|------|------|------|
| | | | | Strikes | Lockouts | Total |
| 1961 | 12,090 | 1,357 | 512 | 2,969 | 1,950 | 4,919 |
| 1966 | 16,192 | 2,556 | 1,410 | 10,377 | 3,469 | 13,846 |
| 1971 | 17,059 | 2,752 | 1,615 | 11,803 | 4,743 | 16,546 |
| 1976 | 20,166 | 1,459 | 736 | 2,799 | 9,947 | 12,746 |
| 1981 | 22,879 | 2,589 | 1,588 | 21,208 | 15,375 | 36,583 |
| 1982 | 23,493 | 2,483 | 1,469 | 52,113 | 22,502 | 74,615 (a) |
| 1983 | 24,008 | 2,488 | 1,461 | 24,921 | 21,937 | 46,858 (a) |
| 1984 | 24,214 | 2,094 | 1,949 | 39,957 | 16,068 | 56,025 |
| 1985 | 24,578 | 1,755 | 1,079 | 11,487 | 17,753 | 29,240 |
| 1986 | 25,056 | 1,892 | 1,645 | 18,824 | 13,925 | 32,749 |
| 1987 | 25,349 | 1,799 | 1,770 | 14,026 | 21,332 | 35,358 |
| 1988 | 25,712 | 1,745 | 1,191 | 12,530 | 21,417 | 33,947 |
| 1989 | 25,986 | 1,793 | 1,351 | 10,700 | 21,990 | 32,680 |
| 1990(P) | n.a. | 1,367 | 1,105 | 10,220 | 13,400 | 23,620 |
| 1991(P) | n.a. | n.a. | n.a. | n.a. | n.a. | 34,120 |

*Notes : (a) Included 41.40 million and 13.38 million mandays lost due to the Bombay textile strike during 1982 and 1983.*
     *(P) Provisional*

❏  Between 1961 and 1984, the loss of mandays due to strikes was larger than that due to lockouts, except during 1966. Thereafter, except in 1986, the mandays loss due to lockouts exceeded that on account of strikes, increasing from 60% in 1987 to 67% in 1989, than only declining to 57% in 1990.

❏  With the prevailing growth rates of population and work force, adding to the backlog of unemployment, such levels of loss of mandays and consequent loss of output are uunaffordable luxuries.

## 7.1 Value Added Per Worker : 1970-71 & 1980-81 Broad Economic Sectors : Rural & Urban

*(Rupees)*

| Economic Sectors | Rural | Urban | Total (average) | Urban : Rural |
|---|---|---|---|---|
| **1970-71** | | | | |
| 1. Agriculture etc. | 1,317 | 1,527 | 1,323 | 1.16 |
| 2. Mining, Manufacturing, etc. | 2,281 | 4,534 | 3,437 | 1.99 |
| 3. Transport, Communications, Trade, etc. | 2,298 | 5,083 | 4,117 | 2.21 |
| 4. Finance & Real Estate | 38,944 | 15,714 | 20,204 | 0.40 |
| 5. Community & Personal Services | 1,745 | 2,579 | 2,165 | 1.48 |
| Commodity Sectors | 1,389 | 3,716 | 1,617 | 2.67 |
| Non-Commodity Sectors | 2,439 | 4,377 | 3,563 | 1.79 |
| Total | 1,477 | 4,071 | 1,936 | 2.76 |
| **1980-81** | | | | |
| 1. Agriculture etc. | 2,203 | 3,245 | 2,239 | 1.47 |
| 2. Mining, Manufacturing etc. | 5,394 | 9,944 | 7,612 | 1.84 |
| 3. Transport, Communications, Trade, etc. | 6,803 | 10,438 | 9,045 | 1.53 |
| 4. Finance & Real Estate | 1,11,923 | 53,078 | 66,719 | 0.48 |
| 5. Community & Personal Services. | 5,211 | 7,022 | 6,182 | 1.35 |
| Commodity sectors | 2,480 | 8,018 | 3,056 | 3.23 |
| Non-Commodity Sector | 7,882 | 10,903 | 9,646 | 1.38 |
| Total | 2,890 | 9,454 | 4,046 | 3.27 |

*Notes : The figures are based on detailed sub sectorwise figures of value added and no. of workers (as on 1 October) published by the CSO in July 1989. Data for later years not available.*

❑ Value added per worker is a more indicative of his productivity than the wages received by him. Connection between the two is not always direct.

❑ Value added per worker in urban areas is more than in rural areas except in real estate and business services both in 1970-71 and 1980-81, and in forestry and logging in 1980-81.

❑ The difference in value added per rural worker and urban worker increased in 1980-81 compared with that in 1970-71.

❑ The relative rural bias in the non-commodity sectors is on account of the larger value added per rural worker in real estate mentioned earlier.

## Growth in Value added per worker : Rural & Urban

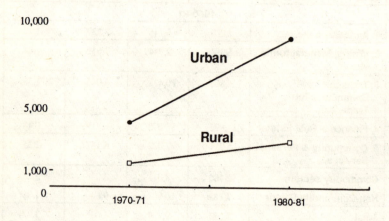

## 7.2 Per Worker Annual Emoluments to Average Per Family National Income : 1960-61 to 1990-91

| Year | NI per Family of three (Rs) | Per worker Emoluments to Per Family National Income | | | | |
|---|---|---|---|---|---|---|
| | | Mining (a) | Manufact-uring (b) | Non-depart-mental enterprise (c) | Railways | Commer-cial banks |
| 1960-61 | 985 | 1.4 | 1.7 | 2.2 | 1.8 | |
| 1961-62 | 1004 | 1.4 | 1.8 | na | na | |
| 1962-63 | 1047 | 1.5 | 1.8 | na | na | |
| 1963-64 | 1173 | 1.4 | 1.7 | na | na | |
| 1964-65 | 1345 | 1.3 | 1.6 | na | | |
| 1965-66 | 1376 | 1.5 | 1.8 | 2.2 | — | |
| 1966-67 | 1528 | 1.4 | 1.8 | 2.3 | 1.7 | |
| 1967-68 | 1763 | 1.6 | 1.6 | 2.2 | 1.6 | |
| 1968-69 | 1814 | 1.6 | 1.8 | 2.3 | 1.6 | |
| 1969-70 | 1952 | 1.6 | 1.8 | 2.4 | 1.6 | |
| 1970-71 | 2024 | 1.3 | 1.6 | 2.7 | 1.7 | 3.9 |
| 1971-72 | 2097 | 1.3 | 1.7 | 2.8 | 1.7 | 4.0 |
| 1972-73 | 2249 | 1.3 | 1.6 | 2.3 | 1.7 | 4.1 |
| 1973-74 | 2708 | 1.3 | 1.6 | 2.1 | 1.5 | 3.9 |
| 1974-75 | 3101 | 1.8 | 1.6 | 2.4 | 1.7 | 4.0 |
| 1975-76 | 3194 | 2.1 | 1.7 | 2.8 | 1.9 | 3.5 |
| 1976-77 | 3364 | 2.2 | 1.6 | 2.7 | 1.9 | 3.5 |
| 1977-78 | 3774 | 2.3 | 1.6 | 2.7 | 1.7 | 3.2 |
| 1978-79 | 3949 | 2.5 | 1.7 | 2.8 | 1.8 | 4.1 |
| 1979-80 | 4171 | 2.6 | 1.7 | 3.0 | 1.8 | 4.0 |
| 1980-81 | 4890 | 2.7 | 1.6 | 2.9 | 1.7 | 3.7 |
| 1981-82 | 5568 | 2.5 | 1.6 | 2.9 | 1.7 | 3.5 |
| 1982-83 | 6003 | 2.6 | 1.7 | 3.0 | 1.8 | 3.5 |
| 1983-84 | 6901 | 2.9 | 1.7 | 3.1 | 1.9 | 3.8 |

| Year | NI per Family of three (Rs) | Per worker Emoluments to Per Family National Income | | | | |
|---|---|---|---|---|---|---|
| | | Mining (a) | Manufacturing (b) | Non-departmental enterprise (c) | Railways | Commercial banks |
| 1984-85 | 7513 | 2.8 | 1.8 | 3.2 | 2.0 | 3.8 |
| 1985-86 | 8178 | 2.8 | 1.8 | 3.2 | 2.1 | 3.8 |
| 1986-87 | 8861 | 2.9 | 1.9 | 3.3 | 2.4 | 3.8 |
| 1987-88 | 9858 | 3.0 | 1.8 | 3.3 | 2.5 | 3.4 |
| 1988-89 | 11626 | | | 3.4 | 2.4 | 3.5 |
| 1989-90 | 12757 | | | 3.4 | 2.3 | 3.8 |
| 1990-91 | 14,688 | | | 3.3 | 2.2 | 3.7 |
| Compound annual rate of increase % | | | | | | |
| 1960-61 to 1989-90 | 9.2 | 12.0 | 9.2 | 10.8 | 10.1 | 9.9 |

Notes : (a) Mining includes mainly coal.
  (b) Manufacturing includes electricity, gas and water supply.
  (c) Non-departmental enterprises of the Central Government.

❑ Compound annual rates of increases relate to the per worker emoluments under respective categories of employment and have been calculated over the period from 1960-61 to the latest available year in each case.

❑ Bank employees are among the highest paid workers getting over three and a half-time the total income of an average family of there persons. Next best paid are the employees in the non-departmental enterprises of the Central Government followed by miners, railways and lastly the manufacturing workers.

❑ Miners have the fatest wage growth rate, next being the non-departmental enterprises. Bank employees get high wages increasing at 10% annually.

## 8.1   Pattern of Agricultural Land Holding : 1960-61 – 1985-86

| Category of farmers | 1960 - 61 | 1970 -71 | 1980 - 81 | 1985 - 86 | 1960 -61 | 1970 -71 | 1980 - 81 | 1985 - 86 |
|---|---|---|---|---|---|---|---|---|
| | A. Number of Holdings | | | | | | | |
| | Million Numbers | | | | As % to total | | | |
| Marginal | 19.90 | 35.68 | 50.12 | 56.75 | 40.7 | 50.6 | 56.4 | 58.1 |
| Small | 10.88 | 13.43 | 16.07 | 17.88 | 22.3 | 19.1 | 18.1 | 18.3 |
| Semi - Medium | 9.22 | 10.68 | 12.46 | 13.25 | 18.9 | 15.2 | 14.0 | 13.5 |
| Medium | 6.97 | 7.93 | 8.07 | 7.92 | 13.4 | 11.2 | 9.1 | 8.1 |
| Large | 2.31 | 2.77 | 2.17 | 1.93 | 4.7 | 3.9 | 2.4 | 2.0 |
| Total | 48.88 | 70.49 | 88.89 | 97.73 | 100.0 | 100.0 | 100.0 | 100.0 |
| | B. Area Operated | | | | | | | |
| | Million Hectares | | | | As % to total | | | |
| Marginal | 8.78 | 14.55 | 19.73 | 21.60 | 6.7 | 9.0 | 12.0 | 13.2 |
| Small | 16.00 | 19.28 | 23.17 | 25.53 | 12.2 | 11.9 | 14.1 | 15.6 |
| Semi - Medium | 26.23 | 30.00 | 34.65 | 36.58 | 20.0 | 18.5 | 21.2 | 22.3 |
| Medium | 40.07 | 48.23 | 48.54 | 47.01 | 30.4 | 29.7 | 29.0 | 28.7 |
| Large | 40.38 | 50.06 | 37.71 | 33.19 | 30.7 | 30.9 | 23.0 | 20.2 |
| Total | 131.46 | 162.12 | 163.80 | 163.91 | 100.0 | 100.0 | 100.0 | 100.0 |
| | C. Average Size of Holding | | | | | | | |
| | Area per operated holding (hectares) | | | | Percentage change over preceding position | | | |
| Marginal | 0.44 | 0.41 | 0.39 | 0.38 | | - 6.8 | - 4.9 | - 2.6 |
| Small | 1.47 | 1.44 | 1.44 | 1.43 | | - 2.0 | - | - 0.7 |
| Semi - Medium | 2.84 | 2.81 | 2.78 | 2.76 | | -1.1 | - 1.1 | - 0.8 |
| Medium | 6.10 | 6.08 | 6.04 | 5.94 | | - 0.3 | - 0.7 | - 1.7 |
| Large | 17.48 | 18.07 | 17.41 | 17.20 | | + 3.4 | - 3.7 | - 1.2 |
| Total | 2.69 | 2.30 | 1.84 | 1.68 | | - 14.5 | - 20.0 | - 8.7 |

*Notes :*    *Marginal = Upto 1 hectare, Small = 1 to 2 hectares, Semi-medium = 2 to 4 hectares, Medium = 4 to 10 hectares, Large = 10 hectares and more.*

❑ Size of operational holding of cultivable land is of fundamental importance in devising any strategy for agricultural development. In our country this poses one of the biggest constraints to improvement of land productivity.

❑ The average size of operational holding was 2.7 hectares in 1960-61; by 1985-86 this had reduced to 1.7 hectares, and the size may have diminished further thereafter.

❑ Fragmentation of holding upon inheritance among the successors, as also the distribution of acquired surplus land among the weaker lots of farming community, increases the number of marginal and small land holdings. What is worse still, these fragments consist of number of tiny plots far scattered away, making the cultivation more labour-intensive and uneconomical.

❑ Thus, in 1985-86, while 49% of the cultivated land belonged to just 10% of the farmers each with large holdings of 4 hectares and more, only 13% of the land was distributed among 58% of the farmers with marginal holdings of one hectare or less.

❑ Productivity gains of technology, mechanisation, irrigation etc. could be reaped if efforts are made for consolidation of fragmented holdings into larger plots.

## Average Size of Operated Holding: 1960-61 & 1985-86

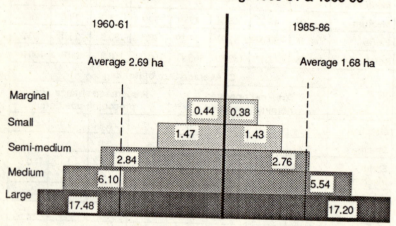

## 8.2    Rainfall : Seasons and Performance

| Performance of Monsoon | | |
|---|---|---|
| Year | Actual Rainfall as % of normal rainfall | Departure from normal rainfall = 100 |
| 1981 | 100 | - |
| 1982 | 85 | - 15 |
| 1983 | 113 | + 13 |
| 1984 | 96 | - 4 |
| 1985 | 93 | - 7 |
| 1986 | 87 | - 13 |
| 1987 | 81 | - 19 |
| 1988 | 119 | + 19 |
| 1989 | 101 | + 1 |
| 1990 | 106 | + 6 |

| Distribution of Annual Normal Rainfall by Period during a year | | | |
|---|---|---|---|
| Rainfall Season | Period | Normal rainfall (mm) | % of annual rainfall |
| Pre-monsoon | 1 Mar - 31May (92 days) | 124 | 10.4 |
| Summer-South-West Monsoon | 1 June - 30 Sept (122 days) | 877 | 73.7 |
| Post-Monsoon | 1 Oct. - 31 Dec. (92 days) | 158 | 13.3 |
| Winter-North-east Monsoon | 1 Jan. - 28 Feb. (59 days) | 31 | 2.8 |
| All-India (35 meteorological divisions) | | 1190 | 100.0 |

❑  In a vast country like India the pattern of rainfall in various regions depends on climatic conditions. The climatic setting is highly diverse, ranging from tropical in the south to temperate and frigid climate in the north. The extreme east receives very high rainfall while in the extreme west, the rainfall is very low and erratic.

❑ Nearly two-thirds of agriculture is in rainfed areas. About one-third of the country receives an annual rainfall of less than 750 mm and these areas are termed as dry lands. Another 42% of the geographical area receives between 750 and 1150 mm rainfall and these areas offer stable conditions for crop production. The remaining 28% area receives between 1150 and 2000 mm of rainfall.

❑ While one-third of the area is prone to vagaries of monsoon like droughts, some parts in excessive rainfall areas (28%) often suffer floods, water logging and soil erosions.

❑ Almost three-fourths of annual rainfall occurs during the south-west monsoon except J&K in extreme north and Tamil Nadu in extreme south. Our agriculture is highly dependent on timely arrival, amount and distribution of the south-west monsoon.

## Seasonwise distribution of Rainfall (%)

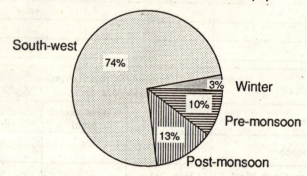

## Deviation from Normal Rainfall

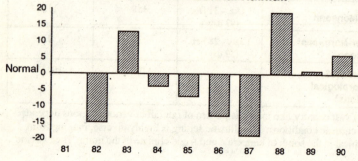

## 8.3  Trends in Area Sown and Irrigated 1950-51 – 1987-88

*(Million. hectares)*

| Year | Area Sown | | | | Area Irrigated | | | |
|---|---|---|---|---|---|---|---|---|
| | Area | | % of geographical area | | Area | | % of area sown | |
| | Net | Gross | Net | Gross | Net | Gross | Net | Gross |
| 1950-51 | 118.8 | 131.9 | 36.1 | 40.1 | 20.9 | 22.6 | 17.6 | 17.1 |
| 1955-56 | 129.3 | 147.3 | 39.3 | 44.8 | 22.8 | 25.6 | 17.7 | 17.4 |
| 1960-61 | 133.2 | 152.8 | 40.5 | 46.5 | 24.7 | 28.0 | 18.5 | 18.3 |
| 1965-66 | 136.2 | 155.3 | 41.4 | 47.2 | 26.3 | 30.9 | 19.3 | 19.9 |
| 1970-71 | 140.8 | 165.8 | 42.8 | 50.4 | 31.1 | 38.2 | 22.1 | 23.0 |
| 1975-76 | 142.2 | 170.9 | 43.2 | 52.0 | 34.5 | 43.2 | 24.3 | 25.3 |
| 1980-81 | 140.0 | 172.6 | 42.6 | 52.5 | 38.7 | 49.8 | 27.6 | 28.9 |
| 1981-82 | 142.1 | 177.1 | 43.2 | 53.9 | 40.0 | 51.6 | 28.2 | 29.1 |
| 1982-83 | 140.8 | 173.8 | 42.8 | 52.9 | 40.7 | 52.0 | 28.9 | 29.9 |
| 1983-84 | 143.2 | 180.8 | 43.6 | 55.0 | 42.1 | 54.2 | 25.4 | 30.0 |
| 1984-85 | 140.9 | 176.4 | 42.8 | 53.6 | 42.0 | 54.7 | 29.8 | 31.0 |
| 1985-86 | 140.9 | 178.8 | 42.9 | 54.4 | 42.1 | 54.7 | 29.9 | 30.6 |
| 1986-87 | 140.2 | 176.9 | 42.7 | 53.8 | 43.1 | 55.6 | 30.7 | 31.4 |
| 1987-88 | 136.2 | 172.9 | 41.5 | 52.6 | 43.0 | 56.2 | 31.6 | 32.5 |
| Compound annual rates of increase (%) | | | | | | | | |
| 1950s | 1.2 | 1.5 | | | 1.7 | 1.2 | | |
| 1960s | 0.6 | 0.8 | | | 2.3 | 2.2 | | |
| 1970s | - 0.06 | 0.4 | | | 2.2 | 2.6 | | |
| 1980-81 to 1987-88 | 0.02 | 0.4 | | | 1.8 | 1.9 | | |
| 1950-51 to 1987-88 | 0.5 | 0.8 | | | 2.0 | 2.5 | | |

❑ Since the seventies, the rate of extension of cropped area has slowed down to less than half a per cent per annum. The growth in agricultural output has been largely obtained through successive improvement in productivity of land. In this, irrigation provides dual advantage in that it enhances the scope for application of modern inputs and techniques to support intensive cultivation, as also it augments the land use through multiple cropping.

❑ The rate of increase in irrigated area has slowed down during the eighties after recording rapid increase of about 2.5% annually during the previous two decades. Thus, as against the irrigation potential of 72 million hectares created till 1986-87, the gross area irrigated was only around 56 million hectares or 77.5% of the potential available.

❑ Again, this irrigation facility was made use of for 43 million hectares of farm land constituting 31% of the net sown area.

❑ Needless to add that if higher production growth targets in agriculture are to be attained then increasing the use of available irrigation potential and extension of the facility over larger cropped land would have to be attended to with due urgency.

## 8.4　Net Area Irrigated by Different Sources 1950-51– 1987-88

*(Million hectares)*

| | Canals | | Tanks | Wells | | Other Sources | Total : Net area irrigated |
|---|---|---|---|---|---|---|---|
| | Govt. | Private | | Tube wells | Other wells | | |
| 1950-51 | 7.2 | 1.1 | 3.6 | ... | 6.0 | 3.0 | 20.9 |
| 1955-56 | 8.0 | 1.4 | 4.4 | ... | 6.8 | 2.2 | 22.8 |
| 1960-61 | 9.2 | 1.2 | 4.6 | 0.2 | 7.2 | 2.4 | 24.8 |
| 1965-66 | 9.8 | 1.1 | 4.4 | ... | 8.6 | 2.5 | 26.4 |
| 1970-71 | 12.0 | 0.9 | 4.1 | 4.5 | 7.4 | 2.3 | 31.2 |
| 1975-76 | 12.9 | 0.9 | 4.0 | 6.8 | 7.6 | 2.4 | 34.6 |
| 1980-81 | 14.5 | 0.8 | 3.2 | 9.5 | 8.2 | 2.6 | 38.8 |
| 1985-86 | 15.7 | 0.5 | 3.1 | 11.5 | 8.6 | 2.7 | 42.1 |
| 1986-87 | 15.8 | 0.5 | 3.0 | 12.2 | 8.8 | 2.7 | 43.0 |
| 1987-88 | 15.0 | 0.5 | 2.8 | 13.2 | 8.7 | 3.0 | 43.2 |
| Compound annual rates of increase % | | | | | | | |
| 1950s | 2.5 | 0.9 | 2.5 | ... | 1.8 | - 2.2 | 1.7 |
| 1960s | 2.7 | - 2.8 | - 1.1 | 36.5 | 0.3 | - 0.4 | 2.3 |
| 1970s | 1.9 | - 1.2 | - 2.5 | 7.8 | 1.0 | 1.2 | 2.2 |
| 1980-81 to 1987-88 | 1.4 | - 7.5 | - 1.1 | 4.3 | 1.2 | 0.6 | 1.7 |
| 1950-51 to 1987-88 | 2.2 | - 2.2 | - 0.5 | 17.1 (a) | 1.1 | - 0.3 | 2.0 |
| % Shares of Sources | | | | | | | |
| 1950-51 | 34.5 | 5.2 | 17.2 | ... | 28.7 | 14.4 | 100.0 |
| 1955-56 | 35.1 | 6.1 | 19.3 | ... | 29.8 | 9.7 | 100.0 |
| 1960-61 | 37.1 | 4.8 | 18.6 | 0.8 | 29.0 | 9.7 | 100.0 |
| 1965-66 | 37.1 | 4.2 | 16.7 | ... | 32.5 | 9.5 | 100.0 |
| 1970-71 | 38.5 | 2.9 | 13.1 | 14.4 | 23.7 | 7.4 | 100.0 |
| 1975-76 | 37.3 | 2.6 | 11.6 | 19.7 | 22.0 | 6.8 | 100.0 |
| 1980-81 | 37.4 | 2.1 | 8.3 | 24.5 | 21.0 | 6.7 | 100.0 |
| 1985-86 | 37.3 | 1.2 | 7.4 | 27.3 | 20.4 | 6.4 | 100.0 |
| 1986-87 | 36.7 | 1.2 | 7.0 | 28.4 | 20.5 | 6.2 | 100.0 |
| 1987-88 | 34.7 | 1.2 | 6.5 | 30.6 | 20.1 | 6.9 | 100.0 |

❑ Wells, including tube wells, are the single most important source of irrigation
while in 1986-87 accounted for 45% of the net irrigated area. With the propa-
gation of tube-wells since 1970-71, for tapping ground water resource, the
share of well water irrigation has surpassed that of canal irrigation.

❑ Canal irrigation is the second large source of irrigation and accounts for 37%
of the net irrigated area. Even with the doubling of net irrigated area, the share
of canal irrigations has remained nearly stable since 1950-51 around 40%.

❑ Role of tanks has progressively declined over the years. By desilting and reno-
vation of tanks their capacity of conserving rainwaters can be enhanced and
their share and the increased.

## Area irrigated by different sources

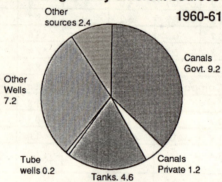

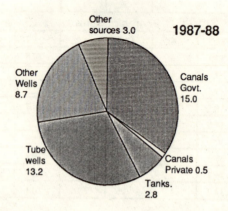

## 8.5 Production and Distribution of Certified/Quality seeds 1983-84 and 1989-90

*(Lakh quintals)*

| Crop groups | Production | | | Distribution | | |
|---|---|---|---|---|---|---|
| | 1983-84 | 1989-90 | CARG. % | 1983-84 | 1989-90 | CARG. % |
| Food grains | 32.0 | 52.1 | 8.5 | 27.8 | 38.3 | 5.5 |
| Cereals | 30.4 | 47.1 | 7.6 | 25.7 | 34.6 | 5.1 |
| Pulses | 1.6 | 5.0 | 20.9 | 2.1 | 3.7 | 9.9 |
| Oilseeds | 5.0 | 9.3 | 10.9 | 6.5 | 9.5 | 6.5 |
| Fibres | 0.8 | 2.0 | 16.5 | 1.9 | 1.7 | - 1.8 |
| Miscellaneous | 3.5 | 4.3 | 3.5 | 8.8 | 7.3 | - 3.1 |
| Total | 41.3 | 67.7 | 8.6 | 45.0 | 56.9 | 4.0 |

❑ Seeds constitute a major item of the cost of cultivation to a farmer. The share of seeds in total value of agricultural inputs ranges between 10 to 11 percent. In the event of resourcing due to prolonged dry spell or floods, the small and marginal farmers are severely hit as they are incapable of affording the right quality of seeds once again.

❑ Seed rates, that is the ratio of quantity of seeds applied per hectare to the yield per hectare, varies between 0.5 to 20% depending upon the type of crop to be cultivated, the lowest rate being for coarse grain like ragi while higher rates apply to cash crops like tobacco and groundnuts and pulses.

❑ While the production of certified quality seeds has been increasing, their distribution has been growing at slower rates and is negative of late in some cases.

## 8.6 Fertilisers : Trends in Production, Imports and Consumption : 1951-52 – 1991-92

*('000 tons of nutrients)*

| Year | Produc-tion | Imports | Consumption | | | | Per hectare of area (kg.) |
|------|------|------|------|------|------|------|------|
| | | | Nitrogenous (N) | Phosphatic (P$_2$O$_5$) | Potassic (K) | Total | |
| 1951-52 | 27 | 52 | 59 | 7 | - | 66 | 0.6 |
| 1955-56 | 89 | 63 | 108 | 13 | 10 | 131 | 0.9 |
| 1960-61 | 166 | 419 | 212 | 53 | 29 | 294 | 1.9 |
| 1965-66 | 357 | 413 | 575 | 133 | 77 | 785 | 5.1 |
| 1970-71 | 1,061 | 630 | 1,479 | 541 | 236 | 2256 | 13.6 |
| 1975-76 | 1,828 | 1,635 | 2,149 | 467 | 278 | 2,894 | 16.9 |
| 1980-81 | 3,005 | 2,759 | 3,678 | 1,214 | 624 | 5,516 | 31.5 |
| 1985-86 | 5,756 | 3,314 | 5,661 | 2,005 | 808 | 8,474 | 47.4 |
| 1986-87 | 7,070 | 2,275 | 5,716 | 2,079 | 850 | 8,645 | 48.9 |
| 1987-88 | 7,131 | 984 | 5,717 | 2,187 | 881 | 8,785 | 49.7 |
| 1988-89 | 8,964 | 1,608 | 7,246 | 2,722 | 1,068 | 11,036 | 62.4 |
| 1989-90 | 8,543 | 3,114 | 7,396 | 3,012 | 1,164 | 11,572 | 65.4 |
| 1990-91 | 9,044 | 2,758 | 8,019 | 3,220 | 1,328 | 12,567 | 70.0 |
| 1991-92 | 10,000 | 2,793 | 8,579 | 3,664 | 1,513 | 13,756 | 75.4 |
| **Compound annual rates of increase (%)** | | | | | | | |
| 1950s | 22.4 | 26.1 | 15.3 | 25.2 | 32.8 (a) | 18.1 | 13.7 |
| 1960s | 20.4 | 4.2 | 21.4 | 26.2 | 23.3 | 22.6 | 21.8 |
| 1970s | 11.0 | 15.9 | 9.5 | 8.4 | 10.2 | 9.4 | 8.8 |
| 1980s | 11.7 | - | 8.1 | 10.2 | 7.8 | 8.6 | 8.3 |
| 1951-52 to 1990-91 | 16.1 | 10.7 | 13.4 | 17.3 | 17.4 (b) | 14.5 | 13.0 |

Notes : (a) Between 1952-53 and 1960-61.
       (b) Between 1952-53 and 1990-91

❑ Assured supply of water is a pre-requisite to the intensive application of fertilisers. Since two-thirds of the gross cropped area depends on rainfed cultivation, this places a constraint on increasing the consumption of fertilisers.

❑ In fact, the rate of growth of fertiliser consumption has almost stagnated during the last two decades at lower levels compared to the earlier period, notwithstanding the increasing subsidy element in cost to the farmers . Until the price revision enforced under the 1991-92 budget, the price of fertiliser had not been revised for almost a decade.

❑ However, it should be noted that per hectare consumption of fertiliser more than doubled from 31.5 kg in 1980-81 to 70 kg in 1990-91.

❑ Fertiliser is a catalyst to the use of other improved techniques for cultivation and improving the agricultural production. Technological transformation in agriculture in future would depend upon our ability to create conditions for raising fertiliser consumption. Rapid increase in indigenous production has enabled to reduce the constraints of dependence on imports of fertilisers.

## Fertilisers : Increased share of Domestic Production

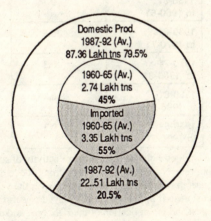

## 8.7 Pesticides Consumption : 1950-51 – 1990-91 (Technical grade material)

*('000 tons)*

| Year | Consumption |
|---|---|
| 1950-51 | 2.35 |
| 1960-61 | 5.62 |
| 1970-71 | 24.32 |
| 1980-81 | 45.00 |
| 1985-86 | 52.00 |
| 1986-87 | 50.00 |
| 1987-88 | 49.00 |
| 1988-89 | 55.00 |
| 1989-90 | 72.00 |
| 1990-91 | 82.36 |

| Compound annual rate of increase (%) | |
|---|---|
| 1950-51 to 1960-61 | 9.1 |
| 1960-61 to 1970-71 | 15.8 |
| 1970-71 to 1980-81 | 6.3 |
| 1980-81 to 1990-91 | 6.2 |
| 1950-51 to 1990-91 | 9.3 |

❑ As fertiliser consumption helps to raise the productivity of seeds, use of pesticides at the proper time ensures against loss of crops due to damage by pests.

❑ The consumption of pesticides has grown rapidly over the years. Advice from agricultural extension staff in this sphere has played a useful role in the matter of detecting the pest and in application of the right type and dosage of pesticides.

## 8.8　Trends in Progress of Farm Mechanisation : 1951-1990

| Year | Gross cropped area (GCA) mln. ha. | Tractors | | Oil engines | | Electrical pumpsets | | Power consumption for agri. Kwh/ '000 ha. |
|---|---|---|---|---|---|---|---|---|
| | | No. in lakhs | Per lakh ha. | No. in lakhs | Per lakh ha. | No. in lakhs | Per lakh ha. | |
| 1951 | 131.9 | 0.09 | 7 | 0.66 | 50 | 0.21 | 16 | 1.5 |
| 1956 | 147.3 | 0.21 | 14 | 1.23 | 84 | 0.56 | 38 | 2.1 |
| 1961 | 152.8 | 0.31 | 20 | 2.30 | 151 | 2.00 | 131 | 5.5 |
| 1966 | 155.3 | 0.54 | 34 | 4.65 | 295 | 5.13 | 330 | 12.4 |
| 1971 | 165.8 | 1.43 | 86 | n.a. | n.a. | 16.20 | 977 | 27.0 |
| 1976 | 171.3 | 2.80 | 163 | n.a. | n.a. | 27.34 | 1,595 | 65.4 |
| 1981 | 172.6 | 5.20 | 301 | 28.10 | 1,623 | 43.24 | 2,505 | 84.0 |
| 1986 | 178.8 | 8.99 | 503 | 37.70 | 2,088 | 61.52 | 3,440 | 131.0 |
| 1987 | 176.9 | 9.79 | 553 | 40.00 | 2,222 | 66.57 | 3,763 | 166.4 |
| 1988 | 177.0 | 10.70 | 605 | 42.50 | 2,400 | 72.26 | 4,082 | 196.7 |
| 1989 | 182.0 | 11.77 | 647 | 45.00 | 2,472 | 78.19 | 4,296 | 214.0 |
| 1990 | 182.5 | 12.97 | 710 | 47.00 | 2,575 | 85.00 | 4,658 | 239.0 |
| Compound annual rate increase (%) | | | | | | | | |
| 1951 to 1961 | 1.5 | 13.2 | 11.1 | 13.3 | 11.7 | 25.3 | 23.4 | 13.9 |
| 1961 to 1971 | 0.8 | 16.5 | 15.7 | .. | .. | 12.0 | 22.3 | 17.2 |
| 1971 to 1981 | 0.4 | 13.8 | 13.3 | .. | .. | 10.3 | 9.9 | 12.0 |
| 1981 to 1990 | 0.6 | 10.7 | 10.0 | 5.9 | 5.3 | 7.8 | 7.1 | 12.3 |
| 1951 to 1990 | 0.8 | 13.6 | 12.6 | 11.6 | 10.6 | 16.6 | 15.7 | 13.9 |

*Notes : GCA = Gross cropped area*

❑ Although there has been a noteworthy progress in farm mechanisation which has been aided by credit facilities and subsidy particularly in electricity rates, the small size and scattered locations of small have deprived small and marginal farmers of the benefits of mechanisation.

❑ The low ratios per lakh of hectares of gross cropped area amply illustrates that the benefit of mechanisation is largely availed by large and medium farmers.

## Increase in poulation of farm equipment & coverage of gross cropped area

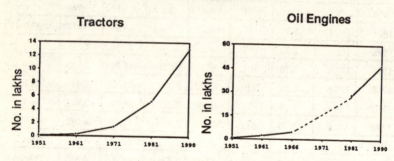

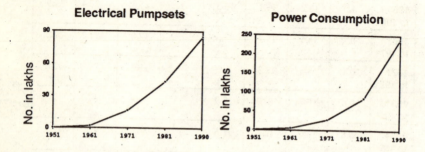

## 8.9 Flow of Institutional Credit for Agriculture : 1950-51 – 1990-91

*(Rs. crores)*

| Year | Co-operatives | | | | Commercial Banks and Regional Rural Bank | | | Grand Total |
|---|---|---|---|---|---|---|---|---|
| | Short term | Medium term | Long term | Total | Short term | Medium term | Total | |
| 1950-51 | 23 (a) | n.a. | 1 | 24 | n.a. | n.a. | n.a. | 24 |
| 1960-61 | 183 | 20 | 11 | 214 | n.a. | n.a. | n.a. | 214 |
| 1970-71 | 519 | 59 | 101 | 679 | n.a. | n.a. | 206 | 885 |
| 1980-81 | 1,526 | 237 | 363 | 2,126 | 517 | 746 | 1,263 | 3,389 |
| 1985-86 | 2,747 | 393 | 543 | 3,683 | 3110 (b) | n.a. | 3,110 | 6,793 |
| 1986-87 | 2,824 | 531 | 560 | 3,915 | 3796 (b) | n.a. | 3,796 | 7,711 |
| 1987-88 | 3,320 | 547 | 690 | 4,557 | 3,914 (b) | n.a. | 3,914 | 8,471 |
| 1988-89 | 3,833 | 381 | 730 | 4,944 | 6,310 (b) | n.a. | 6,310 | 11,254 |
| 1989-90 | 4,222 | 416 | 869 | 5,507 | 3155 | 4,360 | 7,515 | 13,022 |
| 1990-91 | 4,708 | 394 | 957 | 6,059 | 7,181 (b) | n.a. | 7,181 | 13,240 |

| Compound annual rates of increase (%) | | | | | | | | |
|---|---|---|---|---|---|---|---|---|
| 1950-51 to 1960-61 | 23.0 | - | 27.1 | 24.5 | - | - | - | 24.5 |
| 1960-61 to 1970-71 | 11.0 | 11.4 | 24.8 | 12.2 | - | - | - | 15.3 |
| 1970-71 to 1980-81 | 11.4 | 14.9 | 13.6 | 12.1 | - | - | 19.9 | 14.4 |
| 1980-81 to 1990-91 | 11.9 | 5.2 | 10.2 | 11.0 | 30.1 | - | 19.0 | 14.6 |
| 1950-51 to 1990-91 | 14.2 | - | 18.7 | 14.8 | - | - | - | 17.1 |

*Notes : (a) Includes medium term loans,*
*(b) Includes medium and long term loans (1990-91 figures are provisional.)*

❑ Ever since the nationalisation of major scheduled commercial banks in 1969, agriculture has been accorded priority status in allocation of institutional credit and of concessional rates of interests. The credit allocated to agriculture has rapidly increased during the 1980s from Rs 3,389 crores in 1980-81 to Rs 13,240 crores in 1990-91.

❑ The cooperative credit institutions also account for a significant share of the farm credit for which they receive adequate refinance facility from National Bank for Agriculture and Rural Development. But, they are constrained in re-cycling the funds due to persistently high proportion of overdues, of about 40% in recent years.

❑ The scheduled commercial banks which are required to allocate a prescribed 16% share of concessional credit to agriculture also face the problem of mounting overdues and cost of recovery.

❑ In view of the mounting overdues and non-recovery of credit, the Union government decided in 1989 to waive the loans of farmers and artisans upto Rs 10,000. The amount to be so waived is placed at Rs 7,700 crores or so.

❑ It should be noted that benefits of concessions and facilities granted in the agriculture spreads to vast number of beneficiaries spread all over the rural areas of the country, whose contribution in our achieving food self-sufficiency and overall agricultural growth cannot be underestimated.

## Flow of Institutional Credit for Agriculture

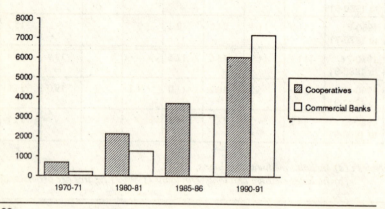

# AGRICULTURE : INPUTS 8

## 8.10 Estimated Gross Value of Inputs in Agriculture : 1980-81 – 1988-89

*(Rs crores at 1980-81 Pricing)*

| Item | 1980-81 | | 1985-86 | | 1988-89 | |
|---|---|---|---|---|---|---|
| | Rs. crores | % | Rs. crores | % | Rs. crores | % |
| Feed of live stock (a) | 2,680 | 21.9 | 2,685 | 17.8 | 2,765 | 16.3 |
| Seeds | 1,682 | 13.8 | 1,815 | 12.1 | 1,947 | 11.5 |
| Chemical fertilisers | 2,308 | 18.9 | 3,780 | 25.1 | 4,777 | 28.1 |
| Organic manures | 679 | 5.6 | 730 | 4.9 | 726 | 4.3 |
| Diesel oil | 453 | 3.7 | 699 | 4.6 | 822 | 4.8 |
| Electricity | 269 | 2.2 | 392 | 2.6 | 732 | 4.3 |
| Irrigation charges | 122 | 1.0 | 149 | 1.0 | 170 | 1.0 |
| Pesticides & Insecticides | 250 | 2.1 | 331 | 2.2 | 394 | 2.3 |
| Market charges | 601 | 4.9 | 678 | 4.5 | 777 | 4.6 |
| Depreciation | 2,410 | 19.7 | 2,865 | 19.1 | 2,893 | 17.0 |
| Current repairs (b) | 758 | 6.2 | 912 | 6.1 | 1,001 | 5.8 |
| Gross value of inputs | 12,212 | 100.0 | 15,036 | 100.0 | 17,004 | 100.0 |
| Value added | 34,066 | | 37,172 | | 42,766 | |
| Total value of output | 46,278 | | 52,208 | | 59,770 | |
| Of inputs as % of value of output | 26.4 | | 28.8 | | 28.4 | |

*Notes: (a) Feed of livestock includes the cost of feed for draught animals only i.e. taken as about one-third of the total given by the CSO.*
*(b) Current repairs includes maintenance of fixed assets and other operational costs.*

❑ Among the costs of various inputs the shares of chemical fertilisers, diesel oil and electricity changes have increased while those of seeds, feedstocks and manure declined between 1980-81 and 1988-89. Pesticides claim nominally more share while irrigation charges, paid mostly to government schemes, remained unchanged at one percent.

## 1980-81

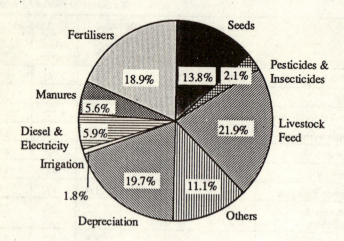

## 1988-89

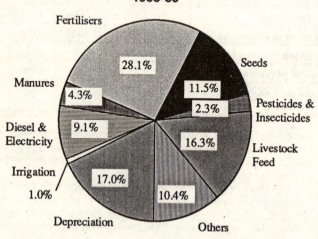

## 8.11 Productivity of Major Inputs in Agriculture : 1980-81 to 1988-89

*(Values at 1980-81 Prices)*

| Year | Value of Output | | Value of Inputs | | Index of productivity of inputs |
|------|-----------|-------|-----------|-------|------|
|      | Rs. crores | Index | Rs. crores | Index | |
| 1980-81 | 46,278 | 100.0 | 12,.212 | 100.0 | 100.0 |
| 1981-82 | 48,872 | 105.6 | 12,940 | 106.0 | 99.6 |
| 1982-83 | 47,999 | 103.7 | 13,229 | 108.3 | 95.8 |
| 1983-84 | 52,730 | 113.9 | 13,772 | 112.8 | 101.0 |
| 1984-85 | 52,421 | 113.3 | 14,507 | 118.8 | 95.4 |
| 1985-86 | 52,208 | 112.8 | 15,036 | 123.1 | 91.6 |
| 1986-87 | 51,175 | 110.6 | 15,551 | 127.3 | 86.9 |
| 1987-88 | 50,555 | 109.2 | 15,134 | 123.9 | 88.1 |
| 1988-89 | 59,770 | 129.2 | 17,004 | 139.2 | 92.8 |
| Compound annual rates of increase (%) | | | | | |
| 1980-81 to 1988-89 | 3.3 | | 4.2 | | - 0.9 |

❑ While there has been impressive growth in inputs of agriculture there is no corresponding improvement in output.

❑ Whereas the inputs cost in real terms accounted for an average 30% of the value of output and increased at the rate of 3.7% per annum during the eighties, the value of real output showed an annual increase at half that rate.

❑ In other words productivity of inputs are not fully realised – rather there was a decline during the eighties. This can be overcome to a great extent by meant of land improvements, conservation of water and extensive afforestation as well as suitable training and awareness among the cultivators so that they could reap the full benefits of the inputs and techniques which they are being induced to adopt over the years.

## 9.1    Trends in Area, Production and Productivity : All Crops : 1950-51 to 1990-91

*(Index : Triennia ended 1981-82 = 100)*

| Year | Area Index | Area % change | Production Index | Production % change | Productivity Index | Productivity % change |
|---|---|---|---|---|---|---|
| 1950 - 51 | 74.1 | 0.1 | 46.2 | -5.5 | 67.8 | -7.9 |
| 1951 - 52 | 75.6 | 2.0 | 46.9 | 1.5 | 67.7 | -0.1 |
| 1952 - 53 | 77.9 | 3.0 | 48.9 | 4.3 | 70.1 | 3.5 |
| 1953 - 54 | 81.9 | 5.1 | 55.5 | 13.5 | 77.7 | 10.8 |
| 1954 - 55 | 83.0 | 1.3 | 57.0 | 2.7 | 77.0 | -0.9 |
| 1955 - 56 | 84.8 | 2.2 | 56.2 | -1.4 | 73.4 | -4.7 |
| 1956 - 57 | 85.8 | 1.2 | 59.8 | 6.4 | 76.0 | 3.5 |
| 1957 - 58 | 84.4 | -1.6 | 55.8 | -6.7 | 71.9 | -5.4 |
| 1958 - 59 | 88.1 | 4.4 | 64.6 | 15.8 | 80.4 | 11.8 |
| 1959 - 60 | 89.3 | 1.4 | 63.0 | -2.5 | 76.4 | -5.0 |
| 1960 - 61 | 89.2 | -01. | 68.8 | 9.2 | 82.7 | 8.2 |
| 1961 - 62 | 91.2 | 2.2 | 68.1 | -1.0 | 79.9 | -3.4 |
| 1962 - 63 | 92.0 | 0.9 | 67.4 | -1.0 | 78.3 | -2.0 |
| 1963 - 64 | 91.8 | -0.2 | 68.3 | 1.3 | 79.3 | 1.3 |
| 1964 - 65 | 91.7 | -0.1 | 76.4 | 11.9 | 88.3 | 11.3 |
| 1965 - 66 | 90.7 | -1.1 | 63.7 | -16.6 | 73.2 | -17.1 |
| 1966 - 67 | 90.6 | -0.1 | 63.0 | -1.1 | 73.6 | 0.5 |
| 1967 - 68 | 94.6 | 4.4 | 77.1 | 22.4 | 86.8 | 17.9 |
| 1968 - 69 | 93.0 | -1.7 | 75.3 | -2.3 | 84.2 | -3.0 |
| 1969 - 70 | 95.7 | 2.9 | 80.4 | 6.8 | 87.1 | 3.4 |
| 1970 - 71 | 96.3 | 0.6 | 85.9 | 6.8 | 92.6 | 6.3 |
| 1971 -72 | 95.8 | -0.5 | 85.2 | -0.8 | 91.6 | -1.1 |

*contd ...*

| Year | Area | | Production | | Productivity | |
|------|-------|-------------|-------|-------------|-------|-------------|
| | Index | % change | Index | % change | Index | % change |
| 1972 - 73 | 92.5 | -3.4 | 78.2 | -8.2 | 86.0 | -6.1 |
| 1973 - 74 | 98.2 | 6.2 | 86.5 | 10.6 | 91.1 | 5.9 |
| 1974 - 75 | 94.8 | -3.5 | 84.0 | -2.9 | 89.6 | -1.6 |
| 1975 - 76 | 99.5 | 5.0 | 96.2 | 14.5 | 99.0 | 10.5 |
| 1976 - 77 | 96.9 | -2.6 | 89.3 | -7.2 | 93.1 | -6.0 |
| 1977 - 78 | 100.1 | 3.3 | 101.6 | 13.8 | 101.6 | 9.1 |
| 1978 - 79 | 101.6 | 1.5 | 105.0 | 3.3 | 104.2 | 2.6 |
| 1979 - 80 | 98.1 | -3.4 | 88.7 | -15.5 | 90.6 | -13.1 |
| 1980 - 81 | 99.7 | 1.6 | 102.1 | 15.1 | 102.9 | 13.6 |
| 1981 - 82 | 102.2 | 2.5 | 109.2 | 7.0 | 106.1 | 3.1 |
| 1982 - 83 | 99.3 | -2.8 | 104.8 | -4.0 | 103.6 | -2.4 |
| 1983 - 84 | 103.6 | 4.3 | 118.6 | 13.2 | 113.3 | 9.4 |
| 1984 - 85 | 100.6 | -2.9 | 117.9 | -0.6 | 114.8 | 1.3 |
| 1985 - 86 | 101.7 | 1.1 | 119.6 | 1.4 | 116.1 | 1.1 |
| 1986 - 87 | 100.3 | -1.4 | 115.2 | -3.7 | 112.5 | -3.1 |
| 1987 - 88 | 96.0 | -4.3 | 115.2 | 0.0 | 114.5 | 1.8 |
| 1988 - 89 | 103.5 | 7.8 | 139.4 | 21.0 | 129.9 | 13.4 |
| 1989 - 90 | 103.4 | -0.1 | 146.6 | 5.2 | 126.8 | -2.4 |
| 1990 - 91 | 105.2 | 1.7 | 154.0 | 5.0 | 126.4 | -0.3 |
| Compound annual rates of increase (%) | | | | | | |
| 1951 - 52 to 1969 - 70 | | 1.3 | | 2.8 | | 1.2 |
| 1969 - 70 to 1988 - 89 | | 0.3 | | 2.5 | | 1.7 |
| 1969 - 70 to 1979 - 80 | | 0.6 | | 2.4 | | 1.4 |
| 1979 - 80 to 1988 - 89 | | 0.0 | | 2.5 | | 2.1 |

❏ The rates are calculated between the triennia ended in the years indicated

❏ Between the triennia ended 1969-70 and 1988-89 the rate of growth of area cultivated was only 0.3% per annum as against the rate of 1.3% between the triennia ended 1950-51 and 1969-70. Particularly since 1979-80 there has been a near-stagnation in this. This trend of low growth of area is unlikely to change significantly in the near future.

❏ Production, being the function of area and yield per unit of area cultivated, has however continued to show a steady rate of growth around 2.5% per annum, entirely because of more rapidly since 1979-80. Seed-fertiliser-irrigation strategy has contributed improvement in productivity growth, significantly enhancing land productivity.

## Growth in Agricultural Productivity

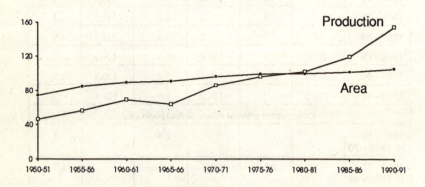

## 9.2 Trends in Area, Production and Productivity : Foodgrains : 1950-51 to 1990-91

*(Index : Triennia ended 1981-82 = 100)*

| Year | Area | | Production | | Productivity | |
|---|---|---|---|---|---|---|
| | Index | % change | Index | % change | Index | % change |
| 1950 - 51 | 76.4 | -2.1 | 46.5 | -9.7 | 64.2 | -8.7 |
| 1951 - 52 | 76.5 | 0.1 | 47.0 | 1.1 | 65.8 | 2.5 |
| 1952 - 53 | 80.5 | 5.2 | 51.7 | 10.0 | 70.1 | 6.5 |
| 1953 - 54 | 86.0 | 6.8 | 60.7 | 17.4 | 77.7 | 10.8 |
| 1954 - 55 | 85.0 | -1.2 | 59.0 | -2.8 | 75.7 | -2.6 |
| 1955 - 56 | 87.0 | 2.4 | 59.0 | 0.0 | 73.3 | -3.2 |
| 1956 - 57 | 87.5 | 0.6 | 61.7 | 4.6 | 75.2 | 2.6 |
| 1957 - 58 | 86.2 | -1.5 | 555.7 | -9.7 | 69.4 | -7.7 |
| 1958 - 59 | 90.3 | 4.8 | 66.7 | 19.7 | 79.6 | 14.7 |
| 1959 - 60 | 91.5 | 1.3 | 64.9 | -2.7 | 75.6 | -5.0 |
| 1960 - 61 | 90.9 | -0.7 | 69.6 | 7.2 | 81.9 | 8.3 |
| 1961 - 62 | 92.0 | 1.2 | 69.4 | -0.3 | 80.2 | -2.1 |
| 1962 - 63 | 92.9 | 1.0 | 67.3 | -3.0 | 76.6 | -4.5 |
| 1963 - 64 | 92.5 | -0.4 | 67.9 | 0.9 | 77.5 | 1.2 |
| 1964 - 65 | 91.6 | -1.0 | 75.4 | 11.0 | 87.8 | 13.3 |
| 1965 - 66 | 90.6 | -1.1 | 60.6 | -19.6 | 71.0 | -19.1 |
| 1966 - 67 | 90.8 | 0.2 | 60.8 | 0.3 | 71.2 | 0.3 |
| 1967 - 68 | 95.7 | 5.4 | 78.3 | 28.8 | 86.6 | 21.6 |
| 1968 - 69 | 94.8 | -0.9 | 76.3 | -2.6 | 84.2 | -2.8 |
| 1969 - 70 | 97.3 | 2.6 | 81.6 | 6.9 | 87.5 | 3.9 |
| 1970 - 71 | 97.9 | 0.6 | 87.9 | 7.7 | 93.2 | 6.5 |
| 1971 - 72 | 96.6 | -1.3 | 86.1 | -2.0 | 91.3 | -2.0 |

*contd ...*

| Year | Area | | Production | | Productivity | |
|---|---|---|---|---|---|---|
| | Index | % change | Index | % change | Index | % change |
| 1972 - 73 | 93.9 | -2.8 | 79.1 | -8.1 | 85.8 | -6.0 |
| 1973 - 74 | 99.6 | 6.1 | 85.3 | 7.8 | 89.0 | 3.7 |
| 1974 - 75 | 95.3 | -4.3 | 81.0 | -5.0 | 87.0 | -2.2 |
| 1975 - 76 | 100.8 | 5.8 | 98.8 | 22.0 | 99.7 | 14.6 |
| 1976 - 77 | 97.8 | -3.0 | 89.6 | -9.3 | 92.4 | -7.3 |
| 1977 - 78 | 100.3 | 2.6 | 103.7 | 15.0 | 103.2 | 11.7 |
| 1978 - 79 | 101.5 | 1.2 | 107.0 | 3.9 | 105.7 | 2.4 |
| 1979 - 80 | 98.5 | -3.0 | 87.5 | -18.2 | 88.7 | -16.1 |
| 1980 - 81 | 99.8 | 1.3 | 104.9 | 19.9 | 105.1 | 18.5 |
| 1981 - 82 | 101.7 | 1.9 | 107.6 | 2.6 | 105.9 | 0.8 |
| 1982 - 83 | 98.6 | -3.0 | 103.7 | -3.6 | 104.9 | -0.9 |
| 1983 - 84 | 103.4 | 4.9 | 122.8 | 18.4 | 117.8 | 12.3 |
| 1984 - 85 | 99.8 | -3.5 | 117.5 | -4.3 | 115.4 | -2.0 |
| 1985 - 86 | 100.9 | 1.1 | 123.4 | 5.0 | 120.0 | 4.0 |
| 1986 - 87 | 100.2 | -0.7 | 116.9 | -5.3 | 115.1 | -4.1 |
| 1987 - 88 | 94.3 | -5.9 | 113.5 | -2.9 | 117.3 | 1.9 |
| 1988 - 89 | 101.1 | 7.2 | 138.4 | 21.9 | 134.0 | 14.2 |
| 1989 - 90 | 99.9 | -1.2 | 140.3 | 1.4 | 137.8 | 2.8 |
| 1990 - 91 | 100.7 | 0.8 | 144.7 | 3.1 | 141.0 | 2.3 |
| Compound annual rates of increase (%) | | | | | | |
| 1951 - 52 to 1969 - 70 | | 1.2 | | 2.7 | | 1.4 |
| 1969 -70 to 1988 - 89 | | 0.1 | | 2.4 | | 1.9 |
| 1969 - 70 to 1979 - 80 | | 0.4 | | 2.3 | | 1.4 |
| 1979 - 80 to 1988 - 89 | | -0.2 | | 2.4 | | 2.3 |

❑ The rates are calculated between the triennia ended in the years indicated

❑ The slow-down in the growth rate of total cultivated area reflects the shifts in cropping pattern where the growth rate of area under foodgrains has declined more rapidly to turn negative since 1979-80 while in case of commercial crops it has been subdued but positive.

❑ Production growth in foodgrains has remained around 2.5% per annum because of better productivity growth.

❑ Among foodgrains a distinct shift in area took place from inferior cereals to more remunerative cereals like wheat, rice and maize where major technological break-through enhanced the yields particularly in regions where extensive irrigation facilities ushered in green revolution. Areas under rainfed crops on the other hand showed negative growth.

## Productivity growth in foodgrains cultivation

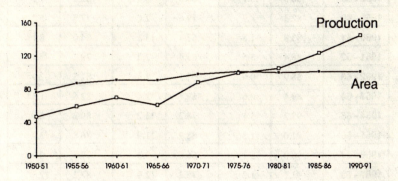

## 9.3 Trends in Area, Production and Productivity : Non-foodgrain Crops : 1950-51 to 1990-91

*(Index : Triennia ended 1981-82 = 100)*

| Year | Area | | Production | | Productivity | |
|---|---|---|---|---|---|---|
| | Index | % change | Index | % change | Index | % change |
| 1950 - 51 | 66.6 | 9.7 | 45.8 | 2.7 | 75.1 | -7.2 |
| 1951 - 52 | 72.5 | 8.9 | 46.9 | 2.4 | 71.2 | -5.2 |
| 1952 - 53 | 69.4 | -4.3 | 44.1 | -6.0 | 70.1 | -1.5 |
| 1953 - 54 | 68.6 | -1.2 | 46.6 | 5.7 | 77.6 | 10.7 |
| 1954 - 55 | 76.5 | 11.5 | 53.6 | 15.0 | 79.4 | 2.3 |
| 1955 - 56 | 77.6 | 1.4 | 51.6 | -3.7 | 73.7 | -7.2 |
| 1956 - 57 | 80.1 | 3.2 | 56.5 | 9.5 | 77.5 | 5.2 |
| 1957 - 58 | 78.4 | -2.1 | 56.1 | -0.7 | 76.5 | -1.3 |
| 1958 - 59 | 80.8 | 3.1 | 60.8 | 8.4 | 82.0 | 7.2 |
| 1959 - 60 | 82.3 | 1.9 | 59.6 | -2.0 | 77.7 | -5.2 |
| 1960 - 61 | 83.8 | 1.8 | 67.4 | 13.1 | 84.0 | 8.1 |
| 1961 - 62 | 88.4 | 5.5 | 65.9 | -2.2 | 79.2 | -5.7 |
| 1962 - 63 | 88.9 | 0.6 | 67.5 | 2.4 | 81.5 | 2.9 |
| 1963 - 64 | 89.4 | 0.6 | 69.1 | 2.4 | 82.6 | 1.3 |
| 1964 - 65 | 92.2 | 3.1 | 78.2 | 13.2 | 89.2 | 8.0 |
| 1965 - 66 | 91.0 | -1.3 | 68.9 | -11.9 | 76.8 | -13.9 |
| 1966 - 67 | 90.0 | -1.1 | 66.6 | -3.3 | 77.5 | 0.9 |
| 1967 - 68 | 91.1 | 1.2 | 75.2 | 12.9 | 87.2 | 12.5 |
| 1968 - 69 | 87.1 | -4.4 | 73.7 | -2.0 | 84.3 | -3.3 |
| 1969 - 70 | 90.3 | 3.7 | 78.3 | 6.2 | 86.3 | 2.4 |
| 1970 - 71 | 91.1 | 0.9 | 82.6 | 5.5 | 91.4 | 5.9 |
| 1971 - 72 | 92.3 | 2.4 | 83.7 | 1.3 | 92.2 | 0.9 |

*contd . . .*

| Year | Area | | Production | | Productivity | |
|---|---|---|---|---|---|---|
| | Index | % change | Index | % change | Index | % change |
| 1972 - 73 | 87.9 | -5.8 | 76.6 | -8.5 | 86.3 | -6.4 |
| 1973 - 74 | 93.7 | 6.6 | 88.6 | 15.7 | 94.7 | 9.7 |
| 1974 - 75 | 93.2 | -0.5 | 89.2 | 0.7 | 94.0 | -0.7 |
| 1975 - 76 | 95.4 | 2.4 | 91.9 | 3.0 | 97.7 | 3.9 |
| 1976 - 77 | 94.1 | -1.4 | 88.8 | -3.4 | 94.3 | -3.5 |
| 1977 - 78 | 99.3 | 5.5 | 99.4 | 11.9 | 99.0 | 5.0 |
| 1978 - 79 | 102.0 | 2.7 | 101.6 | 2.2 | 101.8 | 2.8 |
| 1979 - 80 | 96.6 | -5.3 | 90.8 | -10.6 | 93.9 | -7.8 |
| 1980 - 81 | 99.4 | 2.9 | 97.4 | 7.3 | 99.2 | 5.6 |
| 1981 - 82 | 104.1 | 4.7 | 111.8 | 14.8 | 106.4 | 7.3 |
| 1982 - 83 | 101.8 | -2.2 | 106.6 | -4.7 | 101.3 | -4.8 |
| 1983 - 84 | 104.4 | 2.6 | 111.5 | 4.6 | 105.7 | 4.3 |
| 1984 - 85 | 103.4 | -1.0 | 118.6 | 6.4 | 113.6 | 7.5 |
| 1985 - 86 | 104.2 | 0.8 | 113.0 | -4.7 | 108.2 | -4.8 |
| 1986 - 87 | 100.7 | -3.4 | 112.4 | -0.5 | 108.2 | 0.0 |
| 1987 - 88 | 101.8 | 1.1 | 118.1 | 5.1 | 110.1 | 1.8 |
| 1988 - 89 | 111.3 | 9.3 | 141.2 | 19.6 | 123.6 | 12.3 |
| 1989 - 90 | 115.0 | 3.3 | 135.6 | -4.0 | 121.1 | -2.0 |
| 1990 - 91 | 119.7 | 4.1 | 144.1 | 6.3 | 120.7 | -0.4 |
| Compound annual rates of increase (%) | | | | | | |
| 1951 - 52 to 1969 - 70 | | 1.7 | | 2.8 | | 0.7 |
| 1969 - 70 to 1988 - 89 | | 0.8 | | 2.6 | | 1.5 |
| 1969 - 70 to 1979 - 80 | | 1.0 | | 2.5 | | 1.3 |
| 1979 - 80 to 1988 - 89 | | 0.6 | | 2.7 | | 1.7 |

❑ The rates calculated between the triennia ended at the years indicated

❑ Among the commercial crops, the growth in area was encouraging in case of oilseeds and sugarcane while that under fibre crops declined

❑ Production growth rates were better in oilseeds then in fibre crops and relatively more rapid in case of condiments and spices

## Productivity growth in non-foodgrain crops

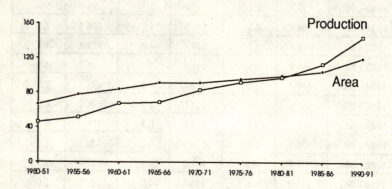

## 9.4 Changes in Shares of Kharif and Rabi Foodgrains Output 1969-70 — 1992-93

| Year | Area (Million hectares) | | | Production (Million tonnes) | | | % shares in production | |
|---|---|---|---|---|---|---|---|---|
| | Kharif | Rabi | Total | Kharif | Rabi | Total | Kharif | Rabi |
| 1969 - 70 | 82.3 | 41.3 | 123.6 | 62.3 | 37.2 | 99.5 | 62.6 | 37.4 |
| 1970 - 71 | 82.4 | 42.0 | 124.4 | 68.9 | 39.5 | 108.4 | 63.6 | 36.4 |
| 1975 - 76 | 83.2 | 45.0 | 128.2 | 73.9 | 47.1 | 121.0 | 61.1 | 38.9 |
| 1979 - 80 | 80.8 | 44.4 | 125.2 | 63.3 | 46.4 | 103.7 | 57.7 | 42.3 |
| 1980 - 81 | 83.2 | 43.5 | 126.7 | 77.7 | 51.9 | 129.6 | 60.0 | 40.0 |
| 1985 - 86 | 81.8 | 46.2 | 128.0 | 85.2 | 65.2 | 150.4 | 56.6 | 43.4 |
| 1986 - 87 | 81.5 | 45.7 | 127.2 | 80.2 | 63.2 | 143.4 | 55.9 | 44.1 |
| 1987 - 88 | 74.9 | 44.8 | 119.7 | 74.6 | 65.8 | 140.4 | 53.1 | 46.9 |
| 1988 - 89 | 82.0 | 45.6 | 127.6 | 95.6 | 74.3 | 169.9 | 56.3 | 43.7 |
| 1989 - 90 | 81.3 | 45.2 | 126.5 | 100.9 | 69.7 | 170.6 | 59.1 | 40.9 |
| 1990 - 91 | - | - | - | 99.4 | 77.0 | 176.4 | 56.3 | 43.7 |
| 1991 - 92 | - | - | - | 91.4 | 75.7 | 167.1 | 54.7 | 45.3 |
| 1992 - 93 | - | - | - | 98.7 | 78.0 | 176.7 | 55.9 | 44.1 |
| Compound annual rates of increase (%) | | | | | | | | |
| 1969 - 70 to 1979 - 80 | 0.1 | 1.1 | 0.4 | 1.8 | 9.5 | 2.5 | | |
| 1979 - 80 to 1989 - 90 | -0.3 | | -0.2 | 2.2 | 3.5 | 2.7 | | |
| 1969 - 70 to 1989 - 90 | -0.1 | 0.6 | 0.1 | 2.0 | 3.5 | 2.6 | | |

❑ The rates are calculated between the triennia ended at the years indicated
❑ The changes in shares of kharif and rabi foodgrains in the total foodgrains production is indicative of the transformation taking place in Indian agriculture. This whole area under kharif foodgrains has been always larger – by 65% – than under rabi grains. There has been some nominal decline in the area under kharif foodgrains in recent years, with same shift in favour of rabi grain sowing.

❑ The shift of area in favour of rabi grains could be explained partly by the improved availability of inputs and partly as a response to technological absorption. Thus, for one thing, the yield rates obtained for rabi foodgrains are higher than for kharif by 25% and the best going even over 45%. Secondly, while there have been increases in yield rates in both kharif as well as rabi foodgrains the rate of increase therein is more rapid for rabi foodgrains. This is reflected in the relative rates of increase in share of rabi foodgrains in total output improving from 34% twenty years ago to the best of 47% in recent years.

## Kharif – Rabi Transformation in Foodgrain Cultivation

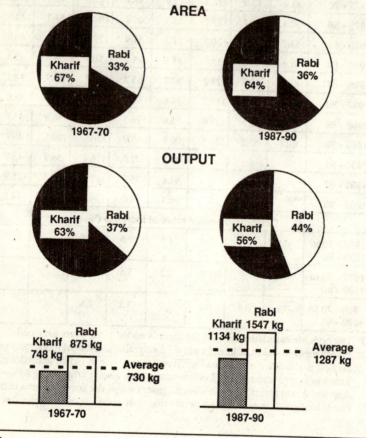

### AREA

Rabi 33%
Kharif 67%
1967-70

Rabi 36%
Kharif 64%
1987-90

### OUTPUT

Kharif 63%
Rabi 37%

Kharif 56%
Rabi 44%

Kharif 748 kg
Rabi 875 kg
Average 730 kg
1967-70

Kharif 1134 kg
Rabi 1547 kg
Average 1287 kg
1987-90

## 9.5    Rates of Changes in Area, Production and Yields of Major Crops : 1969-70 and 1989-90

| Major Crops | Area ('000 hectares) | | | Production ('000 tonnes) | | | Yield per hectares kg. | | |
|---|---|---|---|---|---|---|---|---|---|
| | Triennia ended | | CARG % | Triennia ended | | CARG % | Triennia ended | | CARG % |
| | 1969-70 | 1989-90 | | 1969-70 | 1989-90 | | 1969-70 | 1989-90 | |
| Rice (29-74) | 37,028 | 40,906 | 0.5 | 39,268 | 67,134 | 2.7 | 1,060 | 1,637 | 2.2 |
| Wheat (14.45) | 15,862 | 23,543 | 2.0 | 18,428 | 49,977 | 5.1 | 1,160 | 2,121 | 3.1 |
| Jowar (4.43) | 18,586 | 15,182 | -1.0 | 9,858 | 11,761 | 0.9 | 53.0 | 774 | 1.9 |
| Gram (3.07) | 7,704 | 6,357 | -1.0 | 5,275 | 4,329 | -1.0 | 682 | 678 | – |
| Maize (2.41) | 5,720 | 5,772 | 0.1 | 5,882 | 7,786 | 1.4 | 1,029 | 1,344 | 1.3 |
| Sugar cane (8.11) | 2,443 | 3,338 | 1.6 | 118,400 | 207,467 | 2.8 | 48,337 | 52,124 | 1.3 |
| Ground-nut (Pods) (5.60) | 7,255 | 8,027 | 0.5 | 5,164 | 7,868 | 2.1 | 711 | 972 | 1.6 |
| Cotton (lint) (4.37) | 7,774 | 7,044 | -0.5 | 5,596 (a) | 8,847 (a) | 2.3 | 122 | 212 | 2.8 |
| Tea (1.46) | 351 | 415 | 0.8 | 394 | 684 | 2.8 | 1,123 | 1,649 | 1.9 |
| Rapeseed & Mustard (2.41) | 3,095 | 4,813 | 2.2 | 1,493 | 3,985 | 5.0 | 482 | 827 | 2.7 |

*Note :   a.   In bales of 180 kgs. each*

❏ The ten major crops covered above account for as much as 76% of the total weight in the index of agricultural production for all crops. These together have shown better growth rate than the averages for all crops

❏ Whereas areas under finer grains like wheat and rice have increased at satisfactory rates, that under coarse grains, consumed mainly by the poorer masses in our country, like jowar has declined and that under maize is stagnant.

❏ Thanks to the high yielding seeds and irrigation facilities, the yield rates and output of wheat and rice have recorded impressive growth rate during the two decades under reference whereas these rates are nominally positive for coarse grains. But the area as well as output of gram showed record declines in growth rates.

❏ All the five non-food grain crops covered here have recorded satisfactory growth rates in output and yields, though fall is noted in area under cotton over the period

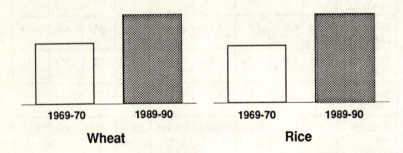

| 1969-70 | 1989-90 | 1969-70 | 1989-90 |

**Wheat**        **Rice**

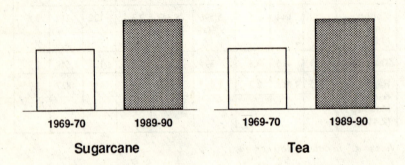

| 1969-70 | 1989-90 | 1969-70 | 1989-90 |

**Sugarcane**        **Tea**

## 9.6    Trends in Yield Rates of Major Crops : 1950-51 — 1989-90

*(Yields in quintals/hectares)*

| Average Triennia (weight) | Foodrains Crops | | | | | Non-foodgrains Crops | | | | |
|---|---|---|---|---|---|---|---|---|---|---|
| | Rice 29.74 | Wheat 14.45 | Jowar 4.43 | Gram 3.07 | Maize 2.4 | Sugar cane 8.11 | Grou ndnut 5.60 | Cot-ton 4.37 | Tea 1.46 | Rape seeds & Must ard 2.41 |
| 1950 - 53 | 7.1 | 6.9 | 3.8 | 5.2 | 6.6 | 315.7 | 6.8 | 0.9 | 9.2 | 3.9 |
| 1960 - 63 | 9.9 | 8.4 | 5.0 | 6.2 | 9.6 | 429.7 | 7.3 | 1.2 | 10.3 | 4.4 |
| 1970 - 73 | 11.1 | 13.2 | 4.6 | 6.5 | 10.9 | 489.2 | 7.5 | 1.3 | 12.2 | 5.1 |
| 1980 - 83 | 12.9 | 17.1 | 6.8 | 6.5 | 11.5 | 575.5 | 8.1 | 1.6 | 14.6 | 5.6 |
| 1987 - 90 | 16.4 | 21.2 | 7.1 | 6.7 | 13.4 | 621.2 | 9.7 | 2.1 | 16.5 | 8.3 |
| Compound annual rates of increase (%) | | | | | | | | | | |
| 1950 - 53 to 1960 - 63 | 3.4 | 2.0 | 2.8 | 1.8 | 3.8 | 3.1 | 0.7 | 2.9 | 1.2 | 1.1 |
| 1960 - 63 to 1970 - 73 | 1.1 | 4.6 | -0.8 | 0.5 | 1.3 | 1.3 | 0.3 | 0.8 | 1.5 | 1.7 |
| 1970 - 73 to 1987 - 90 | 2.3 | 2.8 | 3.1 | 0.2 | 1.2 | 1.4 | 1.5 | 2.9 | 2.9 | 1.8 |
| 1950 - 53 to 1987 - 90 | 2.3 | 3.1 | 1.9 | 0.7 | 1.9 | 1.9 | 1.0 | 2.3 | 2.1 | 1.6 |

❑ Reflecting the gains of technological break-through and seed-fertiliser irrigation strategy, the yield rates in wheat and rice improved rapidly since the 1970s. These advantages were not feasible in coarse cereals mostly grown in rainfed areas. Decline in growth of yield rates of pulses is responsible for the inadequate availability of pulses in the country

❑ Yield rates of commercial crops have been improving in most cases though in sugarcane the growth rate of productivity has stagnated since 1970s. Notwithstanding the rapid growth rate of oilseed yields, shortages of edible oils are increasingly felt. In cotton we have attained overall self-sufficiency, though long-staple cotton for blended fabrics still presents some limitations.

## 9.7    Yield Potentials of High Yield Seeds : 1989-90

*(Kg/hectare)*

| Crop | Potential of High Yielding Varieties (HYV) | Actual Yield Rates | | |
|------|------|------|------|------|
| | | India 1989-90 | Best elsewhere in world | |
| | | | Yield | Country |
| **Foodgrains** | | | | |
| Rice | 4,000-5,810 | 1,756 | 5,475 | North Korea |
| Wheat | 6,000-6,800 | 2,117 | 7,716 | Netherlands |
| Jowar | 3,000-4,200 | 864 | 6,374 | Italy |
| Maize | 6,000-8,000 | 1,606 | 9,091 | Greece |
| Barley | upto 2,500 | 1,481 | 6,499 | France |
| **Non-foodgrains** | | | | |
| Groundnut Pods | 2,000-3,000 | 929 | 4,600 | Israel |
| Rapeseed | 1,500-2,000 | 826 | 5,000 | Netherlands |
| Sesame | upto 2,000 | 304 | 1,043 | Egypt |
| Soyabean | 1,500-2,500 | 804 | 3,453 | Zimbabwe |
| Cotton Lint | 700-850 | 265 | 1,164 | Mexico |
| Jute | 2,500-3,000 | 1,885 | 2,188 | Vietnam |
| Tobacco | 2,530-2,865 | 1,340 | 3,048 | Chile |
| Potato | 23,800-30,900 | 15,817 | 45,349 | Belgium |
| Sugarcane | 96,000-112,000 | 65,383 | 135,448 | Peru |

❑ After 1966, Indian scientists have developed high-yielding variety seeds for a number of crops. Suitable for Indian agro-climatic conditions, these have several times higher yield potentials than the traditional varieties. Such HYV seeds are being applied in increasingly larger areas in various regions of the country.

❑ Although we have reaped higher outputs of various crops due to adoption of HYV seeds, it is sad that in no crop we have been able to achieve even the minimum of the potential obtainable from Indian varieties.

## 9.8 Production, Imports and Availability of Foodgrains 1951 – 1992

*(Million tonnes)*

| Year | Net output | Net Imports | Changes in Govt. Stocks | Availabilty | | Issue through PDS | Internal procurement | |
|------|------------|-------------|-------------------------|-------------|------|-------------------|----------------------|-------|
| | | | | Net | Per capita (gms/per day) | | Million tonnes | % of gross output |
| 1951 | 48.1 | 4.8 | +0.6 | 52.3 | 395 | 8.0 | 3.8 | 6.9 |
| 1956 | 60.7 | 1.4 | -0.6 | 62.7 | 431 | 2.1 | – | – |
| 1961 | 72.0 | 3.5 | -0.2 | 75.7 | 469 | 4.0 | 0.5 | 0.6 |
| 1966 | 63.3 | 10.3 | +0.1 | 73.5 | 408 | 14.1 | 4.0 | 5.5 |
| 1971 | 94.9 | 2.0 | +2.6 | 94.3 | 469 | 7.8 | 8.9 | 8.2 |
| 1976 | 105.9 | 6.9 | +10.7 | 102.1 | 424 | 9.2 | 12.9 | 10.7 |
| 1981 | 113.4 | 0.7 | -0.2 | 114.3 | 454 | 13.0 | 13.0 | 10.0 |
| 1986 | 131.6 | -0.5 | -1.6 | 132.7 | 475 | 17.3 | 19.7 | 13.1 |
| 1987 | 125.5 | -0.2 | -9.5 | 134.8 | 473 | 18.7 | 15.7 | 10.9 |
| 1988 | 122.8 | 3.8 | -4.6 | 131.2 | 451 | 18.6 | 14.1 | 10.0 |
| 1989 | 148.7 | 1.2 | 2.6 | 147.3 | 497 | 15.9 | 19.9 | 11.1 |
| 1990 | 149.6 | 1.3 | 6.2 | 144.7 | 473.8 | 19.3 | 24.0 | 14.1 |
| 1991 | 154.4 | -0.6 | -4.5 | 158.3 | 509.9 | n.a. | n.a. | n.a. |
| 1992 | 146.2 | n.a. | -6.0 | n.a. | n.a. | n.a. | n.a. | n.a. |

PDS = Public distribution system

❑ From an average of 2.9 million tonnes in the fifties, our imports of foodgrains reached an average of 5.8 million tonnes per annum during the sixties with a peak level of over 10 million tonnes imported in 1966.

❑ Thereafter our dependence on imported foodgrains has steadily declined, and in recent years we have been a net exporter of foodgrains.

❑ Besides, per capita availability of foodgrains has improved significantly over the years, though these are as yet far below the norms of recommended diet standards of 490 gms per day of cereals and 53 grams per day of pulses.

❑ Together with higher levels of foodgrains production, the procurement by government agencies has also been enhanced to build up buffer stocks and distribution through public distribution system for the benefits of masses and as a market intervention operation for the farmers.

## 9.9 Public Distribution System : 1971 to 1990

| | Fair price shops for public distribution | | Issuance of foodgrains through PDS | |
|---|---|---|---|---|
| | Number | % change p.a. | Million tonnes | % change p.a. |
| 1971 | 1,22,038 | | 7.8 | |
| 1976 | 2,40,210 | 14.5 | 9.2 | 3.4 |
| 1980 | 2,43,828 | 0.4 | 15.0 | 13..0 |
| 1981 | 2,83,560 | 16.3 | 13.0 | -13.3 |
| 1986 | 3,25.081 | 2.8 | 17.3 | 5.9 |
| 1987 | 3,33,467 | 2.6 | 18.7 | 8.1 |
| 1988 | 3,45,191 | 3.5 | 18.6 | -0.5 |
| 1989 | 3,51,550 | 1.8 | 15.9 | -14.5 |
| 1990 | 3,59,620 | 2.3 | 15.3 | -3.8 |
| Compound annual rates of increase (%) | | | | |
| 1971 to 1981 | | 8.8 | | 5.2 |
| 1980 to 1990 | | 4.0 | | 0.2 |
| 1971 to 1990 | | 5.9 | | 3.6 |

❑ India has one of the largest network of public distribution system in the world for supply of essential commodities at fair prices through retail outlets. The quantities and prices are decided by the government.

❑ The basic objective is to provide food security to the weak and vulnerable sections of the population. However, due to improper spread of network there still exists a good urban-bias in the system and almost half of the villages still remain out of the expanse. Although the government has decided to revamp the system, the magnitude of the task is enormous and it would take a long time for reaching the benefits to all the deserving and needy masses.

## 9.10 Trends in Procurement Prices and Open Market Prices of Foodgrains : 1965-66 to 1991-92

| Year | Procurement price (Rs. per quintal) | | Index of Prices : (1981-82=100) | | | % changes in prices p.a. | | |
|---|---|---|---|---|---|---|---|---|
| | Paddy | Wheat | WPI: Food grains | Procurement Prices | | WPI: Food grains | Procurement Prices | |
| | | | | Paddy | Wheat | | Paddy | Wheat |
| 1965 - 66 | 38.82 | 59.27 | 31.4 | 33.8 | 41.7 | | | |
| 1970 - 71 | 53.30 | 76.00 | 42.1 | 46.3 | 53.5 | 6.0 | 6.5 | 5.1 |
| 1975 - 76 | 74.00 | 105.00 | 73.3 | 64.3 | 73.9 | 11.7 | 6.8 | 6.7 |
| 1980 - 81 | 105.00 | 130.00 | 91.3 | 91.3 | 91.5 | 4.5 | 7.3 | 4.4 |
| 1981 - 82 | 115.00 | 142.00 | 100.0 | 100.0 | 100.0 | 9.5 | 9.5 | 9.3 |
| 1985 - 86 | 142.00 | 162.00 | 124.5 | 123.5 | 114.1 | 5.6 | 5.4 | 3.4 |
| 1986 - 87 | 146.00 | 166.00 | 129.4 | 127.0 | 116.9 | 3.9 | 2.8 | 2.5 |
| 1987 - 88 | 150.00 | 173.00 | 141.3 | 130.4 | 121.8 | 9.2 | 2.7 | 4.2 |
| 1988 - 89 | 160.00 | 183.00 | 161.8 | 139.1 | 128.9 | 14.5 | 6.7 | 5.8 |
| 1989 - 90 | 185.00 | 215.00 | 165.4 | 160.9 | 151.4 | 2.2 | 15.7 | 17.5 |
| 1990 - 91 | 205.00 | 225.00 | 179.01 | 178.3 | 158.5 | 8.2 | 10.8 | 4.7 |
| 1991 - 92 | 230.00 | 250.00 | - | 200.00 | 176.00 | - | 12.2 | 11.1 |
| Compound annual rates of increase (%) | | | | | | | | |
| 1970 - 71 to 1980 - 81 | | | | | | 8.0 | 7.0 | 5.5 |
| 1980 - 81 to 1990 - 91 | | | | | | 7.0 | 6.9 | 5.6 |
| 1965 - 66 to 1990- 91 | | | | | | 7.2 | 6.9 | 5.5 |

❏ The government procures foodgrains, mainly wheat and rice, from the cultivators for distribution through the public distribution network. There is a dual objective, of providing farmers assured prices and proctecting them against the usual post-harvest seasonal dip in open market prices, and providing foodgrains to consumers at a fair price.

❏ Another objective of the procurement and distribution operations to ensure stabilisation of prices in the open markets is often not served to the desired extent. This is because the periodic increases in procurement prices have all along been less than in open market prices.

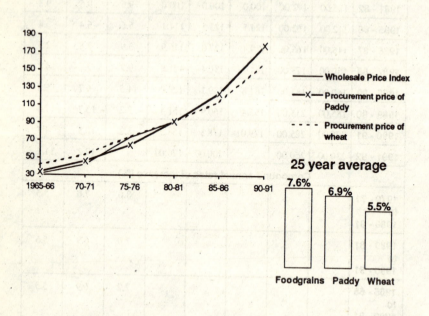

### Relative Trends in Procurement Prices and Open Market Prices of Foodgrains
### Index : 1981-82 = 100

## 9.11 Trends in Production of Milk, Eggs and Fish : 1950-51 to 1990-91

| Year | Milk | | Eggs | | Fish | |
|---|---|---|---|---|---|---|
| | Million tonnes | % change p.a. | Million tonnes | % change p.a. | Lakh tonnes | % change p.a. |
| 1950 - 51 | 17.0 | | 1,032 | | 7.5 | |
| 1955 - 56 | 19.0 | 2.2 | 1,494 | 7.7 | 8.4 | 2.3 |
| 1960 - 61 | 20.1 | 1.1 | 1,900 | 4.9 | 11.6 | 6.7 |
| 1965 - 66 | 19.2 | -0.9 | 2,500 | 5.6 | 13.3 | 2.8 |
| 1970 - 71 | 20.1 | 0.9 | 2,930 | 3.2 | 17.6 | 5.8 |
| 1975 - 76 | 25.4 | 4.8 | n.a. | – | 22.7 | 5.2 |
| 1980 - 81 | 31.6 | 4.5 | 10,600 | – | 24.4 | 1.5 |
| 1985 - 86 | 44.0 | 6.8 | 16,128 | 8.8 | 28.8 | 3.4 |
| 1986 - 87 | 46.1 | 4.8 | 17,310 | 7.3 | 29.4 | 2.1 |
| 1987 - 88 | 46.7 | 1.3 | 17,795 | 2.8 | 29.6 | 0.7 |
| 1988 - 89 | 48.4 | 5.1 | 18,890 | 6.2 | 31.5 | 6.4 |
| 1989 - 90 | 51.4 | 4.9 | 20,204 | 7.0 | 36.8 | 16.8 |
| 1990 - 91 estimate | 54.9 | 6.9 | 21,343 | 5.6 | 38.4 | 4.3 |
| Compound annual rates of increase (%) | | | | | | |
| 1950 - 51 to 1960 - 61 | | 1.7 | | 6.3 | | 4.5 |
| 1960 - 61 to 1970 - 71 | | – | | 4.4 | | 4.3 |
| 1970 - 71 to 1980 - 81 | | 4.6 | | 13.7 | | 3.3 |

*contd ...*

| Year | Milk | | Eggs | | Fish | |
|---|---|---|---|---|---|---|
| | Million tonnes | % change p.a. | Million tonnes | % change p.a. | Lakh tonnes | % change p.a. |
| Compound annual rates of interest (%) | | | | | | |
| 1980 - 81 to 1990 -91 | | 5.7 | | 7.3 | | 4.6 |
| 1950 - 51 to 1990 - 91 | | 3.0 | | 7.9 | | 4.2 |

❑ The Statistics presented above suffer from inadequate coverage because of the lack of reporting /survey system about production in vastly dispersed production sources. All the same these figures illustrate indirectly the trend in consumption of the important sources of protein, particularly of milk versus eggs and fish as the alternative sources of animal protein by a significant section of vegetarian population.

## 9.12 Estimates of Value of Output of Agricultural Commodities : 1988-89

| Group of crops | Gross cropped area | | Prod-uction Million tonnes (a) | Average price realised per tonne (b) | Gross value of output (CSO Estimates) | |
|---|---|---|---|---|---|---|
| | Million hectares | % to total | | | Rs. crores | % to total |
| Foodgrains | 126.53 | 69.5 | 170.62 | 3,000 | 51,178 | 47.9 |
| Cereals | 103.30 | 56.7 | 158.01 | 2,766 | 43,708 | 40.9 |
| Pulses | 23.23 | 12.8 | 12.61 | 5,924 | 7,470 | 7.0 |
| Non - foodgrain crops | 55.47(c) | 30.5 | – | – | 45,934(d) | 43.0 |
| Oilseeds | 24.48 | 13.5 | 18.12 | 6,442 | 11,673 | 10.9 |
| Sugar | 3.41 | 1.9 | 222.63 | 370 | 8,245 | 7.7 |
| Fibres | 8.24 | 4.5 | 3.45 | 15,307 | 4,936 | 4.6 |
| Fruits & Veg. | 2.46 | 1.4 | 31.45 | 3,723 | 11,710 | 11.0 |
| Condiments & Spices | 1.96 | 1.1 | 2.10 | 16,043 | 3,369 | 3.2 |
| Drugs & narcotics | 1.08 | 0.6 | 1.40 | 21,070 | 2,816 | 2.6 |
| Other crops | 2.66 | 1.4 | 0.95 | 33,526 | 3,185 | 3.0 |
| Miscellaneous | 11.18 | 6.1 | – | – | – | – |
| By products | – | – | – | – | 9,670 | 9.1 |
| Total | 182.00 | 100.0 | | | 106,782 | 100.0 |

Notes : (a) Production of non-foodgrains have been only illustratively added up, and is not very meaningful due to heterogenous characters

(b) Average price realisation has been derived as approximate by relating the given value of output to the respective quantity.

(c) Includes areas of miscellaneous crops for which data are not separately available.

(d) Does not include miscellaneous crops.

❑ Cash crops, by their very nature command higher price, and therefore against their share of 24.4% in cropped area, they yield 43% of the gross value of output. Foodgrains on the other hand yield smaller per hectare incomes. Mainly 70% of the total cropped area provide 48% of the gross value of output.

## 10.1   Trends in Industrial Production in Major Segments : 1951-1992 (Organised Sector Only)

| Year | Index of Production : Base - 1980-81 = 100 | | | | |
|---|---|---|---|---|---|
| | Mining & quarrying | Manu-facturing | Electricity | General Index | % change over previous year |
| Weight (%) | 11.46 | 77.11 | 11.43 | 100.00 | |
| 1951 | 28.5 | 22.6 | 5.2 | 21.1 | |
| 1956 | 32.7 | 30.2 | 8.5 | 28.0 | 8.5 |
| 1961 | 47.9 | 41.6 | 16.9 | 39.3 | 9.2 |
| 1966 | 61.9 | 57.9 | 30.3 | 55.1 | - 0.4 |
| 1971 | 68.5 | 69.7 | 52.1 | 67.9 | 4.4 |
| 1976 | 92.7 | 86.9 | 78.0 | 86.9 | 12.1 |
| 1981 | 115.5 | 105.2 | 107.3 | 107.0 | 9.2 |
| 1982 | 127.3 | 108.6 | 115.0 | 111.5 | 4.2 |
| 1983 | 144.3 | 112.7 | 120.9 | 117.2 | 5.1 |
| 1984 | 156.7 | 122.5 | 137.8 | 128.1 | 9.3 |
| 1985 | 164.1 | 134.9 | 148.9 | 139.7 | 9.1 |
| 1986 | 176.1 | 143.2 | 164.0 | 149.4 | 6.9 |
| 1987 | 184.0 | 160.3 | 177.6 | 165.0 | 10.4 |
| 1988 | 193.8 | 173.1 | 192.4 | 178.0 | 7.9 |
| 1989 | 210.3 | 181.2 | 215.6 | 188.4 | 5.8 |
| 1989 - 90 | 211.6 | 190.7 | 219.7 | 196.4 | 8.6 |
| 1990 - 91 | 221.2 | 207.8 | 236.8 | 212.6 | 8.2 |
| 1991 - 92 | 221.8 | 204.4 | 257.0 | 212.4 | -0.1 |

*contd ...*

| Year | Index of Production : Base - 1980-81 = 100 | | | | |
|---|---|---|---|---|---|
| | Mining & quarrying | Manu-facturing | Electricity | General Index | % change over previous year |
| Compound annual rates of increase % | | | | | |
| 1951 - 1961 | 5.3 | 6.3 | 12.5 | 6.4 | |
| 1961 - 1971 | 3.6 | 5.3 | 11.9 | 5.6 | |
| 1971 - 1981 | 5.4 | 4.2 | 7.5 | 4.7 | |
| 1981 - 1990 | 7.1 | 7.7 | 9.0 | 7.7 | |

❑ Although decadewise the highest overall annual growth rate of 7.7% was observed during 1981-90, the best overall growth performance of 9.3% per annum was witnessed during the eight-year phase of 1958-65.

❑ Mining and manufacturing went through their highest annual growth during the latest decade 1981-90, whereas electricity exhibited the highest growth rate during 1951-61. During the eight-year phase of 1958-65, manufacturing and electricity presented the highest ever annual growth rates of 9.3% and 14.3% respectively, while in mining the best of 8.2% per annum was seen during 1980-89.

❑ During the entire period of 40 years, negative overall growth was noted during 1966 (-0.4%) and 1967 (-1.3%) largely due to declines in manufacturing in those two years. The lowest but positive growth of 0.5% was in 1973 owing to a solitary instance of fall (-1.8%) in electricity generation in that year.

❑ After the sustained higher growth during the eighties the industrial production during 1991 is likely to turn out a weak growth rate owing to poor performance in mining and manufacturing, reflecting the impact of import compression and depressed demand.

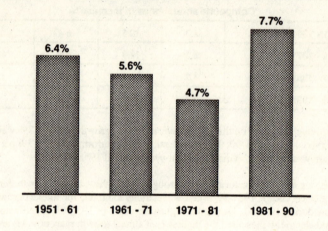

**Growth Rates of Industrial Production : 1951 to 1990
(Index Base : 1980-81 = 100)**

## 10.2 Relative growth of Factory and Non-factory Manufacturing in Real terms Net Value Added. : 1950 - 51 – 1990 - 91.

*(Rs. crores at 1980 - 81 prices)*

| Year | Factory Sector | Non-factory Sector | Total | Share of Non-factory Sector (%) |
|---|---|---|---|---|
| 1950 - 51 | 2,135 | 2,490 | 4,625 | 53.8 |
| 1955 - 56 | 2,780 | 3,275 | 6,055 | 54.1 |
| 1960 - 61 | 3,888 | 4,059 | 7,947 | 51.2 |
| 1965 - 66 | 5,705 | 5,069 | 10,774 | 47.0 |
| 1970 - 71 | 6,946 | 5,817 | 12,763 | 45.6 |
| 1975 - 76 | 7,677 | 7,167 | 14,844 | 48.3 |
| 1980 - 81 | 10,050 | 8,648 | 18,698 | 46.3 |
| 1981 - 82 | 10,876 | 9,383 | 20,259 | 46.3 |
| 1982 - 83 | 12,079 | 9,581 | 21,660 | 44.2 |
| 1983 - 84 | 14,047 | 9,867 | 23,914 | 41.3 |
| 1984 - 85 | 15,291 | 10,128 | 25,419 | 39.8 |
| 1985 - 86 | 15,560 | 10,853 | 26,413 | 41.2 |
| 1986 - 87 | 16,487 | 11,840 | 28,327 | 41.8 |
| 1987 - 88 | 17,716 | 12,696 | 30,412 | 41.7 |
| 1988 - 89 | 19,466 | 13,540 | 33,006 | 41.0 |
| 1989 - 90 | 20,708 | 14,569 | 35,277 | 41.3 |
| 1990 - 91(a) | 22,280 | 15,551 | 37,831 | 41.1 |
| Compound annual rates of increase (%) | | | | |
| 1950 - 51 to 1960 - 61 | 6.2 | 5.0 | 5.6 | |
| 1960 - 61 to 1970 - 71 | 6.0 | 3.7 | 4.9 | |
| 1970 - 71 to 1980 - 81 | 3.8 | 4.0 | 3.9 | |

*contd. . .*

| Year | Factory Sector | Non-factory Sector | Total | Share of Non-factory Sector (%) |
|---|---|---|---|---|
| Compound annual rates of increase (%) | | | | |
| 1980 - 81 to 1990 - 91 | 8.3 | 6.0 | 7.3 | |
| 1980 - 81 to 1985 - 86 | 9.1 | 4.6 | 7.2 | |
| 1985 - 86 to 1990 - 91 | 7.4 | 7.5 | 7.4 | |

*Note :  (a) Quick estimates by the CSO. Figures for a preceding few years are provisional*

❑ Annual growth rate of the non-factory sector in terms of net value added at constant (1980-81) prices, has consistently improved since the sixties, while that of the factory sector had simply declined during the seventies.

❑ Again during the eighties, the real value added growth rate for the non-factory sector improved significantly during the latter half coinciding with the Seventh Plan Period, which that of the factory sector declined to almost equal that of the non-factory sector. In other words, the real value added growth in manufacturing during the Seventh Plan was attributable to the non-factory sector whose share in total is a little over two-fifths.

## Growth Rate of Manufacturing in Factory and Non-factory sectors in Real Value Added Terms (% per annum)

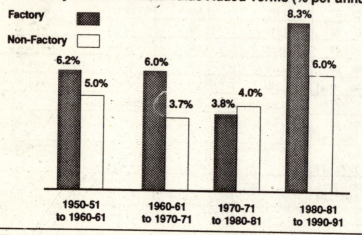

## 10.3 Net Value Added in Manufacturing by factory and Non-factory Sectors : 1950-51 – 1990-91.

*(Rs. crores at current prices)*

| Year | Factory Sector | Non-factory Sector | Total | Share of Non-factory Sector (%) |
|---|---|---|---|---|
| 1950 - 51 | 461 | 533 | 994 | 53.6 |
| 1955 - 56 | 564 | 655 | 1,219 | 53.7 |
| 1960 - 61 | 1,035 | 1,067 | 2,102 | 50.8 |
| 1965 - 66 | 1,796 | 1,580 | 3,376 | 46.8 |
| 1970 - 71 | 2,784 | 2,435 | 5,219 | 46.6 |
| 1975 - 76 | 5,310 | 4,898 | 10,208 | 48.0 |
| 1980 - 81 | 10,050 | 8,648 | 18,698 | 46.3 |
| 1981 - 82 | 11,779 | 9,964 | 21,743 | 45.8 |
| 1982 - 83 | 13,629 | 10,471 | 24,100 | 43.4 |
| 1983 - 84 | 17,019 | 11,534 | 28,553 | 40.4 |
| 1984 - 85 | 19,647 | 12,512 | 32,159 | 38.9 |
| 1985 - 86 | 21,467 | 14,337 | 35,804 | 40.0 |
| 1986 - 87 | 23,415 | 16,032 | 39,447 | 40.6 |
| 1987 - 88 | 26,856 | 18,428 | 45,284 | 40.7 |
| 1988 - 89 | 32,178 | 21,381 | 53,,559 | 39.9 |
| 1989 - 90 | 37,822 | 25,675 | 63,497 | 40.4 |
| 1990 - 91 (a) | 44,069 | 29,757 | 73,826 | 40.3 |
| Compound annual rates of increase (%) | | | | |
| 1950 - 51 to 1960 - 61 | 8.4 | 7.2 | 7.8 | – |
| 1960 - 61 to 1970 - 71 | 10.4 | 8.6 | 9.5 | – |

*contd...*

| Year | Factory Sector | Non-factory Sector | Total | Share of Non-factory Sector (%) |
|---|---|---|---|---|
| Compound annual rates of increase (%) | | | | |
| 1970 - 71 to 1980 - 81 | 13.7 | 13.5 | 13.6 | – |
| 1980 - 81 to 1990 - 91 | 15.9 | 13.2 | 14.7 | – |
| 1980 - 81 to 1985 - 86 | 16.4 | 10.6 | 13.9 | – |
| 1985 - 86 to 1990 - 91 | 15.5 | 15.7 | 15.6 | – |

*Note :*   *(a) Quick estimate by the CSO. Figure for a few preceding years are provisional.*

❑ By net value added in nominal terms, the factory sector has had somewhat higher growth rates than for the non-factory sector. This in part reflects the economies of scale to profits as well as relatively higher wage levels of organised labour in the factory sector, as compared to the non-factory sector where the wages and profits are lower, notwithstanding the concessional interest rates and subsidised input prices in some cases.

❑ This effect is seen in the decline in the share of net value added in the non-factory sector from over fifty percent till 1960-61 to around forty percent since 1983-84.

### Factory & Non-factory Sectors
### Shares in Net Value Added in Manufacturing

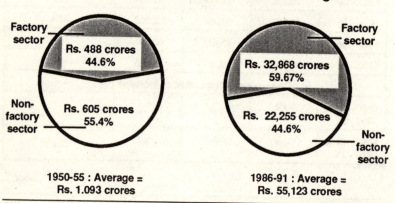

1950-55 : Average = Rs. 1.093 crores      1986-91 : Average = Rs. 55,123 crores

## 10.4  Structure of Industrial Sector : 1986-87
### (Covered by the ASI)

| Employment size : (No. of workers) | No. of factories | Employment '000 persons | Productive capital Rs. crores | Gross value of output Rs. crores | Net value added Rs. crores |
|---|---|---|---|---|---|
| | A : By Size of Employment | | | | |
| | 1 | 2 | 3 | 4 | 5 |
| Less than 50 | 76,416 | 2,336 | 5,586 | 17,690 | 2,391 |
| 50-99 | 10,888 | 1,429 | 4,389 | 10,556 | 1,486 |
| 100-199 | 5,349 | 1,350 | 5,141 | 12,327 | 1,998 |
| 200-499 | 3,178 | 2,316 | 19,560 | 21,713 | 4,759 |
| 500-999 | 1,250 | 1,862 | 22,106 | 24,191 | 4,575 |
| 1,000-1,999 | 537 | 1,552 | 17,298 | 23,288 | 4,811 |
| 2,000-4,999 | 285 | 1,567 | 8,067 | 15,171 | 3,483 |
| 5,000 & above | 54 | 836 | 6,888 | 8,108 | 2,048 |
| Total | 97,957 | 13,248 | 89,035 | 133,044 | 25,551 |
| Smaller : Less than 200 | 92,653 | 5,115 | 15,116 | 40,573 | 5,875 |
| Larger : 200 & more | 5,304 | 8,133 | 73,919 | 92,471 | 19,676 |
| Gross value of plant & machinery Rs. Lakhs | B: By Value of Plant & Machinery | | | | |
| | 1 | 2 | 3 | 4 | 5 |
| upto  1.0 | 32,681 | 1,449 | 826 | 3,580 | 705 |
| 1.0 to 2.5 | 18,205 | 767 | 932 | 3,964 | 587 |
| 2.5 to 5.0 | 13,407 | 709 | 1,079 | 4,399 | 601 |
| 5.0 to 7.5 | 6,066 | 415 | 699 | 2,914 | 475 |

*contd...*

| Gross value of plant & machinery Rs. Lakhs | No. of factories | Employment '000 persons | Productive capital Rs. crores | Gross value of output Rs. crores | Net value added Rs. crores |
|---|---|---|---|---|---|
| | | | B: By Value of Plant & Machinery | | |
| | 1 | 2 | 3 | 4 | 5 |
| 7.5 to 10.0 | 3,843 | 308 | 567 | 2,267 | 295 |
| 10.0 to 20.0 | 7,193 | 734 | 1,754 | 6,410 | 946 |
| 20.0 to 25.0 | 1,835 | 240 | 673 | 2,468 | 369 |
| 25.0 to 35.0 | 1,999 | 327 | 922 | 3,118 | 450 |
| More than 35.0 | 8,463 | 8,002 | 81,308 | 103,104 | 20,919 |
| Unspecified | 4,259 | 297 | 275 | 910 | 204 |
| Total | 97,957 | 13,248 | 89,035 | 133,044 | 25,551 |
| Smaller: Less than 35.0 | 89,494 | 5,246 | 7,727 | 30,030 | 4,632 |
| Larger: More than 35.0 | 8,463 | 8,002 | 81,308 | 103,014 | 20,919 |

❑ By employment size, the smaller industrial units with less than 50 workers constitute the largest segment in terms of number of units (78%) and employment (17.6%), whereas the units employing between 500 to 999 workers have the highest shares of productive capital (24.8%) and value of output (18.2%), and the net value addition claimed the maximum share (18.8%) in the industrial units with employment in the range of 200 to 499 persons.

❑ In terms of the value of plant and machinery, the maximum number of units were of small size with upto Rs 1 lakh value. But in other respects the large size units with RRs.35 lakhs or more value dominate.

## 10.5 Key Parameters of Manufacturing (Factory) Sector : ASI : 1980-81 and 1986-87

| | Indicators | Unit | 1980-81 | 1986-87 | % change per annum (a) |
|---|---|---|---|---|---|
| 1. | Factories : Total | Number | 138,220 | 174,793 | 4.0 |
| | Factories covered by ASI | Number | 92,612 | 93,907 | 0.2 |
| 2. | Workers employed | '000 nos. | 6,587 | 7,149 | 1.4 |
| | Workers covered by ASI | '000 nos. | 5,412 | 5,090 | -1.0 |
| 3. | Capital | | | | |
| | Productive Capital | Rs. crores | 27,579 | 57,284 | 13.0 |
| | Fixed Capital | Rs. crores | 16,734 | 38,267 | 14.8 |
| | Working Capital | Rs. crores | 10,845 | 18,917 | 9.7 |
| | Invested Capital | Rs. crores | 32,584 | 66,706 | 12.7 |
| | Physical working Capital | Rs. crores | 15,850 | 28,339 | 10.2 |
| | Outstanding loans | Rs. crores | 15,667 | 40,479 | 17.1 |
| 4. | Employment | '000 nos | 6,942 | 6,419 | -1.3 |
| | Workers | '000 nos | 5,412 | 5,090 | -1.0 |
| | Supervisors Managers | '000 nos | 1,389 | 1,329 | -0.7 |
| | Others (working proprietors) | '000 nos | 121 | – | – |
| 5. | Mandays worked | Min. nos. | 1,856 | 1,958 | 0.2 |
| 6. | Emoluments | Rs. crores | 5,229 | 10,158 | 11.7 |
| | Wages of workers | Rs. crores | 3,427 | 6,604 | 11.6 |
| | Emoluments of supervisors | Rs. crores | 1,802 | 3,554 | 12.0 |

contd. . .

| Indicators | Unit | 1980-81 | 1986-87 | % change per annum (a) |
|---|---|---|---|---|
| 7. Value of Inputs | Rs. crores | 44,217 | 94,063 | 13.4 |
| Materials consumed | Rs. crores | 34,847 | 76,736 | 14.1 |
| Fuel consumed | Rs. crores | 3,230 | 8,715 | 18.0 |
| Others | Rs. crores | 6,140 | 8,612 | 5.8 |
| 8. Value of Output | Rs. crores | 56,132 | 118,869 | 13.3 |
| Products | Rs. crores | 50,681 | 112,305 | 14.2 |
| Services | Rs. crores | 5,451 | 6,564 | 3.1 |
| 9. Depreciation | Rs. crores | 1,625 | 3,862 | 15.5 |
| 10. Net value added | Rs. crores | 10,290 | 20,944 | 12.6 |
| Emoluments | Rs. crores | 5,229 | 10,158 | 11.7 |
| Interest paid | Rs. crores | 1,999 | 5,015 | 16.6 |
| Rent paid | Rs. crores | 127 | 329 | 17.2 |
| Profits (before tax) | Rs. crores | 2,935 | 5,442 | 10.8 |

*Notes :*

*ASI = Annual Survey of Industries*

*(a)  % change indicates compound annual rate*

❑ Over the six years period represented in the above statistics, the ASI coverage of the factory sector had declined, in terms of number of factories from 67% to 54% and in terms of workers employed from 82% to 71%. While the total number of factories increased at the rate of 4% per annum, those covered by the ASI increased at just 0.2% per annum. As the total number of workers increased at 1.4% per annum, the ASI coverage showed a negative growth of one percent annually during the period.

❑ In terms of various financial parameters the annual growth rates during the period was around 13%.

❑ While the total net value added increased at the rate of 12.6% among its components, interest payment recorded the highest growth rate of 16.6% per annum thereby increasing its share from 19.4% to 23.9%. On the other hand, the largest component of emoluments increased at the rate of 11.7% per annum thus lowering its share of total net value added from 50% in 1980-81 to 48.5% in 1986-87. Profit before tax increased at the lowest rate of 10.8% and as a result its share also declined from 28.5% to 26% per annum over the period.

## Components Gross Value of Manufacturing Output (Factory)

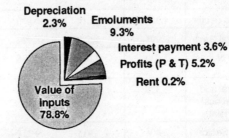

Depreciation 2.3%
Emoluments 9.3%
Interest payment 3.6%
Profits (P & T) 5.2%
Rent 0.2%
Value of inputs 78.8%

**1980-81 = Rs. 56,132 crores**

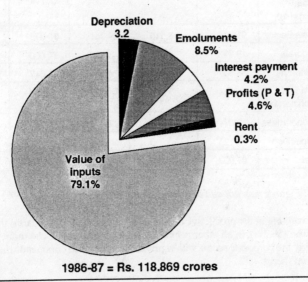

Depreciation 3.2
Emoluments 8.5%
Interest payment 4.2%
Profits (P & T) 4.6%
Rent 0.3%
Value of inputs 79.1%

**1986-87 = Rs. 118.869 crores**

## 10.6 Ownership Pattern of Industrial Units : 1986-87 Covered by ASI

| Ownership category | No. of factories | Employment '000 persons | Productive capital Rs. cr | Gross value of output Rs. cr | Net value added Rs. cr |
|---|---|---|---|---|---|
| Public Sector | 4,353 | 3,818 | 50,010 | 39,818 | 8,518 |
| Central Govt. | 995 | 1,579 | 18,922 | 24,234 | 3,960 |
| State or local govt. | 3,030 | 2,066 | 30,188 | 14,264 | 4,251 |
| Central and State/Local govt. jointly | 328 | 172 | 900 | 1,320 | 307 |
| Joint Sector | 2,404 | 915 | 9,234 | 14,101 | 2,598 |
| Central Govt. & Private enterprises | 1,026 | 469 | 4,724 | 7,015 | 1,065 |
| State and/or Local govt. & private enterprises | 1,378 | 446 | 4,510 | 7,086 | 1,533 |
| Private Sector | 91,077 | 8,510 | 29,781 | 79,073 | 14,426 |
| Corporate | 19,232 | 4,645 | 22116 | 54,600 | 11,288 |
| Partnership | 53,257 | 2,802 | 4,174 | 18,017 | 2,267 |
| Individual proprietorship | 16,514 | 594 | 587 | 2,199 | 346 |
| Co-operatives | 2,074 | 469 | 2,904 | 4,257 | 525 |
| Unspecified | 123 | 5 | 9 | 52 | 10 |
| Total | 97,957 | 13,248 | 69,035 | 133,044 | 25,551 |

*Note : Figures may not add to the indicated totals due to rounding off.*

❑ Excepting in the productive capital where the public sector claims the highest share (56.2%), in all other respects it is the private sector, and more particularly the corporate sector within private sector, which commands the dominant shares.

## 10.7   Small Scale Industries:Key indicators :1973-74 to 1991-92

| Year | No. of units (Lakhs) | Employment (Lakh nos.) | Investment (Rs. crores) | Production at current prices (Rs. crores) | Exports | |
|------|------|------|------|------|------|------|
| | | | | | Rs. crores | % to total exports |
| 1973 - 74 | 4.16 | 39.7 | 2,296 | 7,200 | 393 | 15.6 |
| 1974 - 75 | 4.98 | 40.4 | 2,697 | 9,200 | 541 | 16.3 |
| 1975 - 76 | 5.46 | 45.9 | 3,204 | 11,000 | 532 | 13.2 |
| 1976 - 77 | 5.92 | 49.8 | 3,553 | 12,400 | 766 | 14.9 |
| 1977 - 78 | 6.70 | 54.0 | 3,959 | 14,300 | 845 | 15.6 |
| 1978 - 79 | 7.34 | 63.8 | 4,431 | 15,790 | 1,089 | 18.7 |
| 1979 - 80 | 8.05 | 67.0 | 5,540 | 21,635 | 1,226 | 19.1 |
| 1980 - 81 | 8.74 | 71.0 | 5,850 | 28,060 | 1,643 | 24.5 |
| 1981 - 82 | 9.62 | 75.0 | 6,280 | 32,600 | 2,071 | 26.5 |
| 1982 - 83 | 10.59 | 79.0 | 6,800 | 35,000 | 2,045 | 23.2 |
| 1983 - 84 | 11.58 | 84.2 | 7,360 | 41,620 | 2,164 | 22.1 |
| 1984 - 85 | 12.42 | 90.0 | 8,380 | 50,520 | 2,553 | 21.7 |
| 1985 - 86 | 13.55 | 96.0 | 9,585 | 61,228 | 2,785 | 25.6 |
| 1986 - 87 | 14.64 | 101.4 | 10,881 | 72,250 | 3,631 | 29.2 |
| 1987 - 88 | 15.86 | 107.0 | 12,610 | 87,300 | 4,535 | 28.9 |
| 1988 - 89 | 17.12 | 113.0 | 15,229 | 106,400 | 5,490 | 27.0 |
| 1989 - 90 | 18.23 | 119.6 | 18,196 | 132,320 | 7,626 | 27.6 |
| 1990 - 91 | 19.48 | 125.3 | n.a. | 155,340 | 9,644 | n.a. |
| 1991 - 92 | 20.80 | 129.8 | n.a. | 178,699 | n.a. | n.a. |
| Compound annual rates of increase % | | | | | | |
| 1974 - 75 to 1979 - 80 | 10.1 | 10.6 | 15.5 | 18.7 | 17.8 | |
| 1979 - 80 to 1984 - 85 | 9.1 | 6.1 | 8.6 | 18.5 | 15.8 | |

contd...

| Year | No. of units (Lakhs) | Employ-ment (Lakh nos.) | Invest-ment (Rs. crores) | Product-ion at current prices (Rs. crores) | Exports | |
|---|---|---|---|---|---|---|
| | | | | | Rs. crores | % to total exports |
| Compound annual rates of increase % | | | | | | |
| 1984 - 85 to 1989 - 90 | 8.0 | 5.9 | 16.8 | 21.2 | 24.5 | |
| 1973 - 74 to 1989 - 90 | 9.7 | 7.1 | 13.8 | 20.0 | 20.4 | |

*Note :  Data in this table have been compiled from diverse sources, including the Development commissioner for small scale industries and the Union ministry of industry. The coverage have differs widely from that based on Annual survey of industries.*

## Small Scale Industries

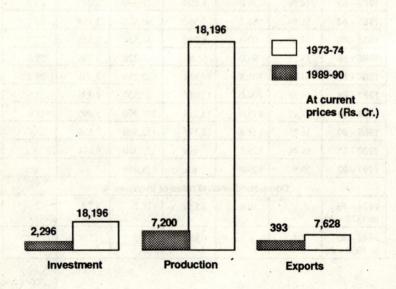

18,196

☐ 1973-74
▓ 1989-90

At current prices (Rs. Cr.)

2,296　18,196
Investment

7,200　18,196
Production

393　7,628
Exports

## 10.8 Growth of Small-Scale Industry in Factory Sector : 1973-74 to 1986-87 covered by ASI

| Year | No. of factories | Employment (Lakh nos.) | Fixed Capital (Rs. crores) | Gross Output (Rs. crore) | Value added (Rs. crores) |
|---|---|---|---|---|---|
| 1973 - 74 | 57,908 | 20.2 | 910 | 5,055 | 816 |
|  | (90.31) | (34.2) | (8.5) | (25.8) | (17.6) |
| 1974 - 75 | 57,335 | 20.4 | 771 | 6,068 | 945 |
|  | (89.3) | (33.6) | (6.5) | (23.3) | (15.5) |
| 1975 - 76 | 65,539 | 24.1 | 1,384 | 7,757 | 1,328 |
|  | (91.4) | (37.8) | (10.2) | (26.1) | (20.8) |
| 1976 - 77 | 74,449 | 24.0 | 1,035 | 8,286 | 1,292 |
|  | (91.6) | (36.1) | (6.4) | (24.3) | (17.7) |
| 1977 - 78 | 77,366 | 25.8 | 1,272 | 9,586 | 1,510 |
|  | (91.1) | (36.4) | (6.5) | (24.7) | (18.6) |
| 1978 - 79 | 79,893 | 25.5 | 1,152 | 9,963 | 1,449 |
|  | (90.7) | (35.2) | (5.0) | (22.5) | (15.2) |
| 1979 - 80 | 86,038 | 26.9 | 1,440 | 11,666 | 1,746 |
|  | (90.5) | (35.0) | (5.4) | (22.3) | (16.1) |
| 1980 - 81 | 90,105 | 29.0 | 2,025 | 15,928 | 2,265 |
|  | (93.4) | (37.6) | (6.8) | (26.1) | (19.0) |
| 1981 - 82 | 98,169 | 30.0 | 2,302 | 17,877 | 2,510 |
|  | (93.5) | (38.5) | (6.6) | (24.3) | (17.2) |
| 1982 - 83 | 85,524 | 30.4 | 2,508 | 19,805 | 2,751 |
|  | (91.8) | (33.7) | (6.1) | (23.0) | (16.5) |
| 1983 - 84 | 87,713 | 28.3 | 3,220 | 15,708 | 3,584 |
|  | (90.7) | (36.2) | (6.6) | (21.0) | (17.8) |

*contd . . .*

| Year | No. of factories | Employment (Lakh nos.) | Fixed Capital (Rs. crores) | Gross Output (Rs. crore) | Value added (Rs. crores) |
|---|---|---|---|---|---|
| 1984-85 | 86,954 | 26.5 | 2,902 | 21,532 | 3,466 |
|  | (89.7) | (33.7) | (5.3) | (20.4) | (16.6) |
| 1985-86 | 93,180 | 30.0 | 3,956 | 29,137 | 4,668 |
|  | (92.2) | (40.2) | (6.6) | (24.2) | (20.1) |
| 1986-87 | 89,494 | 28.6 | 4,663 | 30,030 | 4,633 |
|  | (91.4) | (38.4) | (6.0) | (22.6) | (18.2) |
| Compound annual rates of increase (%) | | | | | |
| 1974-75 to 1979-80 | 8.4 | 5.7 | 13.3 | 14.0 | 13.1 |
| 1979-80 to 1984-85 | 0.2 | -1.0 | 15.0 | 13.0 | 14.7 |
| 1973-74 to 1986-87 | 3.4 | 2.7 | 13.4 | 14.7 | 14.3 |

Notes  (a) Figures within brackets indicate the percentage shares of small scale in the total factory sector
       (b) Definitions of a small scale unit has been changed from time to time but has been generally in terms of the investment in fixed assets of plant and machinery. In 1973-75 the limit was Rs.7.5 lakhs, by June 1990 the limit was raised to Rs.60 lakhs.
       (c) Figures above are more reliable as these are collected under the Annual Survey of Industries.

❑ The share of small scale in the entire factory sector in terms of number of units has been high annual 90%, but in employment it accounts for around 35% share. On the other hand it accounts for about a fourth in gross output and one-fifth of the value added in the entire factory sector.

## 10.9 Industrial Sickness : 1979 to 1988
### A : By size of units

| As at Dec. end | Large Units No. | Large Units Bank credit out-stan-ding (Rs. crore) | Med. Units No. | Med. Units Bank credit out-stan-ding (Rs. crore) | Small-scale Units No. | Small-scale Units Bank credit out-stan-ding (Rs. crore) | Total No. | Total Bank credut out-stan-ding (Rs. crore) |
|---|---|---|---|---|---|---|---|---|
| 1979 | 378 | 1,158 | 1,013 | 202 | 20,975 | 262 | 22,366 | 1,622 |
| 1980 | 409 | 1,324 | 992 | 178 | 23,149 | 306 | 24,550 | 1,808 |
| 1981 | 422 | 1,479 | 994 | 188 | 25,342 | 359 | 26,758 | 2,025 |
| 1982 | 444 | 1,791 | 1,178 | 226 | 58,551(a) | 569(a) | 60,173(a) | 2,586(a) |
| 1983 | 491 | 2,014 | 1,256 | 358 | 78,363 | 729 | 80,110 | 3,101 |
| 1984 | 545 | 2,330 | 1,287 | 429 | 91,450 | 880 | 93,282 | 3,639 |
| 1985 | 637 | 2,980 | 1,186 | 220 | 117,783 | 1,071 | 119,606 | 4,271 |
| 1986 | 714 | 3,287 | 1,250 | 281 | 145,776 | 1,306 | 147,740 | 4,874 |
| 1987 | 1,839(b) | 4,459(b) | n.a. | n.a. | 204,259 | 1,797 | 206,098 | 6,256 |
| 1988 | 2,011(b) | 5,564(b) | n.a. | n.a. | 240,573 | 2,141 | 242,584 | 7,705 |
| **Compound annual rates of increase (%)** | | | | | | | | |
| 1979 & 1988 | 20.4 | 19.1 | 3.0(c) | 4.8(c) | 31.1 | 26.3 | 30.3 | 18.9 |

❑ The number of non-SSI sick units in March 1991 was 1461, according to RBI estimates. The outstanding bank credit to these units was Rs. 5,106 crores.

❑ The number of sick SSI units in March 1991 was 2,21,472 and the bank credit locked up in these units was Rs. 2,792 crores.

## B. Viability Status of Sick Units: 1985 & 1988

| Status | 31 Dec 1985 | | 31 Dec 1988 | |
|---|---|---|---|---|
| | Number | Bank Credit Outstanding Rs. crores | Number | Bank Credit Outstanding Rs. crores |
| Found viable | 8,569 (7.2) | 1,987 (46.5) | 13,712 (5.7) | 2,892 (37.5) |
| Found non-viable | 99,062 (82.8) | 1,791 (41.9) | 224,969 (92.7) | 3,418 (44.4) |
| Viability not determined | 11,975 (10.0) | 493 (11.6) | 3,903 (1.6) | 1,395 (18.1) |
| Total | 119,606 (100.0) | 4,271 (100.0) | 242,584 (100.0) | 7,705 (100.0) |

*Notes : (a) Including small scale units in protest bill/recalled accounts*
*(b) Non-SSI sick and weak units*
*(c) Between 1979 and 1986*
*Figures within brackets in Section 8 above refer to percentages to totals.*

❑ Although number of sick small sale units appears quite large, these accounted for only 28% of the total outstanding bank credit locked up in the sick units at the end of 1988.

❑ Disturbing feature of section B is that the proportion of non-viable units both in terms of number and outstanding bank credit increased between 1985 and 1988. On the other hand, proportions in respect of viable units declined, though their number and outstanding credits amount increased.

❑ These outstanding bank credits locked up in sick units reduce the scope of re-cycling of funds by banks. Besides, these non-performing assets vitiate the accounts of the banks.

❑ As of March 1991, 2,19,138 sick SSI units were studied by the banks, of which 16,140 units were considered viable.

## 10.10 Index of Industrial Production : by Major Groups :1985-86 –1991-92

*(Base : 1980-81 = 100)*

| Weight (%) | Industry groups/ Sub-groups | 1985 - 86 | 1989 - 90 | 1990 - 91 | 1991 - 92 |
|---|---|---|---|---|---|
| 11.46 | Mining | 167.5 | 211.6 | 221.2 | 221.8 |
| 77.11 | Manufacturing | 136.9 | 190.7 | 207.8 | 204.4 |
| 5.33 | Food products | 125.6 | 150.9 | 169.8 | 176.8 |
| 1.57 | Beverages, tobacco & tobacco products | 112.1 | 103.0 | 104.8 | 119.1 |
| 12.31 | Cotton Textiles | 110.4 | 112.3 | 126.6 | 128.2 |
| 2.00 | Jute, hemp, textiles | 97.2 | 97.0 | 101..6 | 90.4 |
| 0.82 | Other textiles | 112.8 | 151.7 | 103.2 | 97.2 |
| 0.45 | Wood & products | 223.2 | 176.0 | 197.2 | 185.0 |
| 3.24 | Paper & products | 148.5 | 181.5 | 198.0 | 205.1 |
| 0.49 | Leather & products | 169.2 | 188.3 | 194.3 | 181.5 |
| 4.00 | Rubber, plastics, Petroleum & Coal | 153.0 | 173.5 | 174.0 | 172.2 |
| 12.51 | Chemicals & products | 154.3 | 247.6 | 254.1 | 261.3 |
| 3.00 | Non-metallic mineral products | 157.3 | 189.9 | 193.1 | 205.2 |
| 9.80 | Basic metals | 117.0 | 143.7 | 158.8 | 168.0 |
| 2.29 | Metal products | 114.7 | 142.6 | 143.0 | 133.1 |
| 6.24 | Non-electrical machinery | 130.2 | 172.0 | 186.9 | 181.4 |
| 5.78 | Electrical machinery | 200.6 | 459.2 | 563.6 | 492.9 |
| 6.39 | Transport equipment | 135.8 | 181.1 | 192.5 | 189.3 |
| 0.91 | Other manufacturing | 152.7 | 333.2 | 321.8 | 269.8 |
| 11.43 | Electricity | 152.4 | 219.7 | 236.8 | 257.0 |
| 100.00 | All industries | 142.1 | 196.4 | 212.6 | 212.4 |

❑ Decadewise, the eighties recorded the highest industrial growth, which accelerated during the latter half in the manufacturing segment.

❑ Mining, chemicals and chemical products and electrical machinery groups were the high growth areas on the industrial scene of the eighties. Engineering industries and within that the capital equipment groups displayed most rapid growth during the second half of the decade, while the growth slowed down during that period in wood products, leather, products, rubber, plastics, petroleum and coal products.

❑ The indices available for February 1993 are as follow :
Mining  241.0; Manufacturing 210.5; Electricity  270.5; All industries  220.8

## Major Contributors to High Industrial Growth : 1980-81 — 1990-91

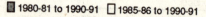

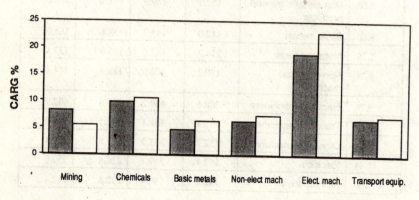

## 10.11 Value of Output in Manufacturing (Factory) Sector : 1970-71, 1980-81 & 1988-89

| Industry groups & subgroups | Value of output at current prices | | | | |
|---|---|---|---|---|---|
| | Rs. crores | | | CARG % | |
| | 1970-71 | 1980-81 | 1988-89 | 1970-71 to 1980-81 | 1980-81 to 1988-89 |
| Food & beverages incl. tobacco products | 3,041 (22.6) | 9,157 (15.6) | 27,963 (15.2) | 11.7 | 15.0 |
| Textiles & products | 2,531 (18.8) | 9.462 (16.1) | 22,314 (12.1) | 14.1 | 11.3 |
| Cotton Textiles | 1,655 (12.3) | 5,562 (9.6) | 9,610 (5.2) | 13.1 | 6.9 |
| Leather & wood products | 719 (5.4) | 2,620 (4.5) | 7,799 (4.3) | 13.8 | 14.6 |
| Paper & products | 451 (3.4) | 1,763 (3.0) | 5,269 (2.9) | 14.6 | 14.7 |
| Chemicals & products | 1,508 (11.2) | 8,165 (13.9) | 27,549 (15.0) | 18.4 | 16.4 |
| Rubber, plastics, petroleum & coal products | 647 (4.8) | 6,171 (10.5) | 21,407 (11.6) | 25.3 | 16.8 |
| Non-metallic mineral products | 412 (3.1) | 1,694 (2.9) | 7,240 (3.9) | 15.2 | 19.9 |
| Engineering industry | 4,015 (29.8) | 19,353 (32.9) | 63,204 (34.4) | 17.0 | 15.9 |
| Basic metals & alloys | 1,334 (9.9) | 7,272 (12.4) | 23,376 (12.8) | 18.5 | 15.7 |
| Metal products | 394 (2.9) | 1,410 (2.4) | 4,488 (2.4) | 13.6 | 15.6 |
| Non-electrical machinery | 718 (5.3) | 3,613 (6.1) | 11,463 (6.2) | 17.5 | 15.5 |
| Electrical machinery | 694 (5.2) | 3,668 (6.2) | 11,968 (6.5) | 18.1 | 15.9 |
| Transport equipment | 875 (6.5) | 3,390 (5.8) | 11,909 (6.5) | 14.5 | 17.0 |

*contd . . .*

| Industry groups & subgroups | Value of output at current prices | | | | |
|---|---|---|---|---|---|
| | Rs. crores | | | CARG % | |
| | 1970-71 | 1980-81 | 1988-89 | 1970-71 to 1980-81 | 1980-81 to 1988-89 |
| Misc: Manufacturing | 584 (4.3) | 1,443 (2.5) | 5,069 (2.8) | 9.5 | 17.0 |
| Total : Manufacturing | 13,455 (100.00) | 58,065 (98.8) | 182,545 (99.3) | 15.7 | 15.4 |
| Total : Repairs & Services | 2 – | 722 (1.2) | 1,292 (0.7) | 8.2 | 7.5 |
| Total | 13,457 (100.00) | 58,787 (100.00) | 183,837 (100.00) | 15.9 | 15.3 |

*CARG = Compound annual rate of growth figures within brackets are percentage to total*

❑ While the output in real terms, as indicated by index of productions, showed that the rate of growth of manufacturing production had accelerated during the eighties the output in money terms shows a lower rate of growth per annum during the eight years ended 1988-89 compound to the seventies implying a lower rate of price rise of manufactured products excepting in food and beverages, non-metalic mineral products, metal productions and transport equipment.

### 1970-71

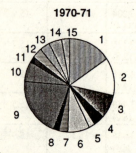

### 1988-89

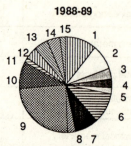

1. Food & beverages; 2.Textiles & products; 3. Cotton Textiles; 4. Leather & wood products; 5. Paper & products; 6. Chemical & products; 7. Rubber, plastics, petroleum & coal products; 8. Non-metallic mineral products; 9. Engineering industry; 10. Basic metals & alloys; 11. Metal products; 12. Non-electrical machinery; 13. Electrical machinery; 14. Transport equipment; 15. Misc: manufacturing.

## 10.12 Gross Value Added in Manufacturing Factory Sector : 1970-71, 1980-81 & 1988-89

| Industry groups & Sub-groups | Value added at current prices | | | | |
|---|---|---|---|---|---|
| | Rs. crores | | | CARG % | |
| | 1970-71 | 1980-81 | 1988-89 | 1970-71 to 1980-81 | 1980-81 to 1988-89 |
| Food & beverages incl. tobacco products | 367 (12.4) | 1,091 (8.6) | 3,949 (9.8) | 11.5 | 17.4 |
| Textiles & products | 597 (20.1) | 2466 (19.5) | 5054 (12.5) | 15.2 | 9.4 |
| Cotton Textiles | 401 (13.5) | 1,567 (12.4) | 2,232 (5.5) | 14.6 | 4.5 |
| Leather & wood products | 204 (6.9) | 674 (5.3) | 1,854 (4.6) | 12.7 | 13.5 |
| Paper & products | 150 (5.1) | 526 (4.2) | 1,406 (3.5) | 13.4 | 13.1 |
| Chemicals & products | 367 (12.4) | 1,854 (14.7) | 6,170 (15.3) | 17.6 | 16.2 |
| Rubber, plastics petroleum & coal products | 129 (4.4) | 614 (4.9) | 3,171 (7.9) | 16.9 | 22.8 |
| Non-metallic mineral products | 114 (3.9) | 474 (3.8) | 2,099 (5.2) | 15.3 | 20.4 |
| Engineering industry | 1,000 (33.7) | 4,829 (38.3) | 15,174 (37.7) | 17.1 | 15.4 |
| Basic metals & alloys | 285 (9.6) | 1,556 (12.3) | 4,417 (11.0) | 18.5 | 13.9 |
| Metal products | 95 (3.2) | 363 (2.9) | 1,169 (2.9) | 14.3 | 15.7 |
| Non-electrical machinery | 194 (6.5) | 985 (7.8) | 3,261 (8.1) | 17.6 | 16.1 |
| Electrical machinery | 182 (6.1) | 918 (7.3) | 3,222 (8.0) | 17.6 | 17.0 |

*contd ...*

| Industry groups & Sub-groups | Value added at current prices | | | | |
|---|---|---|---|---|---|
| | Rs. crores | | | CARG % | |
| | 1970-71 | 1980-81 | 1988-89 | 1970-71 to 1980-81 | 1980-81 to 1988-89 |
| Transport equipment | 244 (8.2) | 1,007 (8.0) | 3,105 (7.7) | 15.2 | 15.1 |
| Misc. manufacturing | 187 (6.3) | 456 (3.6) | 2,242 (5.6) | 9.3 | 22.0 |
| Total Manufacturing | 2,965 (100.00) | 12,458 (98.6) | 39,713 (98.6) | 15.4 | 15.6 |
| Repair & Services | – | 182 (1.4) | 579 (1.4) | – | 15.6 |
| Total Gross value added | 12,965 (100.0) | 12,640 (100.0) | 40,292 (100.0) | 15.6 | 15.6 |

*CARG = Compound annual rate of growth figures within brackets are percentage to total*

❑ Although the rate of growth of overall manufacturing production in value terms slowed down the eighties the growth rate of value addition remained unchanged overall.

❑ The industries which showed accelerated value addition growth during the eighties were food and beverages, non-metallic mineral products, metal product and transport equipment. On the other hand value addition growth declined in cotton textile chemicals group, and other engineering subgroups.

## 10.13 Production Trends in Khadi & Village Industry

| Industry | Value of output (Rs. crores) | | | CARG % | | |
|---|---|---|---|---|---|---|
| | 1980-81 | 1985-86 | 1989-90 | 1980-81 to 1985-86 | 1985-86 to 1989-90 | 1980-81 to 1989-90 |
| KHADI (Rs. Crores) | 182.76 | 321.98 | 406.47 | | | |
| Khadi cloth     Mln Mtr | 91.01 | 104.94 | 107.47 | 2.9 | 0.6 | 1.9 |
| Cotton          Mln Mtr | 79.48 | 87.03 | 87.96 | 1.8 | 0.3 | 1.1 |
| Khadi cloth   Rs. crores | 106.85 | 195.01 | 257.87 | 12.8 | 7.2 | 10.3 |
| Cotton        Rs. crores | 75.93 | 126.97 | 149.60 | 10.8 | 4.2 | 7.8 |
| VILLAGE INDUSTRIES | 451.24 | 929.03 | 1705.39 | 15.5 | 16.4 | 15.9 |
| Mineral based | 33.88 | 100.69 | 196.82 | 24.3 | 18.2 | 21.6 |
| Cottage pottery | 24.14 | 72.60 | 149.36 | 24.6 | 19.8 | 22.4 |
| Forest based | 43.02 | 48.79 | 93.39 | 2.5 | 17.6 | 9.0 |
| Cottage match | 31.05 | 16.55 | 22.57 | -11.2 | 8.1 | -3.5 |
| Bamboo & cane | 4.41 | 20.46 | 57.97 | 35.9 | 29.7 | 33.1 |
| Agro-based & food | 252.75 | 448.86 | 730.47 | 12.2 | 12.9 | 12.5 |
| Ghani oil | 80.20 | 198.54 | 278.08 | 19.9 | 8.8 | 14.8 |
| Cane gur & khandsari | 100.78 | 83.74 | 120.16 | -3.8 | 9.4 | 2.0 |
| Processing cereal & pulses | 27.08 | 72.70 | 127.35 | 21.8 | 15.0 | 18.8 |
| Chemical based | 63.51 | 170.54 | 336.80 | 21.8 | 18.5 | 20.4 |
| Cottage Soaps | 17.25 | 33.89 | 46.28 | 14.5 | 8.1 | 11.6 |
| Cottage Leather | 46.26 | 136.65 | 290.52 | 24.2 | 20.8 | 22.6 |
| Engineering & Craft | 58.66 | 157.03 | 324.49 | 21.8 | 19.9 | 20.9 |
| Carpentry & Blacksmithy | 35.88 | 116.12 | 283.40 | 26.5 | 25.0 | 25.8 |

*contd . . .*

| Industry | Value of output (Rs. crores) | | | CARG % | | |
|---|---|---|---|---|---|---|
| | 1980-81 | 1985-86 | 1989-90 | 1980-81 to 1985-86 | 1985-86 to 1989-90 | 1980-81 to 1989-90 |
| Textiles : Polyvastra | 0.42 | 3.12 | 16.11 | 49.3 | 50.7 | 50.0 |
| Services | – | – | 6.71 | – | – | – |
| Total Khadi & Village Industry | 558.09 | 1124.04 | 1963.11 | 15.0 | 15.0 | 15.0 |

CARG = Compound annual rate of growth

## 11.1 Number of Companies at Work and their Paid-up Capital : 1951 – 1991

| As on 31st March | No. of Companies | | | Paid-up Capital (Rs. Cr.) | | |
|---|---|---|---|---|---|---|
| | Govt. | Non-Govt. | Total | Govt. | Non- Govt. | Total |
| 1951 | 36 | 28,496 | 28,932 | 26 | 749 | 775 |
| 1956 | 61 | 29,813 | 29,874 | 66 | 958 | 1,024 |
| 1961 | 142 | 26,007 | 26,149 | 547 | 1,272 | 1,817 |
| 1966 | 214 | 26,551 | 26,765 | 1,248 | 1,878 | 3,126 |
| 1971 | 314 | 30,008 | 30,322 | 2,064 | 2,439 | 4,503 |
| 1976 | 651 | 42,755 | 43,406 | 6,122 | 3,497 | 9,619 |
| 1981 | 851 | 61,863 | 62,714 | 11,443 | 4,914 | 16,351 |
| 1982 | 894 | 71,508 | 72,402 | 13,309 | 5,626 | 18,935 |
| 1983 | 943 | 81,960 | 82,903 | 16,735 | 6,321 | 23,056 |
| 1984 | 973 | 93,291 | 94,264 | 19,511 | 6,990 | 26,501 |
| 1985 | 980 | 106,389 | 107,369 | 22,447 | 7,639 | 30,086 |
| 1986 | 1,020 | 121,139 | 122,159 | 27,088 | 8,596 | 35,684 |
| 1987 | 1,053 | 137,133 | 138,186 | 32,873 | 9,957 | 42,830 |
| 1988 | 1,104 | 154,445 | 155,549 | 37,169 | 11,308 | 48,477 |
| 1989 | 1,134 | 176,104 | 177,238 | 42,572 | 13,671 | 56,243 |
| 1990 | 1,160 | 197,393 | 198,553 | 44,985 | 14,737 | 59,722 |
| 1991 | 1,179 | 219,542 | 220,721 | 49,424 | 18,686 | 68,110 |

❏ The number of companies increased almost seven times over the past 39 years, but their paid-up capital increased 77 times during the same period.

❏ The average paid-up capital per company in the aggregate increased from Rs.2.72 lakhs at the end of 1950-51 to Rs.30.08 lakhs at the level of March 1990. Within thus, the average paid-up capital per company in the private sector increased from Rs.2.63 lakhs to Rs.7.47 lakhs whereas for the goverment companies the corresponding averages increased from Rs.72.22 lakhs at 1950-51 end to Rs.3878 lakhs at the end of 1989-90.

❏ The number of government companies constitute only a small portion of the total – increasing to maximum of 1.5 percent during 1975-79 and then tapering down to only half a percent of the total number of companies. On the other hand, however, the share of government companies in the total paid up capital increased almost continuously from 3.41 percent at the end of 1950-51 to around 75 percent since 1983-84.

❑ Even with the disinvestment of share capital by the government, initiated in a small way during 1991-92, the dominant share of government companies in the total paid-up capital would not alter much, since the ownership character of the government companies would not change.

### Paid-up Capital 1961

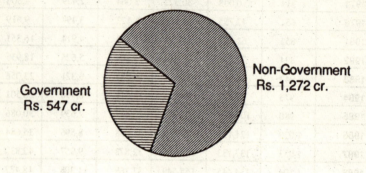

Non-Government Rs. 1,272 cr.

Government Rs. 547 cr.

### Paid-up Capital 1991

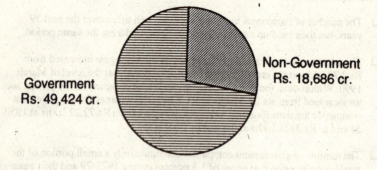

Non-Government Rs. 18,686 cr.

Government Rs. 49,424 cr.

## 11.2 Profile of Corporate Sector in terms of Tax-paying Companies : 1966-67 – 1988-89

*(A = No. of Units, B = Taxable profits Rs. crores)*

| Year | Closely held companies | Widely held companies | Total Indian companies | Foreign companies | Total for Indian & Foreign Co. |
|------|----------|----------|----------|----------|----------|
| **1966-67 A** | 11,193 | 1,625 | 12,818 | 691 | 13,509 |
| **B** | 337.9 | 160.0 | 497.9 | 46.3 | 544.2 |
| **1971-72 A** | 11,669 | 1,376 | 13,045 | 615 | 13,660 |
| **B** | 794.1 | 288.9 | 1083.0 | 64.2 | 1,147.2 |
| **1976-77 A** | 8,617 | 3,548 | 12,165 | 1,454 | 13,619 |
| **B** | 168.8 | 625.2 | 794.0 | 92.4 | 886.4 |
| **1980-81 A** | 7,004 | 2860 | 9,864 | 1,241 | 11,105 |
| **B** | 183.3 | 1,151.6 | 1,334.9 | 129.3 | 1464.2 |
| **1981-82 A** | 7,062 | 2,736 | 9,798 | 1,130 | 10,928 |
| **B** | 286.9 | 1,153.6 | 1,440.5 | 82.9 | 1523.4 |
| **1982-83 A** | 6,312 | 2,519 | 8,831 | 1,334 | 10,165 |
| **B** | 208.2 | 1,670.1 | 1,878.3 | 80.0 | 1,958.3 |
| **1983-84 A** | 5,554 | 2,061 | 7,615 | 624 | 8,239 |
| **B** | 164.7 | 1,442.6 | 1,607.3 | 55.5 | 1,662.8 |
| Series below not comparable with the above | | | | | |
| **1984-85 A** | 21,074 | 4,035 | n.a. | n.a. | 25,109 |
| **B** | 740.0 | 3,642.0 | n.a. | n.a. | 4,382.0 |
| **1985-86 A** | 15,593 | 5,265 | 19,891 | 967 | 20,858 |
| **B** | 1,023.0 | 4,576.0 | 5,199.0 | 400.0 | 5599.0 |
| **1986-87 A** | 13,604 | 3,451 | 16,056 | 999 | 17,055 |
| **B** | 2,773.0 | 4,121.0 | 5,530.0 | 1,364.0 | 6,894.0 |
| **1987-88 A** | 31,884 | 6,706 | 37,549 | 1,041 | 38,590 |
| **B** | 1,590.0 | 8,369.0 | 9,574.0 | 385.0 | 9,959.0 |
| **1988-89 A** | 34,777 | 8,357 | 40,491 | 2,643 | 43,134 |
| **B** | 1,317.0 | 3,449.0 | 4,542.0 | 224.0 | 4,766.0 |

*Note : (a) Data for years upto 1983-84 pertain to assessments completed by the Income Tax department in particular years. These may relate to the particular year or assessment of prior years. Figures from 1984-85 pertain to "returned income" for the particular year, as opposed to the "assessed invoices" in the preceding series.*

*(b) In the later series the totals given for Indian companies do not result from the sum of the two specified constituents. The differences are because of the inclusion of foreign companies under the constituents, without identifying separately the closely held and widely held companies.*

❑  Although the number of closely-held tax-paying companies to predominantly large, their taxable profits are relatively smaller in proportions, both to the trends total of all tax paying companies as also in terms of average taxable profits per company. The widely-held companies generally account for largest share in terms of taxable profits. The foreign companies generally show better average taxable profits per company than the Indian companies.

❑  Public sector companies account for almost half the taxable profits of all companies taken together.

❑  Nearly four-fifths of the taxable profits arise from companies engaged in industrial activities.

❑  About a fourth of taxable profits is set-off against permissible deductions of previous years losses.

## 11.3 Financial Performance Indicators of Medium and Large Public Limited Companies (RBI samples) : 1960-61 – 1988-89

| Year | No. of Cos. in R.B.I. Sample | Profitability Ratios (%) | | | Rate of gross assets formation (%) | Internal resources finance as % of gross assets formation |
|---|---|---|---|---|---|---|
| | | Operating profits to total net assets | Operating profits to sales | Net profits after tax to net worth | | |
| 1960-61 | 1,333 | 10.0 | 10.6 | 11.0 | (N.A.) | (N.A.) |
| 1965-66 | 1,333 | 10.1 | 10.0 | 8.7 | 9.6 | 45 |
| 1966-67 | 1,501 | 9.8 | 10.5 | 9.1 | 11.2 | 41 |
| 1970-71 | 1,501 | 10.4 | 9.9 | 10.1 | 8.8 | 57 |
| 1971-72 | 1,650 | 10.3 | 9.9 | 9.1 | 8.8 | 59 |
| 1975-76 | 1,650 | 10.4 | 9.1 | 8.2 | 9.2 | 43 |
| 1976-77 | 1,720 | 11.0 | 9.0 | 7.9 | 7.4 | 44 |
| 1980-81 | 1,720 | 12.0 | 9.6 | 14.9 | 14.7 | 38 |
| 1981-82 | 1,851 | 11.2 | 9.3 | 13.4 | 17.0 | 29 |
| 1982-83 | 1,838 | 9.9 | 8.9 | 12.1 | 15.0 | 30 |
| 1983-84 | 1,867 | 8.4 | 8.1 | 7.2 | 11.1 | 37 |
| 1984-85 | 1,867 | 8.7 | 8.3 | 7.7 | 12.2 | 41 |
| 1985-86 | 1,942 | 8.8 | 9.0 | 8.3 | 14.7 | 34 |
| 1986-87 | 1953 | 8.0 | 8.5 | 5.7 | 12.2 | 30 |
| 1987-88 | 1953 | 7.4 | 7.8 | 3.5 | 10.1 | 35 |
| 1988-89 | 1885 | 8.7 | 8.9 | 7.8 | 15.6 | 29 |

*Note : (a) Physical stock of assets in real terms.*

❑ In terms of profitability rates, the year 1973-74 (not included in Table) saw the best performance of public limited companies, as the highest levels were reached in that year in operating profit ratio to net assets (13.1%) and to sales (12.0%). The ratio of net profits to net worth in that year was also are the best at 14.3% compared to the highest of 14.9% recorded in 1980-81. On the other hand, 1987-88 recorded the lowest profitability rates mentioned have.

❑  As regards the gross assets formation, i.e. increase in stock of gross assets over the previous year, the 1980s recorded reasonable rates of increases year after year. The highest rate of 17% was recorded in 1981-82 while the lowest of 7.2% was in 1972-73.

❑  While the rate of gross assets formation was high during the 1980s, its financing through internal resources steadily declined. Barring the exception of 72% in 1972-73 the internal resources financed 59% of the gross assets in 1971-72. Whereas the lowest proportions of 29-30 percents were noted during the 1980s.

❑  While additions to gross assets are in current prices, the value of total stock of assets is built up at historic costs. The ratio is further distorted by the variations in prices of capital goods and therefore it does not measure the condition to the physical stock of assets in real terms.

### 11.4 Financial Performance Indicators of Medium and Large Private Limited companies ( RBI Samples) : 1960-61 – 1986-87

| Year | No. of Cos. in R.B.I. Sample | Profitability Ratios (%) | | | Rate of gross assets formation (%) | Internal resources finance as % of gross assets formation |
|---|---|---|---|---|---|---|
| | | Operating profits to total net assets | Operating profits to sales | Net profits after tax to net worth | | |
| 1960-61 | 501 | 11.2 | 6.7 | 13.6 | (N.A.) | (N.A.) |
| 1965-66 | 501 | 13.0 | 8.1 | 9.8 | 10.0 | 33 |
| 1966-67 | 701 | 11.2 | 7.4 | 8.4 | 10.2 | 37 |
| 1970-71 | 701 | 9.7 | 6.4 | 6.6 | 10.0 | 36 |
| 1971-72 | 1,001 | 9.7 | 6.5 | 6.9 | 10.0 | 38 |
| 1975-76 | 1,001 | 9.7 | 6.1 | 4.2 | 4.8 | 46 |
| 1976-77 | 1,011 | 10.6 | 6.4 | 6.8 | 9.9 | 34 |
| 1980-81 | 1,011 | 10.5 | 6.5 | 12.6 | 11.3 | 43 |
| 1981-82 | 1,004 | 8.7 | 5.7 | 7.3 | 19.5 | 19 |
| 1982-83 | 1,004 | 8.4 | 5.6 | 8.0 | 11.9 | 39 |
| 1983-84 | 1,027 | 8.3 | 5.3 | 6.4 | 12.4 | 38 |
| 1984-85 | 1,053 | 7.8 | 5.0 | 8.3 | 13.2 | 36 |
| 1985-86 | 1,096 | 8.7 | 5.8 | 9.5 | 15.1 | 33 |
| 1986-87 | 1,096 | 7.7 | 5.3 | 5.6 | 12.9 | 28 |

❑ As in the case of public limited companies (Table 11.5) the 1980s recorded fairly high levels of gross assets formation by the private limited companies. The highest rate of assets formation of 19.5% was recorded in 1981-82. The lowest of 4.8% was recorded during 1975-76.

❑ The 1980s saw diminishing proportion of internal resources to finance gross assets formation of private limited companies. In part thus reflects the rise in prices of capital goods and in part the greater capital intensive nature of assets formation resorted to by the companies where external funds had to be obtained due to inadequacy of internal resources.

## 11.5 Savings and Capital Formation in Private Corporate Sector : 1960-61 – 1991-92

*(Rs. Crores)*

| Year | Net Savings | Gross Savings | Gross Capital formation | Gross Savings as % of Gross Capital formation | % Shares in the total for the economy | |
|---|---|---|---|---|---|---|
| | | | | | Gross Savings | Gross capital formation |
| | 1 | 2 | 3 | 4 | 5 | 6 |
| 1960-61 | 140 | 276 | 535 | 51.6 | 13.4 | 21.0 |
| 1961-66 | 616 | 1,817 | 3,727 | 48.8 | 12.7 | 22.9 |
| 1966-69 | 140 | 1,240 | 2,181 | 56.9 | 9.0 | 13.8 |
| 1969-74 | 1,226 | 3,797 | 5,939 | 63.9 | 9.6 | 14.2 |
| 1974-79 | 1,407 | 6,629 | 10,719 | 61.8 | 7.4 | 12.8 |
| 1979-80 | 910 | 2,352 | 3,030 | 77.6 | 9.5 | 12.0 |
| 1980-81 | 584 | 2,284 | 3,448 | 66.2 | 7.9 | 12.1 |
| 1981-82 | 495 | 2,496 | 9,118 | 27.4 | 7.5 | 22.8 |
| 1982-83 | 568 | 2,908 | 10,085 | 28.8 | 8.4 | 24.7 |
| 1983-84 | 390 | 3,172 | 6,956 | 45.6 | 7.8 | 16.2 |
| 1984-85 | 795 | 3,991 | 10,111 | 39.5 | 9.2 | 20.7 |
| 1980-85 | 2,832 | 14,851 | 39,718 | 37.4 | 8.2 | 19.7 |
| 1985-86 | 1,277 | 5,208 | 14,405 | 36.2 | 10.1 | 22.9 |
| 1986-87 | 421 | 5,040 | 15,506 | 32.5 | 9.4 | 23.1 |
| 1987-88 | 373 | 5,594 | 12,024 | 46.5 | 8.3 | 15.9 |
| 1988-89 | 1,881 | 8,116 | 16,425 | 49.4 | 9.7 | 17.4 |
| 1989-90 | 4,896 | 12,098 | 19,569 | 61.8 | 12.0 | 18.5 |
| 1985-90 | 8,848 | 36,056 | 77,929 | 46.3 | 10.1 | 19.2 |
| 1990-91 | 5,681 | 14,393 | 20,240 | 71.1 | 11.5 | 14.5 |
| 1991-92 | 5,758 | 16,633 | 23,650 | 70.3 | 11.2 | 15.2 |

❑ The share of depreciation in gross savings of the private corporate sector increased from an average of 66% during 1960-61 to 1965-66 (i.e. the Third Plan) to as much as 80% during 1980-81 to 1985-86 (i.e. the Sixth Plan). Then it came down to around 75% during the Seventh Plan. This is a tax-deductible provision for maintenance of capital assets.

❑ Gross savings (including the depreciation provisions) financed one-half to three-fifths of the gross capital formation of the private corporate sector till the Fifth Plan. Thereafter during the Sixth Plan this share of internal resources declined sharply to around 37%, only to improve to average 46% during the Seventh Plan. This decline in share of gross savings indicates the greater reliance on borrowed funds to finance capital formation by the private corporate sector during the eighties.

❑ The private corporate sector accounts for around one-tenth of the gross domestic savings in the economy. However, its gross capital formation is about a fifth of total capital formation in the economy. Thus during the last decade or so it claimed more than what it contributed to the nation's investible resources.

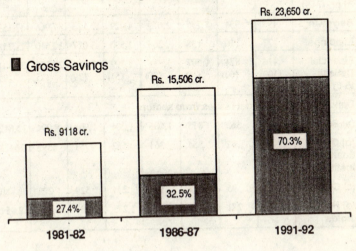

**Gross Savings and Capital Formation**

Gross Savings

Rs. 23,650 cr.

Rs. 15,506 cr.

Rs. 9118 cr.

70.3%

32.5%

27.4%

1981-82     1986-87     1991-92

## 11.6 Financial flows in Private Corporate Sector : 1951-52 to 1989-90

*(Rs. Crores)*

| Item | 1951-52 to 1955-56 | 1956-57 to 1960-61 | 1961-62 to 1965-66 | 1966-67 to 1970-71 | 1971-72 to 1975-76 | 1976-77 to 1980-81 | 1981-82 to 1985-86 | 1986-87 to 1989-90 |
|---|---|---|---|---|---|---|---|---|
| 1. Investment in fixed assets | 404 (100) | 1,374 (100) | 2,663 (100) | 2,588 (100) | 6,254 (100) | 11,616 (100 | 36,446 (100) | 36,440 (100) |
| 2. Savings (i.e. retained earnings) | 178 (44) | 396 (29) | 634 (24) | 618 (24) | 2,043 (33) | 2,481 (21) | 2,938 (8) | 1,397 (4) |
| 3. Capital transfers received (net) | — | — | — | -3 | 402 (6) | 100 (1) | 605 (2) | 2,303 (6) |
| 4. Resource gap (=1-2-3) or (7+9) | 226 (56) | 978 (71) | 2,029 (76) | 1,973 (76) | 3,809 (61) | 9,035 (78) | 32,903 (90) | 32,740 (90) |
| 5. Borrowings | 493 | 934 | 1,735 | 2,079 | 4,929 | 12,173 | 37,966 | 47,159 |
| 6. Lendings | 77 | 110 | 138 | 265 | 1,530 | 3,027 | 10,610 | 13,358 |
| 7. Financial Deficits (5-6) | 416 (103) | 824 (60) | 1,597 (60) | 1,814 (70) | 3,399 (54) | 9,146 (79) | 27,356 (75) | 33,801 (93) |
| 8. Deficits financed by net issues from sectors | | | | | | | | |
| (a) Banking | 63 | 363 | 813 | 1,006 | 1,284 | 1,908 | 8,094 | 12,642 |
| (b) Other financial institutions | 40 | 82 | 354 | 361 | 522 | 1751 | 6599 | 16473 |
| (c) Govt. | 29 | 95 | 115 | 127 | 244 | 529 | 223 | -80 |
| (d) Households | 275 | 281 | 253 | 280 | 1,273 | 3,287 | 6,721 | 2,951 |

| Item | 1951-52 to 1955-56 | 1956-57 to 1960-61 | 1961-62 to 1965-66 | 1966-67 to 1970-71 | 1971-72 to 1975-76 | 1976-77 to 1980-81 | 1981-82 to 1985-86 | 1986-87 to 1989-90 |
|---|---|---|---|---|---|---|---|---|
| (e) Rest of the world | 8 | 61 | 62 | 50 | -107 | -54 | 201 | 356 |
| (f) Others | 1 | -58 | - | -10 | 183 | 1,724 | 5,518 | 1,459 |
| **9. Deficits financed by instruments** | | | | | | | | |
| (a) Currency and deposits | -48 | -28 | -60 | -92 | -465 | -479 | -776 | -485 |
| (b) Securities | 199 | 257 | 457 | 351 | 421 | 1,428 | 5,085 | 10,379 |
| (c) Loans & advances | 239 | 672 | 1,290 | 1,552 | 1,966 | 4,405 | 12,996 | 14,720 |
| (d) Trade credits | 24 | -62 | -90 | -41 | 717 | 1,070 | 1,099 | 327 |
| (e) Others | 2 | -15 | - | 44 | 760 | 2,721 | 8,952 | 8,860 |
| **10. Discrepancy (4-5)** | -190 (-47) | 154 (11) | 432 (16) | 159 (6) | 410 (7) | -111 (-1) | 5,547 (15) | -1,061 (-3) |

Notes : (a) *Figures in brackets are percentages to total investment*
(b) *Sources : Reserve Bank of India, Flow of Funds Accounts of the Indian Economy : 1981-82 to 1985-88*
*Reserve Bank of India Bulletin January 1992 for data for the years 1986-87 to 1989-90.*

❑ The resource gap for financing investment in physical assets increased from 56% during the First Plan to over 70% during the next fifteen years. Again, from 61% during 1971-72 to 1975-76 it increased to 78% during 1976-77 to 1980-81 period. During the eighties the gap has remained high at 90%.

❑ Borrowings by the private corporate sector since the seventies has been over three and a half times its lendings to other sectors during the eighties, banking and financial institutions accounted for two-third share in total borrowings, whereas surpluses of households sector contributed about 15% resources directly by subscribing to securities of the private corporate sector.

## 11.7  Trends in Capital Issues by Private Sector : 1957 – 1991-92

*(RBI compilation)*

|  | Shares Rs. crores | Debentures bonds, etc Rs. crores | Total Capital Issued | |
|---|---|---|---|---|
|  |  |  | Rs. crores | As % of gross domestic saving |
| **Calendar Years** | | | | |
| 1957 | 58.2 | 50.1 | 108.3 | 7.90 |
| 1960 | 80.4 | 31.0 | 111.4 | 5.39 |
| 1965 | 81.0 | 38.3 | 119.3 | 3.15 |
| 1970 | 76.7 | 19.5 | 96.2 | 1.42 |
| 1975 | 68.3 | 38.6 | 106.9 | 0.72 |
| 1980 | 92.9 | 125.2 | 218.1 | 0.76 |
| 1981 | 170.3 | 139.4 | 309.7 | 0.93 |
| 1982 | 124.9 | 300.3 | 425.2 | 1.25 |
| 1983 | 155.5 | 616.2 | 771.7 | 1.98 |
| **Financial Years** | | | | |
| 1983-84 | 244.7 | 644.9 | 909.6 | 2.33 |
| 1984-85 | 244.7 | 613.6 | 858.3 | 2.04 |
| 1985-86 | 899.6 | 845.7 | 1,745.3 | 3.38 |
| 1986-87 | 1,008.2 | 1,555.7 | 2,563.9 | 4.77 |
| 1987-88 | 1,110.9 | 666.3 | 1,777.2 | 2.63 |
| 1988-89 | 1,032.5 | 2,132.4 | 3,164.9 | 3.80 |
| 1989-90 | 1,218.8 | 5,246.4 | 6,465.2 | 5.78 |
| 1990-91 | 1,285.7 | 2,931.4 | 4,217.1 | 3.38 |
| 1991-92 | 1,730.5 | 4,019.8 | 5,750.3 | 3.88 |

❏  Since 1980 the capital market has assumed a vigourous role for providing funds to the corporate sector for project financing as well as for meeting the working capital requirements.

❏  Since 1982, the amounts raised in the form of debenture issues – both convertible and non-convertible – have in most years exceeded the amounts issued for share capital.

❑ According to data compiled by the CMIE, the capital issued in various forms such as shares, debentures, rights or private placements etc. reached an all-time high of Rs.6,787 crores during 1989-90. This constituted 6.75% of the gross domestic saving of the country for that year. Much higher proportion was recorded for once way back in 1957 at 7.90%.

❑ Besides the private sector corporate issues included in the table above, the public sector companies, institutions and mutual funds have increasing taken recource to the capital market particularly since 1985-86. During 1990-91, the funds so raised by public sector amounted to Rs.5,251 crores and were more than the sum issued by the private corporate sector. In 1991-92 the public sector enterprises raised an estimated Rs. 7,116 crores in a total capital issued of Rs.13193 crores. Significant portions of the public sector issues offer many fiscal, tax and other benefits for the investors.

## 11.8   Trends in growth of number of listed companies and their stock values : 1961-1991

| | As at December end | | | | |
|---|---|---|---|---|---|
| | 1961 | 1975 | 1980 | 1990 | 1991 |
| 1. No. of Stock exchanges | 7 | 8 | 9 | 19 | N.A. |
| 2. No. of Companies | | | | | |
| a. (i) Non-government public and private limited companies on 31st March | 26,007 | 40,007 | 55,668 | 1,97,393 | 2,19,542 |
| (ii) of which public limited | 6,663 | 7,275 | 8,864 | 20,234 | N.A. |
| b. Public Limited companies listed on Indian Stock exchanges as on 31 Dec. | 1,203 | 1,852 | 2,265 | 5,968 | N.A. |
| c. Stocks issues[1] of listed companies | 2,111 | 3,230 | 3,697 | 8,289 | N.A. |
| 3. Paid-up Capital (Rs. crores) | | | | | |
| a. (i) Non-government public and private limited companies | 1,272 | 3,235 | 4,536 | 14,738 | 18,686 |
| (ii) As on 31 March ... of which paid - up capital of public limited companies | 915 | 2,484 | 3,445 | 11,439 | N.A. |
| b. Paid-up share capital of listed companies | 675 | 2,142 | 3,212 | 12,864 | N.A. |
| c. Paid-up value of all stock issues[1] | 753 | 2,614 | 3,973 | 27,761 | N.A. |
| d. Market value of all stock issues[1] of listed companies | 1,292 | 3,237 | 6,749 | 70,521 | N.A. |

*Notes : (1) Includes equity and preference share capital and debentures/bonds.*

❑ Companies get their shares listed an stock exchanges because apart from importing easy marketability to their shares, the companies acquire the status of widely-held companies which entitles them to for lower rates of tax on their profits. Besides, this also facilitates easier access to institutional and bank finances.

❑ Over the span of 30 years between 1961 and 1990, the total number of non-government companies increased eight fold. But among than the public limited companies increased three fold in number. During the same period the number of listed companies increased five fold. Yet only 30% of the public limited companies were listed on the stock exchanges at the end of March 1991 compared to 18% at the end of December 1961. The number of stock issues of listed companies expanded four fold.

❑ As against the trend in terms of number of companies, their paid up capital pattern changed during the 30-year span such that the total paid up capital of all non-government companies expanded eleven fold, that of public limited companies 13 fold and of them the paid up capital of listed companies increased 19 fold. The paid-up value of all stock issues increased 37 fold whereas their market value spurted 54 fold.

❑ In view of the concentration of shareholding by public financial institutions, the availability of floating stock for free to trading is limited. Owing to the increasing participation of general public in stock trading, the market price of many a scrips often turn volatile due to surges in demand against limited trading stock. Speculations by big operators leads to unwarranted flare-up in many scrips.

## 11.9  Stock Exchange-wise listed companies and their paid-up capital : 1961-1991

*a. - No. of listed companies    b. Paid-up capital Rs. crores*

| Stock Exchanges | | As at December-end | | | As at March-end |
|---|---|---|---|---|---|
| | | 1961 | 1975 | 1980 | 1990 |
| Bombay | (a) | 297 | 767 | 992 | 2,447 |
| | (b) | 381 | 1,614 | 2,930 | 24,238 |
| Calcutta | (a) | 576 | 730 | 891 | 2,329 |
| | (b) | 326 | 923 | 1,472 | 12,309 |
| Delhi | (a) | 103 | 294 | 452 | 2,003 |
| | (b) | 85 | 428 | 883 | 17,308 |
| Madras | (a) | 249 | 373 | 398 | 586 |
| | (b) | 112 | 702 | 788 | 8,535 |
| Ahmedabad | (a) | 96 | 136 | 169 | 731 |
| | (b) | 84 | 278 | 601 | 12,565 |
| Hyderabad | (a) | 19 | 47 | 81 | 241 |
| | (b) | 63 | 51 | 162 | 2,965 |
| Bangalore | (a) | – | – | 163 | 318 |
| | (b) | – | – | 402 | 7,120 |
| Indore | (a) | 8 | 19 | 26 | 109 |
| | (b) | 3 | 28 | 84 | 989 |
| Cochin | (a) | – | – | – | 79 |
| | (b) | | | | 5202 |
| Pune | (a) | – | – | – | 115 |
| | (b) | | | | 4,566 |
| Lucknow | (a) | – | – | – | 783 |
| | (b) | | | | 5,716 |
| Ludhiana | (a) | – | – | – | 116 |
| | (b) | | | | 1,006 |
| Guwahati | (a) | – | – | – | 170 |
| | (b) | | | | 2,340 |
| Mangalore | (a) | – | – | – | 20 |
| | (b) | | | | 1,887 |
| Magadh | (a) | | | | 14 |
| | (b) | | | | 550 |

| Stock Exchanges | | As at December-end | | | As at March-end |
|---|---|---|---|---|---|
| | | 1961 | 1975 | 1980 | 1990 |
| Jaipur | (a) | | | | 20 |
| | (b) | | | | 85 |
| Total excluding double accounting | (a) | 1,203 | 1,852 | 2,265 | 5,968 |
| | (b) | 753 | 2,614 | 3,973 | 27,761 |

*Note : (a) The figures may not add-up to totals given as companies listed as more than one stock exchange are counted only once in the total.*
*(b) Paid up value includes equity & preference shares, debentures and bonds.*

❑ The increasing number of stock exchanges, the number of companies listed thereon and the volume and value of trading over the years is indicative of the growing equity cut among the household savers and investors, apart from the growing number of companies becoming public limited and widely held companies in order to avail of concessions in taxation rates as well as easier access to institutional and bank finance for funding their expulsion and diversification projects and increasing working capital requirements.

❑ Financial assets in the household sector savings were initially cultivated by commercial banks as bank deposits. These have gradually started transforming into non-deposit form of holding and moving towards direct participation as shares and securities of companies in their primary and secondary markets in search of better returns. Changing profile of intermediary service agencies like merchant banking, mutual funds and stock broking community has played a significant role in this diversification of household savings.

## 11.10 Scrips Turnover on Bombay Stock Exchange : 1985 to 1991.

*(Rs. crores)*

| Year Month | 1985 | 1986 | 1987 | 1988 | 1989 | 1990 | 1991 |
|---|---|---|---|---|---|---|---|
| Jan. | 451.83 | 914.93 | 1492.46 | 820.77 | 1941.08 | 2729.40 | 1111.00 |
| Feb. | 561.66 | 703.31 | 500.99 | 633.59 | 2126.39 | 1414.81 | 837.99 |
| March | 359.64 | 1050.20 | 1215.34 | 702.63 | 1378.30 | 2655.18 | 2426.99 |
| April | 362.08 | 1074.25 | 529.59 | 628.67 | 2982.49 | 2269.62 | 3732.46 |
| May | 455.59 | 1133.44 | 921.21 | 1821.37 | 2222.55 | 3370.20 | 3248.52 |
| June | 468.39 | 1549.45 | 991.94 | 1817.85 | 2109.06 | 3505.75 | 6476.98 |
| July | 753.38 | 1682.31 | 844.62 | 800.82 | 2538.21 | 4737.53 | 6556.70 |
| August | 306.63 | 1108.30 | 424.71 | 1511.82 | 2519.05 | 5157.11 | 4360.57 |
| Sept. | 440.93 | 1223.26 | 751.18 | 1600.27 | 1959.10 | 2768.96 | 8284.46 |
| Oct. | 454.70 | 576.55 | 303.70 | 2863.25 | 2925.39 | 3744.90 | 5630.01 |
| Nov. | 411.18 | 1288.64 | 554.51 | 1380.95 | 2278.74 | 2234.70 | 6631.39 |
| Dec. | 808.48 | 637.19 | 392.65 | 2691.99 | 3851.67 | 1487.35 | 3838.89 |
| Total : | 6139.98 | 13596.18 | 8740.51 | 17053.22 | 28031.96 | 38209.04 | 53135.96 |
| Monthly Avg. | 511.67 | 1133.01 | 728.38 | 1421.10 | 2336.90 | 3164.09 | 4428.00 |
| High | 808.48 | 1682.31 | 1492.46 | 2863.25 | 3851.67 | 5157.11 | 8284.46 |
| Low | 306.63 | 576.55 | 303.70 | 628.67 | 1378.30 | 1414.81 | 837.99 |
| Daily Avg. | 29.92 | 67.98 | 39.55 | 82.38 | 126.84 | 188.22 | 255.46 |

*Notes : (a) Monthly turnovers may not add up to the total for the year.*

❑ The Bombay stock exchange has grown to be the biggest and most dynamic among the stock exchanges in India and has in no small measure contributed towards turning Bombay into the commercial and financial capital of the country.

❏ The number of companies listed on the Bombay stock exchange at the end of March 1991 was the largest in the country.

❏ Between 1985 and 1991 the aggregate value of trading turnover multiplied 8.65 times. While the lowest monthly turnover increased 2.73-fold, the highest monthly turnover multiplied 10.25 times during the period.

❏ Barring the occasional exceptions of speculative behaviour the price behaviour of shares on the Bombay Stock Exchange is quite sensitive to the economic and political developments concerning the country.

❏ In the early years together with real estate, precious metals, shares of reputed companies were preferred modes of investment for appreciation of holding and steady returns. But in recent years quite a large section of investors indulge in stock trading for capital gains. This has in turn imparted volatility to share prices on the stock exchanges, often out of proportion with the fundamental character of many scrips.

## Expanding Turnover on Bombay Stock Exchange

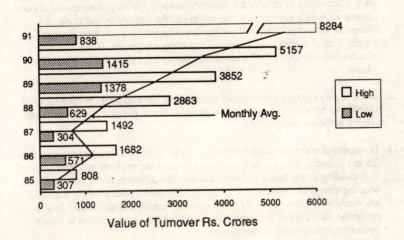

Value of Turnover Rs. Crores

## 11.11 Shareholding Pattern of Private Sector Companies : 1989-90

| Category of Share holding groups | 629 listed on Bombay Stock Exchange | |
|---|---|---|
| | No. of Shares (lakhs) | % to total |
| Individuals and others categories of Shareholders not specified below | 12,225.83 | 29.1 |
| Corporate bodies | 9,962.62 | 23.7 |
| Government/ Financial Institutions | 9,916.90 | 23.6 |
| Foreign | 6,611.73 | 15.8 |
| Directors & their relatives | 1,629.44 | 3.9 |
| Top 50 individual shareholding independent entities | 1,616.19 | 3.9 |
| Total | 41,962.71 | 100.0 |

❏ These data are based on information which the Bombay Stock Exchange has started furnishing in its official directory recently. These pertain to only those companies which have started responding to the enquiry by the stock exchange from each of the listed companies. The information, though representing partial coverage in respect of reporting companies, fills a vital gap which otherwise created all sorts of misconceptions about the shareholding pattern.

❏ Individuals and other unidentified entities hold the maximum portion of shares, but because of their being large in numbers, this group is virtually ineffective in the company affairs.

❏ In respect of effective control or management of companies, the corporate bodies and financial institutions command a controlling position by virtue of their shareholding in the hands of fewer entities. The directors of the companies who together with their relatives, even if supported by the top fifty shareholders would command relatively small quota of almost 8% and would need to recognise the views of the large institutional shareholding entities in issues concerning their managed companies.

❑ Foreign shareholding of 16% represents an average position in the sample companies, but their holding in individual companies under their management would be significantly larger than this average proportion of 16%. They are known to be maintaining little institutional shareholding in their respective companies.

## Shareholding Pattern of Private Sector Companies

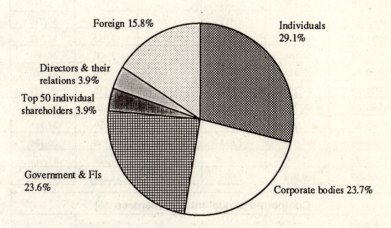

Foreign 15.8%

Individuals
29.1%

Directors & their
relations 3.9%

Top 50 individual
shareholders 3.9%

Government & FIs
23.6%

Corporate bodies 23.7%

## 11.12 Key Financial Indicators of All Non-financial Public Sector Enterprises : 1960-61 – 1989-90

*(Rs. crores)*

| Year | Sales (including other incomes) | Net profits after tax | Net savings | Gross savings | Gross capital formation |
|---|---|---|---|---|---|
| 1960-61 | 1,148 | 90 | 86 | 188 | 579 |
| 1965-66 | 2,971 | 129 | 127 | 335 | 1,580 |
| 1970-71 | 6,721 | 157 | 146 | 588 | 2,175 |
| 1975-76 | 20,678 | 141 | -12 | 901 | 6,419 |
| 1980-81 | 43,677 | - 2,512 | -2,866[1] | 1,232 | 10,789 |
| 1981-82 | 54,096 | - 2,115 | - 2,677[1] | 2,215 | 14,012 |
| 1982-83 | 64,868 | - 1,713 | - 2,393[1] | 3,406 | 16,064 |
| 1983-84 | 73,403 | - 1,907 | - 3,066[1] | 3,608 | 17,163 |
| 1984-85 | 84,399 | - 2,152 | - 3,003[1] | 4,758 | 20,774 |
| 1985-86 | 98,708 | - 2,128 | -3,199[1] | 6,163 | 23,828 |
| 1986-87 | 110,925 | - 1,805 | - 3,433[1] | 7,296 | 27,213 |
| 1987-88 | 127,075 | - 1,878 | - 2,968[1] | 9,198 | 26,181 |
| 1988-89 | 145,896 | - 786 | -2,567[1] | 11,728 | 31,677 |
| 1989-90 | 169,978 | - 1,663 | - 3,760[1] | 13,281 | 38,844 |

| Compound annual rates of increase (%) | | | | | |
|---|---|---|---|---|---|
| 1960-61 to 1989-90 | 18.8 | – | – | 15.8 | 15.6 |

*Notes : (1) Net profits and net savings figures from 1980-81 are not comparable with those for earlier years because of methodological change in provision for depreciation*
*(2) Net Savings = Net profits after tax plus current account transfers*
*Gross Savings = Net Savings plus depreciation*

❑ National accounts statistics is the only source from which limited but dependable data on the financial parameters of operations of public sector as a whole are available.

## 11.13 Key Financial Indicators of Central Government-owned Non-departmental Running Enterprises : 1968-69 to 1990-91

*(Amounts in Rs. crores)*

| Year | No. of enter-prises | Paid-up capital | Reserve and surplus | Capital employ-ed | Sales | Profits after tax | No. of employ-ees (lakhs) | Total emolu-ments |
|------|------|------|------|------|------|------|------|------|
| 1968-69 | 73 | 1,801 | -132 | 3,168 | 2,393 | -28 | 5.54 | 255 |
| 1969-70 | 73 | 1,665 | - 139 | 3,281 | 3,010 | - 3 | 6.13 | 290 |
| 1970-71 | 87 | 1,822 | - 115 | 3,606 | 3,309 | - 3 | 6.60 | 361 |
| 1971-72 | 93 | 2,036 | - 109 | 4,395 | 3,992 | - 19 | 7.01 | 415 |
| 1972-73 | 101 | 2,954 | - 26 | 4,757 | 5,324 | 13 | 9.32 | 541 |
| 1973-74 | 114 | 3,310 | 20 | 5,271 | 6,855 | 59 | 13.44 | 749 |
| 1974-75 | 120 | 3,770 | 150 | 6,654 | 10,185 | 174 | 14.32 | 1,060 |
| 1975-76 | 121 | 4,436 | 340 | 9,006 | 11,688 | 19 | 15.05 | 1,352 |
| 1976-77 | 149 | 5,155 | 465 | 11,097 | 14,911 | 184 | 15.75 | 1,408 |
| 1977-78 | 155 | 6,426 | 426 | 12,065 | 18,020 | - 91 | 16.38 | 1,646 |
| 1978-79 | 159 | 7,108 | 123 | 13,969 | 19,061 | - 40 | 17.03 | 1,908 |
| 1979-80 | 169 | 7,815 | 11 | 16,182 | 23,290 | - 74 | 17.75 | 2,214 |
| 1980-81 | 168 | 8,751 | - 378 | 18,207 | 28,635 | - 203 | 18.39 | 2,619 |
| 1981-82 | 188 | 10,642 | 103 | 21,935 | 36,482 | 445 | 19.39 | 3,133 |
| 1982-83 | 193 | 13,225 | 684 | 26,526 | 41,989 | 613 | 20.25 | 3,649 |
| 1983-84 | 201 | 15,281 | 867 | 29,851 | 47,272 | 241 | 20.12 | 4,465 |
| 1984-85 | 207 | 17,575 | 1,797 | 36,382 | 54,782 | 909 | 21.07 | 5,126 |
| 1985-86 | 211 | 20,501 | 2,875 | 42,965 | 62,360 | 1,172 | 21.54 | 5,576 |
| 1986-87 | 214 | 25,316 | 4,741 | 51,835 | 69,088 | 1,772 | 22.11 | 6,371 |
| 1987-88 | 220 | 26,847 | 7,572 | 55,617 | 81,268 | 2,030 | 22.14 | 7,193 |
| 1988-89 | 226 | 31,171 | 10,503 | 67,629 | 93,137 | 2,994 | 22.09 | 8,683 |
| 1989-90 | 233 | 38,891 | 14,907 | 84,760 | 106,070 | 3,789 | 22.36 | 9,075 |
| 1990-91 | 236 | 42,360 | 17,090 | 101,702 | 118,355 | 2,368 | 22.17 | 10,096 |

| Compound annual rates increase (%) between | | | | | | | |
|---|---|---|---|---|---|---|---|
| 1968-69 & 1990-91 | 15.4 | - | 17.1 | 19.4 | - | 6.5 | 18.2 |

*Notes : (a) Sources : Bureau of Public enterprises,* **Public Enterprises Survey** *(Annual) various issues.*

❏ With gross value added of Rs.31,757 crores, these enterprises account for only 6.7% of the total GDP in 1990-91

❏ In terms of employment, these enterprises account for about one-fourth the number employed in economic enterprise in the public sector or a little less than one-tenth of employment in the organized sector.

❏ 1990-91 was the third year in succession when non-petroleum enterprises taken together recorded net profits. As many as 124 enterprises made profits during 1990-91 of Rs.5431 cores while 109 enterprises incurred a net aggregate loss of Rs.3,063 crores and three others made neither any profit nor any loss during 1990-91. Aggregate net profits to capital employed was only 2.33% and dividend (Rs.365 crores) to paid up capital was only 0.86% since 85% of the net profit was retained.

❏ Net profits of Rs. 2368 crores constituted just 5.6 per cent of the paid-up capital or about 4 per cent of the net worth. As much as 97 per cent of the net profits was earned by the 14 petroleum sector enterprises in 1990-91 (Rs. 2299 crores).

## 11.14 Additional Capital Funds Raised by Financial and Non-financial Public Sector Enterprises Owned by Central Government : 1985-86 to 1992-93

| | Budgetary Support | | | Internal and Extra-Budgetary Resources | |
| | Equity | Loans | Total | Internal resources | Bonds & Debentures |
|---|---|---|---|---|---|
| | 1 | 2 | 3 | 4 | 5 |
| 1985-86 | 3,770 | 2,362 | 6,132 (55.7) | N.A | N.A |
| 1986-87 | N.A | N.A | 7,792 (46.9) | 5,368 (32.3) | 1,364 (8.2) |
| 1987-88 | N.A | N.A | 7,190 (40.3) | 5,700 (31.9) | 2,108 (11.8) |
| 1988-89 | 4,469 (21.0) | 3,382 (15.9) | 7,851 (36.9) | 7,181 (33.8) | 2,476 (11.7) |
| 1989-90 | 4,955 (19.1) | 3,441 13.3 | 8,396 (32.4) | 9,680 (37.4) | 4,493 (17.4) |
| Seventh Plan | | | 3,7361 (40.3) | | |
| 1990-91 | 5,118 (18.2) | 2,447 (8.8) | 595 (27.0) | 10,722 (38.2) | 4,933 (17.6) |
| 1991-92 | 4185 (14.2) | 2735 (9.3) | 6920 (23.5) | 12,007 (40.8) | 5,722 (19.5) |
| 1992-93 (B.E) | 4367 (11.9) | 2477 (6.7) | 6844 (18.6) | 15,084 (41.1) | 6,058 (16.5) |

Notes : (a) Except the figures of 1991-93 and those indicated by asterisk mark, all other figures are only the revised estimates.
(b) B.E.= Budget Estimates.

❏ As part of the Long Term Fiscal policy, the budgetary support to public enterprises has been reduced in each successive year proportions to their total additional capital funds requirement. In turn, they have to rely internal resources increasingly, but the trend shows relatively greater emphasis on raising funds

*(Rs. crores)*

| Internal and Extra-budgetary Resources | | | Total Budgetary & I.E.B.R. (Col. 4 + Col. 7) | Non-plan Budgetary Support | | |
|---|---|---|---|---|---|---|
| External Commercial borrowings / suppliers Credit | Others (deposit & inter-corporate transfers) | Total (Col. 4 to Col. 7) | | Loans | Other Investments | Total (Col. 10 + Col. 11) |
| 6 | 7 | 8 | 9 | 10 | 11 | 12 |
| N.A | N.A | 4,885 (44.3) | 11,017 (100.0) | 608 | 161 | 769 |
| 1,144 (6.9) | 957 (5.7) | 8,833 (53.1) | 16,625 (100.0) | 1,942 | 75 | 2,017 |
| 577 (3.3) | 2,272 (12.71) | 10,657 (59.7) | 17,847 (100.0) | 572 | 51 | 623 |
| 1,056 (5.0) | 2,682 (12.6) | 13,395 (63.1) | 21,246 (100.0) | 867 | 76 | 943 |
| 1,922 (7.4) | 1,384 (5.4) | 174.79 (67.6) | 25,875 (100.0) | 1,131 | 161 | 1292 |
| | | 55,249 (59.7) | 92,610 (100.0) | 5,120 | 524 | 5644 |
| 2,553 (9.1) | 2,251 (8.1) | 20,459 (73.0) | 28,054 (100.0) | 1,067 | 23 | 1,090 |
| 1,854 (6.3) | 2,981 (9.9) | 22,501 (76.5) | 29,421 (100.0) | 758 | 25 | 783 |
| 5,922 (16.1) | 2,842 (7.7) | 29,906 (81.4) | 36.750 (100.0) | 445 | 22 | 467 |

through bonds and external commercial borrowings. Together, the share of internal and extra-budgetary resources (IEBR) could have nearly doubled since the beginning of the Seventh Plan to the end of 1992-93

## 12.1 Trends in Gross National Product and Gross Domestic Product : 1950-51 – 1991-92

*(At current Prices)*

| Year | Gross National Product (GNP) (a) Rs. crores | Gross Domestic Product (GDP) (b) Rs. crores | Mid-Year Population (1 Oct.) crores | Per Capita | |
|---|---|---|---|---|---|
| | | | | GNP Rs. | GDP Rs. |
| | (1) | (2) | (3) | (4) | (5) |
| 1950-51 | 9,325 | 8,979 | 35.9 | 260 | 250 |
| 1955-56 | 10,248 | 9,717 | 39.3 | 261 | 247 |
| 1960-61 | 16,129 | 15,254 | 43.4 | 372 | 351 |
| 1965-66 | 25,981 | 24,063 | 48.5 | 536 | 496 |
| 1970-71 | 42,879 | 39,708 | 54.1 | 793 | 734 |
| 1975-76 | 75,506 | 71,201 | 60.7 | 1,293 | 1,173 |
| 1980-81 | 136,358 | 122,427 | 67.9 | 2,008 | 1,803 |
| 1981-82 | 159,800 | 143,216 | 69.4 | 2,303 | 2,064 |
| 1982-83 | 177,498 | 159,395 | 70.9 | 2,503 | 2,248 |
| 1983-84 | 206,645 | 186,723 | 72.4 | 2,854 | 2,579 |
| 1984-85 | 229,963 | 208,577 | 73.9 | 3,112 | 2,822 |
| 1985-86 | 260,491 | 233,476 | 75.5 | 3450 | 3,052 |
| 1986-87 | 290,169 | 259,055 | 77.0 | 3,768 | 3,364 |
| 1987-88 | 329,997 | 294,266 | 78.5 | 4,204 | 3,749 |
| 1988-89 | 392,373 | 351,724 | 80.0 | 4,905 | 4,397 |
| 1989-90 | 446,428 | 450,601 | 82.0 | 5,444 | 5,495 |
| 1990-91 | 465,827 | 472,660 | 83.9 | 5,552 | 5,634 |
| 1991-92 | 535,055 | 541,888 | 85.6 | 6,251 | 6,330 |
| 1992-93 | 610,000 | 694,800 | 87.3 | 6,987 | 7,959 |

| Year | Gross National Product (GNP) (a) Rs. crores | Gross Domestic Product (GDP) (b) Rs. crores | Mid-Year Population (1 Oct.) crores | Per Capita | |
|---|---|---|---|---|---|
| | | | | GNP Rs. | GDP Rs. |
| Compound annual rates of increase (%) | | | | | |
| | (1) | (2) | (3) | (4) | (5) |
| 1950-51 to 1960-61 | 5.6 | 5.4 | 1.9 | 3.6 | 3.5 |
| 1960-61 to 1970-71 | 10.3 | 10.0 | 2.2 | 7.9 | 7.7 |
| 1970-71 to 1980-81 | 12.3 | 11.9 | 2.3 | 9.7 | 9.4 |
| 1980-81 to 1990-91 | 14.4 | 14.5 | 2.1 | 12.1 | 12.1 |
| 1950-51 to 1990-91 | 10.6 | 10.4 | 2.1 | 8.3 | 8.1 |

Notes : (a) GNP at market prices
     (b) GDP at factor cost
     (c) Data for the last three years are provisional and subject to revisions

❑ The difference between figures in Col.1 and Col.2 is to be explained for the following equation :-
Gross domestic product at factor cost + net factor incomes from rest of the world + indirect taxes – subsidy = Gross national product at market prices.

❑ The net factor income from abroad has been negative since 1982-83 and growing year after year. In 1982-83 it was – Rs.634 crores which increased to – Rs.4173 crores by 1989-90. This drain of factor incomes was largely due to . growing burden of interest payments on external debt of the country. The outward flow of about one percent of the gross domestic product adversely affects our domestic saving and investing capacity.

❑ Indirect taxes, after setting off the growing subsidy, add about 11 to 12% to the domestic product at factor cost, for the price at which various goods and services are obtainable in the marketplace valued in current purchasing power of the rupee.

## 12.2 Trends in Real National Income and Per Capita Income : 1950-51 – 1991-92.

*(At 1980-81 prices)*

| Year | National Income: Net National Product at Factor cost | | | | | |
|---|---|---|---|---|---|---|
| | Total National Income | | | Per Capita Income | | |
| | Rs. Crores | Index | % Change | Rupees | Index | % Change |
| 1950-51 | 40,454 | 100.0 | – | 1,127 | 100.0 | – |
| 1953-56 | 48,288 | 119.4 | 2.5 | 1,229 | 109.0 | 0.6 |
| 1960-61 | 58,602 | 144.9 | 7.0 | 1,350 | 119.8 | 5.0 |
| 1965-66 | 65,734 | 162.5 | -4.7 | 1,355 | 120.3 | -6.8 |
| 1970-71 | 82,211 | 193.2 | 5.2 | 1,520 | 134.9 | 2.8 |
| 1975-76 | 95,433 | 235.9 | 9.5 | 1,572 | 139.5 | 7.0 |
| 1980-81 | 110,685 | 273.6 | 7.5 | 1,630 | 144.7 | 5.2 |
| 1981-82 | 117,140 | 289.6 | 5.8 | 1,688 | 149.8 | 3.5 |
| 1982-83 | 119,704 | 295.9 | 2.2 | 1,688 | 149.8 | 0.0 |
| 1983-84 | 129,392 | 319.8 | 8.1 | 1,787 | 158.6 | 5.9 |
| 1984-85 | 133,844 | 330.9 | 3.4 | 1,811 | 160.7 | 1.3 |
| 1985-86 | 139,059 | 343.7 | 3.9 | 1,842 | 163.5 | 1.7 |
| 1986-87 | 143,682 | 355.2 | 3.3 | 1,866 | 165.6 | 1.3 |
| 1987-88 | 149,408 | 369.3 | 4.0 | 1,903 | 168.9 | 2.0 |
| 1988-89 | 166,200 | 410.8 | 11.2 | 2,078 | 184.4 | 9.2 |
| 1989-90 | 176,159 | 435.4 | 6.0 | 2,148 | 191.4 | 3.8 |
| 1990-91 | 184,460 | 455.0 | 5.2 | 2,227 | 197.6 | 3.7 |
| 1991-92 | 186,135 | 460.0 | 0.9 | 2,174 | 192.9 | -1.1 |
| 1992-93 | 193,940 | 479.0 | 4.2 | 2,222 | 197.1 | 2.2 |
| Compound annual rates of increase (%) | | | | | | |
| 1950-51 to1960-61 | | | 3.8 | | | 1.8 |
| 1960-61 to 1970-71 | | | 3.4 | | | 1.2 |
| 1970-71 to 1980-81 | | | 3.0 | | | 0.7 |
| 1980-81 to 1990-91 | | | 5.4 | | | 3.2 |
| 1950-51 to 1990-91 | | | 3.9 | | | 1.7 |

*Note :* *(a) Data for the latest three years are provisional*
*(b) National income at constant prices is net national product at factor cost*
*= Gross National Product – Depreciation of fixed assets in use for*
*producing goods and services. It is a measure of quantitative output.*

❑ During the forty years ended 1990-91, India's real national income increased
by 370%. During the same period, the population increased by 133%. As a result the per capita real income increased by 98.5%. This explains the rather
low growth of our real per capita income at barely 1.7% per annum. Most of
this meagre increase has benefited the upper 20 to 30% of the population including the employees in the organised sector.

❑ Because of the rising rate of population growth during 1950-51 to 1980-81,
coupled with the decelerating growth rate of national income, the per capita income growth also declined from 1.8% per annum in the 50s to 1.2% and 0.7%
in the 60s and 70s respectively. The per capita income growth improved only
during the 80s, to 3.2% per annum.

## Growth of National Income and of Per Capita Income

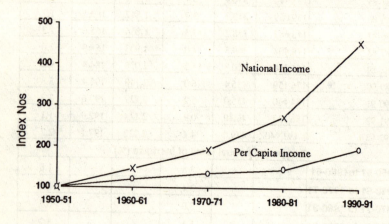

## 12.3 Sectorwise shares in Gross Domestic Product : 1950-51 to 1990-91

*(At Current Prices)*

| Year | Gross Domestic Product at Factor Cost | | | | | | |
|---|---|---|---|---|---|---|---|
| | Rs. crores | | | | % Share in GDP | | |
| | Agricultural Sectors | Industrial Sectors | Services Sectors | Total GDP | Agricultural | Industrial | Services |
| 1950-51 | 5,009 | 1,366 | 2,604 | 8,979 | 55.8 | 15.2 | 29.0 |
| 1955-56 | 4,579 | 1,780 | 3,358 | 9,717 | 47.10 | 18.3 | 34.6 |
| 1960-61 | 6,990 | 3,157 | 5,107 | 15,254 | 45.8 | 20.7 | 33.5 |
| 1965-66 | 10,600 | 5,268 | 8,195 | 24,063 | 44.1 | 21.9 | 34.0 |
| 1970-71 | 17,937 | 8,703 | 13,068 | 39,708 | 45.2 | 21.9 | 32.9 |
| 1975-76 | 28,839 | 16,898 | 25,464 | 71,201 | 40.5 | 23.7 | 35.8 |
| 1980-81 | 46,649 | 31,715 | 44,063 | 122,427 | 38.1 | 25.9 | 36.0 |
| 1981-82 | 52,685 | 38,195 | 52,336 | 143,216 | 36.8 | 26.7 | 36.5 |
| 1982-83 | 56,151 | 43,392 | 59,852 | 159,395 | 35.2 | 27.2 | 37.6 |
| 1983-84 | 67,498 | 50,737 | 68,488 | 186,723 | 36.1 | 27.2 | 36.7 |
| 1984-85 | 71,994 | 57,850 | 78,733 | 208,577 | 34.5 | 27.7 | 37.8 |
| 1985-86 | 77,280 | 65,435 | 90,761 | 233,476 | 33.1 | 28.0 | 38.9 |
| 1986-87 | 82,515 | 73,481 | 103,059 | 259,055 | 31.8 | 28.4 | 39.8 |
| 1987-88 | 92,458 | 83,544 | 118,264 | 294,266 | 31.4 | 28.4 | 40.2 |
| 1988-89 | 114,758 | 97,919 | 139,047 | 351,724 | 32.6 | 27.8 | 39.6 |
| 1989-90 | 127,201 | 113,469 | 160,899 | 401,569 | 31.7 | 28.2 | 40.1 |
| 1990-91 | 153,119 | 130,143 | 189,337 | 472,599 | 32.4 | 27.5 | 40.1 |
| Average Sector at shares (%) | | | | | | | |
| 1951-52 to 1960-61 | – | – | – | – | 50.1 | 17.7 | 32.2 |
| 1961-62 to 1970-71 | – | – | – | – | 45.4 | 21.4 | 33.2 |

| 1971-72 to 1980-81 | – | – | – | – | 40.8 | 24.2 | 35.0 |
|---|---|---|---|---|---|---|---|
| 1981-82 to 1990-91 | – | – | – | – | 33.6 | 27.7 | 38.7 |
| 1951-52 to 1990-91 | – | – | – | – | 42.4 | 22.8 | 34.8 |

❑ The long term growth trend of real GDP has exhibited definite improvement from about 3.5% per annum till the middle of seventies to nearly 5% in the following period, with a significant break at 1979-80 whereafter there has been a consistently positive and accelerated growth averaging around 5.5% during the eighties.

❑ The improvement in the overall GDP growth rate has been accompanied by a perceptible change in the sectoral composition of the domestic output such that the share of agricultural sectors has steadily declined, which has been offset by rise in shares of industrial sectors and services sectors. During the eighties, the services sectors have become as important as agricultural sector, and the share of services sectors has steadily surpassed that of the agricultural sectors.

## Structural Transformation of the Economy
## Sectorwise Shares in GDP

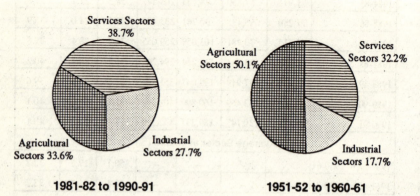

Services Sectors 38.7%

Agricultural Sectors 33.6%

Industrial Sectors 27.7%

**1981-82 to 1990-91**

Agricultural Sectors 50.1%

Services Sectors 32.2%

Industrial Sectors 17.7%

**1951-52 to 1960-61**

## 12.4 Sectorwise Growth Rates of Gross Domestic Product : 1950-51 – 1990-91

*(At 1980-81 Prices)*

| Year | Gross Domestic Product at Factor Cost | | | | | | | |
|---|---|---|---|---|---|---|---|---|
| | Rs. crores | | | | % Change over previous year | | | |
| | Agricultural Sectors | Industrial Sectors | Services Sectors | Total GDP | Agricultural | Industrial | Services | Total |
| 1950-51 | 23,741 | 6,914 | 12,216 | 42,811 | – | – | – | – |
| 1955-56 | 27,318 | 9,214 | 14,641 | 51,173 | -0.9 | 9.7 | 5.1 | 2.6 |
| 1960-61 | 31,995 | 12,588 | 18,321 | 62,904 | 6.7 | 10.2 | 5.6 | 7.1 |
| 1965-66 | 31,208 | 17,520 | 23,394 | 72,122 | -11.0 | 3.1 | 2.7 | -3.7 |
| 1970-71 | 40,214 | 21,380 | 28,832 | 90,426 | 7.1 | 1.4 | 4.9 | 5.0 |
| 1975-76 | 44,668 | 25,024 | 35,278 | 104,968 | 12.9 | 5.5 | 6.8 | 9.0 |
| 1980-81 | 46,649 | 31,715 | 44,063 | 122,427 | 12.9 | 3.5 | 4.2 | 7.2 |
| 1981-82 | 49,406 | 34,233 | 46,250 | 129,889 | 5.9 | 7.9 | 5.0 | 6.1 |
| 1982-83 | 48,803 | 35,858 | 49,254 | 133,915 | -1.2 | 4.7 | 6.5 | 3.1 |
| 1983-84 | 54,080 | 38,992 | 51,793 | 144,865 | 10.8 | 8.7 | 5.2 | 8.2 |
| 1984-85 | 54,097 | 41,330 | 55,092 | 150,469 | 0.0 | 6.0 | 6.4 | 3.9 |
| 1985-86 | 54,252 | 43,225 | 59,123 | 156,600 | 0.3 | 4.6 | 7.3 | 4.1 |
| 1986-87 | 53,335 | 46,252 | 63,124 | 162,711 | -1.7 | 7.0 | 6.8 | 3.9 |
| 1987-88 | 53,549 | 49,250 | 67,242 | 170,041 | 0.4 | 6.5 | 6.5 | 4.5 |
| 1988-89 | 61,789 | 63,244 | 72,692 | 187,725 | 15.4 | 28.4 | 8.1 | 10.4 |
| 1989-90 | 63,940 | 56,684 | 78,705 | 199,329 | 3.5 | - 10.4 | 8.3 | 6.0 |
| 1990-91 | 66,292 | 52,913 | 90,586 | 209,791 | 3.7 | - 6.7 | 15.1 | 5.2 |
| 1991-92 | 65,398 | 52,455 | 94,483 | 212,316 | - 1.4 | - 0.9 | 4.3 | 1.2 |
| 1992-93 | – | – | – | 221,168 | – | – | – | 4.2 |
| Compound annual rates of increase (%) | | | | | | | | |
| 1950-51 to 1960-61 | – | – | – | – | 3.0 | 6.2 | 4.1 | 3.9 |

| | | | | | | | |
|---|---|---|---|---|---|---|---|
| 1960-61 to 1970-71 | – | – | – | – | 2.3 | 5.4 | 4.6 | 3.7 |
| 1970-71 to 1980-81 | – | – | – | – | 1.5 | 4.0 | 4.3 | 3.1 |
| 1980-81 to 1990-91 | – | – | – | – | 3.6 | 6.7 | 6.6 | 5.6 |
| 1950-51 to 1974-75 | – | – | – | – | 2.2 | 5.3 | 4.2 | 3.4 |
| 1974-75 to 1990-91 | – | – | – | – | 3.3 | 6.0 | 6.0 | 5.0 |
| 1950-51 to 1990-91 | – | – | – | – | 2.6 | 5.6 | 4.9 | 4.1 |

❑ The perceptible changes in sectoral share in the GDP mentioned in the preceding table came about due to changes in relative rates of growth of real output of different sectors over the years. The growth rate of agricultural output has been consistently below those of the other two broad sectors, namely, industrial and service sectors. The eighties witnessed the highest growth rates in all the three sectors, but the improvements were more marked in the industrial and services sectors.

## Sectorwise Growth Rate of Real GDP % per annum

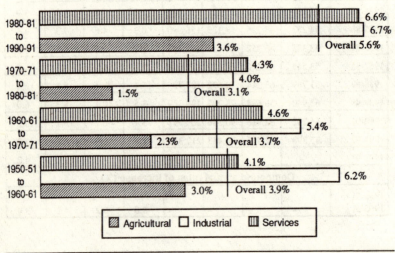

## 12.5 Net Domestic Product by Industry of origin : 1950-51 – 1990-91

### A. Absolute figures

*(At current Prices)*

| Activity | | Rs. crores | | | | |
|---|---|---|---|---|---|---|
| | | 1950-51 | 1960-61 | 1970-71 | 1980-81 | 1990-91 |
| **1** | **Agricultural Sectors** | **4,906** | **6,727** | **17,261** | **44,091** | **144,613** |
| a | Agriculture | 4,590 | 6,314 | 16,190 | 40,056 | 136,927 |
| b | Forestry & logging | 278 | 345 | 864 | 3,229 | 7665 |
| c | Fishing | 38 | 68 | 207 | 806 | 4021 |
| **2** | **Industrial Sector** | **1,317** | **2900** | **7,597** | **26,855** | **107,141** |
| a | Mining & Quarrying | 57 | 133 | 318 | 1,474 | 5,973 |
| b | Manufacturing | 994 | 2,102 | 5,219 | 18,698 | 73,826 |
| | Factory | 461 | 1,035 | 2,784 | 10,050 | 44,069 |
| | Non-factory | 533 | 1,067 | 2,435 | 8,648 | 29,757 |
| c | Electricity, gas & water supply | 18 | 56 | 216 | 912 | 3,345 |
| d | Construction | 248 | 609 | 1,844 | 5,771 | 23,997 |
| **3** | **Services Sector** | **2,343** | **4,605** | **11,788** | **39,394** | **168,768** |
| a | Transport, Storage & Communications | 211 | 419 | 1,115 | 3,724 | 25,104 |
| | Railway | 75 | 160 | 288 | 559 | 4,141 |
| | Other transport | 96 | 193 | 599 | 2,438 | 16,866 |
| | Storage | 6 | 9 | 27 | 114 | 373 |
| | Communications | 34 | 57 | 201 | 613 | 3,724 |
| b | Trade, hotels & restaurants | 580 | 1,184 | 3,438 | 14,322 | 58,046 |
| | Trade | 548 | 1,120 | 3,241 | 13,555 | 55,069 |
| | Hotels & Restaurant | 32 | 64 | 197 | 767 | 2977 |
| c | Finance & real estate | 764 | 1,611 | 3,569 | 9,264 | 33,535 |
| | Banking & insurance | 70 | 159 | 642 | 3,344 | 20,272 |
| | Real estate etc. | 694 | 1,452 | 2,927 | 5,920 | 13,263 |

| Activity | Rs. crores | | | | |
|---|---|---|---|---|---|
| | 1950-51 | 1960-61 | 1970-71 | 1980-81 | 1990-91 |
| d  Community & personal services | 788 | 1,391 | 3,666 | 12,084 | 52,083 |
|     Public administration & defence | 256 | 538 | 1,635 | 5,307 | 25,343 |
|     Other Services | 532 | 853 | 2,031 | 6,777 | 26,740 |
| Commodity Sectors (1+2) | 6,223 | 9,627 | 24,858 | 70,946 | 251,754 |
| Non-commodity Sector (3) | 2,343 | 4,605 | 11,788 | 39,394 | 168,768 |
| **Total** | **8,566** | **14,232** | **36,646** | **110,340** | **420,522** |

## B. Percentages

*(At current Prices)*

| Activity | Percentage Shares in total NDP | | | | |
|---|---|---|---|---|---|
| | 1950-51 | 1960-61 | 1970-71 | 1980-81 | 1990-91 |
| 1  **Agricultural Sectors** | **57.2** | **47.2** | **47.1** | **40.0** | **34.4** |
|   a  Agriculture | 53.6 | 44.4 | 44.2 | 36.3 | 31.6 |
|   b  Forestry & logging | 3.2 | 2.4 | 2.4 | 2.9 | 1.8 |
|   c  Fishing | 0.4 | 0.4 | 0.5 | 0.8 | 1.0 |
| 2  **Industrial Sector** | **15.4** | **20.4** | **20.7** | **24.3** | **25.5** |
|   a  Mining & Quarrying | 0.7 | 0.9 | 0.9 | 1.3 | 1.4 |
|   b  Manufacturing | 11.6 | 14.8 | 14.2 | 16.9 | 17.6 |
|     Factory | 5.4 | 7.3 | 7.6 | 9.1 | 10.5 |
|     Non-factory | 6.2 | 7.5 | 6.6 | 7.8 | 7.1 |
|   c  Electricity, gas & water supply | 0.2 | 0.4 | 0.6 | 0.8 | 0.8 |
|   d  Construction | 2.9 | 4.3 | 5.0 | 5.2 | 5.7 |

| Activity | Percentage Shares in total NDP | | | | |
|---|---|---|---|---|---|
| | 1950-51 | 1960-61 | 1970-71 | 1980-81 | 1990-91 |
| **3  Services Sector** | **27.4** | **32.4** | **32.2** | **35.7** | **40.1** |
| a  Transport, Storage & Communications | 2.5 | 2.9 | 3.0 | 3.4 | 6.0 |
| Railway | 0.9 | 1.1 | 0.8 | 0.5 | 1.0 |
| Other transport | 1.1 | 1.4 | 1.6 | 2.2 | 4.0 |
| Storage | 0.1 | 0.1 | 0.1 | 0.1 | 0.1 |
| Communications | 0.4 | 0.4 | 0.5 | 0.6 | 0.9 |
| b  Trade, hotels & restaurants | 6.8 | 8.3 | 9.4 | 13.0 | 13.8 |
| Trade | 6.4 | 7.9 | 8.8 | 12.3 | 13.1 |
| Hotels & Restaurant | 0.4 | 0.4 | 0.5 | 0.7 | 0.7 |
| c  Finances & real estate | 8.9 | 11.3 | 9.7 | 8.4 | 8.0 |
| Banking & insurance | 0.8 | 1.1 | 1.8 | 3.0 | 4.8 |
| Real estate etc. | 8.1 | 10.2 | 8.0 | 5.4 | 3.2 |
| d  Community & personal services | 9.2 | 9.8 | 10.0 | 11.0 | 12.4 |
| Public administration & defence | 3.0 | 3.8 | 4.5 | 4.8 | 6.0 |
| Other Services | 6.2 | 6.0 | 5.5 | 6.1 | 6.4 |
| Commodity Sectors (1+2) | 72.6 | 67.6 | 67.8 | 64.3 | 59.9 |
| Non-commodity Sector (3) | 27.4 | 32.4 | 32.2 | 35.7 | 40.1 |
| **Total** | **100.0** | **100.0** | **100.0** | **100.0** | **100.0** |

❑ The contribution of agricultural sectors to NDP has significantly decreased from 57% to 34.5% over the 40 years. There has been noteworthy increases in the shares of transport and trade.

❑ The share of large-scale manufacturing has almost doubled and so also of mining.

## 12.6  Growth Rates of Real Net Domestic Product by Industry of Origin 1950-51 – 1990-91

### A. Absolute figures                                    *(At 1980-81 prices)*

| Activity | | Rs. Crores | | | | |
|---|---|---|---|---|---|---|
| | | 1950-51 | 1960-61 | 1970-71 | 1980-81 | 1990-91 |
| **1** | **Agricultural Sectors** | **23,262** | **31,054** | **38,711** | **44,091** | **63,178** |
| a | Agriculture | 20,401 | 27,982 | 34,545 | 40,056 | 58,921 |
| b | Forestry & logging | 2,586 | 2,644 | 3,547 | 3,229 | 2,887 |
| c | Fishing | 275 | 428 | 619 | 806 | 1,370 |
| **2** | **Industrial Sector** | **6,593** | **11,472** | **18,628** | **26,855** | **50,183** |
| a | Mining & Quarrying | 438 | 760 | 1,027 | 1,474 | 2,067 |
| b | Manufacturing | 4,625 | 7,947 | 12,763 | 18,698 | 37,831 |
| | Factory | 2,135 | 3,888 | 6,946 | 10,050 | 22,280 |
| | Non-factory | 2,490 | 4,059 | 5,817 | 8,648 | 15,551 |
| c | Electricity, gas & water supply | 116 | 240 | 567 | 912 | 2,232 |
| d | Construction | 1,414 | 2,525 | 4,271 | 5,711 | 8,053 |
| **3** | **Services Sector** | **10,826** | **16,448** | **25,833** | **39,394** | **75,155** |
| a | Transport, Storage & Communications | 734 | 1,278 | 1,946 | 3,724 | 7,556 |
| | Railway | 149 | 279 | 400 | 559 | 909 |
| | Other transport | 455 | 783 | 1,160 | 2,438 | 5,488 |
| | Storage | 30 | 39 | 48 | 114 | 160 |
| | Communications | 100 | 177 | 338 | 613 | 999 |
| b | Trade, hotels & restaurants | 3,598 | 6,006 | 9,556 | 14,322 | 25,856 |
| | Trade | 3,384 | 5,652 | 9,015 | 13,555 | 24,457 |
| | Hotels & Restaurant | 214 | 354 | 541 | 767 | 1,399 |
| c | Finance & real estate | 2,979 | 4,198 | 6,096 | 9,264 | 19,459 |
| | Banking & insurance | 485 | 955 | 1,783 | 3,344 | 10,795 |
| | Real estate etc. | 2,494 | 3,243 | 4,313 | 5,920 | 8,664 |
| d | Community & personal services | 3,515 | 4,966 | 8,235 | 12,084 | 22,284 |
| | Public administration & defence | 922 | 1,492 | 3,179 | 5,307 | 10,702 |
| | Other Services | 2,593 | 3,474 | 5,056 | 6,777 | 11,582 |

*Contd....*

| Activity | Rs. Crores | | | | |
|---|---|---|---|---|---|
| | 1950-51 | 1960-61 | 1970-71 | 1980-81 | 1990-91 |
| Commodity Sectors (1+2) | 29,855 | 42,526 | 57,339 | 70,946 | 113,361 |
| Non-commodity Sector (3) | 10,826 | 16,448 | 25,833 | 39,394 | 75,155 |
| **Total** | **40,681** | **58,974** | **83,172** | **110,340** | **188516** |

## B. Percentages

| Activity | Compound annual rates of growth % | | | | |
|---|---|---|---|---|---|
| | 1950-51 to 1960-61 | 1960-61 to 1970-71 | 1970-71 to 1980-81 | 1980-81 to 1990-91 | 1950-51 to 1990-91 |
| **1 Agricultural Sectors** | **2.9** | **2.2** | **1.3** | **3.7** | **2.5** |
| a Agriculture | 3.2 | 2.1 | 1.5 | 3.9 | 2.7 |
| b Forestry & logging | 0.2 | 3.0 | -0.9 | -1.1 | 0.3 |
| c Fishing | 4.5 | 3.8 | 2.7 | 5.4 | 4.1 |
| **2 Industrial Sector** | **5.7** | **5.0** | **3.7** | **6.5** | **5.2** |
| a Mining & Quarrying | 5.7 | 3.1 | 3.7 | 3.4 | 4.0 |
| b Manufacturing | 5.6 | 4.9 | 3.9 | 7.3 | 5.4 |
| Factory | 6.2 | 6.0 | 3.8 | 8.3 | 6.0 |
| Non-factory | 5.0 | 3.7 | 4.0 | 6.0 | 4.7 |
| c Electricity, gas & water supply | 7.5 | 9.0 | 4.9 | 9.4 | 7.7 |
| d Construction | 6.0 | 5.4 | 3.1 | 3.4 | 4.4 |
| **3 Services Sector** | **4.3** | **4.6** | **4.3** | **6.7** | **5.0** |
| a Transport, Storage & Communications | 5.7 | 4.3 | 6.7 | 7.3 | 6.0 |
| Railway | 6.5 | 3.7 | 3.4 | 5.0 | 4.6 |
| Other transport | 5.6 | 4.0 | 7.7 | 8.5 | 6.4 |
| Storage | 2.7 | 2.1 | 9.0 | 3.4 | 4.3 |
| Communications | 5.9 | 6.7 | 6.1 | 5.0 | 5.9 |
| b Trade, hotels & restaurants | 5.3 | 4.8 | 4.1 | 6.1 | 5.1 |
| Trade | 5.3 | 4.8 | 4.2 | 6.1 | 5.1 |
| Hotels & Restaurant | 5.2 | 4.3 | 3.6 | 6.2 | 4.8 |

| Activity | Compound annual rates of growth % | | | | |
|---|---|---|---|---|---|
| | 1950-51 to 1960-61 | 1960-61 to 1970-71 | 1970-71 to 1980-81 | 1980-81 to 1990-91 | 1950-51 to 1990-91 |
| c  Finance & real estate | 3.5 | 3.8 | 4.3 | 7.7 | 4.8 |
| Banking & insurance | 7.0 | 6.4 | 6.5 | 12.4 | 8.1 |
| Real estate etc. | 2.7 | 2.9 | 3.2 | 3.9 | 3.2 |
| d  Community & personal services | 3.5 | 5.2 | 3.9 | 6.3 | 4.7 |
| Public administration & defence | 4.9 | 7.9 | 5.3 | 7.3 | 6.3 |
| Other Services | 3.0 | 3.8 | 3.0 | 5.5 | 3.8 |
| Commodity Sectors (1+2) | 3.6 | 3.0 | 2.2 | 4.8 | 3.4 |
| Non-commodity Sector (3) | 4.3 | 4.6 | 4.3 | 6.7 | 5.0 |
| **Total** | **3.8** | **3.5** | **2.9** | **5.5** | **3.9** |

❑ Considering the prevailing standard of living, what we need is a steady aeecleration in the growth rates of commodity sectors. Unfortunately what we had was a deceleration in the growth rates of these sectors till 1970s. During the 1980s rising standards of living reflected the sharp spurt in the growth rates of large-scale manufacturing, power and agriculture. Three successive good monsoons boosted the agricultural growth rate during the eighties to an unprecedented 3.9%.

❑ There has also been an acceleration in the growth rate of the service sector in 1980s.

## 12.7  Supply and Disposal of Nation's Economic Resources : 1960-61 – 1990-91

*(At current prices)*

| A. Supply of Economic Resources | | | | |
|---|---|---|---|---|
| Sources | Rs. Crores | | | |
| | 1960-61 | 1970-71 | 1980-81 | 1990-91 |
| 1. Agriculture etc. | 6,727 | 17,261 | 44,091 | 144,613 |
| 2. Mining, manufacturing | 2,900 | 7,597 | 26,855 | 107,141 |
| 3. Transport, Communications and trade | 1,603 | 4,553 | 18,046 | 83,150 |
| 4. Finance and real estate | 1,611 | 3,569 | 9,264 | 33,535 |
| 5. Community and personal services | 1,391 | 3,666 | 12,084 | 52,083 |
| 6. Net domestic product at factor cost (1 to 5) | 14,232 | 36,646 | 110,340 | 420,522 |
| 7. Consumption of fixed capital (i.e. depreciation) | 1,022 | 3,062 | 12,087 | 52,077 |
| 8. Gross domestic product at factor cost | 15,254 | 39,708 | 122,427 | 472,599 |
| 9. Indirect taxes-subsidies | 947 (5.7) | 3,455 (8.0) | 13,586 (9.7) | 56,938 (10.5) |
| 10. Gross domestic product at market prices | 16,201 | 43,163 | 136,013 | 529,537 |
| 11. Net imports of goods and services | 452 | 45 | 4,567 | 13,088 (a) |
| Total Supply | 16,653 | 43,208 | 140,580 | 542,625 |

| B. Disposal of Economic Resources | | | | |
|---|---|---|---|---|
| **Uses** | **Rs. Crores** | | | |
| 1. Government consumption expenditure | 1,072 (6.4) | 3,838 (8.9) | 13,084 (9.3) | 63,325 (11.7) |
| 2. Private consumption expenditure | 13,442 (80.7) | 32,545 (75.3) | 98,128 (69.8) | 341,822 (63.0) |
| 3. Gross fixed captial formation | 2,156 | 6,305 | 26,276 | 116,868 |
| (a) Public Sector | 1,055 | 2,394 | 11,693 | 51,637 |
| (b) Private Sector | 1,101 | 3,911 | 14,583 | 65,231 |
| 4. Increase in Stocks | 427 | 1,074 | 2,177 | 10,221 |
| 5. Statistical discrepency | -444 | -554 | 915 | 10,389 (a) |
| Total uses | 16,653 | 43,208 | 140,580 | 542,625 |

Notes : (a) *Estimated as current account deficit*
     (b) *Includes net purchase of expatriates.*
       *Figures within brackets indicate percent of total.*

❑ The difference between the GDP at factor cost and at market prices is caused by the sharp increase in the net indirect taxes on purchase of goods and services out of the factor incomes earned. The increasing indirect taxes affect lower income groups most.

❑ The claim of government consumption expenditure on nation's resources increased from 6.4% in 1960-61 to 11.7% in 1990-91. Likewise, the resources used for gross fixed capital formation increased from 12.9% in 1960-61 to 21.5% in 1990-91. Consequently the share of private consumption shrank from 80.7% to 63.0%, a drop of about a fourth in the share of resources.

## 12.8 Composition and growth of Private Consumption Expenditure : 1960-61 and 1990-91

| Item groups | A : At 1980-81 Prices | | |
|---|---|---|---|
| | Rs. Crores | | Compound annual rate of increase (%) |
| | 1960-61 | 1990-91 | |
| 1. Food, beverages, tobacco | 35,009 | 85,069 | 3.0 |
|     Food | 31,181 | 78,928 | 3.1 |
|     Beverages, pan, intoxicants | 1,825 | 2,338 | 0.8 |
|     Tobacco & its products | 1,738 | 2,209 | 0.8 |
|     Hotels & restaurants | 265 | 1,594 | 6.2 |
| 2. Clothing & footwear | 3,755 | 17,611 | 5.3 |
| 3. Gross rent, fuel, power | 7,486 | 18,055 | 3.0 |
| 4. Furniture, furnishing, appliances & services | 1,248 | 5,809 | 5.3 |
| 5. Medical care & health services | 824 | 3,636 | 5.1 |
| 6. Transport & Communications | 1,467 | 13,941 | 7.8 |
| 7. Recreation, education & cultural services | 1,009 | 5,928 | 6.1 |
| 8. Miscellaneous goods & services | 1,916 | 7,441 | 4.6 |
| Private final consumption in domestic market | 52,714 | 157,490 | 3.7 |
| Per capita consumption (Rs.) | 1,215 | 1,882 | 1.5 |

| Item groups | B : At Current Prices | | | | |
|---|---|---|---|---|---|
| | Rs. crores | | (%) Share | | CARG 1960-61 to 1990-91 |
| | 1960-61 | 1990-91 | 1960-61 | 1990-91 | |
| 1. Food, beverages, tobacco | 8,117 | 190,053 | 60.4 | 55.6 | 11.1 |
|     Food | 7,073 | 173,510 | 52.6 | 50.8 | 11.3 |
|     Beverages, pan, intox. | 385 | 5,016 | 2.9 | 1.5 | 8.9 |
|     Tobacco & products | 562 | 8,051 | 4.2 | 2.4 | 9.3 |
|     Hotels & restaurants | 97 | 3,476 | 0.7 | 1.0 | 12.7 |
| 2. Clothing & footwear | 1,191 | 33,977 | 8.9 | 9.9 | 11.8 |

| Item groups | | B: At Current Prices | | | |
|---|---|---|---|---|---|
| | | Rs. crores | | (%) Share | | CARG 1960-61 to 1990-91 |
| | | 1960-61 | 1990-91 | 1960-61 | 1990-91 | |
| 3. | Gross rent, fuel, power | 2,437 | 36,871 | 18.1 | 10.8 | 9.5 |
| 4. | Furniture, furnishing, appliances & services | 307 | 10,689 | 2.3 | 3.1 | 12.6 |
| 5. | Medical care & health services | 205 | 8,182 | 1.5 | 2.4 | 13.1 |
| 6. | Transport & Communications | 394 | 36,238 | 2.9 | 10.6 | 16.3 |
| 7. | Recreation, education & cultural services | 341 | 11,534 | 2.5 | 3.4 | 12.5 |
| 8. | Miscellaneous goods & services | 450 | 14,278 | 3.3 | 4.2 | 12.2 |
| | Private final consumption in domestic market | 13,442 | 341,822 | 100.0 | 100.0 | 11.4 |
| | Per capita consumption (Rs.) | 310 | 4,084 | – | – | 9.0 |

*Note : CARG = Compound Annual Rate of Growth*

❑  Between 1960-61 and 1990-91, the private final consumption expenditure in real terms increased at the rate of 3.7% per annum. The lowest increases of 3.0% were recorded in the groups "Food, beverages and tobacco" and "Gross rent, fuel and power", while the highest growth rate was on "transport, communications and storage" (7.8%) followed by "Recreation, education and cultural services" (6.1%).

❑  Within "Food etc." group the expenditure on hotels and restaurants increased at a high rate of 6.2% per annum in real terms. In the "Transport" group, the largest growth occured in the personalised transport facilities.

❑  In money terms, the growth rate of expenditure was again the highest on transport etc. facilities followed by medical care.

❑  The annual rate of increase in private consumption of 3.7% per annum is to be viewed against the average annual population growth rate of 2.2% during the period. As a result, the annual rate of increase in per capita consumption increased at the rate of only 1.5% in real terms.

## 13.1 Gross Domestic Saving and Gross Domestic Capital Formation : 1950-51 – 1991-92

*(At current prices)*

| Year | Rs. crores | | | As % of G.D.P. | | |
|---|---|---|---|---|---|---|
| | Gross domestic saving | Gross domestic capital formation | Net capital inflow | Gross domestic saving | Gross domestic capital formation | Net capital inflow |
| **1950- 51** | 975 | 954 | -21 | 10.4 | 10.2 | -0.2 |
| **1955 - 56** | 1,430 | 1,469 | 39 | 13.9 | 14.3 | 0.4 |
| **1960 - 61** | 2,063 | 2,544 | 481 | 12.7 | 15.7 | 3.0 |
| **1965 - 66** | 3,791 | 4,390 | 599 | 14.5 | 16.8 | 2.3 |
| **1970 - 71** | 6,783 | 7,177 | 394 | 15.7 | 16.6 | 0.9 |
| **1975 - 76** | 14,928 | 14,811 | -117 | 19.0 | 18.8 | -0.2 |
| **1980 - 81** | 28,786 | 30,880 | 2,094 | 21.2 | 22.7 | 1.5 |
| **1981 - 82** | 33,478 | 36,069 | 2,591 | 21.0 | 22.6 | 1.6 |
| **1982 - 83** | 34,068 | 36,634 | 2,566 | 19.1 | 20.6 | 1.5 |
| **1983 - 84** | 38,971 | 41,488 | 2,517 | 18.8 | 20.0 | 1.2 |
| **1984 - 85** | 42,158 | 45,450 | 3,293 | 18.2 | 19.6 | 1.4 |
| **1985 - 86** | 51,664 | 57,898 | 6,234 | 19.7 | 22.1 | 2.4 |
| **1986 - 87** | 53,738 | 60,093 | 6,355 | 18.4 | 20.6 | 2.2 |
| **1987 - 88** | 67,561 | 74,386 | 6,825 | 20.3 | 22.4 | 2.1 |
| **1988 - 89** | 83,298 | 94,432 | 11,134 | 21.1 | 23.9 | 2.8 |
| **1989 - 90** | 100,471 | 111,192 | 10,721 | 22.3 | 24.7 | 2.4 |
| **1990 - 91** | 125,109 | 139,793 | 14,684 | 26.5 | 29.6 | 3.1 |
| **1991 - 92** | 148,039 | 155,407 | 7,368 | 27.3 | 28.7 | 1.4 |

*Notes:*    *Data for the latest four to five years are provisional.*

❑ In recent years our rate of gross domestic capital formation has been between 21% and 24%. This is a pretty high figure. But it should be noted that in most years our domestic saving has been insufficient to finance this high rate of investment. Consequently, we have to supplement the domestic saving by inflow of capital from rest of the world which consists of long-term investment funds and draw down on foreign exchange reserves necessitated by deficits on current account in the balance of payments.

❑ The inflow of capital reached a peak level of 3.7% of the GDP in 1957-58. It steadily declined for some years, until the Sixth Plan when it averaged 1.4%, but again rose during the Seventh Plan to average 2.4% of GDP.

❑ All owing for the leakages of capital expenditure, corruptions and high cost of investment goods, the remainder has given us over 5% annual growth rate in recent years. If we can reduce such drains of investible funds and also improve the productivity of assets created over the years, we could attain much higher growth rates. Getting more output from assets, is what we need badly.

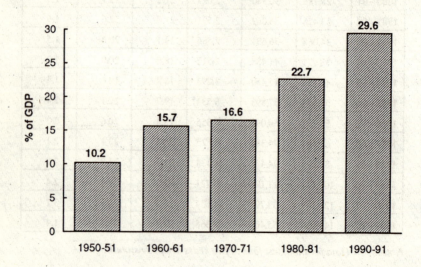

**Gross Domestic Capital Formation as % of GDP**

## 13.2 Shares of Public and Private Sectors in Gross Domestic Savings and Gross Capital Formation : Annual Average.

A : Gross Domestic Savings (At current prices)

| Plan Periods | By broad sectors (Rs. crores) | | | % shre in total savings | | As % of GDP at market prices | | |
|---|---|---|---|---|---|---|---|---|
| | Public Sector | Private Sector | Total | Public Sector | Private Sector | Public Sector | Private Sector | Total |
| First Plan 1951 - 56 | 169 | 874 | 1,043 | 16.2 | 83.8 | 1.7 | 8.6 | 10.3 |
| Second Plan 1956 - 61 | 273 | 1,368 | 1,641 | 16.6 | 83.4 | 1.9 | 9.8 | 11.7 |
| Third Plan 1961 - 66 | 679 | 2,185 | 2,864 | 23.7 | 76.3 | 3.1 | 10.1 | 13.2 |
| Annual Plan 1966 - 69 | 731 | 3,838 | 4,569 | 16.0 | 84.0 | 2.2 | 11.4 | 13.6 |
| Fourth Plan 1969 - 74 | 1,341 | 6,759 | 7,920 | 16.9 | 83.1 | 2.8 | 13.5 | 16.3 |
| Fifth Plan 1974 - 79 | 3,830 | 14,181 | 18,010 | 21.3 | 78.7 | 4.4 | 16.2 | 20.6 |
| Annual Plan 1979 - 80 | 4,967 | 19,731 | 24,698 | 20.1 | 79.9 | 4.3 | 17.3 | 21.6 |
| Sixth Plan 1980 - 85 | 6,607 | 28,885 | 35,492 | 18.6 | 81.4 | 3.6 | 15.8 | 19.4 |
| Seventh Plan 1985 - 90 | 7,701 | 63,645 | 71,346 | 10.8 | 89.2 | 2.3 | 18.1 | 20.4 |
| Annual Plan 1990 - 91 | 5,591 | 1,19,518 | 1,25,109 | 4.5 | 95.5 | 1.2 | 25.3 | 26.5 |
| Annual Plan 1991 - 92 | 10,176 | 1,37,863 | 1,48,039 | 6.9 | 93.1 | 1.9 | 25.4 | 27.3 |

contd. . .

## B : Gross Domestic Capital Formation

| Plan Periods | By broad sectors (Rs. crores) | | | % shre in total capital | | As % of GDP at market prices | | |
|---|---|---|---|---|---|---|---|---|
| | Public Sector | Private Sector | Total | Public Sector | Private Sector | Public Sector | Private Sector | Total |
| First Plan 1951 - 56 | 357 | (a)724 | 1,082 | 33.0 | 67.0 | 3.5 | 7.2 | 10.7 |
| Second Plan 1956 - 61 | 871 | 1,154 | 2,025 | 43.0 | 57.0 | 6.2 | 8.3 | 14.5 |
| Third Plan 1961 - 66 | 1,687 | 1,662 | 3,349 | 50.4 | 49.6 | 7.8 | 7.7 | 15.5 |
| Annual Plan 1966 - 69 | 2,211 | 3,084 | 5,295 | 41.8 | 58.2 | 6.6 | 9.3 | 15.9 |
| Fourth Plan 1969 - 74 | 3,370 | 4,911 | 8,280 | 40.7 | 59.3 | 6.6 | 10.1 | 16.9 |
| Fifth Plan 1974 - 79 | 7,891 | 9,698 | 17,588 | 44.9 | 55.1 | 9.0 | 11.1 | 20.1 |
| Annual Plan 1979 - 80 | 11,818 | 13,460 | 25,278 | 46.8 | 53.2 | 10.3 | 11.8 | 22.1 |
| Sixth Plan 1980 - 85 | 18,789 | 19,315 | 38,104 | 49.3 | 50.7 | 10.3 | 10.6 | 20.9 |
| Seventh Plan 1985 - 90 | 36,609 | 42,991 | 79,600 | 46.0 | 54.0 | 10.6 | 12.1 | 22.7 |
| Annual Plan 1990- 91 | 49,798 | 72,775 | 122,573 | 40.6 | 59.4 | 10.5 | 15.4 | 25.9 |
| Annual Plan 1991 - 92 | 54,966 | 81,118 | 1,36,084 | 40.4 | 59.6 | 10.1 | 15.0 | 25.1 |

*Notes: (a) Adjusted for errors and omissions.*

❑  A rapid expansion of the public sector investment was accepted as the corner stone of the Indian development strategy in the earlier stage of planning. As a result, the share of public sector in gross domestic capital formation increased from about a quarter around 1950-51 to about a half during the closing years of the Third Plan.

❏ The official aim was to further increase the share of public sector investment. However, mainly because of the failure to raise resources through non-inflationary instruments, the uptrend in the share of pubic sector in gross capital formation was reversed after 1965-66, barring some exceptional years. During recent years, the shares of public and private sectors hovered around 49% and 51% respectively.

❏ It is noted that throughout the Seven Plan periods the share of public sector in gross domestic capital formation was much higher than that in total savings. Thus it has always remained a deficit sector drawing upon the surplus savings of other sectors, mainly household sector.

## 13.3 Shares of Public and Private Sectors in Real Gross Domestic Capital Formation : 1960-61 to 1991-92

*(At 1980-81 prices)*

| Year | Rs. crores | | | % share in total | |
|------|-----------|-----------|-------|-----------|-----------|
| | Public Sector | Private Sector | Total | Public Sector | Private Sector |
| 1960 - 61 | 4,805 | 7,543 | 12,348 | 38.9 | 61.1 |
| 1961 - 62 | 4,815 | 6,510 | 11,325 | 42.5 | 57.5 |
| 1962 - 63 | 5,731 | 7,458 | 13,189 | 43.5 | 56.5 |
| 1963 - 64 | 6,473 | 7,403 | 13,878 | 46.6 | 53.4 |
| 1964 - 65 | 6,822 | 8,367 | 15,189 | 44.9 | 55.1 |
| 1965 - 66 | 7,412 | 9,476 | 16,888 | 43.9 | 56.1 |
| Average | 6,251 | 7853 | 14,094 | 44.4 | 55.6 |
| 1966 - 67 | 6,569 | 11,182 | 17,751 | 37.0 | 63.0 |
| 1967 - 68 | 6,662 | 9,565 | 16,227 | 41.1 | 58.9 |
| 1968 - 69 | 6,002 | 9,294 | 15,296 | 39.2 | 60.8 |
| Average | 6,411 | 10,014 | 16,425 | 39.0 | 61.0 |
| 1969 - 70 | 5,997 | 11,584 | 17,581 | 34.1 | 65.9 |
| 1970 - 71 | 6,984 | 11,944 | 18,928 | 36.9 | 63.1 |
| 1971 - 72 | 7,650 | 12,249 | 19,899 | 38.4 | 61.6 |
| 1972 - 73 | 9,053 | 9,570 | 18,623 | 48.6 | 51.4 |
| 1973 - 74 | 8,969 | 14,695 | 23,664 | 37.9 | 62.1 |
| Average | 7,731 | 12,008 | 19,739 | 39.2 | 60.8 |
| 1974 - 75 | 8,757 | 12,576 | 21,333 | 41.0 | 59.0 |
| 1975 - 76 | 11,030 | 10,984 | 22,014 | 50.1 | 49.9 |
| 1976 - 77 | 12,326 | 11,849 | 24,175 | 51.0 | 49.0 |
| 1977 - 78 | 10,445 | 15,866 | 26,311 | 39.7 | 60.3 |
| 1978 - 79 | 12,519 | 19,249 | 31,768 | 39.4 | 60.6 |
| Average | 11,015 | 14,105 | 25,120 | 43.9 | 56.1 |

*contd...*

| Year | Rs. crores | | | % share in total | |
|------|------------|--|--|------------------|--|
|      | Public Sector | Private Sector | Total | Public Sector | Private Sector |
| **1979 - 80** | 13,029 | 15,372 | 28,401 | 45.9 | 54.1 |
| **1980 - 81** | 11,767 | 19,113 | 30,880 | 38.1 | 61.9 |
| **1981 - 82** | 15,178 | 17,207 | 32,385 | 46.9 | 53.1 |
| **1982 - 83** | 16,635 | 13,948 | 30,583 | 54.4 | 45.6 |
| **1983 - 84** | 15,502 | 15,572 | 34,074 | 49.9 | 56.1 |
| **1984 - 85** | 17,588 | 13,406 | 30,994 | 56.7 | 43.3 |
| **Average** | **15,334** | **15,849** | **31,183** | **49.2** | **50.8** |
| **1985 - 86** | 18,216 | 18,167 | 36,383 | 50.1 | 49.9 |
| **1986 - 87** | 19,831 | 14,637 | 34,468 | 57.5 | 42.5 |
| **1987 - 88** | 18,842 | 21,159 | 40,001 | 47.1 | 52.9 |
| **1988 - 89** | 19,173 | 27,948 | 47,121 | 40.7 | 59.3 |
| **1989 - 90** | 20,859 | 30,758 | 51,617 | 40.4 | 59.6 |
| **Average** | **19,384** | **22,534** | **41,918** | **46.2** | **53.8** |
| **1990 - 91** | 21,091 | 35,157 | 56,248 | 37.5 | 62.5 |
| **1990 - 91** | 20,749 | 30,323 | 51,072 | 40.63 | 59.37 |
| **1991 - 92** | 18,760 | 27,686 | 46,446 | 40.39 | 59.61 |

❏ Increase in gross capital formation at current prices in an earlier table reflects the combined result of the real increase in terms of valuable of capital goods and in their prices.

❏ Gross capital formation in real terms reflects by and large the availability of investment goods in the economy i.e. domestic output minus exports plus imports.

❏ Irrespective of the money outlay increases for investment, the real investment would be determined by the availability of the capital goods and capacity of the economy to absorb them. So, when availability of investment goods increases at, say, 5 per cent per annum, the increase in outlays at the rate of 14% would only lead to increase in prices of capital goods.

Thus between 1980-81 and 1990-91 money outlay increased at the average rate of 15.5% per annum, whereas in real terms the gross capital formation increased at the rate of 6.2% per annum. Obviously the difference reflects the 8.8% annual price rise of capital goods.

## 13.4   Gross Domestic Capital Formation by types of Assets : 1950-51 – 1990-91

*(Rs. crores at current prices)*

| Year | Gross fixed capital formation | | | Change in stocks | Gross domestic capital formation | | |
|---|---|---|---|---|---|---|---|
| | Const-ruction | Machin-ery | Total | | Unadju-sted | Errors & Omissi-ons | Adjusted |
| 1950 - 51 | 633 | 241 | 874 | 160 | 1,034 | -80 | 954 |
| 1955 - 56 | 810 | 473 | 1,283 | 133 | 1,416 | 53 | 1,469 |
| 1960 - 61 | 1,331 | 819 | 2,156 | 427 | 2,583 | -39 | 2,544 |
| 1965 - 66 | 2,360 | 1,772 | 4,132 | 295 | 4,427 | -37 | 4,390 |
| 1970 - 71 | 3,960 | 2,345 | 6,305 | 1,074 | 7,379 | -202 | 7,177 |
| 1975 - 76 | 7,340 | 5,990 | 13,330 | 3,076 | 16,406 | -1,595 | 14,811 |
| 1980 - 81 | 13,649 | 12,627 | 26,276 | 2,177 | 28,453 | 2,427 | 30,880 |
| 1981 - 82 | 16,400 | 15,055 | 31,455 | 8,558 | 40,013 | -3944 | 36,069 |
| 1982 - 83 | 18,327 | 17,442 | 35,769 | 5,015 | 40,784 | -4,150 | 36,634 |
| 1983 - 84 | 19,649 | 20,342 | 39,991 | 3,070 | 43,061 | -1,573 | 41,488 |
| 1984 - 85 | 22,719 | 22,849 | 45,568 | 3,220 | 48,788 | -3,338 | 45,450 |
| 1985 - 86 | 27,453 | 26,802 | 54,255 | 8,691 | 62,946 | -5,048 | 57,898 |
| 1986 - 87 | 29,781 | 31,479 | 61,260 | 5,970 | 67,230 | -7,137 | 60,093 |
| 1987 - 88 | 34,053 | 36,785 | 70,838 | 45,458 | 75,386 | -1,000 | 74,386 |
| 1988 - 89 | 39,257 | 43,948 | 83,205 | 11,162 | 94,367 | 85 | 94,432 |
| 1989 - 90 | 44,793 | 51,615 | 96,408 | 9,463 | 105,811 | 5,321 | 111,192 |
| 1990 - 91 | 51,074 | 65,794 | 116,868 | 10,221 | 127,089 | 3,181 | 130,270 |

*contd...*

| Year | Gross fixed capital formation | | | Change in stocks | Gross domestic capital formation | | |
|---|---|---|---|---|---|---|---|
| | Const-ruction | Machin-ery | Total | | Unadju-sted | Errors & Omissi-ons | Adjusted |
| Compound annual rate of increase (%) | | | | | | | |
| 1980 - 81 to 1990 -91 | 14.1 | 17.9 | 16.1 | 16.7 | 16.1 | | 15.5 |
| 1950 - 51 to 990 - 91 | 11.6 | 15.1 | 13.0 | 11.0 | 12.8 | | 13.1 |

*Notes :*     *Errors & omissions = Domestic savings plus net capital inflow from abroad minus gross domestic capital formation.*

❑ Construction accounted for about half of the total investment for fixed assets since the early eighties, declining from around 60% during the early sixties. This activity however involves high degree of wastage, thefts and leakages of funds through corruption. If, only these abuses could be diminished, there could be substantial gains of costs and time in bringing such assets to use for productive purposes.

❑ In early years more than half the investment in machinery and equipment was utilised for imported machinery. It is heartening that in recent years this import component has been brought down to 15 to 16%.

## 13.5   Gross Domestic Capital Formation by industry of use : 1960-61 and 1990-91

*(At current prices)*

| Industry of use | Gross domestic capital formation (Rs. crores) | | % Share in total | | As % of GDP of the industry | |
|---|---|---|---|---|---|---|
| | 1960-61 | 1990-91 | 1960-61 | 1990-91 | 1960-61 | 1990-91 |
| 1.  Agriculture etc | 448 | 12,159 | 16.7 | 10.8 | 2.8 | 2.3 |
|     Agriculture | 424 | 10,988 | 15.8 | 9.8 | 2.6 | 2.1 |
|     Forestry & logging | 8 | 367 | 0.3 | 0.3 | 0.1 | 0.1 |
|     Fishing | 16 | 804 | 0.6 | 0.7 | 0.1 | 0.1 |
| 2.  Industry etc | 996 | 55,171 | 37.1 | 49.2 | 6.1 | 10.4 |
|     Mining & quarries | 43 | 7,297 | 1.6 | 6.5 | 0.3 | 1.4 |
|     Manufacturing | 717 | 32,281 | 26.7 | 28.8 | 4.4 | 6.1 |
|     Factory | 650 | 23,609 | 24.2 | 21.1 | 4.0 | 4.5 |
|     Non-factory | 67 | 8,672 | 2.5 | 7.7 | 0.4 | 1.6 |
|     Construction | 113 | 1,749 | 4.2 | 1.6 | 0.7 | 0.3 |
|     Electricity,gas etc | 123 | 13,844 | 4.6 | 12.3 | 0.7 | 2.6 |
| 3.  Transport, Communications, trade | 505 | 19,988 | 18.9 | 17.8 | 3.1 | 3.8 |
|     Railways | 176 | 3,159 | 6.6 | 2.8 | 1.1 | 0.6 |
|     Other transport & storage | 157 | 8,637 | 5.9 | 7.7 | 1.0 | 1.6 |
|     Communications | 17 | 2,870 | 0.6 | 2.6 | 0.1 | 0.6 |
|     Trade, hotels etc | 155 | 5,322 | 5.8 | 4.7 | 0.9 | 1.0 |
| 4.  Finance & Real Estate | 347 | 14,887 | 12.9 | 13.3 | 2.2 | 2.8 |

*contd...*

| Industry of use | Gross domestic capital formation (Rs. crores) | | % Share in total | | As % of GDP of the industry | |
|---|---|---|---|---|---|---|
| | 1960-61 | 1990-91 | 1960-61 | 1990-91 | 1960-61 | 1990-91 |
| Banking & Insurance | 10 | 2,741 | 0.4 | 2.4 | 0.1 | 0.5 |
| Real estate | 337 | 12,146 | 12.5 | 10.8 | 2.1 | 2.3 |
| 5. Community & personal services | 386 | 9,938 | 14.4 | 8.9 | 2.4 | 1.9 |
| Public adminis-tration & defencce | 307 | 7,281 | 11.4 | 6.5 | 1.9 | 1.4 |
| Other services | 79 | 2,657 | 3.0 | 2.4 | 0.5 | 0.5 |
| Commodity sectors | 1,444 | 67,330 | 53.8 | 60.0 | 8.9 | 12.7 |
| Non-commodity sectors | 1,238 | 44,813 | 46.2 | 40.0 | 7.7 | 8.5 |
| Total by industry | 2,682 | 112,143 | 100.00 | 100.00 | 16.6 | 21.2 |
| Total by type of assets | 2,544 | 130,270 | | | 15.7 | 24.6 |
| Difference | -138 | 18,127 | | | -0.9 | 3.4 |

*Note :*   *Figures of total capital formation by "industry of use" appearing here differ from total by "type of asset appearing in a foregoing table. This is because the estimates by "type of assets" are prepared on the basis of "commodity flow" approach while those by "Industry of use" are prepared on the basis of "expenditure flow" approach.*

❑ Notice the significant decline in the share of investment in the agriculture sector, as opposed to the increased in the share of industrial sector, particularly for mining and electricity. Agricultural sector is primarily in the private sector while industrial sector investment by public sector is in more capital intensive industries and where mining and electricity are almost entirely under the public sector.

# 13                  SAVING & INVESTMENT

## 13.6 Gross Financial Saving and Liabilities of Household sector : 1970-71, 1980-81 & 1989-90

| Items of Savings/ Liabilities | 1970-71 | | 1980-81 | | 1989-90 | |
|---|---|---|---|---|---|---|
| | Rs. crores | % | Rs. crores | % | Rs. crores | % |
| 1. Gross financial savings | 2,110 | 100.0 | 12,117 | 100.00 | 55,706 | 100.00 |
| a. Currency | 355 | 16.8 | 1,625 | 13.4 | 7655 | 13.8 |
| b. Bank deposits | 754 | 35.7 | 5,550 | 45.8 | 21,947 | 39.5 |
| c. Non-banking deposits | 67 | 3.2 | 378 | 3.1 | 1,224 | 2.2 |
| d. Trade debt (Net) | 50 | 2.4 | 373 | 3.1 | 130 | 0.2 |
| e. Shares & debentures | 68 | 3.2 | 412 | 3.4 | 1,923 | 3.5 |
| f. Units of UTI | 14 | 0.7 | 31 | 0.3 | 1,856 | 3.3 |
| g. Claims on govt. | 105 | 5.0 | 711 | 5.9 | 7,024 | 12.6 |
| h. LIC fund | 207 | 9.8 | 915 | 7.6 | 4,440 | 8.0 |
| i. Provident/pension funds | 450 | 23.2 | 2,122 | 17.5 | 9,507 | 16.9 |
| 2. Financial liabilities | 591 | 280 | 3,508 | 29.0 | 13,891 | 25.0 |
| a. Bank advances | 509 | 24.1 | 3,093 | 25.5 | 12,508 | 22.5 |
| b. Loans & advances from other financial institutions | 38 | 1.8 | 182 | 1.5 | 1,007 | 1.8 |
| c. Loans & advances from govt. | 69 | 3.3 | 151 | 1.2 | 268 | 0.5 |
| d. Loans & advances from co-operatives | -25 | -1.2 | 82 | 0.7 | 108 | 0.2 |
| Net financial savings (1-2) | 1,519 | 72.0 | 8,609 | 71.0 | 41,815 | 75.0 |

*Notes :* (a) The figures have been compiled from the Reserve bank of India publications namely the Report on Currency and finance and monthly Bulletin incorporating its study on flow of funds.

(b) Figures for 1989-90 are provisional estimates of the RBI

(c) These figures of the RBI on household sector savings do not tally precisely with those compiled by the Central Statistical Organization because of time-lag in communication and conceptual differences in classification of claims in the household sector, although the RBI estimates are by far the best known compilation of household sector savings, which contributes a large component of total domestic financing savings.

(d) Gross financial savings for 1990-91 was Rs. 45,058 crores and that for 1991-92 was Rs. 58,563 crores.

(e) In 1990-91, Life Insurance fund Provident fund were Rs. 5,627 crores and Rs. 11,058 crores respectively.

## 13.7 Price Deflators of Gross Domestic Product and Gross Domestic Capital Formation : 1960-61 – 1990-91

*Base 1980-81 = 100*

| | Index of Price Deflators | | | | | Rates of Gross Domestic Capital Formation | |
|---|---|---|---|---|---|---|---|
| | Gross National Product | Gross Domestic Product | | | Gross Domestic Capital Formation | | |
| | | Total | Commo-dities | Services | | Nominal | Real |
| 1960 - 61 | 23.8 | 24.2 | 22.8 | 27.9 | 20.6 | 15.7 | 18.1 |
| 1965 - 66 | 32.3 | 33.4 | 32.6 | 35.0 | 26.0 | 16.8 | 20.8 |
| 1970 - 71 | 42.7 | 43.9 | 43.3 | 45.3 | 37.4 | 16.6 | 18.7 |
| 1975 - 76 | 67.5 | 67.8 | 65.6 | 72.2 | 67.3 | 18.8 | 18.9 |
| 1980 - 81 | 100.0 | 100.0 | 100.0 | 100.0 | 100.0 | 22.7 | 22.7 |
| 1981 - 82 | 110.3 | 110.2 | 108.6 | 111.0 | 111.4 | 22.6 | 22.3 |
| 1982 - 83 | 118.5 | 119.0 | 117.6 | 121.5 | 119.8 | 20.6 | 20.3 |
| 1883 - 84 | 128.7 | 128.9 | 127.0 | 132.2 | 133.5 | 20.0 | 19.2 |
| 1984 - 85 | 138.2 | 138.6 | 136.1 | 142.9 | 146.6 | 19.6 | 18.5 |
| 1985 - 86 | 148.4 | 149.1 | 146.4 | 153.5 | 159.1 | 22.1 | 20.6 |
| 1986 - 87 | 158.6 | 159.2 | 156.6 | 163.4 | 174.3 | 20.6 | 18.7 |
| 1987 - 88 | 172.4 | 172.1 | 171.2 | 175.9 | 186.0 | 22.4 | 20.6 |
| 1988 - 89 | 186.4 | 187.4 | 184.9 | 191.3 | 200.4 | 23.9 | 22.2 |
| 1989 - 90 | 199.9 | 201.9 | 199.5 | 204.4 | 215.4 | 24.7 | 22.9 |
| 1990 - 91 | 222.5 | 224.8 | 222.9 | 227.1 | 231.6 | 24.6 | 23.6 |
| Compound annual rate of increase (%) Average | | | | | | | |
| 1960 - 61 to 1970- 71 | 6.0 | 6.1 | 6.6 | 5.0 | 6.3 | 15.6 | 18.5 |
| 1970 - 71 to 1980 - 91 | 8.9 | 8.6 | 8.7 | 8.2 | 10.2 | 19.1 | 20.4 |
| 1980 - 91 to 1990 - 91 | 8.3 | 8.4 | 8.3 | 8.5 | 8.8 | 22.2 | 21.1 |
| 1960 - 61 to 1990 - 91 | 7.7 | 7.7 | 7.9 | 7.2 | 8.4 | 19.1 | 20.0 |

❏ Because of the differential in relative rates of increase in prices of gross domestic product and of capital goods, the rates of gross domestic capital formation (as % of GDP) in real terms were higher than the nominal rates before 1979-80. But thereafter the real rates have been lower than the nominal rates of capital formation.

❏ When prices of capital goods rise faster, the investible savings for fixed investments would buy lower quantum of investment goods.

## 14.1 Trends in structure of Government expenditure – Centre, States and Union Territories 1960-61 — 1992-93

*(Rs. crores)*

| | 1960-61 | 1970-71 | 1980-81 | 1991-92(RE) | 1992-93(BE) |
|---|---|---|---|---|---|
| A. Development Expdt. | 1,599 | 4,718 | 24,426 | 140,802 | 149,172 |
| % to total | 61.8 | 56.5 | 66.3 | 60.0 | 59.2 |
| B. Non-development Expdt. | 987 | 3,636 | 12,419 | 91,690 | 102,691 |
| % to total | 38.2 | 43.5 | 33.7 | 39.4 | 40.8 |
| 1. Defence | 281 | 1,199 | 3,867 | 16,350 | 17,500 |
| % to total | 10.9 | 14.4 | 10.5 | 7.0 | 6.9 |
| 2. Interest payments | 218 | 746 | 2,957 | 39,281 | 46,598 |
| % to total | 8.4 | 8.9 | 8.0 | 16.9 | 18.5 |
| 3. Police | 99 | 335 | 1,163 | n.a | n.a |
| % to total | 3.8 | 4.0 | 3.2 | | |
| 4. Others | 389 | 1,356 | 4,432 | n.a | n.a |
| % to total | 15.0 | 16.2 | 12.0 | | |
| Total expenditure | 2,586 | 8,352 | 36,845 | 232,492 | 251,863 |
| | 100.0 | 100.0 | 100.0 | 100.0 | 100.0 |
| **Govt. expdt. as % of GNP** | | | | | |
| Developmental | 10.7 | 11.8 | 17.9 | 26.3 | 24.4 |
| Non-Developmental | 6.6 | 9.1 | 9.1 | 17.1 | 16.8 |
| Total | 17.3 | 20.9 | 27.0 | 43.4 | 41.2 |

\* *Estimated by CMIE*
*Note : BE = Budget Estimates; RE= Revised Estimates*

❑ The overall government expenditure has expanded at a breath-taking place by 216 times between 1950-51 and 1991-92.
❑ The revised estimate for 1991-92 may reach Rs.205,000 crores and claim one third of GNP for the year. What is more, the incremental government expenditure would take away two-fifths of the increment of GNP over the previous year.
❑ The proportion of development expenditure has been more or less stable amount 60-65% of the total government expenditure since 1960-61.
❑ The pace of increase in non-development expenditure has been faster than that of GNP. Thus the proportion of non-development expenditure to GNP has more than doubled between 1960-61 and 1991-92.

❑ While the shares of other components of non-development expenditure have declined since 1960-61 the share of interest payment has increased sharply, particularly doubling since 1980-81 from 8.0% to 16.1% in 1991-92, to become the largest component of non-development expenditure.

❑ Contrary to general impression, the defence expenditure has been stable around 3% of GNP since 1970-71. On the other hand, the interest payment burden on GNP has increased sharply from 1.5% in 1960-61 to 5.3% of GNP in 1991-92. While resources devoted to national security can be controlled, mounting burden of interest cannot be so altered in the short-run.

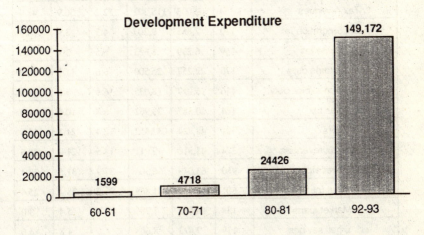

Development Expenditure

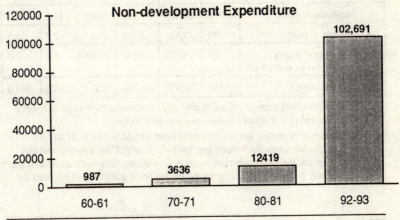

Non-development Expenditure

## 14.2 Structure of Government Incomes : Centre, States & Union Territories : 1960-61 and 1992-93

| | Rs. crores | | | % to total | | |
|---|---|---|---|---|---|---|
| | 1960-61 | 1991-92 (Accts) | 1992-93 (RE) | 1960-61 | 1991-92 | 1992-93 |
| **A. Current revenues** | 1,724 | 145,813 | 168,213 | 66.7 | 72.7 | 69.6 |
| 1. Tax revenues | 1,350 | 102,003 | 118,302 | 52.2 | 50.9 | 48.9 |
| a. Corporation tax | 110 | 7,853 | 9,200 | 4.3 | 3.9 | 3.8 |
| b. Income tax | 169 | 6,269 | 8,653 | 6.5 | 3.1 | 3.6 |
| c. Customs duty | 170 | 22,257 | 25,500 | 6.6 | 11.1 | 10.5 |
| d. Union excise duty | 416 | 16,017 | 18,035 | 16.1 | 8.0 | 7.5 |
| e. Sales tax | 164 | 20,887 | 23,962 | 6.3 | 10.4 | 9.9 |
| f. Others | 321 | 48,724 | 32,952 | 12.4 | 24.1 | 13.6 |
| 2. Non-tax revenues | 374 | 43,810 | 49,911 | 14.5 | 21.9 | 20.6 |
| **B. Capital receipts** | 980 | 63,079 | 66,303 | 37.9 | 31.5 | 27.4 |
| 3. Internal (net) | 601 | 56,950 | 61,869 | 23.2 | 28.4 | 25.6 |
| g. Market loans | 138 | 10,822 | 7,286 | 5.3 | 5.4 | 3.0 |
| h. Small savings | 119 | 9,673 | 8,608 | 4.6 | 4.8 | 3.6 |
| i. Miscellaneous | 285 | 36,455 | 45,975 | 11.0 | 18.2 | 19.0 |
| 4. External (net) | 379 | 5,421 | 4,434 | 14.7 | 2.7 | 1.8 |
| **C. Overall budgetary surplus (+) or deficit (-)** | -118 | -8,522 | +7,242 | -4.6 | -4.2 | 3.0 |
| Total incomes | 2,586 | 200,370 | 241,758 | 100.0 | 100.0 | 100.0 |

❑ The proportions of current revenues and capital receipts have generally been two-thirds and one-third of the total government incomes.

❑ Within current revenues the tax revenues have varied between 51 to 57% though in recent years their share has been declining. Union excise and customs duties are the two main components accounting for over a quarter of the total income. Sales tax generally levied by the State government account for

around 10% the burden of these indirect taxes fall on almost all categories of
people the extent being dependent upon their consumption purchases.

❏ The proportion of direct taxes has been steadily declining even though its burden falls on the upper income strata of people in the taxable income levels.

❏ The reliance on internal capital receipts has been increasing.

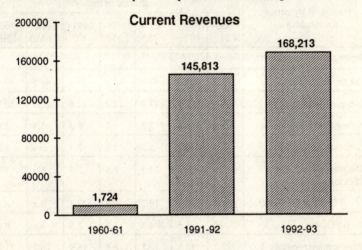

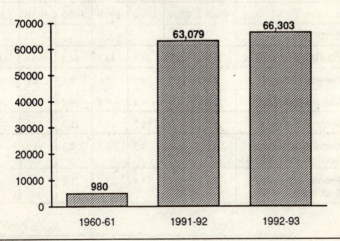

## 14.3 Pattern of Central Government Income and Expenditure through Budgetary Transactions on Revenue and Capital Accounts : 1950-51 – 1993-94

| Heads of income/ expenditure | % shares in totals | | | | | | |
|---|---|---|---|---|---|---|---|
| | 1950-51 | 1960-61 | 1970-71 | 1980-81 | 1991-92 | 1992-93(RE) | 1993-94(BE) |
| **INCOME** | | | | | | | |
| Tax revenue | 71.3 | 44.3 | 49.9 | 47.1 | 48.9 | 49.5 | 49.4 |
| Non-tax revenue | 14.4 | 13.6 | 13.8 | 12.3 | 14.6 | 17.1 | 16.9 |
| Market loans (Net) | -1.9 | 3.6 | 2.2 | 9.7 | 5.4 | 3.1 | 2.9 |
| External loans (Net) | 0.5 | 10.7 | 5.2 | 4.8 | 3.7 | 3.8 | 4.3 |
| Recovery of loans & advances from : | 1.8 | 6.2 | 14.3 | 8.8 | 5.4 | 5.3 | 5.2 |
| (i) State & UT Govts. | 1.4 | 4.7 | 10.2 | 6.6 | 3.1 | n.a. | n.a. |
| (ii) Others | 0.4 | 1.5 | 4.1 | 2.2 | 2.3 | n.a. | n.a. |
| Other capital receipts | 13.2 | 15.9 | 10.1 | 8.1 | 16.9 | 20.2 | 21.2 |
| Uncovered gap | 0.7 | 5.8 | 4.4 | 9.2 | 5.1 | – | – |
| Total : Income | 100.0 | 100.0 | 100.0 | 100.0 | 100.0 | 100.0 | 100.0 |
| **EXPENDITURE** | | | | | | | |
| **Directly Used by Centre** | 76.6 | 62.0 | 54.0 | 64.2 | 64.7 | 67.0 | 68.7 |
| General Services | 4.9 | 4.9 | 9.0 | 9.6 | 9.1 | n.a. | n.a. |
| Interest payments | 12.5 | 9.5 | 9.4 | 9.3 | 19.8 | 26.0 | 28.9 |
| Defence Services | 29.6 | 13.9 | 18.7 | 13.8 | 11.9 | 9.9 | 10.4 |
| Social & Community Services (Incl. loans) | n.a. | n.a. | 3.5 | 3.7 | 2.8 | 4.2 | 4.9 |
| Economic Services (Incl. loans) | n.a. | n.a. | 13.4 | 27.7 | 21.1 | n.a. | n.a. |

*contd* . . .

| Heads of income/expenditure | % shares in totals | | | | | | |
|---|---|---|---|---|---|---|---|
| | 1950-51 | 1960-61 | 1970-71 | 1980-81 | 1991-92 | 1992-93(RE) | 1993-94(BE) |
| **Transferred and lent to States & UTs** | **22.2** | **30.0** | **37.4** | **34.8** | **34.2** | **32.2** | **30.3** |
| Share out of Centre's tax revenue | 8.5 | 8.2 | 11.7 | 13.6 | 12.5 | 16.5 | 16.8 |
| Grants-in-aid | 3.0 | 5.1 | 9.7 | 10.0 | 11.7 | 14.8 | 15.1 |
| Loans and advances | 10.7 | 16.8 | 16.0 | 11.2 | 10.0 | 9.9 | 9.0 |
| **Transferred or lent to others** | **1.2** | **8.0** | **8.5** | **1.0** | **1.1** | **0.8** | **1.0** |
| Grants-in-aid | n.a. | 0.2 | 0.4 | 0.4 | 0.1 | n.a. | n.a. |
| Loans and advances | 1.2 | 7.8 | 8.2 | 0.7 | 1.0 | n.a. | n.a. |
| Total Expenditure | 100.0 | 100.0 | 100.0 | 100.0 | 100.0 | 100.0 | 100.0 |

❑ On the income side, there has been a general stability in the proportions contributed from tax and non-tax revenues to the centre's resource pool. Reliance on external borrowings has been steadily reduced in relative terms. But the share of domestic market borrowings increased sharply since 1980-81 though in 1991-92 its proportion got reduced significantly as other capital receipts contributed larger share. However, resort to borrowings from the RBI increased sharply during the eighties, thus bridging the budgetary gap in an increasingly inflationary manner; some little abatement in 1991-92 would be meaningful only if there is sustained gradual effort at reducing its proportion.

❑ The centre uses a little less than two-thirds of its resources and the rest is transferred mostly to states and Union Territories. Massive increase in share of interest payment has surpassed that of defence services in recent years. Thus increased share has caused reduction in the share of allocations to social and economic services.

## 14.4 Structure of Central Government Incomes on revenue and capital accounts 1970-71 – 1992-93

*(Rs. crores)*

| Heads of incomes | 1970-71 Accts. | 1980-81 Accts. | 1990-91 (RE) | 1992-93 (BE) |
|---|---|---|---|---|
| **A. Revenue Account** | 3,342 (58.9) | 12,829 (53.1) | 60,112 (53.8) | 79,725 (52.3) |
| 1. Taxes on Income & Expt. | 844 | 2,908 | 11,985 | 15,995 |
| a. Corporation Tax | 371 | 1,311 | 6,350 | 8,125 |
| b. Income Tax | 473 | 1,506 | 5,560 | 7,870 |
| c. Others | – | 91 | 75 | – |
| 2. Taxes on Property & Capital Transactions | 33 | 100 | 196 | 1,158 |
| d. Estate duty | 8 | 16 | 4 | 3 |
| e. Wealth tax | 15 | 68 | 190 | 300 |
| f. Others | 10 | 16 | 2 | 855 |
| 3. Taxes on Commodity & Services | 2,330 | 10,172 | 46,735 | 59,371 |
| g. Customs duty | 524 | 3,409 | 20,800 | 25,212 |
| h. Union excise duty | 1,759 | 6,500 | 24,500 | 32,211 |
| i. Others | 47 | 263 | 1,435 | 1,948 |
| 4. Gross Tax Revenue | 3,207 (56.5) | 13,180 (54.5) | 58,916 (52.7) | 76,524 (50.2) |
| Less : States' share | 755 | 3,792 | 14,535 | 19,992 |
| Net tax revenue | 2,452 (43.2) | 9,388 (38.8) | 44,381 (39.7) | 56,532 (37.1) |
| 5. Fiscal Services | 26 | 143 | 668 | 820 |
| 6. Interest Receipts | 589 (10.4) | 1,795 (7.4) | 9.573 (8.6) | 13,464 (8.8) |
| 7. Dividend & Profits | 121 (2.1) | 292 (1.2) | 779 (0.7) | 2,622 (1.7) |

*contd . . .*

| Heads of incomes | 1970-71 Accts. | 1980-81 Accts. | 1990-91 (RE) | 1992-93 (BE) |
|---|---|---|---|---|
| 8. Other revenue receipts | 154 (2.7) | 1,211 (5.0) | 4,711 (4.2) | 6,287 (4.1) |
| B. Capital Account | 2,046 (36.1) | 8,771 (36.3) | 40,904 (36.3) | 47,394 (31.1) |
| 9. Internal debt : Net market loans | 144 (2.5) | 2,716 (11.2) | 8,000 (7.2) | 5000 (3.3) |
| 10. External debt (Net) | 332 (5.9) | 1,334 (5.5) | 3,984 (3.6) | 4,509 (3.0) |
| 11. Recovery of loans and advances | 923 (16.3) | 2,462 (10.2) | 7,095 (6.3) | 7,608 (5.0) |
| 12. Other Capital receipts | 647 (11.4) | 2,259 (9.3) | 21,825 (19.5) | 30,277 (19.9) |
| C. Budgetary deficit financing | 285 (5.0) | 2,577 (10.7) | 10,772 (9.6) | 5,389 (3.5) |
| Total Incomes | 5,673 (100.0) | 24,177 (100.0) | 111,788 (100.0) | 152,499 (100.0) |

*Figures within brackets are percentage shares.*

❑ The debate on annual union budgets are mostly confined to the year to year changes in the tax proposals and in the process some important features of the budget get overlooked such as the general basic stability of the structure of the centre's receipts as also some long term significant changes therein.

❑ Thus, in 1970-71, the revenue receipts formed 58.9% of the total receipts; in 1980-81 and 1990-91 these had declined to around 53% share of tax revenue steadily declined although the states' share of centre's tax revenue has been maintained around 13% of the total receipts of centre.

❑ On the capital account internal debt in the form of market loans raised from captive market of the government-owned financial institutions,was the most rapidly expanding source of funds till 1990-91. Thereafter reliance on this has been reduced.

Part of the increased borrowings was from the non-inflationary source of the genuine savings of the community. But a significant portion represented the most deplorably growing inflationary means like borrowing from the RBI to meet the overall budgetary deficit. This tendency is sought to be drastically curbed in the budget for 1992-93.

## 14.5 Structure of Central Government Development Expenditure on Revenue and capital accounts : 1970-71 – 1992-93

*(Rs. crores)*

| Heads of expenditure | 1970-71 (Accts) | 1980-81 (Accts) | 1990-91 (RE) | 1992-93 (BE) |
|---|---|---|---|---|
| 1. Social & Community Services | 227 (4.0) | 1,008 (4.2) | 3,547 (3.4) | (4,016) (3.0) |
| 2. Economic Services | 864 (15.2) | 5,406 (22.4) | 26,083 (20.2) | 24,718 (18.7) |
| a. General ecooimic services | 36 | 89 | 4,323 | 1,992 |
| b. Agricultural & allied activities | 77 | 1,279 | 5,711 | 6,717 |
| c. Industry & minerals | 297 | 2,067 | 6,086 | 6,236 |
| d. Energy | n.a. | n.a. | 3,870 | 2,889 |
| e. Water, rural development | 70 | 532 | 632 | 701 |
| f. Science, technology | n.a. | n.a. | 1,278 | 1,507 |
| g. Transport & Communication | 144 | 653 | 2,596 | 2,751 |
| h. Railway | 136 | 645 | 1,587 | 1,925 |
| i. Others | 103 | 141 | – | – |
| 3. General Services | – – | 12 – | 241 (0.2) | 255 (0.2) |
| 4. Grants-in-aid to States & UT Govts | 386 (6.8) | 2,121 (8.8) | 10,692 (10.7) | 14,271 (10.8) |
| 5. Loans & Advances | 1,553 (27.4) | 4,968 (20.5) | 9,551 (8.6) | 10,494 (7.9) |
| j. L & A to States & UTs | 1,028 | 2,630 | 6,384 | 7,177 |
| k. Loans to Social & Community Services | 525 | 38 | 4 | 90 |
| l. Loans to eco-services | – | 2,300 | 2,819 | 2,780 |

*contd . . .*

| Heads of expenditure | 1970-71 (Accts) | 1980-81 (Accts) | 1990-91 (RE) | 1992-93 (BE) |
|---|---|---|---|---|
| m. Loans of UTs without legislatures | – | – | 344 | 448 |
| 6. Expenditure of UTs | – | – | 1,615 (1.5) | 1,931 (1.5) |
| Total : Development Expenditure | 3,030 (53.4) | 13,515 (55.9) | 51,729 (44.6) | 55,691 (42.0) |
| Total : Non-development Expenditure | 2,643 (46.6) | 10,662 (44.1) | 60,060 (55.4) | 76,817 (58.0) |
| Total Expdt on Revenue & Capital Accounts | 5,673 (100.0) | 24,177 (100.0) | 111,788 (100.0) | 132,507 (100.0) |

*Figures within brackets indicate percentages to totals.*

❑ Certain imbalances are noticeable as between shares of allocations for certain sectors. Thus while the share of "agriculture" and "industry" together increased from 6.6% in 1970-71 to 9.6% in 1990-91. The share of "transport" and "railways" together declined from 4.9% in 1970-71 to 3.7% in 1990-91. There was no point in devoting larger proportions of resources and building up the commodity sectors, unless there was matching development of infrastructure.

## 14.6 Structure of Central government Non-development Expenditure on Revenue and Capital Accounts : 1970-71 – 1992-93

| Heads of expenditure | 1970-71 (Accts) | 1980-81 (Accts) | 1990-91 (RE) | 1992-93 (BE) |
|---|---|---|---|---|
| 1.  General Services | 2,381 (42.0) | 9,401 (38.9) | 46,681 (45.4) | 66,947 (50.5) |
| a. Organs of state | 72 | 98 | 364 | 475 |
| b. Fiscal services | 111 | 825 | 1,949 | 9,453 |
| c. Interest payments | 606 | 2,664 | 21,850 | 32,000 |
| d. Admn. Services | 166 | 584 | 3,541 | 4,834 |
| e. Pensions & misc. general services | 14 | 1,185 | 3,227 | 2,685 |
| f. Defence services | 1,199 | 3,867 | 15,750 | 17,500 |
| g. Others | 213 | 178 | – | – |
| 2.  Grants-in-aid, contribution etc. | 262 (4.6) | 750 (3.1) | 2,771 (2.0) | 2,288 (1.7) |
| h. Grants to States & UT govts | 226 | 663 | 2,481 | 2,092 |
| i. Aid to other countries | 24 | 57 | 223 | 190 |
| j. Other grants | 12 | 30 | 7 | 7 |
| 3.  Loans & Advances | – | 551 (2.1) | 10,668 (8.0) | 7,582 (5.7) |
| k. L & A to States & UTs | – | 211 | 8,056 | 6,500 |
| l. Adv. to foreign govts | – | 73 | 1,238 | 294 |
| m. Loans for Social & Community Services | – | 135 | 23 | 8 |
| n. Loans for eco. services | – | – | 1,154 | 545 |
| o. Other loans | – | 92 | 198 | 235 |
| Total : Non - Development Expenditure | 2,643 (46.6) | 10,662 (44.1) | 9,814 (55.4) | 76,819 (58.0) |

*contd . . .*

| Heads of expenditure | 1970-71 (Accts) | 1980-81 (Accts) | 1990-91 (RE) | 1992-93 (BE) |
|---|---|---|---|---|
| Total : Development Expenditure | 3,030 (53.4) | 13,515 (55.9) | 51,729 (44.6) | 36,879 |
| Total : Expenditrure on Revenue & Capital Accounts | 5,673 (100.0) | 24,177 (100.0) | 111,788 (100.0) | 113,698 (100.0) |

*Figures within brackets indicate percentages to total*

❑ Interest payments have been increasing rapidly and claiming ever larger share to the central government resources rising for 10.7% in 1970-71 to 22.5% in 1990-91 and expected to claim nearly a quarter of the total resources in 1992-93. Unless the tendency of the government to go on borrowing without restraint is curbed, this trend would continue unabated, for once the loans are contracted, interest thereon has to be paid, and if assets created out of such borrowing do not yield sufficient returns, the interest burden becomes oppressive.

## 14.7 Economic Classification of Central Budget Expenditure : 1980-81 – 1992-93

*(Rs. crores)*

| Major Heads of expenditure | 1980-81 (Accts) | 1984-85 (Accts) | 1989-90 (Accts) | 1991-92 (BE) | 1992-93 (BE) |
|---|---|---|---|---|---|
| 1. Consumption expenditure | 5,174 (23.0) | 9,428 (21.5) | 20,784 (21.9) | 24,655 (20.8) | 27,130 (22.1) |
| 2. Transfer payments | 6,911 (30.7) | 14,937 (34.0) | 37,877 (39.8) | 51,207 (43.2) | n.a. |
| 3. Gross capital formation | 1,907 (8.5) | 4,124 (9.4) | 8,137 (8.6) | 9,750 (8.2) | 11,787 (9.6) |
| 4. Capital transfers | 1,302 (5.8) | 2,958 (6.7) | 6,835 (7.2) | 8,144 (6.9) | n.a. |
| 5. Investment in Shares | 1,407 (6.3) | 2,791 (6.4) | 3,736 (3.9) | 3,223 (2.7) | n.a. |
| 6. Loans for capital formation | 4,521 (20.1) | 7,884 (18.0) | 15,159 (15.9) | 17,121 (14.4) | n.a. |
| 7. Other loans | 704 (3.1) | 1,379 (3.1) | 1,601 (1.7) | 884 (0.8) | n.a. |
| 8. Subscription to international financial organisations | 568 (2.5) | 376 (0.9) | 916 (1.0) | 3,515 (3.0) | n.a. |
| 9. Net purchase of gold and silver | -2 | 2 | 4 | 2 | n.a. |
| Total | 22,492 (100.0) | 43,879 (100.0) | 95,049 (100.0) | 118,501 (100.0) | 122,878 (100.0) |

*Figures within brackets indicate percentages to total expenditure.*

❑ This classification explains the manner in which the Central government uses its budgetary resources for various objectives.

❑ During the eleven years ended 1991-92 the consumption expenditure of the central government increased nearly five fold, but its share in total expenditure declined somewhat to about one-fifth. Within the consumption expenditure about half is used for paying wages and salaries.

❑ Little less than one third of the central government resources are used for capital formation either directly by itself or through grants and loans provided to other bodies.

❑ Within the transfer payments on revenue account, which claims two-fifths of the total expenditure, the two large items are interest payments and subsidies whose claim increased from 8.5% in 1980-81 in 29.2% in 1991-92.

## 14.8 Trends in Tax Revenue of Centre, States and Union Territories : 1950-51 – 1990-91

| Year | Tax revenue : Rs. crores | | | % shares | | Tax revenue as % of GNP | | |
|---|---|---|---|---|---|---|---|---|
| | Direct | Indirect | Total | Direct | Indirect | Direct | Indirect | Total |
| 1950 - 51 | 231 | 428 | 659 | 35 | 65 | 2.5 | 4.6 | 7.1 |
| 1955 - 56 | 255 | 558 | 813 | 31 | 69 | 2.5 | 5.4 | 7.9 |
| 1960 - 61 | 420 | 1,040 | 1,460 | 29 | 71 | 2.6 | 6.4 | 9.0 |
| 1965 - 66 | 775 | 2,273 | 3,048 | 25 | 75 | 3.0 | 8.7 | 11.7 |
| 1970 - 71 | 1,091 | 3,864 | 4,955 | 22 | 78 | 2.5 | 9.0 | 11.5 |
| 1975 - 76 | 2,643 | 8,834 | 11,477 | 23 | 77 | 3.4 | 11.3 | 14.7 |
| 1980 - 81 | 3,575 | 16,746 | 20,321 | 18 | 82 | 2.6 | 12.3 | 14.9 |
| 1981 - 82 | 4,461 | 20,089 | 24,550 | 18 | 82 | 2.8 | 12.6 | 15.4 |
| 1982 - 83 | 4,835 | 22,985 | 27,820 | 17 | 83 | 2.7 | 12.9 | 15.6 |
| 1983 - 84 | 5,355 | 26,471 | 31,826 | 17 | 83 | 2.6 | 12.8 | 15.4 |
| 1984 - 85 | 5,806 | 30,640 | 36,446 | 16 | 84 | 2.5 | 13.3 | 15.8 |
| 1985 - 86 | 6,574 | 36,987 | 43,561 | 15 | 85 | 2.5 | 14.2 | 16.7 |
| 1986 - 87 | 7,328 | 42,714 | 50,042 | 15 | 85 | 2.5 | 14.7 | 17.2 |
| 1987 - 88 | 8,001 | 49,847 | 57,848 | 14 | 86 | 2.4 | 15.1 | 17.5 |
| 1988 - 89 | 10,363 | 57,403 | 67,766 | 15 | 85 | 2.6 | 14.6 | 17.2 |
| 1989 - 90 | 11,351 | 66,875 | 78,226 | 15 | 85 | 2.5 | 15.0 | 17.5 |
| 1990 - 91 | 14,378 | 75,925 | 90,303 | 16 | 84 | 2.7 | 14.5 | 17.2 |

❑ Total tax revenue as percentage of GNP has increased over the 40 years from 7.1% in 1950-51 to 17.5% in 1989-90. The ratio sharply increased in recent years since 1985-86 and has remained above 17% ever since.

❑ The proportion of direct taxes to GNP peaked to 3.4% in 1975-76, which level it had touched in 1963-64. In both cases the proportion declined in subsequent years, even though the income that should have fallen in the tax net must have increased in both the phases with the increase in the national income during those periods. This phenomenon could be a pointer to increasing tax evasion, even after discounting for the tax-exempt incomes, concessions and incentives available for reducing tax liability and to promote savings at the same time.

❑ The proportion of indirect taxes in total tax reverse has increased over the years from 69% in 1951-52 to 86% in 1987-88 and remaining at 85% thereafter. This reflects the wider commodity coverage, increased real output of taxable commodities as also the enhanced rates of indirect taxes.

## Changing Ratio of Direct & Indirect Taxation

**1950 - 51**　　　　　　**1990 - 91**

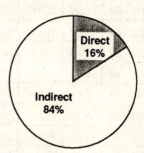

## 14.9 Revenue from Major Taxes of Centre : 1950-51 – 1992-93 (Before Transfer of States' Shares)

| Years | Direct taxes : Rs. crores | | | | | |
| --- | --- | --- | --- | --- | --- | --- |
| | Income tax | Corporate tax | Other taxes | Total Direct | Total tax revenue | As % of total tax revenue |
| 1950 - 51 | 134 | 39 | 4 | 177 | 405 | 43.7 |
| 1955 - 56 | 131 | 37 | 4 | 172 | 485 | 35.5 |
| 1960 - 61 | 169 | 110 | 10 | 289 | 895 | 32.3 |
| 1965 - 66 | 272 | 305 | 27 | 604 | 2,061 | 29.3 |
| 1970 - 71 | 473 | 371 | 25 | 869 | 3,207 | 27.1 |
| 1975 - 76 | 1,214 | 862 | 130 | 2,206 | 7,609 | 29.0 |
| 1980 - 81 | 1,440 | 1,377 | 84 | 2,901 | 13,149 | 22.1 |
| 1981 - 82 | 1,476 | 1,970 | 309 | 3,755 | 15,816 | 23.7 |
| 1982 - 83 | 1,570 | 2,185 | 345 | 4,100 | 17,657 | 23.2 |
| 1983 - 84 | 1,699 | 2,493 | 272 | 4,464 | 20,687 | 21.6 |
| 1984 - 85 | 1,928 | 2,556 | 270 | 4,754 | 23,472 | 20.3 |
| 1985 - 86 | 2,511 | 2,865 | 247 | 5,621 | 28,670 | 19.6 |
| 1986 - 87 | 2,879 | 3,160 | 197 | 6,235 | 32,838 | 19.0 |
| 1987 - 88 | 3,192 | 3,433 | 128 | 6,753 | 37,666 | 17.9 |
| 1988 - 89 | 4,241 | 4,407 | 186 | 8,830 | 44,474 | 19.9 |
| 1989 - 90 | 5,010 | 4,729 | 270 | 10,003 | 51,636 | 19.4 |
| 1990 - 91 | 5,371 | 5,335 | 318 | 11,024 | 57,576 | 19.1 |
| 1991 - 92(RE) | 6,788 | 7,300 | 912 | 15,000 | 67,300 | 22.3 |
| 1992 - 93(BE) | 7,870 | 8,125 | 1,158 | 17,157 | 76,524 | 22.4 |

| Years | Indirect taxes Rs. crores | | | | | |
|---|---|---|---|---|---|---|
| | Union excise | Customs | Others | Total indirect | Total tax revenue | As % of total tax revenue |
| 1950 - 51 | 68 | 157 | 3 | 228 | 405 | 56.3 |
| 1955 - 56 | 145 | 167 | 1 | 313 | 485 | 64.5 |
| 1960 - 61 | 416 | 170 | 20 | 606 | 895 | 67.7 |
| 1965 - 66 | 898 | 539 | 20 | 1457 | 2061 | 70.7 |
| 1970 - 71 | 1759 | 524 | 55 | 2338 | 3207 | 72.9 |
| 1975 - 76 | 3,845 | 1,419 | 139 | 5,403 | 7,609 | 71.0 |
| 1980 - 81 | 6,500 | 3,409 | 273 | 10,182 | 13,149 | 77.4 |
| 1981 - 82 | 7,421 | 4,300 | 340 | 12,061 | 15,816 | 76.3 |
| 1982 - 83 | 8,059 | 5,119 | 379 | 13,557 | 17,657 | 76.8 |
| 1983 - 84 | 10,222 | 5,583 | 418 | 16,223 | 20,687 | 78.4 |
| 1984 - 85 | 11,151 | 7,041 | 526 | 18,718 | 23,472 | 79.7 |
| 1985 - 86 | 12,956 | 9,526 | 568 | 23,050 | 28,670 | 80.4 |
| 1986 - 87 | 14,470 | 11,475 | 657 | 26,602 | 32,838 | 81.0 |
| 1987 - 88 | 16,426 | 13,702 | 785 | 30,913 | 37,666 | 82.1 |
| 1988 - 89 | 18,841 | 15,805 | 998 | 35,644 | 44,474 | 80.1 |
| 1989 - 90 | 22,406 | 18,036 | 1,191 | 41,633 | 51,636 | 80.6 |
| 1990 - 91 | 24,514 | 20,644 | 1,394 | 46,552 | 57,576 | 80.9 |
| 1991 - 92 (RE) | 27,696 | 22,895 | 1,709 | 52,300 | 67,300 | 77.7 |
| 1992 - 93 (BE) | 32,211 | 25,212 | 1,948 | 59,371 | 76,524 | 77.6 |

## 14.10 Transfer of Resources from Centre to States and Union Territories : 1951-52 – 1992-93

*(Rs. crores)*

| | Share in taxes | Grants | Loans | Total | Loan repay-ment | Net transfer | |
|---|---|---|---|---|---|---|---|
| | | | | | | Amt. | % of Centre's total expdt. |
| 1951 - 52 | 53 | 34 | 60 | 147 | 12 | 135 | 22.1 |
| 1955 - 56 | 74 | 48 | 250 | 372 | 25 | 347 | 35.6 |
| 1960 - 61 | 165 | 103 | 339 | 607 | 95 | 512 | 35.2 |
| 1965 - 66 | 276 | 349 | 836 | 1,461 | 276 | 1,185 | 29.3 |
| 1970 - 71 | 755 | 624 | 1,028 | 2,407 | 658 | 1,749 | 30.4 |
| 1975 - 76 | 1,599 | 1,289 | 1,295 | 4,183 | 746 | 3,437 | 27.3 |
| 1980 - 81 | 3,791 | 2,796 | 3,146 | 9,733 | 1,855 | 7,878 | 32.6 |
| 1981 - 82 | 4,274 | 2,855 | 3,460 | 10,589 | 1,264 | 9,325 | 35.3 |
| 1982 - 83 | 4,640 | 3,635 | 4,298 | 12,573 | 1,444 | 11,129 | 34.5 |
| 1983 - 84 | 5,246 | 4,402 | 5,059 | 14,707 | 1,941 | 12,766 | 33.8 |
| 1984 - 85 | 5,777 | 5,220 | 6,177 | 17,174 | 2,454 | 14,720 | 32.1 |
| 1985 - 86 | 7,491 | 7,067 | 8,473 | 23,031 | 1,625 | 21,406 | 42.0 |
| 1986 - 87 | 8,476 | 7,744 | 7,895 | 24,114 | 2,909 | 21,205 | 34.4 |
| 1987 - 88 | 9,598 | 9,210 | 9,414 | 28,222 | 3,562 | 24,660 | 36.9 |
| 1988 - 89 | 10,669 | 10,076 | 10,046 | 30,791 | 3,316 | 27,475 | 35.7 |
| 1989 - 90 | 13,232 | 8,713 | 11,625 | 33,570 | 3,356 | 30,214 | 32.5 |
| 1990 - 91 | 14,535 | 13,295 | 14,885 | 42,713 | 4,653 | 38,060 | 36.1 |
| 1991 - 92 (RE) | 17,199 | 16,079 | 13,804 | 47,082 | 4,297 | 42,785 | 37.8 |
| 1992 - 93 (BE) | 19,992 | 16,363 | 14,125 | 50,480 | 4,692 | 45,788 | .38.4 |

❑ On a net basis about a quarter to one-third of Centre's resources are transferred to state and UT governments. Such transfers finance about 40% of the total expenditure of state governments.

## 14.11 Expenditure on Subsidies by Governments : 1950-51 – 1990-91

|  | Rs. crores | | | As % of | | |
|---|---|---|---|---|---|---|
|  | Central | States | Total | Indirect tax revenue | Total tax revenue | Combined govt. expdt. |
| 1950 - 51 | 26 | 15 | 41 | 9.6 | 6.2 | 4.3 |
| 1960 - 61 | 31 | 62 | 93 | 8.9 | 6.4 | 3.2 |
| 1970 - 71 | 94 | 243 | 337 | 8.7 | 6.8 | 3.8 |
| 1975 - 76 | 470 | 650 | 1,120 | 12.7 | 9.8 | 5.6 |
| 1980 - 81 | 2,028 | 1,132 | 3,160 | 18.9 | 15.6 | 8.1 |
| 1981 - 82 | 1,941 | 1,604 | 3,545 | 17.6 | 14.4 | 8.0 |
| 1982 - 83 | 2,262 | 1,986 | 4,248 | 18.5 | 15.3 | 8.2 |
| 1983 - 84 | 2,749 | 2,856 | 5,605 | 21.2 | 17.6 | 9.3 |
| 1984 - 85 | 4,038 | 3,792 | 7,830 | 25.6 | 21.5 | 10.9 |
| 1985 - 86 | 4,796 | 3,747 | 8,543 | 23.1 | 19.6 | 10.1 |
| 1986 - 87 | 5,451 | 4,344 | 9,795 | 22.9 | 19.6 | 9.6 |
| 1987 - 88 | 5,980 | 5,517 | 11,497 | 23.1 | 19.9 | 10.3 |
| 1988 - 89 | 7,732 | 6,403 | 14,135 | 24.6 | 20.9 | 11.0 |
| 1989 - 90 | 10,474 | 7,369 | 17,843 | 26.7 | 22.8 | 12.1 |
| 1990 - 91 | 12,121 | 6,866 | 18,987 | 25.0 | 21.0 | 11.2 |
| 1991 - 92 (RE) | 12,290 | 6,960(a) | 19,250(a) | – | – | 9.4(a) |
| 1992 - 93 (BE) | 10,487 | 6,013(a) | 16,500(a) | – | – | 7.8(a) |

*Notes : (a) CMIE Estimates*

❑ A disturbing feature of our government finances has been the rapid increase in subsidies both at the centre and state government levels.

❏ These subsidies account for roughly 10% of the Central government expenditure in recent years. About a fourth of the indirect tax revenue of the government is drained in the form of subsidies.

❏ Of late, there has been some appreciation of the pernicious effects of subsidies not only on the public finance but also on the economy in general. That every effort should be made to cut down most of the subsidies is now generally conceded and the central government has taken bold steps in the direction in the last two annual budgets.

❏ It should be noted that the table shows only the explicitly mentioned subsidies. The losses incurred by state-owned commercial enterprises which run into crores of rupee are not included here. To the extent that the losses represent the effect of below-cost administered prices, rates, fares etc. of goods provided to the consumers, would also constitute an implicit subsidy.

## 14.12 Expenditure on Major Explicit Subsidies by Central Government : 1980-81 – 1992-93

*(Rs. crores)*

| | 1980-81 | 1985-86 | 1990-91 | 1991-92 (RE) | 1992-93 (BE) |
|---|---|---|---|---|---|
| **Major Subsidies** | 1,554 | 4,177 | 9,550 | 9,829 | 7,980 |
| Food | 650 | 1,650 | 2,450 | 2,850 | 2,500 |
| Fertiliser | 505 | 1,924 | 4,400 | 5,205 | 5,000 |
|   Indigenous | 170 | 1,600 | 3,650 | 3,500 | 3,500 |
|   Imported | 335 | 324 | 750 | 1,300 | 1,500 |
| Fertiliser subsidy to small farmers | – | – | – | 405 | – |
| Export promotion & market development | 399 | 603 | 2,700 | 1,774 | 480 |
| **Other Subsidies** | 474 | 619 | 2,571 | 2,461 | 2,507 |
| Railways | 69 | 128 | 276 | 313 | 339 |
| Mill-made cloth | 76 | 51 | 10 | 15 | 15 |
| Handloom cloth | 36 | 86 | 188 | 187 | 205 |
| Import/export of sugar, edible oils etc. | – | 23 | – | – | – |
| Interest subsidies | 253 | 271 | 379 | 316 | 325 |
| Debt relief to farmers | – | – | 1,500 | 1,425 | 1,500 |
| Other subsidies | 40 | 60 | 218 | 205 | 123 |
| **Total** | 2,028 | 4,796 | 12,121 | 12,290 | 10,487 |

*Notes : Central subsidies account for roughly two-thirds of all explicitly mentioned subsidies extended by the government.*

❑ Within the Central Subsidies, food and fertiliser together account for almost three-fourths of the total.

❑ But for the debt relief to farmers during the recent three years in succession, the total central government subsidy burden on the exchequer could have reduced during the period.

## 14.13 India's Defence Expenditure : 1975-76 to 1992-93

| Year | Rs. crores | | | As % of GNP | | | As % of total Govt. expdt. |
|---|---|---|---|---|---|---|---|
| | Revenue | Capital | Total | Revenue | Capital | Total | |
| 1975 - 76 | 2,251 | 221 | 2,472 | 2.8 | 0.3 | 3.1 | 12.4 |
| 1976 - 77 | 2,347 | 215 | 2,582 | 2.8 | 0.2 | 3.0 | 11.5 |
| 1977 - 78 | 2,386 | 248 | 2,634 | 2.5 | 0.3 | 2.8 | 10.8 |
| 1978 - 79 | 2,614 | 254 | 2,868 | 2.5 | 0.2 | 2.7 | 10.2 |
| 1979 - 80 | 2,902 | 262 | 3,164 | 2.5 | 0.2 | 2.8 | 10.0 |
| 1980 - 81 | 3,278 | 326 | 3,604 | 2.4 | 0.2 | 2.6 | 9.2 |
| 1981 - 82 | 3,844 | 485 | 4,329 | 2.4 | 0.3 | 2.7 | 9.7 |
| 1982 - 83 | 4,494 | 527 | 5,021 | 2.5 | 0.3 | 2.8 | 9.6 |
| 1983 - 84 | 5,189 | 642 | 5,831 | 2.5 | 0.3 | 2.8 | 9.7 |
| 1984 - 85 | 6,324 | 737 | 7,061 | 2.8 | 0.3 | 3.1 | 9.9 |
| 1985 - 86 | 7,020 | 967 | 7,988 | 2.7 | 0.4 | 3.0 | 9.5 |
| 1986 - 87 | 9,178 | 1,299 | 10,477 | 3.2 | 0.4 | 3.6 | 10.3 |
| 1987 - 88 | 8,860 | 3,108 | 11,968 | 2.7 | 0.9 | 3.6 | 10.8 |
| 1988 - 89 | 9,558 | 3,783 | 13,341 | 2.4 | 1.0 | 3.4 | 10.3 |
| 1989 - 90 | 10,194 | 4,222 | 14,416 | 2.3 | 0.9 | 3.2 | 9.8 |
| 1990 - 91 | 10,874 | 4,553 | 15,427 | 2.0 | 0.8 | 2.9 | 9.1 |
| 1991 - 92 (RE) | 11,467 | 4,883 | 16,350 | 1.9 | 0.8 | 2.7(a) | 8.0(a) |
| 1992 - 93 (BE) | 12,153 | 5,347 | 17,500 | – | – | – | – |

*Notes : (a) Estimated by CMIE*

❑ Notwithstanding its enormous frontiers bordering generally hostile neighbor-
hood and the vast coastlines exposed to two oceans, it is a measure of sagacity
of India's national leadership that the defence expenditure has been contained

between 2.5% and 3.5% of GNP over the past several years. This is a commendable performance on international comparison as well, since in many other countries much higher proportions of their GNP are devoted to defence expenditure.

☐ It should be borne in mind that defence expenditure offers little scope for short-term adjustments to relate it with the years to year variations in GNP or the total government expenditure. Therefore, the trend in respective ratios in the above table should be viewed in the light of this limitation. While efficiency in use of allocated resources should be ensured, austerity should not be over-stretched in defence expenditure.

## Remarkable Reduction in Defence Expenditure

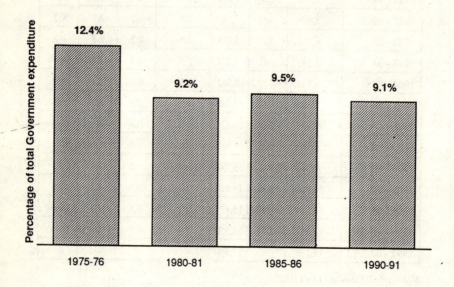

## 14.14 Outstanding Debt and Interest Burden of Central Government : 1980-81 – 1992-93

*(Rs. crores)*

| | 1980-81 (Accts) | 1985-86 (Accts) | 1990-91 (Accts) | 1991-92 (RE) | 1992-93 (BE) | Increase No. of times 1980-81 to 1992-93 |
|---|---|---|---|---|---|---|
| **Internal debts : Bearing interests** | | | | | | |
| Outstanding | 30,864 | 71,039 | 152,903 | 169,058 | 186,973 | 6.06 |
| Interest paid | 1,422 | 3,920 | 9,414 | 11,191 | 13,264 | 9.33 |
| Average rate of interest (%) | 4.61 | 5.52 | 6.16 | 6.62 | 7.09 | 1.54 |
| **External debts** | | | | | | |
| Outstanding | 11,298 | 18,153 | 31,525 | 35,501 | 39,565 | 3.50 |
| Interest paid | 231 | 537 | 1,809 | 2,635 | 2,916 | 12.62 |
| Average rate of interest (%) | 2.05 | 2.96 | 5.74 | 7.42 | 7.37 | 3.60 |
| **Total Public debt** | | | | | | |
| Outstanding | 42,162 | 89,192 | 184,428 | 204,559 | 116,538 | 5.37 |
| Interest paid | 1,653 | 4,457 | 11,223 | 13,826 | 16,180 | 9.79 |
| Average rate of interest (%) | 3.92 | 5.00 | 6.09 | 6.76 | 7.14 | 1.82 |
| **Small Savings Provident Funds** | | | | | | |
| Outstanding | 13,953 | 36,859 | 107,040 | 122,725 | 140,453 | 10.07 |
| Interest paid | 901 | 2,889 | 9,807 | 12,741 | 15,086 | 16.74 |
| Average rate of interest (%) | 6.46 | 7.78 | 9.16 | 10.38 | 10.74 | 1.66 |

*contd . . .*

|  | 1980-81 (Accts) | 1985-86 (Accts) | 1990-91 (Accts) | 1991-92 (RE) | 1992-93 (BE) | Increase No. of times 1980-81 to 1992-93 |
|---|---|---|---|---|---|---|
| **Reserves, deposits & other obligations** | | | | | | |
| Outstanding | 1,832 | 8,574 | 10,799 | 13,034 | 14,854 | 8.11 |
| Interest paid | 49 | 186 | 441 | 683 | 734 | 14.98 |
| Average rate of interest (%) | 2.67 | 2.17 | 4.08 | 5.24 | 4.94 | 1.85 |
| **Total debt & obligations bearing interest** | | | | | | |
| Outstanding | 57,947 | 134,825 | 302,267 | 340,718 | 381,845 | 6.59 |
| Interest paid | 2,604 | 7,512 | 21,471 | 27,250 | 32,000 | 12.29 |
| Average rate of interest (%) | 4.49 | 5.52 | 7.10 | 8.01 | 8.38 | 1.87 |

❑ In a short span of 12 years between 1980-81 and 1992-93, our total debt and interest bearing obligations would have become six-fold (6.59 times) and the interest burden therefrom over 12-fold (12.29 times), since the average rate of interest has nearly doubled (1.87 times) over the period.

❑ Increase in liabilities on account of voluntary small savings induced by tax-saving incentives/revenue sacrifice may not be criticised because of their beneficial side-effects of curbing consumption and demand growths. However, what could be termed most deplorable are the increased resort to debts, and most particularly to the external debts where the average interest rate has multiplied by a much higher factor than in the case of any other debt and obligations, the implications or consequent deterioration of our balance of payments are too well-known presently to warrant any further comment.

## 15.1 Overall Growth Targets and Achievements during Plan Periods.

| Plan | Plan period | Growth Performance | | |
| | | Indicator | % per annum | |
| | | | Target | Actual |
|---|---|---|---|---|
| First Plan | 1951-52 to 1955-56 | N.I. | 2.1 | 3.6 |
| Second Plan | 1956-57 to 1960-61 | N.I. | 4.5 | 4.0 |
| Third Plan | 1961-62 to 1965-66 | N.I. | 5.6 | 2.2 |
| Fourth Plan | 1969-70 to 1973-74 | NDP | 5.7 | 3.3 |
| Fifth Plan | 1974-75 to 1978-79 | GDP | 4.4 | 5.1 |
| Sixth Plan | 1980-81 to 1984-85 | GDP | 5.20 | 5.66 |
| Seventh Plan | 1985-86 to 1989-90 | GDP | 5.0 | 5.8 |
| Eighth Plan | 1992-93 to 1996-97 | GDP | 5.6 | |

Notes : (a) There were virtual Plan holidays during the periods : 1966-67 to 1968-69, 1979-80 and 1990-91 and 1991-92, when development programmes were carried through Annual Plans
(b) Growth targets over performance rates are at factor costs and at constant prices.
(c) N.I. = National Income

## 15.2  Key Macro Indicators of Economic Performance

| Period | Annual growth rate of Real GDP at factor cost | Savings rate (% of GDP) | Investment rate (% of GDP) | Incremental capital output ratio (ICOR) | Current A/C deficit in BOP |
|---|---|---|---|---|---|
| 1951-52 to 1955-56 | 3.61 | 10.28 | 10.64 | 2.9 | 0.36 |
| 1956-57 to 1960-61 | 4.27 | 11.73 | 14.50 | 3.4 | 2.77 |
| 1961-62 to 1965-66 | 2.84 | 13.21 | 15.46 | 5.4 | 2.25 |
| 1966-67 to 1970-71 | 4.66 | 14.35 | 15.98 | 3.4 | 1.63 |
| 1971-72 to 1975-76 | 3.08 | 17.98 | 17.88 | 5.8 | 0.6 |
| 1976-77 to 1980-81 | 3.20 | 21.65 | 21.46 | 6.7 | -0.19 |
| 1981-82 to 1985-86 | 5.20 | 19.82 | 21.42 | 4.1 | 1.60 |
| 1985-86 to 1989-90 | 5.8 | 20.36 | 22.74 | 3.9 | 2.38 |
| Eighth Plan : 1992-93 to 1996-97 (Targets) | 5.6 | 21.6 | 23.0 | 4.1 | 1.4 |

*Notes : Source : C. Rangarajan "Macro economic dimensions of the
Eighth Five Year Plan", 15 Feb. 1992.*

## 15.3 Sectoral Growth Rates and Shares of Gross Value Added at Factor Cost : Sixth Plan, Seventh Plan & Eighth Plan

| A: Sectoral growth Rates (% per annum) | | | | | |
|---|---|---|---|---|---|
| Sector | Sixth Plan 1980-85 | | Seventh Plan 1985-90 | | Eighth Plan 1992-97 |
| | Target | Actual | Target | Actual | |
| 1. Agriculture | 3.83 | 5.53 | 2.5 | 3.4 | 3.0 |
| 2. Mining and Quarrying | 11.25 | 8.13 | 11.75 | 7.0 | 7.5 |
| 3. Manufacturing | 6.50 | 6.18 | 5.5 | 6.7 | 7.3 |
| 4. Electricity etc | 7.15 | 7.88 | 7.9 | 9.6 | 8.2 |
| 5. Construction | 5.10 | 4.80 | 4.8 | 4.1 | 4.3 |
| 6. Transport | | 6.25 | | 8.4 | 7.2 |
| 7. Transpt. & Communication | 5.46 | 6.36 | 7.1 | 8.0 | 7.0 |
| 8. Communication | | 7.04 | | 5.5 | 6.3 |
| 9. Other Services | 5.44 | 5.28 | 6.1 | 7.3 | 6.1 |
| Overall growth rate | 5.20 | 5.66 | 5.0 | 5.8 | 5.6 |

| B: Sectoral Share in GDP : Targets and Actuals (%) | | | | | | | |
|---|---|---|---|---|---|---|---|
| | | Sixth Plan | | Seventh Plan | | Eighth Plan | |
| | | 1979-80 | 1984-85 | 1985-86 | 1989-90 | 1991-92 | '96-97 |
| 1. Agriculture | Assumed | 35.1 | 32.9 | 36.9 | 32.7 | 27.66 | 24.22 |
| | Actual | 36.4 | 35.9 | 34.6 | 32.1 | | |
| 2. Mining and Quarrying | Assumed | 1.5 | 2.0 | 3.5 | 4.8 | 2.04 | 2.23 |
| | Actual | 1.5 | 1.7 | 1.7 | 1.7 | | |
| 3. Manufacturing | Assumed | 18.1 | 19.2 | 14.6 | 15.0 | 21.50 | 23.29 |
| | Actual | 18.9 | 19.4 | 19.4 | 20.2 | | |

*Contd....*

| B: Sectoral Share in GDP : Targets and Actuals (%) | | Sixth Plan | | Seventh Plan | | Eighth Plan | |
|---|---|---|---|---|---|---|---|
| | | 1979-80 | 1984-85 | 1985-86 | 1989-90 | 1991-92 | '96-97 |
| 4. Electricity etc | Assumed | 1.7 | 1.9 | 2.0 | 2.3 | 2.40 | 2.71 |
| | Actual | 1.7 | 1.9 | 2.0 | 2.3 | | |
| 5. Construction | Assumed | 5.1 | 5.1 | 6.2 | 6.2 | 5.13 | 4.82 |
| | Actual | 4.7 | 4.5 | 4.6 | 4.2 | | |
| 6. Transport | Assumed | 4.9 | 5.0 | 5.6 | 6.2 | 5.94 | 6.40 |
| | Actual | 4.7 | 4.8 | 5.1 | 5.4 | | |
| 7. Communication | Assumed | | | | | 1.17 | 1.21 |
| | Actual | | | | | | |
| 8. Other Services | Assumed | 33.6 | 34.0 | 31.2 | 32.9 | 34.16 | 34.92 |
| | Actual | 32.3 | 31.8 | 32.6 | 34.1 | | |
| Total | | 100.00 | 100.00 | 100.00 | 100.00 | 100.00 | 100.00 |

Notes : a : While the assumed targets and shares for Sixth and Seventh Plans are based on "Old Series" of National Accounts Statistics, then in use, the actuals have been worked out on the basis of "New Series" only in order to compare with the Eighth Plan Targets.

## 15.4  Planwise Public Sector Plan Outlays and Actual Expenditures

*(Rs. crores)*

| Five Year Plans | Period | Approved Outlays | Actual expenditures |
|---|---|---|---|
| First Plan | 1950-51 to 1955-56 | 2,358 | 1960 |
| Second Plan | 1956-57 to 1960-61 | 4,500 | 4,672 |
| Third Plan | 1961-62 to 1965-66 | 8,099 | 8,577 |
| Annual Plan | 1966-67 to 1968-69 | 6,757 | 6,625 |
| Fourth Plan | 1969-70 to 1973-74 | 15,902 | 15,779 |
| Fifth Plan | 1974-75 to 1978-79 | 39,303 | 39,426 |
| Annual Plan | 1979-80 | 12,601 | 12,177 |
| Sixth Plan | 1980-81 to 1984-85 | 97,500 | 109,291 (110,467) (a) |
| Seventh Plan | 1985-86 to 1989-90 | 180,000 | 218,730 (221,435) (a) |
| Annual Plans | 1990-91 & 1991-92 | 135,793 | 150,777 |
| Eight Plan | 1992-93 to 1996-97 | 434,100 | |

*Notes : (a) Includes Rs.1,176 crores and Rs.2,705 crores as expenditure on works financed by Central assistance for relief from natural calamities during the respective Five Year Plans*

❑ The figures of approved Plan outlays are in terms of constant prices of the respective base year, while those of actual expenditures are totals of annual plan at respective year's current prices. Since there has been a general tendency of prices to rise throughout the Plan periods, the actual expenditures would have to be deflated to make than comparable with the corresponding approved outlays.

## 15.5   Aggregate Resources for Sixth and Seventh Plans : Public and Private Sectors

| | | Sixth Plan 1980-85 at 1979-80 prices | | Seventh Plan 1985-90 at 1984-85 prices | |
|---|---|---|---|---|---|
| | | Rs. crores | % | Rs. crores | % |
| I | Public Sector Savings | 34,200 | 19.9 | 57,422 | 16.4 |
| | 1. Budgetary savings of the government | 13,430 | 7.8 | 13,671 | 3.9 |
| | a) Balance form current revenues | 14,478 | 8.4 | - 5,249 | - 1.5 |
| | b) Addl : resource mobilisation | 12,452 | 7.2 | 44,702 | 12.8 |
| | c) Less : Current development outlays of public sector | 13,500 | 7.8 | 25,782 | 7.4 |
| | 2. Public enterprises : Non-Financial | 18,245 | 10.6 | 35,485 | 10.2 |
| | 3. Public enterprises : Financial | 2,525 | 1.5 | 8,266 | 2.3 |
| | d) RBI | 2,200 | 1.3 | n a | |
| | e) Nationlised Banks | 175 | 0.1 | n a | |
| | f) Others | 150 | 0.1 | n a | |
| II | Private Sector Savings | 1,15,447 | 67.0 | 224,944 | 70.4 |
| | 1. Household Sector | 104,859 | 60.9 | 216,165 | 62.1 |
| | g) Financial assets | 49,731 | 28.9 | 102,253 | 29.4 |
| | h) Non-financial assets | 55,128 | 32.0 | 113,912 | 32.7 |
| | 2. Private corporate sector | 9,053 | 6.2 | | 8.3 |
| | i) Financial enterprises | 183 | 0.1 | | |
| | j) Non-financial enterprises | 8,870 | 5.1 | 28,779 | |
| | 3. Cooperative sector | 1,535 | 0.9 | | |
| | k) Financial cooperatives | 910 | 0.5 | | |
| | l) Non-financial cooperatives | 625 | 0.4 | | |
| III | Aggregate domestic savings | 149,647 | 86.9 | 302,366 | 86.8 |
| IV | Net Capital inflow | 9,063 | 5.3 | 20,000 | 5.8 |
| V | Total savings available for domestic investment | 158,710 | 92.2 | 322,366 | 92.6 |
| VI | Current development outlays of public sector | 13,500 | 7.8 | 25,762 | 7.4 |
| | Aggregate resources for the plan | 172,210 | 100.0 | 348,148 | 100.00 |

*Notes : (a) Table specially compiled by CMIE with supporting data from plan documents.*

❑ The importance of public sector savings for financing the total plan outlays diminished while household sector provided increased share.

❑ For the first time a negative contribution from the balance of current budgetary revenues of the government was assumed in the Seventh Plan.

## 6th Plan

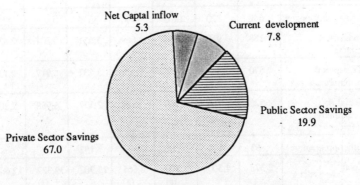

Net Captal inflow
5.3

Current development
7.8

Public Sector Savings
19.9

Private Sector Savings
67.0

## 7th Plan

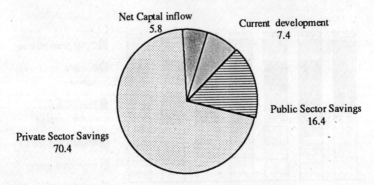

Net Captal inflow
5.8

Current development
7.4

Public Sector Savings
16.4

Private Sector Savings
70.4

## 15.6 Public Sector Plan outlays & Expenditures by Broad Economic Sectors : First Plan to Fifth Plan & 1979-80.

### A : Plan Outlays : Rs. crores

| Heads of development | First Plan : 1951-56 | Second Plan : 1956-61 | Third Plan : 1961-66 | Annual Plans : 1966-69 | Fourth Plan : 1969-74 | Fifth Plan : 1974-79 | Annual Plan : 1979-80 |
|---|---|---|---|---|---|---|---|
| Agriculture & allied activities | 354 | ·510 | 1086 | 1037 | 2728 | 4766 | 1815 |
| Irrigation & power | 648 | 820 | 1662 | 1490 | 3535 | 10,450 | 3707 |
| Industry & minerals | 188 | 950 | 1,784 | 1,669 | 3,631 | 10,201 | 2,837 |
| Transport & communications | 570 | 1,340 | 1,486 | 1,273 | 3,237 | 6,917 | 2,136 |
| Social & community services | 525 | 766 | 1,300 | 859 | ´2,579 | 6,988 | 2,107 |
| Other programmes | 93 | 114 | 200 | 337 | 192 | | |
| Total | 2,378 | 4,500 | 7,500 (a) | 6,665 (a) | 15,902 | 39,322 (a) | 12,601 |

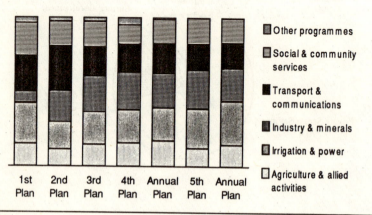

- ▨ Other programmes
- ▤ Social & community services
- ■ Transport & communications
- ▦ Industry & minerals
- ▨ Irrigation & power
- ☐ Agriculture & allied activities

1st Plan   2nd Plan   3rd Plan   4th Plan   Annual Plan   5th Plan   Annual Plan

## B : Actual Expenditures : Rs. crores.

| Heads of development | First Plan : 1951-56 | Second Plan : 1956-61 | Third Plan : 1961-66 | Annual Plans : 1966-69 | Fourth Plan : 1969-74 | Fifth Plan : 1974-79 | Annual Plan : 1979-80 |
|---|---|---|---|---|---|---|---|
| Agriculture & allied activities | 290 | 549 | 1,089 | 1,107 | 2,320 | 4,865 | 1,996 |
| Irrigation & power | 583 | 882 | 1,917 | 1,683 | 4,286 | 11,276 | 3,528 |
| Industry & minerals | 97 | 1,125 | 1,967 | 1,636 | 3,107 | 9,581 | 2,640 |
| Transport & communications | 518 | 1,261 | 2,112 | 1,222 | 3,080 | 6,870 | 2,045 |
| Social & community services | 408 | 733 | 1,320 | 861 | 2,508 | 6,834 | 1,967 |
| Other programmes | 64 | 122 | 173 | 116 | 478 | - | - |
| Total | 1960 | 46,732 | 8,577 | 6,625 | 15,779 | 39,426 | 12,176 |

Notes : *Totals may not tally due to rounding*
  (a) *These figures do not tally with outlays given elsewhere due to reclassification of development heads and inclusion of some expenditures ad-hoc.*

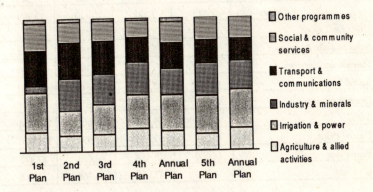

□ Other programmes

▤ Social & community services

■ Transport & communications

▦ Industry & minerals

▨ Irrigation & power

□ Agriculture & allied activities

1st Plan  2nd Plan  3rd Plan  4th Plan  Annual Plan  5th Plan  Annual Plan

## 15.7 Public Sector Plan Outlays and Expenditures by Broad Sectors : Sixth and Seventh Plans

*(Rs. crores)*

| Heads of Development | Sixth Plan 1980-85 | | Seventh Plan 1985-90 | |
|---|---|---|---|---|
| | Outlays (1979-80 prices) | Actual expndts. | Outlays (1984-85 prices) | Actual expndts. |
| Agriculture and allied activities | 5,695 | 6,624 | 10,524 | 12,793 |
| Rural development | 5,364 | 6,997 | 8,901 | 15,247 |
| Special area programmes | 1,480 | 1,580 | 2,804 | 3,470 |
| Irrigation & flood control | 12,160 | 10,930 | 16,979 | 16,590 |
| Energy | 26,535 | 30,751 | 54,822 | 61,689 |
| Power | 19,265 | 18,299 | 34,274 | 37,895 |
| Petroleum | 4,300 | 8,482 | 12,628 | 16,009 |
| Coal | 2,870 | 3,807 | 7,401 | 7,122 |
| Non-conventional energy | 100 | 163 | 519 | 663 |
| Industry & minerals | 15,018 | 16,947 | 22,416 | 29,220 |
| Village & Small ind. | 1,781 | 1,945 | 2,753 | 3,249 |
| Other Industries | 13,237 | 15,002 | 19,663 | 25,971 |
| Transport | 12,412 | 14,209 | 22,645 | 29,548 |
| Railways | 5,100 | 6,587 | 12,335 | 16,545 |
| Others | 7,312 | 7,621 | 10,310 | 12,799 |
| Communications | 3,134 | 3,470 | 4,475 | 8,425 |
| Science, tech. & enviro. | 865 | 1,020 | 2,463 | 3,024 |
| General eco. services | N.A. | N.A. | 1,396 | 2,250 |
| Social services | 14,035 | 15,917 | 31,545 | 34,960 |
| General services | 802 | 847 | 1,028 | 1,514 |
| **Total** | **97,500** | **109,291** | **180,000** | **218,730** |
| Central Plans | 47,250 | 57,825 | 95,534 | 127,520 |
| State Plans | 48,600 | 45,458 | 80,698 | 87,492 |
| UT Plans | 1,650 | 42,008 | 3,768 | 3,718 |

*Notes : (a) While the outlays are at constant prices of the base year of respective plans, the actual expenditures are the sum totals of each year's current prices.*

*(b) Sectorwise break-up of the Seventh Plan outlays has been taken here as appearing in the latest issue of annual economic surveys issued by the Ministry of Finance. These figures differ from those given in the Seventh Plan document of the Planning Commission which are used in the next table (15.7).*

❏ Notice the predominantly large share of the energy sector, and within that of power which is larger than outlay or expenditure for any other sector individually. Transport claimed the most highest share during the Seventh Plan. These infrastructure sectors almost entirely in the public sector are most capital intensive and have long gestation periods. Same is true and evident about irrigation and flood control. Social services is the basic responsibility though not entirely, of the public sector, which justifies large allocation of resources.

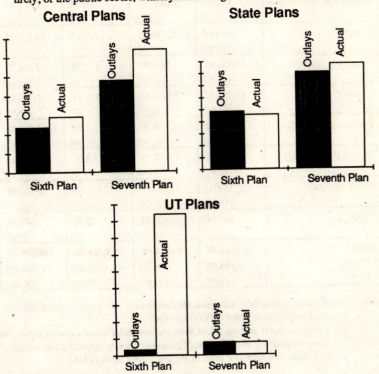

## 15.8 Sectoral Distribution of Seventh Plan Outlays of Centre, States & UTs

*(Rs. crores at 1984-85 prices)*

| Heads of development | Centre | States | Union Territories | Total |
|---|---|---|---|---|
| Agriculture | 4,056.71 (4.25) | 6248.40 (7.74) | 268.51 (7.13) | 10,573.62 (5.87) |
| Rural development | 1901.59 (5.13) | 4142.84 (5.13) | 29.79 (0.79) | 9074.22 (5.04) |
| Special area programmes | - - | 3144.69 (3.90) | - - | 3,144.69 (1.75) |
| Irrigation & flood control | 834.93 (0.87) | 15,949.77 (19.77) | 193.95 (5.15) | 16,978.65 (9.43) |
| Energy | 31,492.14 (32.96) | 22786.15 (28.24) | 542.97 (14.41) | 54,821.26 (30.45) |
| Industry & minerals | 18,552.97 (19.42) | 3785.88 (4.69) | 121.98 (3.24) | 22,460.83 (12.48) |
| Transport | 16,459.37 (17.23) | 5772.50 (7.15) | 739.15 (19.61) | 22971.02 (12.76) |
| Communication I&B | 6,385.82 (6.66) | 99.33 (0.12) | 7.31 (0.19) | 6,472.46 (3.60) |
| Science & technology | 2303.43 (2.41) | 157.28 (0.20) | 5.29 (0.14) | 2466.00 (1.37) |
| Social services | 10,350.90 (10.84) | 17,182.88 (21.29) | 1816.68 (48.21) | 29350.46 (16.31) |
| Others | 216.14 (0.23) | 1428.28 (1.77) | 42.37 (1.13) | 1686.79 (0.94) |
| Total | 95,534.00 (100.00) (53.07) | 80,698.00 (100.00) (44.83) | 3,768.00 (100.00) (2.10) | 180,000.00 (100.00) (100.00) |

*Note : (a) Figures within brackets indicate percentage shares of sectoral outlays for Centre, States and UTs respectively.*
*(b) These sectoral outlays taken from the Seventh Plan document differ from those appearing in the annual Economic Survey issued by the Ministry of Finance, which are used in the preceding table (15.6).*

## 15.9 Inter-Sectoral Capital Flows for Plan Investments : Sixth, Seventh & Eighth Plans

| Sources of Capital | | Investments by | | | |
|---|---|---|---|---|---|
| | | Public Sector | Private Sector | | Total |
| | | | Corporate & Cooperative Sectors | Household Sector | |
| **Sixth Plan : 1980-85 (Rs. crores at 1979-80 Prices)** | | | | | |
| 1. | Own Savings | 34,200 (21.5) | 10,588 (6.7) | 104,859 (66.1) | 149,647 (94.3) |
| 2. | Transfers from other domestic sectors | 38,811 (24.5) | 8,994 (5.7) | -47,865 (-30.2) | – – |
| 3. | Inflow from rest of the world | 10,929 (6.9) | - - | - 1,866 (-1.2) | 9,063 (5.7) |
| | Investment | 84,000 (52.9) | 19,582 (12.4) | 55,128 (34.7) | 158,710 (100.00) |
| **Seventh Plan : 1985-90 (Rs. crores at 1984-85 Prices)** | | | | | |
| 1. | Own Savings | 57,422 (17.8) | 28,779 (8.9) | 216,165 (67.1) | 302,366 (93.8) |
| 2. | Transfers from other domestic sectors | 78,796 (24.4) | 23,457 (7.3) | -102,253 (-31.7) | - |
| 3. | Inflow from rest of the world | 18,000 (5.6) | 2000 (0.6) | - - | 20,000 (6.2) |
| | Investment | 154,218 (47.8) | 54,236 (16.8) | 113,912 (35.4) | 322,366 (100.00) |
| **Eighth Plan : 1992-97 (Rs. crores at 1991-92 Prices)** | | | | | |
| 1. | Own Savings | 68,900 (8.7) | 68,930 (8.7) | 605,170 (76.4) | 743,000 (93.8) |

| Sources of Capital | | Investments by | | | Total |
|---|---|---|---|---|---|
| | | Public Sector | Private Sector | | |
| | | | Corporate & Cooperative Sectors | Household Sector | |
| Eighth Plan : 1992-97 (Rs. crores at 1991-92 Prices) | | | | | |
| 2. | Transfers from other domestic sectors | 239,400 | 63,770 | -303,170 | - |
| | | (30.2) | (8.1) | (-38.3) | - |
| 3. | Inflow from rest of the world | 33,700 | 15,300 | - | 49,000 |
| | | (4.3) | (1.9) | - | (6.2) |
| | Investment | 342,000 | 148,000 | 302,000 | 792,000 |
| | | (43.2) | (18.7) | (38.1) | (100.0) |

❑ Notice the shift in proportions of investments between public and private sectors — the share of public sector has been declining.

❑ Household sector has been an important growing surplus sector while public sector remains a large deficit sector drawing ever increasing surplus of the household sector as well as of the rest of the world; its own savings financed about 40% of its investment during the Sixth and Seventh Plans and this is expected to decline to 20% during the Eighth Plan.

❑ Private corporate sector too would increase its dependence on surpluses of household sector for its investment requirements. Its own savings would contribute less than half of the investment during the Eighth Plan.

❑ A part from the plan investment the public sector needs funds for financing its current outlays on plans which would constitute 12% of the Eighth Plan outlay for the public sector. This was around 14% of Sixth and Seventh Plan outlays.

## 16.1 Financial Flow in the Indian Economy : Sectorwise 1968-69 and 1989-90

*Rs. Crores*

| Sources \ Users | Banking | Financial Institution | Private Corporate Sector | Government | Rest of the world | Households | Total Users |
|---|---|---|---|---|---|---|---|
| **1968-69** | | | | | | | |
| 1. Banking | - | 6 | 198 | 495 | 25 | 403 | 1127 |
| | - | (0.2) | (5.4) | (13.5) | (0.7) | (11.0) | (30.7) |
| 2. Financial Institutions | 31 | - | 66 | 171 | - | 27 | 295 |
| | (0.8) | - | (1.8) | (4.7) | - | (0.7) | (8.0) |
| 3. Private Corporate Sector | 35 | - | - | 6 | -1 | 73 | 113 |
| | (1.0) | - | - | (0.2) | - | (2.0) | (3.1) |
| 4. Government | 123 | 54 | 20 | - | 30 | 11 | 238 |
| | (3.4) | (1.5) | (0.5) | - | (0.8) | (0.3) | (6.5) |
| 5. Rest of the World | -2 | 1 | 6 | 418 | - | - | 423 |
| | (-0.1) | - | (0.2) | (11.4) | - | - | (11.5) |
| 6. Household | 790 | 343 | 20 | 164 | - | - | 1317 |
| | (21.5) | (9.4) | (0.5) | (4.5) | - | - | 35.9 |
| 7. Items not classified elsewhere | 18 | 25 | 1 | 115 | -1 | - | 158 |
| | (0.5) | (0.7) | - | (3.1) | - | - | (4.3) |
| a. Total Sources | 995 | 429 | 311 | 1369 | 53 | 514 | 3671 |
| | (27.1) | (11.7) | (8.5) | (37.3) | (1.4) | (14.0) | (100.0) |
| b. Surplus/Deficit (Sources-Uses) | -84 | 29 | 246 | 1109 | -479 | -859 | -38 |
| c. Total Uses | 1079 | 400 | 85 | 260 | 532 | 1373 | 3709 |
| Instrumentwise | (29.1) | (10.8) | (1.8) | (7.0) | (14.3) | (37.0) | (100.0) |

*contd....*

*Rs. Crores*

| Users / Sources | Banking | Financial Institution | Private Corporate Sector | Government | Rest of the world | Households | Total Users |
|---|---|---|---|---|---|---|---|
| **1989-90** | | | | | | | |
| 1. Banking | - | 3947 | 4187 | 19605 | -1594 | 12508 | 38653 |
| | - | (2.6) | (2.7) | (12.9) | (-1.0) | (8.2) | (25.4) |
| 2. Financial Institutions | 3387 | - | 5173 | 11294 | - | 1007 | 20861 |
| | (2.2) | - | (3.4) | (7.4) | - | (0.7) | (13.7) |
| 3. Private Corporate Sector | 1244 | 3273 | - | -3 | 27 | 108 | 4649 |
| | (0.8) | (2.1) | - | - | - | (0.1) | (3.0) |
| 4. Government | 2625 | 1183 | 324 | - | -6 | 268 | 4394 |
| | 1.7 | 0.8 | (0.2) | - | - | (0.2) | (2.9) |
| 5. Rest of the World | 3534 | 1350 | 110 | 6891 | - | - | 11885 |
| | (2.3) | (0.9) | (0.1) | (4.5) | - | - | (7.8) |
| 6. Household | 29528 | 13617 | 1035 | 11391 | - | - | 55571 |
| | (19.4) | (8.9) | (0.7) | (7.5) | - | - | (36.5) |
| 7. Items not classified elsewhere | 4066 | 968 | 3032 | 8551 | -351 | - | 16266 |
| | (2.7) | (0.6) | (2.0) | (5.6) | -0.2 | - | (10.7) |
| a. Total Sources | 44384 | 24338 | 13861 | 57729 | -1924 | 13891 | 152279 |
| | (29.1) | (15.9) | (9.1) | (37.9) | (-1.2) | (9.2) | (100.0) |
| b. Surplus/ Deficit (Sources-Uses) | -1361 | -3122 | 10150 | 46917 | -10956 | -41680 | -52 |
| c. Total Uses | 45145 | 27460 | 3711 | 10812 | 9032 | 55571 | 152331 |
| Instrumentwise | (30.0) | (18.0) | (2.4) | (7.1) | (5.9) | (36.5) | (100.0) |

❑ The flow of funds accounts studied in this Table indicate the changes in financial activities in the economy, and describe the lending and borrowing transactions of different sectors.

❑ The two reference years are to facilitate the study of changes since the nationalisation of major banks, which are an important intermediary in financial flows.

❑ The household sector is the main surplus sector in the domestic economy. It comprises all individuals, non-government, non-corporate enterprises of farm and non-farm business, like proprietary, partnership and non-profit firms. This sector's contribution has been around 35% in the economy. The contribution mainly to the banking sector declined to 66.5% in 1989-90 after peaking to 77.2% in 1987-88; pre-nationalisation, it was 79.4%, although its overall surplus has been steadily on the rise.

❑ The investment needs of government and private corporate business far exceed than savings. Therefore they borrow from the surplus sectors directly by creating primary issues and indirectly from the financial sector through secondary. The surplus household sector meets most of the gap and the deficiency is further met from net capital inflow from rest of the world. The banks and financial institutions serve as secondary sources out of funds mobilised by them.

## 16.2   Financial Flows in the Indian Economy by Instruments 1968-69 and 1989-90

*(Rs. crores)*

| Sectors / Instruments | Banking | Financial Institution | Private Corporate Sector | Government | Rest of the world | Households | Total |
|---|---|---|---|---|---|---|---|
| **1968-69** | | | | | | | |
| 1. Currency and Deposits | - <br> - | 37 <br> (1.0) | 52 <br> (1.4) | 34 <br> (0.9) | 22 <br> (0.6) | 782 <br> (21.1) | 979 <br> (25.0) |
| 2. Investments Securities | 355 <br> (9.6) | 207 <br> (5.6) | -2 <br> (-0.1) | 60 <br> (1.6) | -99 <br> (-1.6) | -1 <br> - | 560 <br> (15.1) |
| 3. Loans & Advances | 742 <br> (20.0) | 132 <br> (3.5) | 16 <br> (0.4) | 133 <br> (3.6) | 570 <br> (15.4) | 99 <br> (2.7) | 1692 <br> (45.6) |
| 4. Small Savings | - <br> - | 29 <br> (0.8) | - <br> - | - <br> - | - <br> - | 84 <br> (2.2) | 113 <br> (3.0) |
| 5. Life Fund | - <br> - | - <br> - | - <br> - | - <br> - | 2 <br> (0.1) | 184 <br> (4.9) | 186 <br> (5.0) |
| 6. Provident Funds | - <br> - | - <br> - | - <br> - | - <br> - | - <br> - | 225 <br> (6.1) | 225 <br> (6.1) |
| 7. Compulsory Deposits | - <br> - | - <br> - | - <br> - | - <br> - | - <br> - | - <br> - | - <br> - |
| 8. Trade Debt | - <br> - | - <br> - | - <br> - | 15 <br> (0.4) | - <br> - | - <br> - | 15 <br> (0.4) |
| 9. Foreign claims n.e.c | -24 <br> (-0.6) | - <br> - | - <br> - | 7 <br> (0.2) | - <br> - | - <br> - | -17 <br> (-0.4) |
| 10. Other Items n. e. c. | 6 <br> (0.1) | -5 <br> (-0.1) | -1 <br> - | 11 <br> (0.3) | -3 <br> (-0.1) | - <br> - | 8 <br> (0.2) |
| Total Uses | 1079 <br> (20.1) | 400 <br> (10.8) | 55 <br> (1.8) | 260 <br> (7.0) | 532 <br> (14.3) | 1373 <br> (37.0) | 3709 <br> (100.0) |

*Notes: n.e.c. = not elsewhere classified*

*Rs. crores*

| Sectors \ Instruments | Banking | Finan-cial Institu-tion | Private Corpo-rate Sector | Govern-ment | Rest of the world | House-holds | Total |
|---|---|---|---|---|---|---|---|
| **1989-90** | | | | | | | |
| 1. Currency and Deposits | -4 - | 8410 (5.5) | 707 (0.5) | 1128 (0.7) | 2062 (1.4) | 3096 (20.3) | 43271 (28.4) |
| 2. Investmnets in Securities | 23536 (15.5) | 6561 (4.3) | 309 (0.2) | 3842 (2.5) | 228 (0.1) | 4194 (2.8) | 38,670 (25.4) |
| 3. Loans & Advances | 22,512 (14.8) | 10,562 (6.9) | 2,669 (1.8) | 3,050 (2.0) | 5,015 (3.3) | - - | 43,808 (28.8) |
| 4. Small Savings | - - | 1349 (0.9) | - - | - - | - - | 6609 (4.3) | 7958 (5.2) |
| 5. Life Fund | - - | - - | - - | - - | 25 - | 4415 (2.9) | 4440 (2.9) |
| 6. Provident Funds | - - | - - | - - | - - | - - | 9397 (6.2) | 9397 (6.2) |
| 7. Complusory Deposits | - - | - - | - - | - - | - - | - 142 -0.1 | - 142 -0.1 |
| 8. Trade Debt | - - | - - | - - | 1348 (0-.9) | - - | 130 (0.1) | 1478 (1.0) |
| 9. Foreign Earning n.e.c. | - 299 (-0.2) | - - | - - | 921 (0.6) | 1702 (1.1) | - - | 2324 (1.5) |
| 10. Other Items n. e. c. | - - | 578 (0.4) | 26 - | 523 (0.3) | - - | - - | 1,127 (0.7) |
| Total Uses | 45745 (30.0) | 27460 (18.0) | 3711 (2.4) | 10812 (7.1) | 9032 (5.9) | 55571 (36.5) | 152331 (100.0) |

*Notes: n.e.c. = not elsewhere classified*

❏ The government and private corporate sectors directly from the household sector as well as indirectly through financial intermediaries. The government's direct draft as net savings of the household sector takes the form of small savings, provident funds and investments in special bonds, etc. This averages around 28% of the net savings of the household sector.

❏ The private corporate business sector draws on the savings of the household sector in the form of subscription share capital, debentures, deposits. This is about 2.5%.

❏ Over the years, the household sector's savings through bank deposits has declined in favour of investments in securities.

❏ Share of benefit induced small savings and the household sector has significantly improved while that of life fund has declined.

## 16.3 Assistance sanctioned and disbursed by all financial institutions : 1964-65 & 1970-71 to 1990-91

|  | Sanctions | | Disbursements | |
|---|---|---|---|---|
|  | Rs. crores | % increase | Rs. crores | % increase |
| 1964-65 | 118.1 |  | 90.5 |  |
| 1970-71 | 254.2 |  | 159.9 |  |
| 1971-72 | 342.7 | 34.8 | 191.4 | 19.7 |
| 1972-73 | 325.9 | -4.9 | 218.8 | 14.3 |
| 1973-74 | 446.7 | 37.1 | 301.6 | 37.8 |
| 1974-75 | 545.6 | 23.0 | 425.0 | 40.9 |
| 1975-76 | 648.3 | 18.0 | 435.2 | 2.4 |
| 1976-77 | 988.9 | 52.5 | 602.0 | 38.3 |
| 1977-78 | 1224.8 | 23.9 | 713.0 | 18.4 |
| 1978-79 | 1404.3 | 14.7 | 347.5 | 32.9 |
| 1979-80 | 2060.5 | 46.7 | 1352.2 | 42.7 |
| 1980-81 | 2513.0 | 22.0 | 1603.4 | 18.6 |
| 1981-82 | 2724.6 | 8.4 | 2065.6 | 28.8 |
| 1982-83 | 3218.0 | 18.1 | 2371.9 | 14.8 |
| 1983-84 | 4097.9 | 27.3 | 2936.4 | 23.8 |
| 1984-85 | 5517.8 | 34.6 | 3502.6 | 19.3 |
| 1985-86 | 6363.5 | 15.3 | 4925.9 | 40.6 |
| 1986-87 | 7892.3 | 24.0 | 5656.0 | 14.8 |
| 1987-88 | 9124.8 | 15.6 | 6852.3 | 21.2 |
| 1988-89 | 14,165.9 | 55.2 | 9171.3 | 33.8 |
| 1989-90 | 15,747.4 | 11.2 | 10,007.4 | 9.1 |
| 1990-91 | 20,032.7 | 27.2 | 12470.5 | 24.6 |
| Cumulative upto March 1991 | 98385.2 |  | 69372.1 |  |

*contd....*

| Compound annual rate of increase | | |
|---|---|---|
| 1964-65 to 1990-91 | 21.8 | 20.9 |
| 1980-81 to 1990-91 | 23.1 | 22.8 |

❑ Over the years an integrated structure of financial institutions has been evolved for providing term finance and other assistance to industrial sector. The all-India development banks comprise the IDBI, IFCI, ICICI and the newly set up SIDBI for small industries. The investment institutions comprise LIC, UTI and LIC. The IRBI provides mainly the term finance for rehabilitations of industrial units.

❑ RCTC, TDICI, SCICI and TFCI are specialised financial institutions providing, risk capital, secondary finance, shipping and tourism related industries respectively.

❑ Besides there is also a network of state-level institutions the SCFs and SIDCs.

❑ Over the years, the institutions have been involved in industrial development process through various schemes of financial assistance and promotional and development activities.

❑ The cumulative figures shown here include rupee loans, foreign currency loans, underwriting or direct subscription of share capital and guarantees.

## 16.4 Institutionwise Cumulative Assistance Sanctioned and Disbursed upto March 1991

| | Sanction | | Disbursements | |
|---|---|---|---|---|
| | Rs. crores | % | Rs. crores | % |
| Industrial Development Bank of India | 34,451 | 35.0 | 25,463 | 36.7 |
| Industrial Finance Corp. of India | 11,453 | 11.6 | 6,948 | 10.0 |
| Industrial Credit and Investment Corp. of India | 16,822 | 17.1 | 10,597 | 15.3 |
| Small Industrial Development Bank of India | 1,214 | 1.2 | 1,095 | 1.6 |
| Industrial Reconstruction Bank of India | 1,244 | 1.3 | 919 | 1.3 |
| Life Insurance Corpn. of India | 4,334 | 4.4 | 3,296 | 4.7 |
| Unit Trust of India | 8,577 | 8.7 | 6,198 | 8.9 |
| General Insurance Corp. of India | 1,621 | 1.6 | 1,184 | 1.7 |
| Risk Capital & Technology Finance Corpn. | 43 | 0.1 | 30 | 0.1 |
| Technology Development and Information Corpn. of India | 39 | 0.1 | 25 | 0.1 |
| Shipping Credit & Investment Corpn. of India | 1,109 | 1.1 | 591 | 0.8 |
| Tourism Finance Corpn. of India | 138 | 0.2 | 52 | 0.1 |
| State Financial Corpn. | 11,635 | 11.8 | 8,756 | 12.6 |
| State Industrial Development Corpn. | 5,705 | 5.8 | 4,218 | 6.1 |
| Total | 98,385 | 100.0 | 69,372 | 100.0 |

## 16.5 Industrywise Shares of Cumulative Assistance Sanctioned and Disbursed by FIs, upto March 1991

| Industry | | Sanction | | Disbursements | |
|---|---|---|---|---|---|
| | | Rs. crores | % | Rs. crores | % |
| 1. | Food products | 4,975 | 5.3 | 3,820 | 5.7 |
| 2. | Textiles | 11,128 | 11.8 | 8,186 | 12.2 |
| 3. | Paper | 2,522 | 2.7 | 2,074 | 3.1 |
| 4. | Rubber | 1,836 | 1.9 | 1,184 | 1.8 |
| 5. | Fertilisers | 3,803 | 4.0 | 2,434 | 3.6 |
| 6. | Chemicals and products | 13,941 | 14.8 | 8,851 | 13.2 |
| 7. | Cement | 4,749 | 5.0 | 8,336 | 5.0 |
| 8. | Basic metals: | 6,827 | 7.2 | 4,516 | 6.7 |
| | Iron & Steels | 6,083 | 6.4 | 4,014 | 6.0 |
| | Non-ferous | 744 | 0.8 | 502 | 0.7 |
| 9. | Metal products | 2,403 | 2.6 | 1,871 | 2.8 |
| 10. | Machinery | 6,007 | 6.4 | 3,999 | 6.0 |
| 11. | Electrical & electronic equipment | 4,367 | 4.6 | 2,999 | 4.5 |
| 12. | Transport equipment | 3,031 | 3.2 | 2,038 | 3.0 |
| 13. | Electricity generation | 6,660 | 7.0 | 4,549 | 6.8 |
| 14. | Services | 10,779 | 11.4 | 8,477 | 12.6 |
| 15. | Others | 11,452 | 12.1 | 8,735 | 13.0 |
| | Total | 94,478 | 100.0 | 67,053 | 100.0 |

Note : (a) Totals are adjusted for inter-institutional flow and therefore smaller than the totals shown in other tables.

❑ Chemicals and textiles are the two largest recipients of institutional assistence accounting together for cumulative 26.6% of sanctions and 25.4% of disbursements. Capital equipment group gets 14.2% of sanctions and 13.5% of disbursed. Electricity claims about 7%, but services dominate with one-eighth share of total finance.

## 16.6 Growth of Deposits and Credit of Scheduled Commercial Banks : 1950-51 — 1991-92

| As on Last Friday of March | Aggregrate deposits | | | Total Credit | | |
|---|---|---|---|---|---|---|
| | Rs. crores | % Change | As % of GNP | Rs. crores | % Change | As % of Deposits |
| 1951 | 881 | - | 9.4 | 546 | - | 62.0 |
| 1956 | 1,043 | 10.6 | 10.2 | 761 | 24.3 | 73.0 |
| 1961 | 1,746 | -8.2 | 10.8 | 1,320 | 17.1 | 75.6 |
| 1966 | 2,950 | 14.2 | 11.4 | 2,288 | 12.5 | 77.6 |
| 1971 | 5,950 | 17.5 | 13.8 | 4,684 | 18.0 | 79.3 |
| 1976 | 14,155 | 19.7 | 18.0 | 10,877 | 24.1 | 76.8 |
| 1981 | 37,988 | 19.6 | 27.9 | 25,371 | 17.8 | 66.8 |
| 1982 | 43,733 | 15.1 | 27.4 | 29,681 | 17.0 | 67.9 |
| 1983 | 51,358 | 17.4 | 28.9 | 35,493 | 19.6 | 69.1 |
| 1984 | 60,596 | 18.0 | 29.3 | 41,294 | 16.3 | 68.1 |
| 1985 | 72,245 | 19.2 | 31.4 | 48,953 | 18.5 | 67.8 |
| 1986 | 85,404 | 18.2 | 32.8 | 56,067 | 14.5 | 65.6 |
| 1987 | 102,724 | 20.3 | 35.4 | 63,300 | 12.9 | 61.6 |
| 1988 | 118,045 | 14.9 | 35.8 | 70,536 | 11.4 | 69.8 |
| 1989 | 140,150 | 18.7 | 35.7 | 84,719 | 20.1 | 60.4 |
| 1990 | 166,959 | 19.1 | 37.4 | 101,453 | 19.8 | 60.8 |
| 1991 1992 | 192,542 | 15.3 | 36.6 | 116,301 | 14.6 | 60.4 |

*contd....*

| Compound annual rates of increase (%) | | | | | |
|---|---|---|---|---|---|
| 1951 to 1961 | | 7.1 | | | 9.2 |
| 1961 to 1971 | • | 13.0 | | | 13.5 |
| 1971 to 1981 | | 20.5 | | | 18.4 |
| 1981 to 1991 | | 17.6 | | | 16.4 |
| 1951 to 1991 | | 14.4 | | | 14.3 |

❑ The aggregate deposits expressed as percent of GNP have increased at a steady pace from 9.4% in 1950-51 to 36.6% by 1990-91. This four fold increase can be taken as a measure of bankisation of the Indian economy.

❑ The rapid absolute increase in deposits during recent years, particularly during the eighties reflects the increase of money supply which in turn reflects the massive deficit finance by government.

❑ After persistent increase for three decades, the slow-down in deposits and credit of banks during the eighties point towards the dilution of the intermediary role of banks in mobilisation of savings and deployment of credit.

## 16.7 Sectoral Shares of Gross Bank Credit : March 1977 and March 1991

*(50 Major Banks)*

| Sectors | Outstanding as on Last Friday of March | | | | Variations between March 1977 and 1991 | | |
|---|---|---|---|---|---|---|---|
| | 1977 | | 1991 | | Rs. crores | % Chan-ges | % shares |
| | Rs. crores | % shares | Rs. crores | % shares | | | |
| A. Priority Sectors: | 3,382 | 29.3 | 42,880 | 36.4 | 39,498 | 1,168 | 37.9 |
| Agriculture | 1,343 | 10.1 | 16,756 | 14.2 | 15,413 | 1,148 | 14.8 |
| Small Scale industries | 1,403 | 10.5 | 17,151 | 14.6 | 15,748 | 1,122 | 15.1 |
| Other Sectors | 636 | 4.8 | 8,973 | 7.6 | 8,337 | 1,311 | 8.0 |
| B. Directly identifiable public sector agencies : | | | | | | | |
| Public total : | 2,374 | 17.8 | 4,871 | 4.2 | 2,497 | 105 | 2.4 |
| procurement credit | 2,190 | 16.4 | 4,506 | 3.8 | 2,316 | 106 | 2.2 |
| Cotton Corpn. of India | 132 | 1.0 | 91 | 0.1 | -41 | -31 | - |
| Food Corpn. of India | 23 | 0.2 | 212 | 0.2 | 189 | 822 | 0.2 |
| Jute Corporation | 29 | 0.2 | 62 | 0.1 | 33 | 114 | - |
| C. Other trade (mainly private) | 815 | 6.1 | 5,519 | 4.7 | 4,704 | 577 | 4.5 |
| D. Industry (Medium, large, including PSUs) | 5,539 | 41.5 | 44,425 | 37.7 | 38,886 | 702 | 37.2 |
| E. Other Sectors | 1,247 | 9.3 | 20,028 | 17.0 | 18781 | 1,506 | 18.0 |
| Gross Bank Credit | 13,357 | 100.0 | 117,723 | 100.0 | 104,336 | 1781 | 100.0 |

❑ The share of priority sectors in outstanding gross credit increased from 25.3% to 36.4%, but in the incremental credit their share was the largest about 38%.

❑ Apart from the directly identifiable public sectors agencies which had 4.2% share in total credit, there are many public sector agencies/undertakings under category C,D and E which could not be segregated for want of such separate credit figures. In view of the recent importance attached to the total borrowings of the public and ceiling sought to be prescribed for it, rather than only to be limited to pure government borrowings (stipulations of IMF), the RBI should now set the practice of reporting data for entire public sector credit— commercial and governmental.

❑ Under the reforms of the financial sector the priority sector lending is to be drastically reduced.

## 16.8   Industry-wise Deployment of Gross Bank Credit : March 1981 and March 1991

| Industry (Small Medium & Large scale) | Outstanding as on last Friday of March | | | | Variations between 1981 and 1991 | |
|---|---|---|---|---|---|---|
| | 1981 | | 1991 | | | |
| | Rs. crores | % Share | Rs. crores | % Share | Rs. crores | % Share |
| 1. Coal | 66 | 0.5 | 2,411 | 0.4 | 175 | 0.4 |
| 2. Iron and Steel | 738 | 5.6 | 3,277 | 5.3 | 2,539 | 5.2 |
| 3. Other metals and metal products | 451 | 3.4 | 2,216 | 3.6 | 1,765 | 3.6 |
| 4. All engineering of which electronics | 3,222 n.a. | 24.4 | 13,939 (1852) | 22.6 (3.0) | 10,717 (1852) | 22.1 |
| 5. Electricity | 163 | 1.2 | 1,158 | 1.9 | 995 | 2.1 |
| 6. Cotton Textiles | 1,155 | 8.7 | 4,063 | 6.6 | 2,908 | 6.0 |
| 7. Jute Textiles | 159 | 1.2 | 348 | 0.6 | 189 | 0.4 |
| 8. Other Textiles | 729 | 5.5 | 3,756 | 6.1 | 3,027 | 6.3 |
| 9. Sugar | 342 | 2.6 | 624 | 1.0 | 282 | 0.6 |
| 10. Tea | 226 | 1.7 | 575 | 0.9 | 349 | 0.7 |
| 11. Food processing | n.a. | - | 1,214 | 2.0 | 1,214 | 2.5 |
| 12. Vegetable Oils & vanaspati | 185 | 1.4 | 864 | 1.4 | 679 | 1.4 |
| 13. Tobacco & products | 142 | 1.1 | 392 | 0.6 | 250 | 0.5 |
| 14. Paper & products | 285 | 2.2 | 1,478 | 2.4 | 1,193 | 2.5 |
| 15. Rubber & products | 251 | 1.9 | 982 | 1.6 | 731 | 1.5 |

*contd....*

| Industry (Small Medium & Large scale) | Outstanding as on last Friday of March | | | | Variations between 1981 and 1991 | |
|---|---|---|---|---|---|---|
| | 1981 | | 1991 | | | |
| | Rs. crores | % Share | Rs. crores | % Share | Rs. crores | % Share |
| 16. Chemicals dyes, paints: | 1,501 | 11.4 | 7,716 | 12.5 | 6,215 | 12.8 |
| Of which fertilisers | (278) | (2.1) | (1,298) | (2.1) | (1,020) | |
| Petrochemicals | n.a. | - | (681) | (1.1) | (681) | |
| Drugs & pharmaceuticals | n.a. | - | (989) | (1.6) | (989) | |
| 17. Cement | 121 | 0.9 | 899 | 1.5 | 778 | 1.6 |
| 18. Leather & products | 219 | 1.7 | 996 | 1.6 | 777 | 1.6 |
| 19. Gems & jewellery | n.a. | - | 1,242 | 2.0 | 1,242 | 2.6 |
| 20. Construction | 119 | 0.9 | 1,314 | 2.2 | 1,195 | 2.5 |
| 21. Petroleum | 723 | 5.5 | 54 | 0.1 | -669 | -1.4 |
| 22. Shipping | 300 | 2.3 | 87 | 0.1 | -213 | -0.4 |
| 23. Other Industry | 2,092 | 15.9 | 14,141 | 23.0 | 12,049 | 24.9 |
| Total | 13,189 | 100.0 | 61,576 | 100.0 | 48,387 | 100.0 |

❑ Partly as the combined result of impounding of ever-larger proportions of bank resources by the RBI and of directed credit for priority sector on the one hand, and various restrictions for expansion of non food credit on the other, from time to time, the share of medium and large industries in gross bank credit has declined over the years from 41.5% at March 1971 to 37.7% at March 1991. However, the share of small scale industry, falling under the priority sector, has increased correspondingly from 10.5% to 14.6% over the same period. Consequently, the overall share of the industrial sector appears to have remained unaffected around 52% between these two reference points.

❑ Among the medium and large industry segment those industries whose credit shares have declined are cotton and jute textiles, tobacco and sugar while the gainss are chemicals, cement and construction.

## 16.9 Ownership and Spatial Distribution of Deposits of Scheduled Commercial Banks : 1971 & 1988

| Ownership of deposits | 1971 | | 1988 | | Variation between 1971 & 1988 | |
|---|---|---|---|---|---|---|
| | Last Friday of March | | | | | |
| | Rs. crores | % Share | Rs. crores | % Share | Rs. crores | % Share |
| **A : Ownership of Deposits** | | | | | | |
| A. Government Sector | 877 | 14.3 | 9,425 | 7.7 | 8,548 | 7.3 |
| a Central and State Govt. & Local authorities | 360 | 6.0 | 4,115 | 3.4 | 3,747 | 3.2 |
| b Departmental and autonomous govt. undertakings | 331 | 5.4 | 2,155 | 1.8 | 1,824 | 1.6 |
| c Public sector banks | 67 | 1.1 | 2,076 | 1.7 | 2,009 | 1.7 |
| d Govt. financial institutions | 111 | 1.8 | 1,079 | 0.9 | 968 | 0.8 |
| B. Corporate Sector | 478 | 7.8 | 10,575 | 8.6 | 10,097 | 8.7 |
| C. Household Sector | 4,769 | 77.9 | 102,473 | 83.7 | 97,704 | 84.0 |
| a Individuals & professionals | 3,593 | 58.7 | 92,004 | 75.1 | 88,411 | 76.0 |
| b Non-corporate business partnerships etc. | 1,176 | 19.2 | 10,469 | 8.5 | 9,293 | 8.0 |
| Total | 6,124 | 1,000 | 122,473 | 100 | 116,349 | 100 |

*contd....*

| Ownership of deposits | 1971 Last Friday of March | | 1988 Last Friday of March | | Variation bewteen 1971 & 1988 | |
|---|---|---|---|---|---|---|
| | Rs. crores | % Share | Rs. crores | % Share | Rs. crores | % Share |
| B : Distribution by Type of Deposit | | | | | | |
| Type of Deposits Current | 1,507 | 24.6 | 17,761 | 14.5 | 16,254 | 14.0 |
| Savings | 1,541 | 25.2 | 34,440 | 28.1 | 32,899 | 28.3 |
| Term/time | 3,076 | 50.2 | 70,272 | 57.4 | 67,196 | 57.7 |
| Total | 6,124 | 100.0 | 122,473 | 100.0 | 116,349 | 100.0 |
| C : Spatial Distribution of Deposits | | | | | | |
| Rural | 447 | 7.3 | 17,620 | 14.4 | 17,173 | 14.8 |
| Semi-urban | 1,396 | 22.8 | 27,160 | 22.2 | 25,764 | 22.1 |
| Urban | 1,562 | 25.2 | 31,650 | 25.8 | 30,088 | 25.9 |
| Metropolitan | 2,719 | 44.4 | 46,043 | 37.6 | 43,324 | 37.2 |
| Total | 6,124 | 100.0 | 122,473 | 100.0 | 116,349 | 100.0 |

❏ According to the biennial RBI survey of ownership of bank deposits, the share of government sector had declined considerably rom 14.3% at March 1971 to 7.7% by March 1988, while that of the corporate sector had improved marginally – 7.8% to 8.6%. On the other hand, the share of deposits of individuals in the household sector had substantially increased from 58.7% to 75.1% over the same period.

❏ Examination of disintegrated data shows that among "individuals", increase in share of total deposits was registered by all sub-sectors viz. non-residents and residents, and within residents, by "farmers" and "businessmen & traders".

❏ By types of deposits, the share of "farmers" continued to increase in all the three types of deposits, and increase in their share of term deposits in particular was the maximum.

❏ The observed increase in share of farmers in deposits in 1987-88 is strange, as the year was one of severe drought. One would think the deposit growth would slow down, as farmers would tend to liquidate their deposits.

## 16.10 Distribution of Scheduled Commercial Bank Branches 1969 – 1991

| Year | Areas of branch locations | | | | | Population per bank branch ('000) |
|------|-------|---------------|-------|--------------|-------|--------|
|      | Rural | Semi-Urban | Urban | Metropolitan | Total | |
| 1969 | 1,822 (22.2) | 3,322 (40.2) | 1,447 (17.5) | 1,661 (20.1) | 8,262 (100.0) | 64.03 |
| 1970 | 3,062 (30.2) | 3,695 (36.5) | 1,583 (15.6) | 1,791 (17.7) | 10,131 (100.0) | 53.40 |
| 1975 | 8,806 (36.3) | 5,569 (29.7) | 3,267 (17.4) | 3,088 (16.5) | 18,730 (100.0) | 32.41 |
| 1980 | 15,101 (46.6) | 8,078 (24.9) | 4,856 (15.0) | 4,384 (13.5) | 32,419 (100.0) | 20.94 |
| 1981 | 17,650 (49.3) | 8,426 (23.6) | 5,186 (14.5) | 4,505 (12.6) | 35,767 (100.0) | 19.12 |
| 1982 | 20,394 (52.1) | 8,764 (22.4) | 5,359 (13.7) | 4,660 (11.9) | 39,177 (100.0) | 17.89 |
| 1983 | 22,678 (53.9) | 9,036 (21.5) | 55.77 (13.3) | 4,778 (11.4) | 42,089 (100.0) | 17.00 |
| 1984 | 25,372 (56.0) | 9,262 (20.4) | 5,769 (12.7) | 4,929 (10.9) | 45,332 (100.0) | 16.13 |
| 1985 | 28,782 (55.4) | 10,460 (20.1) | 7,542 (14.5) | 5,194 (10.0) | 51,978 (100.0) | 14.35 |
| 1986 | 29,718 (55.8) | 10,567 (19.6) | 7,195 (13.5) | 5,785 (10.9) | 53,265 (100.0) | 14.29 |
| 1987 | 30,022 (55.8) | 10,692 (19.9) | 7,684 (14.3) | 5,374 (10.0) | 53,772 (100.0) | 14.43 |
| 1988 | 30,798 (55.8) | 11,204 (0.9) | 7,782 (14.1) | 5,414 (9.8) | 55,198 (100.0) | 14.35 |
| 1989 | 33,010 (57.2) | 11,165 (19.4) | 7,524 (13.0) | 5,995 (10.4) | 57,698 (100.0) | 13.99 |
| 1990 | 34,494 (58.1) | 11,255 (19.0) | 7,582 (12.7) | 6,057 (10.2) | 59,388 (100.0) | 13.78 |
| 1991 | 35,187 (58.4) | 11,269 (18.7) | 7,615 (12.7) | 6,119 (10.2) | 60,190 (100.0) | 11.00 |

*contd....*

| Compound annual rate of increase (%) between | | | | | | |
|---|---|---|---|---|---|---|
| 1969 & 1991 | 14.4 | 5.7 | 7.8 | 6.1 | 9.4 | |
| 1991-92 | | | | | | |

❑ Of the total bank branches in the country the proportion in rural areas has increased from 22.2% in June 1969 to 58.4% in June 1991. This reflects the substantial progress made towards the spread of banking overall as well as to hitherto unbanked rural areas. As a result, the population coverage per bank branch has come down from about 65,000 at the time of nationalisation to 11,000 in a span of 22 years.

❑ The branch licensing policy for the future would lay emphasis on improving the operational efficiency and financial strength of banks while continuing the consolidation of efforts already made. Therefore the future growth of bank branch network would be guided by well-established need, business potential and financial viability of every proposed new branch. While moderating the branch expansion, spatial gaps in rural areas would be considered.

## 16.11 Progress of Regional Rural Banks : 1975 to 1990

| Year | No. of R.R.Bs | No. of Districts covered | No. of branches | Deposits Rs. lakhs | Ratio of Outstanding advance to deposits | |
|---|---|---|---|---|---|---|
| | | | | | Rs. Lakhs | Ratios |
| 1975 | 6 | 12 | 17 | 20 | 10 | 50 |
| 1976 | 40 | 84 | 489 | 772 | 702 | 91 |
| 1977 | 48 | 99 | 1,187 | 3,304 | 4,235 | 128 |
| 1978 | 51 | 102 | 1,753 | 7,411 | 12,202 | 165 |
| 1979 | 60 | 111 | 2,420 | 12,322 | 16,741 | 136 |
| 1980 | 85 | 144 | 3,279 | 19,983 | 24,338 | 122 |
| 1981 | 107 | 182 | 4,795 | 33,600 | 40,659 | 121 |
| 1982 | 124 | 214 | 6,191 | 50,226 | 57,711 | 115 |
| 1983 | 150 | 265 | 7,795 | 67,785 | 75,084 | 111 |
| 1984 | 173 | 307 | 10,245 | 95,997 | 108,077 | 113 |
| 1985 | 188 | 333 | 12,606 | 128,582 | 140,767 | 109 |
| 1986 | 194 | 351 | 12,838 | 171,494 | 178,484 | 104 |
| 1987 | 196 | 363 | 13,353 | 230,552 | 223,226 | 97 |
| 1988 | 196 | 369 | 13,920 | 296,588 | 280,429 | 95 |
| 1989 (Sept.) | 196 | 370 | 14,279 | 346,799 | 315,493 | 91 |
| 1990 (Sept.) | 196 | 380 | 14,511 | 426,752 | 355,517 | 83 |

❑ The Regional Rural Banks were established basically with the objective of providing to the weaker sections of society access to institutional credit, including credit against government sponsored programmes such as IRDP and DRI.

❑ The RRBs account for about 24% of the total bank branches in the country. Their aggregate deposits at the of September 1991 formed about 2% of the aggregate bank deposits and their advances were 3% of the total bank credit. But the percentage of their overdues to outstanding advances was fairly high at 32% at the end of September 1991. Their aggregate borrowings from NABARD, IDBI and other financial institutions formed nearly 50% of their total outstanding advances.

## 16.12 Liquidity and Reserves Ratios Prescribed for Commercial Banks

| A : Statutory Liq[uidity Ratio] | | | |
|---|---|---|---|
| Effective from | Rate as percent of net Demand and Time Liabilities (DTL) of banks | Effective from | Rate as percent of net Demand and Time Liabilities (DTL) of banks |
| 1949 | 20.00 | 25 Sept. 1981 | 34.50 |
| Sept. 1964 | 25.00 | 30 Oct. 1981 | 35.00 |
| 5 Feb. 1970 | 25.00 to 26.00 | 28 July 1984 | 35.50 |
| April 1970 (Last Friday) | 27.00 | 1 Sept. 1984 | 36.00 |
| August 1970 (Last Friday) | 28.00 | 8 June 1985 | 36.50 |
| | | 6 July 1985 | 37.00 |
| August 1972 | 29.00 | 27 April 1987 | 37.50 |
| 17 Nov. 1972 | 30.00 | 2 Jan. 1988 | 38.00 |
| 8 Dec. 1973 | 32.00 | 22 Sept. 1990 | 38.50 |
| 29 June 1974 | 33.00 | 3 April 1992 | Reduced to 30.00 only on incremental net DTL over 3 April |
| 1 Dec. 1978 | 34.00 | | |

| B : Cash Reserves Ratio | | | |
|---|---|---|---|
| Effective from | Rate as percent of net DTL of banks | Effective from | Rate as percent of net DTL of banks |
| 31 May 1973 | From 3.00 to 5.00 | 14 Jan. 1977 till 31 Oct. 1980 | Additional CRR of 10% of incremental net DTL accuring after Jan. 1977 |
| 8 Sept 1973 | 6.00 | | |
| 22 Sept. 1973 | 7.00 | 1 June 1978 till 5 June 1979 | Impounding of addl. one-half of net aggregate amount received after 1 June 1978 under non-resident external rupee a/c and foreign currency non-resident a/c |
| 29 June 1974 | 5.00 | | |
| 14 Dec. 1974 | 4.50 | | |
| 28 Dec. 1974 | 4.00 | | |
| 4 Sept. 1976 | 5.00 | | |
| 13 Nov. 1976 | 6.00 | 31 July 1981 | 6.50 |

*contd....*

| serves Ratio | | | |
|---|---|---|---|
| Effective from | Rate as percent of net DTL of banks | Effective from | Rate as percent of net DTL of banks |
| 21 Aug. 1981 | 7.00 | 4 Feb. 1984 | 9.00 |
| 27 Nov. 1981 | 7.25 | 28 Feb. 1987 | 9.50 |
| 25 Dec. 1981 | 7.50 | 24 Oct. 1987 | 10.00 |
| 29 Jan. 1982 | 7.75 | 2 July 1988 | 10.50 |
| 9 April 1982 | 7.25 | 30 July 1988 | 11.00 |
| 11 June 1982 | 7.00 | 1 July 1989 | 15.00 |
| 27 May 1983 | 7.50 | 4 May 1991 | Incremental CRR of 10% of increase in net DTL over 3 May |
| 29 July 1983 | 8.00 | | |
| 27 Aug. 1983 | 8.50 | | |
| 12 Nov. 1983 | Incremental CRR of 10% of increase in net DTL over 11 Nov. | | |

❑ The SLR highlights the commandeering of resources of banks by central and state governments by way of subscription to their market loans floated every year for bridging their resource gaps.

❑ In effect this means shifting the use of banks' resources from non-government to government sector over and above what is mopped up under small savings schemes of the government.

❑ The committee for reforms of financial sector has recommended phased reduction of SLR to 25% over a period of five years.

❑ The banks, in order to safeguard their profitability, have of late started diversifying their activity of raising and deploying resources to areas which do not attract SLR stipulations.

❑ The CRR requires the banks to deposit with RBI prescribed portions of their deposits. The objective is to control expansion of credit and thereby satisfy the monetary policy stipulations of the RBI. The reforms committee has also recommended reduction of the CRR from its present high level.

## 17.1  Components of Money Supply with Public : 1950-51 – 1992-93

| Year (Last Friday of March) | Money Supply (M1) | | Currency with Public | | Deposit with Public | | Monetary Resources (M3) Rs. crores |
|---|---|---|---|---|---|---|---|
| | Rs. crores | % change | Rs. crores | % of M1 | Rs. crores | % of M1 | |
| Old Series | | | | | | | |
| 1950 - 51 | 2,016 | 7.8 | 1,407 | 69.8 | 609 | 30.2 | 2,280 |
| 1955 - 56 | 2,217 | 13.4 | 1,571 | 70.9 | 646 | 29.1 | 2,683 |
| 1960 - 61 | 2,869 | 5.5 | 2,098 | 73.1 | 771 | 26.9 | 3,964 |
| 1965 - 66 | 4,529 | 11.0 | 3,034 | 67.0 | 1,495 | 33.0 | 6,134 |
| 1969 - 70 | 6,387 | 10.5 | 4,011 | 62.8 | 2,376 | 37.2 | 9,336 |
| New Series | | | | | | | |
| 1969 - 70 | 6,536 | – | 3,995 | 61.1 | 2,541 | 38.9 | 9,639 |
| 1970 - 71 | 7,321 | 12.0 | 4,367 | 59.7 | 2,954 | 40.3 | 10,958 |
| 1975 - 76 | 13,143 | 10.3 | 6,704 | 51.0 | 6,439 | 49.0 | 22,286 |
| 1977 - 78 | 18,383 | 17.5 | 8,602 | 46.8 | 9,781 | 53.2 | 32,906 |
| Revised Series | | | | | | | |
| 1977 - 78 | 14,388 | – | 8,831 | 80.0 | 5,757 | 40.0 | 32,906 |
| 1980 - 81 | 23,117 | 15.9 | 13,464 | 58.2 | 9,653 | 41.8 | 55,358 |
| 1981 - 82 | 24,729 | 7.0 | 14,492 | 58.6 | 10,237 | 41.4 | 62,426 |
| 1982 - 83 | 28,535 | 15.4 | 16,659 | 58.4 | 11,876 | 41.6 | 72,868 |
| 1983 - 84 | 33,066 | 15.9 | 19,553 | 59.1 | 13,513 | 40.9 | 85,899 |

*contd. . .*

| Year (Last Friday of March) | Money Supply (M1) | | Currency with Public | | Deposit with Public | | Monetary Resources (M3) Rs. crores |
|---|---|---|---|---|---|---|---|
| | Rs. crores | % change | Rs. crores | % of M1 | Rs. crores | % of M1 | |
| 1984 - 85 | 39,649 | 19.9 | 22,864 | 57.2 | 16,985 | 42.8 | 101,957 |
| 1985 - 86 | 43,599 | 10.0 | 25,168 | 57.7 | 18,431 | 42.3 | 118,338 |
| 1986 - 87 | 51,177 | 17.4 | 28,585 | 55.9 | 22,592 | 44.1 | 140,633 |
| 1987 - 88 | 57,802 | 12.9 | 33,650 | 58.2 | 24,152 | 41.8 | 162,660 |
| 1988 - 89 | 66,607 | 15.2 | 38,415 | 57.7 | 28,192 | 42.3 | 192,085 |
| 1989 - 90 | 81,060 | 21.7 | 46,300 | 57.1 | 34,760 | 42.9 | 230,950 |
| 1990 - 91 | 92,770 | 14.4 | 53,087 | 57.2 | 39,683 | 42.8 | 265,436 |
| 1991 -92 | 114,838 | 23.8 | 61,098 | 53.2 | 52,855 | 46.0 | 317,481 |
| 1992 - 93 | 123,181 | 7.3 | 68,533 | 55.6 | 53,145 | 43.1 | 362,364 |

*Note :  All the three series of data presented above are non-comparable. However data within each series are fully comparable.*

❏ In general, in an "under-bankised" economy currency forms a relatively large portion of the total money supply. On the other hand, in developed countries generally deposits from such a large part of money supply that much of the monetary discussion runs in terms of deposit money only.

❏ In the data above it is observed that share of currency has been falling more or less steadily.

## 17.2 Sources of Expansion of Money Supply : 1956-57 – 1991-92

*(Rs. Crores)*

| Year | Variations in Normally expansionary factors | | | | Variations in Normally contractionary factors | | | Variation in money supply (M1) |
|---|---|---|---|---|---|---|---|---|
| | Bank Credit to govt. sector | Bank Credit to Commercial sector | Net foreign exchange assets | Total (1+2+3) | Time deposits | Impact of all other factors | Total (5+6) | |
| | 1 | 2 | 3 · | 4 | 5 | 6 | 7 | |
| Old Series | | | | | | | | |
| 1956-57 | 310 | 103 | -262 | 151 | 61 | -35 | 26 | 125 |
| 1960-61 | -17 | 253 | -63 | 173 | -15 | 39 | 24 | 149 |
| 1965-66 | 467 | 100 | -24 | 543 | 187 | -93 | 94 | 449 |
| 1970-71 | 511 | 889 | -25 | 1,375 | 498 | -77 | 421 | 954 |
| New Series | | | | | | | | |
| 1970-71 | 512 | 1,048 | -25 | 1,535 | 534 | 216 | 750 | 785 |
| 1975-76 | 579 | 2,721 | 658 | 3,958 | 1,592 | 1,134 | 2,726 | 1,232 |
| 1977-78 | 1,951 | 2,496 | 1,991 | 6,438 | 6,848 | 852 | 7,700 | -1,262 |
| Revised Series | | | | | | | | |
| 1977-78 | 1,872 | 2,707 | 1,916 | 6,495 | 6,847 | 910 | 7,757 | -1,262 |
| 1980-81 | 1,409 | 5,602 | -785 | 6,226 | 5,393 | 1,669 | 7,062 | -836 |
| Revised Series | | | | | | | | |
| 1981-82 | 5,408 | 6,677 | -2,086 | 9,999 | 5,456 | 2,931 | 8,387 | 1,612 |
| 1982-83 | 4,609 | 8,249 | -895 | 11,963 | 6,636 | 2,193 | 8,829 | 3,134 |
| 1983-84 | 5,757 | 8,830 | -104 | 14,483 | 8,500 | 1,452 | 9,952 | 4,531 |
| 1984-85 | 8,445 | 10,809 | 1,633 | 20,887 | 9,475 | 4,829 | 14,304 | 6,583 |
| 1985-86 | 9,572 | 11,051 | 195 | 20,818 | 12,431 | 4,437 | 16,868 | 3,950 |

*contd...*

| Year | Variations in Normally expansionary factors | | | | Variations in Normally contractionary factors | | | Variation in money supply (M1) |
|---|---|---|---|---|---|---|---|---|
| | Bank Credit to govt. sector | Bank Credit to Commercial sector | Net foreign exchange assets | Total (1+2+3) | Time deposits | Impact of all other factors | Total (5+6) | |
| | 1 | 2 | 3 | 4 | 5 | 6 | 7 | |
| 1986-87 | 12,776 | 11,294 | 1,314 | 25,384 | 13,492 | 3,089 | 16,581 | 8,803 |
| 1987-88 | 12,811 | 12,389 | 673 | 25,873 | 15,343 | 3,846 | 19,189 | 6,684 |
| 1988-89 | 12,771 | 21,687 | 1,199 | 35,657 | 18,362 | 5,670 | 24,032 | 11,625 |
| 1989-90 | 19,630 | 23,183 | 69 | 42,882 | 23,052 | 5,016 | 28,068 | 14,814 |
| 1990-91 | 23,043 | 20,065 | 1,854 | 44,962 | 23,046 | 5,084 | 28,130 | 11,832 |
| 1991-92 | 18,097 | 19,423 | 10,855 | 48,379 | 28,079 | 13,020 | 41,094 | 21,186 |
| Increase between 1980-81 and 1991-92 | | | | | | | | |
| | 135,328 | 159,257 | 13,922 | 308,583 | 1,69,265 | 53,236 | 222,506 | 163,918 |

❑ Between 1980-81 and 1991-92, additional bank credit to government sector totalled Rs.135,328 crores and that to commercial sector totalled Rs.159,257 crores. Net foreign exchange assets of banking sector increased by Rs.13,922 crores. Had other things remained unchanged this would have resulted in expansion of money supply by Rs.308,513 crores. However, increase in time deposits and contractionary impact of other factors resulted in a contraction of Rs.222,502 crores. As a result, money supply increased by Rs.86,011 crores (Rs.308,513 crores minus Rs.222,502 crores).

❑ Thus any effort at controlling money supply can be effective only to the extent it succeeds in controlling the expansionary factors.

❑ The primary expansionary factor is the galloping government expenditure, which in turn leads to ever larger resort by the government to banking credit obtained by selling securities to the banking sector. It is therefore the excessive increase in credit-financed government expenditure that has added to the expansion of money supply which is at the root of inflation during the eighties and nineties.

## 17.3  Mechanics of Price Inflation : 1960-61 – 1990-91

| Year | Index of Money Supply | Index of Real National Income | Movement of Price Index | | |
|---|---|---|---|---|---|
| | | | Computed $\frac{Col1}{Col2} \times 100$ | National Income deflator | Consumer Prices (Average) |
| 1960 - 61 | 100.0 | 100.0 | 100.0 | 100.0 | 100 |
| 1965 - 66 | 155.4 | 112.1 | 138.6 | 139.1 | 132 |
| 1970 - 71 | 246.8 | 133.3 | 185.1 | 182.7 | 186 |
| 1975 - 76 | 446.1 | 162.8 | 274.0 | 278.6 | 313 |
| 1980 - 81 | 765.4 | 188.8 | 405.4 | 411.5 | 401 |
| 1981 - 82 | 877.4 | 199.9 | 438.9 | 452.7 | 451 |
| 1982 - 83 | 974.4 | 204.2 | 477.2 | 487.7 | 486 |
| 1983 - 84 | 1,117.0 | 220.7 | 506.1 | 529.6 | 547 |
| 1984 - 85 | 1,321.9 | 228.4 | 578.8 | 569.1 | 582 |
| 1985 - 86 | 1505.6 | 237.2 | 634.7 | 609.1 | 620 |
| 1986 - 87 | 1727.9 | 245.1 | 705.0 | 651.4 | 674 |
| 1987 - 88 | 1979.2 | 254.9 | 776.5 | 710.7 | 736 |
| 1988 - 89 | 2279.0 | 283.5 | 803.9 | 767.5 | 805 |
| 1989 - 90 | 2732.1 | 300.5 | 909.2 | 821.8 | 853 |
| 1990 - 91 | 3214.1 | 317.9 | 1011.0 | 918.9 | 951 |
| Compound annual rate of increase (%) between | | | | | |
| 1960 - 61 & 1990 - 91 | 12.3 | 3.9 | 8.0 | 7.7 | 7.8 |

❑ In an economy as a whole, money supply is a reasonably good measure of aggregate demand for goods and services while real national income is equally a good indicator of aggregate supply of goods and services. Any imbalance between the growth of aggregate demand and supply suggested by these indicators translates itself into inflation after some time lag.

❑ Thus between 1960-61 and 1990-91, while money supply expanded at the annual rate of 12.3%, the real national income increased at the rate of only 3.9% per annum. This differential in growth rates resulted in inflation of consumer prices at the annual rate of around 8% during the period.

❑ Persistently excessive expansion of money supply carries a hangover effect on prices even into a year of reasonably good growth of real output.

## 17.4   Index Numbers of Wholesale Prices : 1950 - 1991

### A : Average Overall Index (Base : 1981-82 = 100)

| Average Index for Calendar Year | Index | % change over previous year | Average Index for Calendar Year | Index | % change over previous year |
|---|---|---|---|---|---|
| 1950 | 16.2 | 5.2 | 1981 | 97.2 | 12.1 |
|  |  |  | 1982 | 99.7 | 2.5 |
| 1955 | 14.1 | -9.4 | 1983 | 110.8 | 11.1 |
|  |  |  | 1984 | 118.5 | 6.9 |
| 1960 | 18.9 | 6.2 | 1985 | 124.0 | 4.6 |
|  |  |  |  |  |  |
| 1965 | 24.9 | 8.3 | 1986 | 130.9 | 5.6 |
|  |  |  | 1987 | 140.0 | 7.0 |
| 1970 | 34.6 | 6.1 | 1988 | 152.2 | 8.7 |
|  |  |  | 1989 | 162.5 | 6.8 |
| 1975 | 61.4 | 3.9 | 1990 | 176.7 | 8.7 |
|  |  |  |  |  |  |
| 1980 | 86.7 | 20.2 | 1991 | 199.4 | 12.8 |
|  |  |  |  |  |  |
| 1950 to 1960 |  | 1.6 | 1980 to 1990 |  | 7.4 |
| 1960 to 1970 |  | 6.2 |  |  |  |
| 1970 to 1980 |  | 9.6 | 1950 to 1991 |  | 6.3 |

*contd* ..

## B : Average index of major commodity groups (Base : 1981-82 = 100)

| Average Index for | Primary articles (32.30%) | | Fuel group (10.66%) | | Manufactured products (57.04%) | | All commoditites (100.0%) | |
|---|---|---|---|---|---|---|---|---|
| Financial Year | Index | % change | Index | % change | Index | % change | Index | % change |
| 1982 - 83 | 106.7 | 6.7 | 106.5 | 6.5 | 103.5 | 3.5 | 104.9 | 4.9 |
| 1983 - 84 | 118.2 | 10.8 | 112.5 | 5.6 | 109.8 | 6.1 | 112.8 | 7.5 |
| 1984 - 85 | 125.5 | 6.2 | 117.3 | 4.3 | 117.5 | 7.0 | 120.1 | 6.5 |
| 1985 - 86 | 125.7 | 0.2 | 129.8 | 10.7 | 124..4 | 5.9 | 125.4 | 4.4 |
| 1986 - 87 | 137.1 | 9.1 | 138.6 | 6.8 | 129.2 | 3.9 | 132.7 | 5.8 |
| 1987 - 88 | 152.6 | 11.3 | 143.3 | 3.4 | 138.5 | 7.2 | 143.6 | 8.2 |
| 1988 - 89 | 160.1 | 4.9 | 151.2 | 5.5 | 151.5 | 9.4 | 154.3 | 7.5 |
| 1989 - 90 | 163.6 | 2.2 | 156.6 | 3.6 | 168.6 | 11.3 | 165.7 | 7.4 |
| 1990 - 91 | 184.9 | 13.0 | 175.8 | 12.3 | 182.6 | 8.3 | 182.7 | 10.3 |
| 1991 - 92 (Provisional) | 218.3 | 18.0 | 199.0 | 13.2 | 203.4 | 11.4 | 207.8 | 13.7 |
| Annual rate of increase (%) between | | | | | | | | |
| 1981-82 & 1991-92 | | 8.1 | | 7.1 | | 7.2 | | 7.5 |

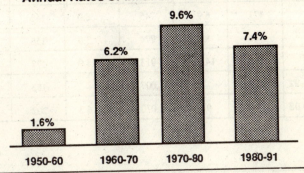

## Wholesale Price Index
## Annual Rates of Inflation – 1950 to 1991

1950-60: 1.6%
1960-70: 6.2%
1970-80: 9.6%
1980-91: 7.4%

## 17.5 Index Numbers of Consumer Prices 1960-1993.

| Average for the year | Industrial Workers | | Agricultural Labourers | | Urban Non-manual Employees | |
|---|---|---|---|---|---|---|
| | Index 1982=100 | % change | Index 1960-61 =100 | % change | Index 1984-85 =100 | % change |
| 1960 | 20 | | | | 19 | |
| 1965 | 28 | 12.0 | 149 | | 24 | 4.3 |
| 1970 | 37 | 5.7 | 194 | 4.3 | 33 | 6.5 |
| 1975 | 65 | 4.8 | 360 | 8.4 | 52 | 6.1 |
| 1980 | 79 | 11.3 | 383 | 15.0 | 67 | 11.7 |
| 1981 | 89 | 12.7 | 436 | 13.8 | 76 | 13.4 |
| 1982 | 100 | 12.4 | 458 | 5.0 | 82 | 7.9 |
| 1983 | 108 | 8.0 | 511 | 11.6 | 90 | 9.6 |
| 1984 | 117 | 8.3 | 521 | 2.0 | 98 | 8.9 |
| 1985 | 123 | 5.1 | 538 | 3.3 | 105 | 7.1 |
| 1986 | 134 | 8.9 | 567 | 5.4 | 113 | 7.6 |
| 1987 | 146 | 9.0 | 608 | 7.2 | 123 | 8.8 |
| 1988 | 160 | 9.6 | 690 | 13.5 | 133 | 8.1 |
| 1989 | 171 | 6.9 | 745 | 8.0 | 143 | 7.5 |
| 1990 | 186 | 8.8 | 774 | 3.9 | 156 | 9.1 |
| 1991 | 212 | 14.0 | 913 | 18.0 | 177 | 13.5 |
| 1991 - 92 | 219 | – | 1,007 | – | 183 | – |
| 1992 - 93 | 240 | 9.6 | 1,070 | 6.3 | 202 | 10.4 |

*contd* ..

| Average for the year | Industrial Workers | | Agricultural Labourers | | Urban Non-manual Employees | |
|---|---|---|---|---|---|---|
| | Index 1982=100 | % change | Index 1960-61 =100 | % change | Index 1984-85 =100 | % change |
| Compound annual rate of increase (%) | | | | | | |
| 1960 to 1970 | | 6.3 | | 6.9 | | 5.7 |
| 1970 to 1980 | | 7.8 | | 7.0 | | 7.3 |
| 1980 to 1990 | | 8.9 | | 7.3 | | 8.8 |
| 1960 to 1991 | | 7.9 | | 7.2 | | 7.5 |

❑ The cost of index for the three categories of workers show a long term growth rate of between 7.2% and 7.5% per annum between 1960 and 1991.

❑ The year 1991 average index showed the maximum rise leaping to double digit rates exactly after one decade.

❑ There has been a steady acceleration in the rate of inflation, culminating in the highest annual rates of increase recorded during the eighties.

## Accelerating Rate of Inflation
### Average annual rate of rise in Consumer Price Index for Industrial Workers.

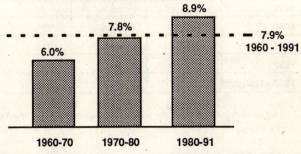

## 17.6   Inflation and Erosion of purchasing power of Rupee 1950-1993

| Year (Average index for) | Consumer Price Index for Industrial Workers | | Purchasing power of today's Rupee (i.e. March 1993) in the year indicated | Loss of value of Rupee by Feb 1992 since the year indicated (%) |
|---|---|---|---|---|
| | Average index base 1982=100 | % variation over previous year | | |
| 1950 | 17 | | 8 | 92 |
| 1955 | 16 | -5.9 | 8 | 92 |
| 1960 | 20 | – | 10 | 90 |
| 1965 | 28 | 12.0 | 14 | 86 |
| 1970 | 37 | 5.7 | 18 | 82 |
| 1975 | 65 | 4.8 | 32 | 68 |
| 1980 | 79 | 11.3 | 38 | 62 |
| 1981 | 89 | 12.7 | 43 | 57 |
| 1982 | 100 | 12.4 | 49 | 51 |
| 1983 | 108 | 8.0 | 53 | 47 |
| 1984 | 117 | 8.3 | 57 | 43 |
| 1985 | 123 | 5.1 | 60 | 40 |
| 1986 | 134 | 8.9 | 65 | 35 |
| 1987 | 146 | 9.0 | 71 | 29 |
| 1988 | 160 | 9.6 | 78 | 22 |
| 1989 | 171 | 6.9 | 83 | 17 |
| 1990 | 186 | 8.8 | 91 | 9 |
| 1991 | 212 | 14.0 | 103 | -3 |
| 1992 | 198 | -6.6 | 97 | 3 |
| 1993 - March | 205 | 3.5 | 100 | 0 |

❏   This table tries to answer the often asked question as to what is the value of rupee today.

❑ The real value of rupee today can be related to a particular base year's value of rupee taken equal to 100 paise.

❑ Thus taking 1950 as the base year, the cost of living index today i.e. by March 1993 has increased from 17 to 205. So, one can buy today for 100 paise the same quantity of real goods and services which one could buy in 1950 for only 8 paise. Thus in terms of purchasing power of one rupee in 1950 the value of rupee today is just 8 paise. In other words there is 92% erosion in the value of rupee over the period between 1950 and today.

## 18.1 Trends in India's Imports, Exports & Trade Balance : 1950-51 – 1991-92

*(Rs. crores)*

| Year | Imports | Exports | Trade Balance | Exports as % of World exports | As % GNP | | |
|---|---|---|---|---|---|---|---|
| | | | | | Import | Exports | Trade Balance |
| 1950-51 | 650 | 601 | -49 | 1.88 | 6.97 | 6.45 | -0.52 |
| 1955-56 | 774 | 609 | -165 | 1.35 | 7.55 | 5.94 | -1.61 |
| 1960-61 | 1,122 | 642 | -480 | 1.03 | 6.96 | 3.98 | -2.98 |
| 1965-66 | 1,401 | 806 | -603 | 0.81 | 5.42 | 3.10 | -2.32 |
| 1970-71 | 1,634 | 1,535 | -99 | 0.63 | 3.81 | 3.58 | -0.23 |
| 1975-76 | 5,265 | 4,042 | -1,223 | 0.49 | 6.71 | 5.15 | -1.56 |
| 1980-81 | 12,549 | 6,711 | -5,838 | 0.43 | 9.20 | 4.92 | -4.28 |
| 1981-82 | 13,608 | 7,806 | -5,802 | 0.42 | 8.51 | 4.88 | -3.63 |
| 1982-83 | 14,293 | 8,803 | -5,490 | 0.50 | 8.05 | 4.96 | -3.09 |
| 1983-84 | 15,831 | 9,771 | -6,060 | 0.50 | 7.66 | 4.73 | -2.93 |
| 1984-85 | 17,134 | 11,744 | -5,390 | 0.52 | 7.45 | 5.12 | -2.34 |
| 1985-86 | 19,658 | 10,895 | -8,763 | 0.47 | 7.54 | 4.18 | -3.36 |
| 1986-87 | 20,096 | 12,452 | -7,644 | 0.43 | 6.92 | 4.29 | -2.63 |
| 1987-88 | 22,244 | 15,674 | -6,570 | 0.46 | 6.74 | 4.75 | -1.99 |
| 1988-89 | 28,235 | 20,232 | -8,003 | 0.46 | 7.20 | 5.16 | -2.04 |
| 1989-90 | 35,416 | 27,681 | -7,735 | 0.54 | 7.93 | 6.20 | -1.73 |
| 1990-91 | 43,193 | 32,553 | -10,640 | 0.56 | 8.22 | 6.20 | -2.02 |
| 1991-92 | 47,851 | 44,042 | -3,809 | N.A. | 8.07 | 8.94 | -0.71 |
| Compound annual rates of increase % | | | | | | | |
| 1950-51 to 1960-61 | 5.6 | 0.7 | — | — | — | — | — |
| 1960-61 to 1970-71 | 3.8 | 9.1 | — | — | — | — | — |

| Compound annual rates of increase % | | | | | | | |
|---|---|---|---|---|---|---|---|
| 1970-71 to 1980-81 | 22.6 | 15.9 | — | — | — | — | — |
| 1980-81 to 1990-91 | 13.2 | 17.1 | — | — | — | — | — |

❑ During the entire period of 40 years of planning era, there have been only two years in which we had some small external trade surplus – in 1972-73 and 1976-77. In other words, our imports growth in value terms was faster than that of exports. The peculiar contradiction to this observation during the decade of 1960-61 to 1970-71 should be ignored because of the abnormal growth behaviours of imports and exports in the terminal years of the decade.

❑ During the eighties, even though exports recorded higher growth than imports in most of the years, the trade gap in 1990-91 reached an all time high of Rs.10,640 crores, implying that exports earnings financed only 75% of our import bill in that year. The average import finance through exports during the eighties was also high at 68% resulting in a sharp deterioration of our overall balance of payments position.

❑ The share of our exports in total world exports which was around 2% during the post independents years steadily declined to about half a percent towards the close of eighties.

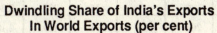

## Dwindling Share of India's Exports In World Exports (per cent)

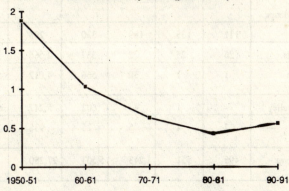

## 18.2   India's Export Earnings by Major Commodities for Select Years : 1950-51 – 1991-92

*(Rs. crores)*

| Commodities | 1950-51 | 1960-61 | 1970-71 | 1980-81 | 1990-91 | 1991-92 |
|---|---|---|---|---|---|---|
| Cashew Kernel | | 19 | 52 | 123 | 447 | 672 |
| Coffee | 1 | 7 | 25 | 214 | 253 | 310 |
| Marine products | 2 | 5 | 31 | 217 | 960 | 1374 |
| Oilcake | - | 15 | 55 | 125 | 609 | 871 |
| Raw cotton | 17 | 12 | 16 | 177 | 846 | 316 |
| Rice | - | - | 6 | 224 | 440 | N.A. |
| Spices | 26 | 17 | 39 | 111 | 234 | 370 |
| Sugar | - | 3 | 29 | 41 | 38 | 144 |
| Tea | 80 | 124 | 148 | 426 | 1,070 | 1132 |
| Tobacco, Unmfr. | 14 | 15 | 31 | 124 | 193 | 312 |
| Tobacco Mfrs. | 4 | 1 | 1 | 16 | 70 | N.A. |
| Iron ore | - | 17 | 117 | 303 | 1,049 | 1432 |
| Engineering goods | 2 | 13 | 184 | 874 | 3,221 | N.A. |
| Chemicals & prods. | 6 | 7 | 36 | 235 | 2,345 | 3677 |
| Cotton yarn Fabrics Madeups | 201 | 130 | 133 | 429 | 2,100 | 3209 |
| Jute mfrs. | 111 | 135 | 189 | 330 | 298 | 388 |
| Leather mfrs. | 26 | 25 | 72 | 337 | 2,566 | 3076 |
| Readymade garments | 1 | 1 | 30 | 566 | 4,012 | 5411 |
| Gem & jewelley | - | 1 | 43 | 602 | 5,247 | 6750 |
| Petroleum products | 2 | 4 | 5 | 25 | 938 | 1022 |
| Total of above items | 495 | 551 | 1,243 | 5,503 | 27,280 | – |

| Share to total exports from India | 82.4 | 85.8 | 80.9 | 82.0 | 83.9 | – |
|---|---|---|---|---|---|---|
| Other exports | 106 | 91 | 292 | 1,208 | 5,247 | – |
| Total exports | 601 | 642 | 1,535 | 6,711 | 32,553 | 44,042 |

❑ Whereas the share of 20 listed items in India's total exports has ranged between 80% and 86% during the period, the main items that have recorded significant growth of exports are gems & jewellery, readymade garments, leather manufactures, engineering goods, and chemical products. These five commodities/groups together contribute as much as 54% to out total export earnings today as Export growth of traditional has slowed down over the years against only 6% in 1950-51.

## Years : 1950-51 to 1991-92 Total Exports

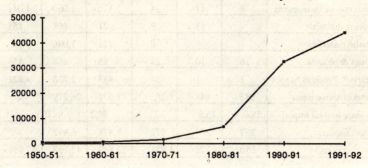

## 18.3 India's Import Bill by Major Commodities for select years : 1950-51 – 1991-92

*(Rs. crores)*

| Commodities | 1950-51 | 1960-61 | 1970-71 | 1980-81 | 1990-91 | 1991-92 |
|---|---|---|---|---|---|---|
| Cereals & preparations | 95 | 181 | 213 | 100 | 182 | 141 |
| Pulses | - | - | - | 30 | 481 | 254 |
| Edible Oils | 3 | 4 | 23 | 683 | 326 | 240 |
| Fertilsers | 12 | 12 | 84 | 652 | 1,141 | 1520 |
| Crude oil & products | 55 | 69 | 135 | 5,263 | 10,820 | 13,129 |
| Coal | - | - | - | 27 | 789 | 1,037 |
| Paper, boards & pulp | 10 | 19 | 37 | 187 | 456 | 488 |
| Iron & steel | 16 | 122 | 147 | 852 | 2,113 | 2,154 |
| Non-ferrous metals | 26 | 47 | 119 | 477 | 1,102 | 840 |
| Ores & metal scrap | 2 | 3 | 11 | 116 | 1,528 | 1,015 |
| Capital goods | 132 | 356 | 404 | 1,910 | 10,465 | 10,394 |
| Professional instruments | 8 | 11 | 24 | 176 | 1,060 | 1,041 |
| Dyeing materials | - | 13 | 9 | 21 | 168 | 155 |
| Plastic materials | - | - | 8 | 121 | 1,096 | N.A. |
| Drugs & pharma. | 10 | 10 | 24 | 85 | 468 | 456 |
| Pearls & Precious Stones | 1 | 1 | 24 | 417 | 3,738 | 4,822 |
| Total of above items | 383 | 848 | 1,262 | 11,071 | 36,279 | – |
| % share in total imports | 58.9 | 75.6 | 77.2 | 88.2 | 84.0 | – |
| other imports | 267 | 274 | 372 | 1,478 | 6,892 | – |
| Total imports | 650 | 1,122 | 1,634 | 12,549 | 43,193 | 47,851 |

❑ Unlike in the composition of exports, the 15 major commodities of imports listed above have come to claim increasing share of our total import bill rising from 59% in 1950-51 to 88.2% in 1980-81 before declining slightly to 84% in 1990-91.

❑ Crude oil and products and capital goods are the two largest items of our imports costing 49% of total imports in 1990-91. Iron and steel fertilisers and ores are the next three in order. Together these five top commodities amount for over 60% of the import bill against 33% in 1950-51.

## 18.4 Top 20 Destinations of India's Exports in 1990-91

*(Rs. crores)*

| Countries | 1951-52 | 1960-61 | 1970-71 | 1980-81 | 1990-91 |
|---|---|---|---|---|---|
| USA | 7 | 29 | 210 | 1,226 | 5,266 |
| USSR | 132 | 103 | 207 | 743 | 4,796 |
| Japan | 15 | 35 | 203 | 508 | 3,025 |
| Germany W. | 9 | 20 | 32 | 385 | 2,535 |
| U. K. | 190 | 172 | 170 | 395 | 2,133 |
| Belgium | 8 | 5 | 20 | 144 | 1,254 |
| Hongkong | 7 | 3 | 17 | 141 | 1,074 |
| Italy | 8 | 9 | 14 | 152 | 1002 |
| UAE | 1 | 2 | - | 152 | 780 |
| France | 11 | 9 | 18 | 147 | 765 |
| Singapore | 12 | 7 | 18 | 109 | 679 |
| Netherlands | 8 | 8 | 14 | 152 | 650 |
| Bangladesh | 3 | 6 | - | 75 | 547 |
| Thailand | 9 | 3 | 6 | 45 | 443 |
| Saudi Arabia | 2 | 3 | 15 | 165 | 418 |
| Switzerland | 2 | 1 | 7 | 111 | 401 |
| Korea south | - | - | 2 | 44 | 327 |
| Australia | 48 | 22 | 24 | 92 | 321 |
| Spain | - | 1 | 3 | 16 | 281 |
| Canada | 16 | 18 | 28 | 62 | 268 |
| Total of Top 20 | 488 | 456 | 1,008 | 4,864 | 26,965 |
| % share in total exports | 66.6 | 71.0 | 65.7 | 72.5 | 82.9 |
| Exports to other countries | 245 | 186 | 527 | 1,847 | 5,562 |
| Total exports to all countries | 733 | 642 | 1,535 | 6,711 | 32,527 (a) |

*Notes : (a) Un-revised*

❏ The top 20 countries accounted for 83% of our total exports.

❏ The top 5 importers of Indian goods accounted for 55% of total exports during 1990-91 from 48% in 1950-51.

❏ While UK was the largest buyer till the early sixties, USA took the top place thereafter USSR consistently ranked second till 1990-91 whereas UK slid to fourth place since the seventies and to fifth place by 1990-91.

❏ Australia and Canada which were the third and fourth largest importers of Indian goods are how placed at almost the bottom of the list.

## Changing Shares of top 5 importing countries

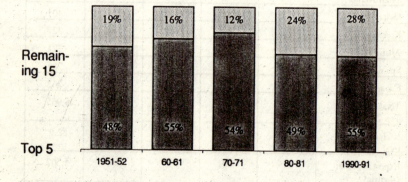

## 18.5   Top 20 Sources of India's Imports in 1990-91

*(Rs. crores)*

| Countries | 1951-52 | 1960-61 | 1970-71 | 1980-81 | 1990-91 |
|---|---|---|---|---|---|
| USA | 28 | 290 | 446 | 1,519 | 5,237 |
| Germany W | 24 (a) | 124 | 107 | 657 | 3,477 |
| Japan | 16 (a) | 59 | 92 | 749 | 3,245 |
| U. K. | 162 | 211 | 126 | 731 | 2,920 |
| Saudi Arabia | 10 | 14 | 24 | 540 | 2,898 |
| Belgium | 10 | 15 | 11 | 296 | 2,717 |
| USSR | 1 | 15 | 105 | 1,014 | 2,552 |
| UAE | - | - | - | 350 | 1,899 |
| Australia | 12 (a) | 17 | 36 | 170 | 1,487 |
| Singapore | 18 | 10 | 1 | 428 | 1,430 |
| France | 11 | 20 | 21 | 280 | 1,305 |
| Italy | 18 | 25 | 29 | 242 | 1,094 |
| Iran | 29 | 37 | 92 | 1,339 | 1,018 |
| Malaysia | - | - | 9 | 266 | 999 |
| Netherlands | 11 | 10 | 19 | 215 | 795 |
| Taiwan | - | - | 1 | 44 | 676 |
| Korea south | - | - | 1 | 135 | 646 |
| Canada | 19 | 16 | 117 | 332 | 559 |
| Iraq | 4 | 2 | 3 | 753 | 497 |
| Switzerland | 10 | 10 | 11 | 121 | 482 |
| Total of above countries | 383 | 875 | 1,251 | 10,181 | 36,033 |
| Share in total imports | 40.6 | 78.0 | 76.6 | 81.1 | 83.5 |
| Imports from other countries | 560 | 247 | 383 | 2,368 | 7,138 |
| Total imports from all countries | 943 | 1,122 | 1,634 | 12,549 | 43,171 (b) |

Notes : (a) Related to 1952-53
      (b) Un-revised.

- ❑ The top five countries of India's imports accounted for 41% of an total import bill, i.e. about half of the total share of the top 20 source countries.

- ❑ Our reliance on the listed top 20 countries has been more than three-fourths of our total imports since 1960-61.

- ❑ There is no definite movement of the position of countries as our sources of imports. Thus USSR which was the second largest supplier of goods to us in 1980-81 skipped to seventh pace in 1990-91

- ❑ Most countries which improved their share in our imports during the eighties, did so on account of our greater reliance on them for supplies of crude oil and petroleum products; Saudi Arabia, Iran and UAE are important among them. The top four have also been the major sources for import of capital goods.

## 18.6 India's Share in World Exports of Engineering Goods : 1956-57 – 1989-90

| Year | World exports of Engg. goods (b) | | India's exports of engineering goods (c) | | |
|---|---|---|---|---|---|
| | US $ billion | As % of total world exports | Rs. crores | As % of world exports of engg. goods | As % of India's total exports |
| 1956-57 | 19.59 (a) | 21.0 | 5 | — | 0.81 |
| 1960-61 | 31.10 | 24.1 | 10 | — | 1.56 |
| 1970-71 | 102.90 | 32.5 | 117 | 0.15 | 7.56 |
| 1975-76 | 279.08 | 31.7 | 408 | 0.18 | 10.09 |
| 1980-81 | 596.30 | 29.8 | 874 | 0.19 | 13.49 |
| 1981-82 | 610.50 | 31.0 | 1,043 | 0.20 | 13.36 |
| 1982-83 | 594.70 | 32.1 | 1,011 | 0.22 | 14.03 |
| 1983-84 | 600.95 | 33.2 | 1,000 | 0.19 | 11.97 |
| 1984-85 | 647.85 | 33.9 | 1,150 | 0.15 | 9.79 |
| 1985-86 | 686.70 | 35.5 | 1000 | 0.12 | 10.05 |
| 1986-87 | 827.85 | 38.9 | 1,150 | 0.11 | 9.15 |
| 1987-88 | 978.30 | 39.3 | 1,432 | 0.11 | 9.10 |
| 1988-89 | 1,016.00 | 35.5 | 2,258 | 0.15 | 11.13 |
| 1989-90 | 1,095.00 | 34.5 | 3,115 | 0.17 | 11.25 |

| Compound annual rate of increase (%) | | |
|---|---|---|
| Between 1970-71 & 1989-90 | 14.3 | 18.9 |

Notes : (a) *Relate to 1955*
(b) *World exports relate to calendar year basis ie. 1975-76 = 1975.*
(c) *Source for Indian data is the Engineering Export Promotion Council and therefore the data would not compare with data appearing in an earlier table.*

❑ The world market for engineering goods has been expanding at the highest rate. India must try to increase its share in the growing world market.

## 19.1 Balance of Payments 1989-90 to 1993-94

*(US $ million))*

| | 1989-90 | 1990-91 | 1991-92 | 1992-93 | 1993-94 |
|---|---|---|---|---|---|
| **A: Earning by Sources** | | | | | |
| Exports | 16,955 | 18,491 | 18,135 | 18,500 | 20,350 |
| Imports | 24,411 | 26,241 | 21,213 | 24,000 | 27,600 |
| Trade balance | -7,456 | -7,750 | -3,078 | -5,500 | -7,250 |
| Tourist earnings (net) | 1,031 | 862 | 850 | 900 | 900 |
| Remittances (net) | 2,284 | 2,000 | 2,200 | 2,200 | 2,500 |
| Interst and other invest income (net) | -2928 | -3,100 | -3,200 | -3,400 | -3,500 |
| Official tranfers (net) | 539 | 457 | 451 | 450 | 450 |
| Others invisibles (net) | -308 | -196 | -249 | -250 | -200 |
| Total invisibles (net) | 618 | 23 | 52 | -100 | 150 |
| Current account balance | -6,838 | -7,727 | -3,026 | -5,600 | -7,100 |
| Foreign assistance (net) | 1,856 | 2,268 | 2,803 | 2,500 | 2,800 |
| Commercial borrowings (net) | 1,777 | 729 | 1,805 | 50 | 75 |
| NRI deposists (net) | 2,403 | 1,259 | -747 | 650 | 650 |
| IMF (net) | -877 | 1,214 | 781 | 1,500 | 325 |
| Other capital (net) inc. foreign investment | 938 | 979 | 1,767 | 2,300 · | 2,400 |
| Total capital (net) | 6,097 | 6,449 | 6,409 | 7,000 | 6,250 |
| Change in reserves | -741 | -1,278 | 3,383 | 1,400 | -850 |
| Reserves outstanding | 3,368 | 2,236 | 5,361 | 6,434 | 5,584 |
| External Debt | 57,737 | 67,070 | 68,670 | 75,670 | 81,920 |
| Debt service ratio | 24.90 | 25.20 | 26.20 | 29.00 | 30.0 |
| GROWTH RATE (%) Export | 18.92 | 9.06 | -1.93 | 2.01 | 10.0 |
| Import | 3.36 | 7.50 | -19.16 | 13.14 | 15.0 |
| Current account as % of GDP | - 2.7 | - 2.5 | - 1.0 | - 2.4 | - 3.0 |

*Note : The last two year's figures are CMIE estimates and projections.*

## 19.2   Balance of Payments : April-September 1991 & 1992

*($ million)*

|  | April-September | | | April-September | |
|---|---|---|---|---|---|
|  | 1991-92 | 1992-93 |  | 1991-92 | 1992-93 |
| **Current account balance** | -2,638 | -3,996 | Capital account (net) | 1,580 | 3,228 |
| Exports | 8,275 | 8,720 | External assistance (net) | 1,353 | 228 |
| Imports | 10,535 | 13,003 | Disbursement | 1,914 | 969 |
| Trade balance | -2,260 | -4,283 | Amortisation | 561 | 741 |
| Official transfers (net) | 187 | 166 | Commercial borrowings (net) | 45 | -88 |
| Other invisibles (net) | -565 | 121 | Disbursement | 556 | 514 |
|  |  |  | Amortisation | 511 | 602 |
|  |  |  | NRI deposits (net) | -818 | 44 |
|  |  |  | Other capital (net) | 1,000 | 3,044 |
|  |  |  | IMF (net) | 626 | 472 |
|  |  |  | Total capital account incl. IMF | 2,206 | 3,700 |
|  |  |  | Reserves & monetary gold | 432 | 296 |

❑ According to the Quick Estimates released by the RBI, the current account deficit during April-September 1992 amounted to nearly $ 4 billion. This was a rise of over 50% compared with the deficit of $ 2.6 billion in the first half of 1991-92. The substantial increase in the current account deficit was due mainly to a surge in imports by 23% (in dollar terms), following a year of strong import compression in 1991-92. The trade deficit in the first half of 1992-93 increased by 90% over that in the corresponding period of 1991-92, reaching $ 4.3 billion. While there was a net outflow of $ 378 million on the invisible account in April-September 1991, positive earnings of $ 287 million were recorded in April-September 1992, (This was a result of the inclusion of $ 575 million as a counter entry against the import of gold by NRIs.)

❑ For the financial year 1992-93 as a whole, the current account deficit is projected by CMIE to reach $ 6 billion, as compared with $ 2.8 billion in 1991-92. The trade deficit for 1992-93 is expected to be $ 6.2 billion, compared with $ 3.1 billion in 1991-92. The trade deficit in the second half of 1992-93 is likely to be lower than in the first half because non-oil imports are expected to shrink during October-March 1992-93.

☐ Net external assistance during April-September 1992 was less than one-fifth that received in the corresponding period of 1991. This source financed only 6% of the current account deficit in April-September 1992 whereas it had financed more than half the current account deficit in April-September 1991. During the second half of 1992-93, "other capital" (net) amounting to $ 3,044 million financed more than 75% of the current account deficit. "Other capital" receipts included FCBOD receipts of $ 1,446 million, movements in bilateral balances of $ 635 million and short-term credits of $ 333 million.

☐ During the second half of 1992-93, net external assistance is expected to finance a major portion of the current account deficit.

## 19.3 Ratio of External Trade and Net Current and Capital Accounts Balances to GDP 1955-56 – 1990-91

| Year | Exports | Imports | Trade Balance | Gross invisible earnings | Net invisible earnings | Current account balance | Net capital inflow |
|---|---|---|---|---|---|---|---|
| 1955-56 | 6.26 | 7.29 | -1.03 | 2.36 | 1.23 | 0.20 | 0.23 |
| 1960-61 | 3.90 | 6.72 | -2.82 | 1.58 | 0.56 | -2.26 | 1.89 |
| 1965-66 | 2.99 | 5.11 | -2.12 | 1.34 | 0.31 | -1.89 | 1.53 |
| 1970-71 | 3.26 | 4.23 | -0.97 | 1.15 | -0.09 | -1.06 | 1.16 |
| 1975-76 | 5.30 | 6.02 | -0.72 | 2.04 | 1.09 | 0.37 | 0.72 |
| 1980-81 | 4.84 | 9.24 | -4.40 | 4.34 | 3.17 | -1.23 | 0.67 |
| 1981-82 | 4.87 | 8.71 | -3.84 | 3.65 | 2.39 | -1.45 | 0.31 |
| 1982-83 | 5.15 | 8.40 | -3.25 | 3.44 | 1.96 | -1.29 | 0.46 |
| 1983-84 | 4.92 | 7.75 | -2.83 | 3.33 | 1.74 | -1.09 | 1.06 |
| 1984-85 | 5.18 | 8.09 | -2.91 | 3.57 | 1.67 | -1.24 | 1.47 |
| 1985-86 | 4.41 | 8.06 | -3.65 | 3.00 | 1.38 | -2.27 | 1.86 |
| 1986-87 | 4.54 | 7.73 | -3.19 | 2.82 | 1.20 | -1.99 | 2.01 |
| 1987-88 | 4.93 | 7.73 | -2.80 | 2.62 | 0.90 | -1.90 | 2.25 |
| 1988-89 | 5.23 | 8.66 | -3.43 | 2.77 | 0.80 | -2.63 | 2.60 |
| 1989-90 | 6.32 | 9.10 | -2.78 | 2.80 | 0.58 | -2.20 | 2.32 |
| 1990-91 | 6.32 | 9.20 | -2.88 | n.a. | 0.39 | -2.49 | 1.64 |

Notes : (a) *An aspect of over economy which has been a source of major concern of late relates to the balance of payments situation which has dictated the formulation of our economic agenda. The Seventh Plan period (1985-90) saw a widening of our current account deficit. As against the targeted ratio of 1.6 percent to GDP, the current account deficit for the period averaged 2.2 percent of the GDP. Despite a robust growth of exports the current account deficit increased because of increase in imports on one hand and a steady decline in net invisible receipts on the other hand.*

❑ This position did not improve even during 1990-91, with the current account deficit at 2.5 per cent of the GDP. No doubt this was largely the result of a sharp rise in crude oil prices and other effects of the gulf war. But the consequences of our efforts to obtain finance for this widening current account deficit are by now widely known, following the exceptional mode of finance that had to be sought from the IMF and World Bank.

## 19.4   A : Foreign Exchange Reserves of India 1950 – 1991

| At the end of Dec. | In US $ million | | | | | Rs. crore's | |
| | Gold | Reserves positions in IMF | SDRs | Foreign exchange | Total | Excluding gold & SDRs | |
| | | | | | | Total | No. of months imports |
|---|---|---|---|---|---|---|---|
| 1950 | 247 | – | – | 1810 | 2057 | n.a. | – |
| 1951 | 245 | – | – | 1699 | 1944 | n.a. | – |
| 1955 | 247 | – | – | 1620 | 1867 | 814 (a) | – |
| 1960 | 247 | – | – | 423 | 670 | 245 | 2 |
| 1965 | 280 | – | – | 319 | 599 | 116 | 2 |
| 1970 | 241 | 21 | 44 | 698 | 1004 | 546 | 3 |
| 1975 | 204 | – | 248 | 841 | 1293 | 611 | 3 |
| 1980 | 284 | 420 | 480 | 6043 | 7227 | 5164 | 5 |
| 1981 | 248 | 384 | 545 | 3764 | 4941 | 4822 | 3 |
| 1982 | 234 | 402 | 374 | 3539 | 4549 | 3354 | 4 |
| 1983 | 215 | 510 | 110 | 4318 | 5153 | 4265 | 4 |
| 1984 | 184 | 477 | 331 | 5034 | 6026 | 5498 | 5 |
| 1985 | 203 | 535 | 336 | 5549 | 6623 | 6817 | 5 |
| 1986 | 209 | 596 | 356 | 5444 | 6605 | 7384 | 5 |
| 1987 | 213 | 691 | 159 | 5604 | 6667 | 7645 | 4 |
| 1988 | 183 | 656 | 96 | 4148 | 5083 | 7287 | 3 |
| 1989 | 161 | 640 | 113 | 3105 | 4019 | 6605 | 2 |
| 1990 | 3667 | – | 316 | 1205 | 5188 | 5787 | 1 |
| 1991 | | | | | | 9287 | |

Notes : (a) Data in US dollars are taken from the IMF sources, where figures for 1991 were not available.

❏  Level of foreign exchange reserves at any point in time is the net result of all transactions in the external sector.

❏ As said in the preceding table (19.3) the 1980s witnessed mounting trade deficits and precipitous fall in invisible receipts, thereby worsening current account deficits. The effect of this was seen in depletion of reserves as inflow of capital became scarce and difficult to obtain.

❏ Conventionally it is considered prudent to maintain foreign exchange reserves equivalent to three months value of imports. However, during 1991, there was a steep decline in reserves to the low of Rs. 2,387 crores by June 1991, which was then enough to hardly finance about a fortnight's imports.

❏ As a result of the BOP adjustment strategy followed since July 1991 there has been a distinct improvement in our reserves position reaching Rs.10,958 crores by mid-February 1992. It should be noted however that this was attained mainly through large scale borrowings abroad rather than an improvement of export earnings.

## B: Foreign Currency Reserves 1991-92 and 1992-93

| End of month | US $ million | | Months of imports covered | |
|---|---|---|---|---|
| | 1991-92 | 1992-93 | 1991-92 | 1992-93 |
| April | 1,269 | 5,476 | 0.89 | 2.75 |
| May | 1,271 | 5,458 | 0.90 | 2.72 |
| June | 1,124 | 6,224 | 0.70 | 2.88 |
| July | 1,286 | 6,457 | 0.98 | 3.00 |
| August | 1,141 | 6,309 | 0.77 | 3.36 |
| September | 1,722 | 5,769 | 1.12 | 2.82 |
| October | 2,325 | 5,467 | 1.43 | 3.03 |
| November | 2,707 | 4,861 | 1.81 | 2.42 |
| December | 3,580 | 5,359 | 2.08 | 2.65 |
| January | 3,774 | | 2.35 | |
| February | 4,162 | | 2.46 | |
| March | 5,631 | | 3.08 | |

*Note :  To calculate the number of months of imports covered, the rupee equival ent of foreign currency reserves (at the official exchange rate) is divided by imports in that month*

❑  By December-end, foreign currency reserves stood at $ 5,359 million — nearly 50% higher than the level a year earlier. Compared with the position at the end of 1991-92, however, the reserves at the and of calendar year 1992 were lower by $ 272 million. The reserves at December-end were $ 272 million higher than at November-end 1992. The reserves position strengthened due to the release of around one billion dollars by the IMF, ADB and World Bank in December 1992. The IMF released two tranches worth $ 646 mln. under the Standby Arrangement, bringing drawals from the IMF in the current financial year to $ 1,293 million.

❑  With the net outflow of funds on the external aid account during April-November 1992, it is evident that the build-up of reserves has a high cost in terms of interest and debt servicing.

❑  Reserves have also suffered because of a net outflow of NRI funds. The net outflow of funds from NRI bank deposits between April-November 1992 was $ 248 million — approximately 15% the net outflow in the corresponding period of 1991. In fact, there was a net inflow of $ 64 mln. into FCNR accounts in November 1992. However, there was net outflow from NRER accounts for the fifth consecutive month in November 1992, resulting in a total net inflow of $ 40 mln. during the month.

## 19.5    Remittances of Profits, Interests etc. from India : 1956-57 – 1986-87

| Year | Profits | Dividends | Royalties | Technical know-how fees | Interest payments by private sector | Total |
|---|---|---|---|---|---|---|
| 1956-57 | 19.40 | 7.10 | 1.20 | – | 2.70 | 30.40 |
| 1960-61 | 18.90 | 12.60 | 2.50 | – | 7.60 | 41.60 |
| 1965-66 | 13.50 | 19.40 | 2.95 | 6.98 | – | 42.83 |
| 1970-71 | 13.12 | 43.48 | 5.23 | 20.63 | 12.80 | 95.26 |
| 1975-76 | 20.36 | 24.84 | 10.49 | 25.66 | 24.65 | 106.00 |
| 1980-81 | 21.10 | 55.92 | 8.88 | 104.93 | 22.32 | 204.15 |
| 1981-82 | 12.16 | 58.92 | 15.99 | 270.70 | 41.08 | 398.85 |
| 1982-83 | 19.12 | 70.31 | 39.72 | 258.58 | 80.23 | 467.96 |
| 1983-84 | 20.00 | 62.11 | 27.60 | 314.89 | 81.51 | 506.11 |
| 1984-85 | 16.68 | 74.58 | 28.49 | 300.80 | 123.91 | 544.26 |
| 1985-86 | 11.80 | 75.20 | 23.50 | 367.90 | 218.70 | 697.10 |
| 1986-87 | 10.60 | 85.50 | 40.10 | 358.40 | 318.90 | 813.50 |

❑ That the foreign-based multinational corporations have exploited India's natural resources and cheap labour had been for long a favourite excuse for the politicians and academicians when it came to any policy changes for allowing foreign participation. Such criticism was not adequately supported by factual information. For instance, remittances from India by such enterprises in recent years was less than half-a-percent of GNP.

❑ While this may not be a sufficient ground to throw wide open all areas of business for unlimited investment by foreign firms, liberalisation in selective areas is needed for obtaining technical know-how and promoting foreign exchange earnings. In this respect Japan's is an ideal case to emulate : rather than devoting scarce resources to develop one's own technical know-how, it would be preferable to adopt what could be readily available through tie-ups with foreign firms.

## 19.6    A Comparison with other Asian Countries

| | Real GDP/GNP growth | Inflation rate | Exports | Imports | Current account balance (US $ bln.) | Exchange rate (Currency per US $) |
|---|---|---|---|---|---|---|
| **China** | | | | | | |
| 1991 | 7.7 | 2.9 | 15.8 | 19.5 | 13.3 | 5.45 |
| 1992 | 10.3 | 5.7 | 14.5 | 18.2 | 10.3 | 5.50 |
| 1993 | 9.2 | 9.5 | – | – | 6.0 | 5.68 |
| **Hong Kong** | | | | | | |
| 1991 | 4.2 | 12.0 | 19.7 | 21.2 | 2.7 | 7.78 |
| 1992 | 4.7 | 9.7 | 20.0 | 21.9 | 1.5 | 7.72 |
| 1993 | 5.4 | 10.3 | – | – | 0.5 | 7.72 |
| **INDIA** | | | | | | |
| 1991 | 5.6 | 13.6 | -1.7 | -19.4 | 7.7 | 22.74 |
| 1992 | 1.5 | 13.9 | 6.9 | 22.5 | -2.6 | 29.51 |
| 1993 | 4.0 | 11.0 | – | – | -6.0 | 30.90 |
| **Indonesia** | | | | | | |
| 1991 | 6.6 | 9.4 | 13.5 | 18.5 | -4.4 | 1992.00 |
| 1992 | 5.7 | 7.5 | 10.0 | 5.5 | -3.3 | 2033.00 |
| 1993 | 6.2 | 5.5 | – | – | -3.0 | 2043.00 |
| **Malaysia** | | | | | | |
| 1991 | 8.7 | 4.4 | 18.9 | 27.8 | -4.5 | 2.72 |
| 1992 | 8.1 | 4.7 | 15.3 | -1.5 | -3.4 | 2.52 |
| 1993 | 7.6 | 4.3 | – | – | -2.8 | 2.59 |
| **Philippines** | | | | | | |
| 1991 | -0.1 | 17.7 | 6.8 | -2.0 | -1.0 | 27.48 |
| 1992 | 1.8 | 9.3 | 12.8 | 30.6 | -1.4 | 24.73 |
| 1993 | 3.7 | 8.5 | – | – | -2.2 | 24.60 |
| **Singapore** | | | | | | |
| 1991 | 6.7 | 3.4 | 7.9 | 4.5 | 4.2 | 1.63 |
| 1992 | 5.4 | 2.4 | 2.0 | 1.8 | 4.9 | 1.60 |
| 1993 | 6.5 | 2.7 | – | – | 5.2 | 1.65 |
| **South Korea** | | | | | | |
| 1991 | 8.4 | 9.3 | 10.5 | 16.7 | -8.7 | 733.40 |
| 1992 | 5.6 | 6.2 | 12.8 | -3.7 | -4.0 | 787.30 |
| 1993 | 6.9 | 5.5 | – | – | -1.0 | 782.10 |

*Contd....*

| | Real GDP/GNP growth | Inflation rate | Exports | Imports | Current account balance (US $ bln.) | Exchange rate (Currency per US $) |
|---|---|---|---|---|---|---|
| **Taiwan** | | | | | | |
| 1991 | 7.3 | 3.6 | 13.3 | 14.9 | 12.0 | 25.75 |
| 1992 | 6.0 | 4.8 | 2.4 | 16.5 | 6.5 | 25.19 |
| 1993 | 6.3 | 4.5 | – | – | 5.8 | 25.37 |
| **Thailand** | | | | | | |
| 1991 | 7.5 | 5.7 | 23.4 | 15.4 | -7.6 | 25.51 |
| 1992 | 6.8 | 4.2 | 12.4 | 11.9 | -6.1 | 25.19 |
| 1993 | 8.0 | 4.4 | – | – | -7.8 | 25.45 |

Notes: (1) Figures are year-on-year percentage changes
(2) Figures of export, import, and exchange rate for the 1992 are of the latest quarter/month of the year.
(3) Exchange rate figures for 1993 are of January 1993

## 20.1 Inflow of External Assistance : 1960-61 to 1992-93

*(Rs. crores)*

| Year | Aid pledged by Aid-India Consortium | Aid from Consortium & Non-consortium sources | | | | | |
|------|------|------|------|------|------|------|------|
| | | Gross aid utilisation | Amortis-ation Payment | Interest payment | Total debt services (3+4) | Debt service as % of col. 2 | Net aid inflow (2-5) |
| | (1) | (2) | (3) | (4) | (5) | (6) | (7) |
| 1961-62 | | 532 | 91 | 52 | 143 | 26.9 | 389 |
| 1962-63 | | 699 | 76 | 61 | 137 | 19.6 | 562 |
| 1963-64 | | 929 | 85 | 72 | 157 | 16.9 | 772 |
| 1964-65 | | 1,139 | 109 | 82 | 191 | 16.8 | 948 |
| 1965-66 | | 1,216 | 121 | 106 | 227 | 18.7 | 989 |
| 1966-67 | | 1,132 | 157 | 115 | 272 | 24.0 | 860 |
| 1967-68 | | 1,177 | 194 | 122 | 316 | 26.8 | 861 |
| 1968-69 | | 913 | 207 | 137 | 344 | 37.7 | 569 |
| 1969-70 | | 837 | 238 | 142 | 380 | 45.4 | 457 |
| 1970-71 | | 780 | 254 | 158 | 412 | 52.8 | 368 |
| 1971-72 | 940 | 823 | 271 | 175 | 446 | 54.2 | 377 |
| 1972-73 | 950 | 605 | 302 | 177 | 479 | 79.2 | 126 |
| 1973-74 | 852 | 803 | 300 | 184 | 484 | 60.3 | 319 |
| 1974-75 | 1,134 | 1,314 | 368 | 201 | 569 | 43.3 | 745 |
| 1975-76 | 1,483 | 1,718 | 427 | 224 | 651 | 37.9 | 1,067 |
| 1976-77 | 1,523 | 1,531 | 471 | 242 | 713 | 46.6 | 818 |
| 1977-78 | 1,853 | 1,268 | 561 | 260 | 821 | 64.8 | 447 |
| 1978-79 | 2,015 | 1,216 | 600 | 286 | 886 | 72.9 | 330 |
| 1979-80 | 2,698 | 1,353 | 570 | 301 | 871 | 64.4 | 482 |
| 1980-81 | 2,681 | 2,162 | 518 | 286 | 804 | 37.2 | 1,358 |
| 1981-82 | 3,089 | 1,865 | 538 | 311 | 849 | 45.5 | 1,016 |
| 1982-83 | 3,585 | 2,252 | 587 | 360 | 947 | 42.1 | 1,305 |
| 1983-84 | 3,980 | 2,266 | 616 | 417 | 1,033 | 45.6 | 1,233 |
| 1984-85 | 4,707 | 2,359 | 647 | 529 | 1,176 | 49.9 | 1,183 |
| 1985-86 | 4,748 | 2,936 | 776 | 591 | 1,367 | 46.6 | 1,569 |
| 1986-87 | 5,626 | 3,605 | 1,176 | 853 | 2,029 | 56.3 | 1,576 |

*contd...*

| Year | Aid pledged by Aid-India Consortium | Aid from Consortium & Non-consortium sources | | | | | |
| --- | --- | --- | --- | --- | --- | --- | --- |
| | | Gross aid utilisation | Amortis-ation Payment | Interest payment | Total debt services (3+4) | Debt service as % of col. 2 | Net aid inflow (2-5) |
| 1987-88 | 7,003 | 5,052 | 1,581 | 1,043 | 2,624 | 51.9 | 2,428 |
| 1988-89 | 8,741 | 5,304 | 1,646 | 1,300 | 2,946 | 55.5 | 2,358 |
| 1989-90 | 11,000 | 5,802 | 1,987 | 1,699 | 3,686 | 63.5 | 2,116 |
| 1990-91 | 11,350 | 6,660 | 2,395 | 1,955 | 4,350 | 65.0 | 2,310 |
| 1991-92 | 17,300 | 11,670 | 3,559 | – | – | – | – |
| 1992-93 | 18,600 | – | – | – | – | – | – |

Note :  *The above figures do not include loans received by government from the IMF under Extended Fund Facility and Compensatory Financing Facility.*

❑ At the annual Aid-India consortium meetings the donor countries only make aid pledges which does not means corresponding aid availability to us, since such meetings are followed by country negotiations for signing of agreements. So, often the aid agreed is smaller than aid pledged. Then out of the agreed and funds are released when purchases are made, while project-linked amounts are released over several years. Besides a good part of the aid is used for repayment of outstanding of earlier aids and interest payments thereon. Thus only a small part of the aid utilised in a year is out of the aid authorised during the year. Therfore, debt servicing which absorbed around one sixth of the gross aid utilised during early sixties increased over the years to form three-fifths in 1990-91.

**Gross External Assistance Utilisation & Servicing 1961-65 to 1985-90 & 1990-91**

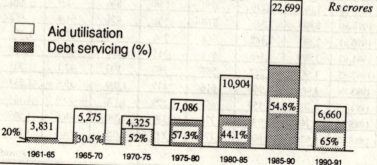

*Rs crores*

Aid utilisation
Debt servicing (%)

22,699

10,904

7,086

5,275

4,325

3,831

6,660

20%  30.5%  52%  57.3%  44.1%  54.8%  65%

1961-65  1965-70  1970-75  1975-80  1980-85  1985-90  1990-91

## 20.2 External Assistance Authorised and utilised : 1974-75 to 1990-91

*(Rs crores)*

| Year | Loans | Grants | Total | PL 480/665 Repayable in | | Total Including PL 480/665 |
|---|---|---|---|---|---|---|
| | | | | Rupees | Convert-ible currencies | |
| **Authorisation** | | | | | | |
| Upto 4th plan | 9,665 | 753 | 10,418 | 2,307 | 330 | 13,056 |
| 1974-75 | 1,481 | 190 | 1,671 | | | 1,671 |
| 1975-76 | 2,193 | 441 | 2,631 | | 20 | 2,651 |
| 1976-77 | 807 | 386 | 1,193 | | 94 | 1,287 |
| 1977-78 | 1,536 | 337 | 1,873 | | 23 | 1,896 |
| 1978-79 | 1,895 | 441 | 2,336 | | | 2,336 |
| 1979-80 | 1,295 | 564 · | 1,859 | | | 1,860 |
| 1980-81 | 3,771 | 76 | 3,847 | | | 3,847 |
| 1981-82 | 2,767 | 207 | 2,974 | | | 2,974 |
| 1982-83 | 2,549 | 423 | 2,972 | | | 2,973 |
| 1983-84 | 1,701 | 387 | 2,088 | | | 2,088 |
| 1984-85 | 4,409 | 471 | 4,880 | | | 4,880 |
| 1985-86 | 5,337 | 313 | 5,650 | | | 5,650 |
| 1986-87 | 5,730 | 430 | 6,160 | | | 6,160 |
| 1987-88 | 8,203 | 4,062 | 9,265 | | | 9,265 |
| 1988-89 | 12,856 | 214 | 13,070 | | | 13,070 |
| 1989-90 | 10,106 | 720 | 10,826 | | | 10,826 |
| 1990-91 | 7,601 | 522 | 8,123 | | | 8,123 |
| **Utilisation** | | | | | | |
| Upto 4th plan | 8,573 | 713 | 9,285 | 2,312 | 325 | 11,922 |
| 1974-75 | 1,220 | 94 | 1,314 | | | 1,314 |
| 1975-76 | 1,465 | 253 | 1,748 | | 92 | 1,840 |
| 1976-77 | 1,285 | 246 | 1,531 | | 68 | 1,599 |

*contd...*

| Year | Loans | Grants | Total | PL 480/665 Repayable in | | Total Including PL 480/665 |
| | | | | Rupees | Convert-ible currencies | |
|------|-------|--------|-------|--------|------------------|------|
| 1977-78 | 1,008 | 261 | 1,268 | | 22 | 1,290 |
| 1978-79 | 942 | 273 | 1,216 | | | 1,216 |
| 1979-80 | 1,049 | 305 | 1,353 | | | 1,353 |
| 1980-81 | 1,765 | 397 | 2,162 | | | 2,162 |
| 1981-82 | 1,519 | 346 | 1,865 | | | 1,865 |
| 1982-83 | 1,909 | 343 | 2,252 | | | 2,252 |
| 1983-84 | 1,962 | 303 | 2,266 | | | 2,266 |
| 1984-85 | 1,962 | 397 | 2,359 | | | 2,359 |
| 1985-86 | 2,493 | 443 | 2,936 | | | 2,936 |
| 1986-87 | 3,176 | 429 | 3,605 | | | 3,605 |
| 1987-88 | 4,574 | 478 | 5,052 | | | 5,052 |
| 1988-89 | 4,739 | 566 | 5,304 | | | 5,304 |
| 1989-90 | 5,138 | 665 | 5,803 | | | 5,803 |
| 1990-91 | 6,170 | 534 | 6,704 | | | 6,704 |

❑ Over the years, the proportion of grants in total external assistance has been di-minishing.

❑ The increasing proportion as well as the absolute sums of loans entails that much increase in interest burden.

❑ Of course, as compared to authorisation our ability to utilise the loan has been at a slower pace. This is mostly due to our ability to find the rupee counter-parts for project linked loans. As a result, there is an ever larger amount of unutilised loans building up in the pipeline. At the end of 1989-90 the total of unutilised loan amounted to Rs 48,000 crores.

❑ In most cases, the unutilised loans attract only the commitment charges. But once the loan is utilised the interest payments and loan repayments commence.

## 20.3   Shares of IDA and IBRD in Aid to India : 1980 to 1991-92

| Fiscal Year | IDA's share in total aid authorised from IBRD & IDA | IDA'S aid to India as % of IDA's aid to all countries | IDA's share in total aid authorised from all sources | IBRD's share in total aid authorised from IBRD & IDA | IBRD's aid to India as % of IBRD's aid to all countries | IBRD's share in total aid authorised from all sources |
|---|---|---|---|---|---|---|
| 1980 | 92.5 | 40.0 | 40.0 | 7.5 | 1.6 | 10.1 |
| 1981 | 74.9 | 36.8 | 46.0 | 25.1 | 4.9 | 18.8 |
| 1982 | 41.6 | 33.5 | 25.8 | 58.4 | 12.2 | 36.9 |
| 1983 | 49.4 | 31.8 | 29.1 | 50.6 | 9.8 | 25.0 |
| 1984 | 36.8 | 28.0 | 24.6 | 63.2 | 14.4 | 43.9 |
| 1985 | 28.7 | 22.2 | 20.3 | 71.3 | 14.7 | 39.3 |
| 1986 | 26.4 | 19.9 | 8.0 | 73.6 | 13.2 | 28.9 |
| 1987 | 24.2 | 19.4 | 14.0 | 75.8 | 15.0 | 36.2 |
| 1988 | 24.1 | 16.1 | 6.7 | 75.9 | n.a. | n.a. |
| 1989 | 29.6 | 18.2 | 9.1 | 70.4 | 13.0 | 40.3 |
| 1990 | 42.9 | 15.1 | 13.5 | 57.1 | 7.3 | 41.0 |
| 1990-91 | 38.9 | 14.9 | 20.9 | 61.1 | 6.8 | 32.8 |
| 1991-92 | 50.5 | N.A. | 27.9 | 49.5 | N.A. | 27.4 |

❑ The World Bank comprises of the IBRD ( International Bank for Reconstruction & Development) and the IDA ( International Development Agency), which is the soft-lending affiliate of the World Bank.

❑ Ever since the US drastically cut down aid to India in the wake of Indo-Pakistan war giving rise to the emergence of Bangladesh, the World Bank has been a major source of external assistance to India. With the shrinking of IDA resources the aid pattern for India has changed requiring higher borrowing from the IBRD. The respective shares of these have almost reversed during the eighties.

## 20.4  Commercial Borrowing from Abroad : Approved and Utilised : 1980-81 to 1991-92.

*(Rs crores)*

| Year | Public Sector | Financial institutions | Procurement of ships | Private Sector | Total approvals | Utilisation |
|---|---|---|---|---|---|---|
| 1980-81 | 810 (78.0) | – – | 90 (8.7) | 138 (13.3) | 1,038 (100.0) | |
| 1981-82 | 391 (32.5) | 151 (12.5) | 270 (22.4) | 392 (32.6) | 1,204 (100.0) | |
| 1982-83 | 1,544 (76.2) | 133 (6.6) | 109 (5.4) | 240 (11.8) | 2,026 (100.0) | |
| 1983-84 | 459 (42.3) | 120 (11.1) | 344 (31.7) | 162 (14.9) | 1,085 (100.0) | |
| 1984-85 | 1,085 (57.0) | 159 (8.3) | 282 (14.8) | 379 (19.9) | 1,905 (100.0) | 1,472 |
| 1985-86 | 951 (55.9) | 380 (22.3) | 74 (4.4) | 295 (17.4) | 1,700 (100.0) | 1,827 |
| 1986-87 | 784 (56.2) | 250 (17.9) | 65 (4.7) | 297 (21.2) | 1,396 (100.0) | 3,115 |
| 1987-88 | 1,598 (60.2) | 809 (30.5) | 32 (12.1) | 215 (8.1) | 2,654 (100.0) | 1,946 |
| 1988-89 | 2,413 (55.9) | 1,353 (31.4) | 198 (4.6) | 350 (8.1) | 4,314 (100.0) | 4,069 |
| 1989-90 | 3,504 (63.9) | 1,332 (24.3) | 191 (3.5) | 452 (8.3) | 5,479 (100.0) | 4,196 |
| 1990-91 | 1,689 | 1,149 | N.A. | 576 | 3,414 | 3,050 |
| 1991-92 | 1,577 | 2,132 | 56 | 661 | 4,427 | N.A. |

❑ Although the share of public sector in total external commercial borrowings from high of over 75% in 1980-81 and 1982-83, it still claims over 55% shares. Financial institutions account for one-fourth to one third share whereas the private sector, gets a little over 8% from high of around 20% in mid-eighties.

❑ With the liberalisation of foreign investment regulations the private sector is likely to claim larger shares in the coming years.

## 20.5 External Debt Outstanding and Debt Servicing : 1984-85 to 1990-91

*(Rs crores)*

| Year | Debt outstanding | Amortisation | Interest payment | Total debt servicing |
|---|---|---|---|---|
| | | External Assistance | | |
| | | a) On Govt. Account | | |
| 1984-85 | 24,004 | 555 | 470 | 1,025 |
| 1985-86 | 26,638 | 698 | 544 | 4,242 |
| 1986-87 | 32,312 | 1,029 | 772 | 1,801 |
| 1987-88 | 36,578 | 1,249 | 981 | 2,230 |
| 1988-89 | 46,838 | 1,554 | 1,244 | 2,798 |
| 1989-90 | 54,100 | 1,881 | 1,618 | 3,499 |
| 1990-91 | 66,314 | 2,234 | 1,863 | 4,097 |
| | | b) On Non-Govt. Account | | |
| 1984-85 | 758 | 93 | 59 | 152 |
| 1985-86 | 741 | 78 | 47 | 125 |
| 1986-87 | 889 | 147 | 81 | 228 |
| 1987-88 | 848 | 332 | 62 | 394 |
| 1988-89 | 1,164 | 92 | 56 | 148 |
| 1989-90 | 1,608 | 106 | 81 | 187 |
| 1990-91 | 2,273 | 95 | 90 | 185 |
| | | Total (a + b) | | |
| 1984-85 | 24,762 | 648 | 529 | 1,177 |
| 1985-86 | 27,379 | 776 | 591 | 1,367 |
| 1986-87 | 33,201 | 1,176 | 853 | 2,029 |
| 1987-88 | 37,426 | 1,581 | 1,043 | 2,624 |
| 1988-89 | 48,002 | 1,646 | 1,300 | 2946 |
| 1989-90 | 55,708 | 1,987 | 1,699 | 3,686 |
| 1990-91 | 68,587 | 2,329 | 1,953 | 4,282 |

*contd...*

| Year | Debt outstanding | Amortisation | Interest payment | Total debt servicing |
|------|-----------------|--------------|------------------|---------------------|
| c) External Commercial Borrowing | | | | |
| 1984-85 | 6,413 | 392 | 290 | 682 |
| 1985-86 | 7,647 | 565 | 610 | 1,175 |
| 1986-87 | 10,321 | 796 | 769 | 1,565 |
| 1987-88 | 12,876 | 871 | 865 | 1,736 |
| 1988-89 | 18,034 | 1,103 | 1,121 | 2,224 |
| 1989-90 | 22,065 | 1455 | 1,586 | 3,041 |
| 1990-91 | 26,706 | 2,137 | 1,869 | 4,006 |
| d) IMF Liabilities | | | | |
| 1984-85 | 4,550 | 156 | 509 | 665 |
| 1985-86 | 5,285 | 256 | 391 | 647 |
| 1986-87 | 5,547 | 666 | 356 | 1,022 |
| 1987-88 | 4,732 | 1,206 | 346 | 1,552 |
| 1988-89 | 3,696 | 1,549 | 288 | 1,837 |
| 1989-90 | 2,572 | 1,456 | 281 | 1,737 |
| 1990-91 | 5,132 | 1,165 | 240 | 1,405 |
| Total (a + b + c + d) | | | | |
| 1984-85 | 35,725 | 1,195 | 1,328 | 2,523 |
| 1985-86 | 40,311 | 1,597 | 1,592 | 3,189 |
| 1986-87 | 49,069 | 2,638 | 1,978 | 4,616 |
| 1987-88 | 55,034 | 3,658 | 2,254 | 5,912 |
| 1988-89 | 69,732 | 4,298 | 2,709 | 7,007 |
| 1989-90 | 80,345 | 4,898 | 3,566 | 8,464 |
| 1990-91 | 100,425 | 5,631 | 4,062 | 9,693 |

*Note : The figures relate to medium and long-term debt*

❑ Our medium and long term external debt outstanding at Rs.1,00,425 crores at the end of March 1991 constituted almost 19% of the GDP for 1990-91. If the total NRI deposits held at Rs.20,446 crores are included than the corresponding external debt of Rs.1,20,871 crores was 22.8% of the GDP. Further, adding short term debt of maturity upto one year estimated at Rs.9,500 crores, our aggregate external outstanding debt was about Rs.130371 crores at the end of March 1991, forming 24.6% of the GDP.

❑ The short term debt generally in the nature of suppliers' credit to finance normal imports, as well as bankers' acceptance facility largely for the public sector canalising agencies, formed 7.3% of our aggregate external debt.

## 20.6   External Debt - to - Service Ratios  1984-85 to 1990-91

*(per cent)*

| Year | Total external debt to gross exchange earnings | Total external debt to gross national product | Debt Service ratio (a) | Total interest payments to gross exchange earning | Exchange reserves to total debt servicing | Exchange reserves to total extenal debt |
|------|------|------|------|------|------|------|
| 1984-85 | 177 | 15.5 | 13.6 | 6.6 | 270 | 18.5 |
| 1985-86 | 204 | 15.2 | 17.5 | 8.1 | 234 | 16.6 |
| 1986-87 | 224 | 16.7 | 21.8 | 9.1 | 168 | 15.8 |
| 1987-88 | 213 | 16.6 | 24.0 | 8.8 | 124 | 13.3 |
| 1988-89 | 220 | 17.7 | 25.0 | 8.6 | 95 | 9.5 |
| 1989-90 | 207 | 18.2 | 21.0 | 9.2 | 69 | 7.2 |
| 1990-91 | 229 | 19.4 | 22.0 | 9.3 | 46 | 4.4 |

*Notes : All figures are provisional and subject to revisions, because of the time-lags in compilation and operating of external accounts. Statistics by the RBI.*

❑ The most disturbing aspect of our external accounts is the rapid rise in debt-service ratio during the eighties. Conventionally, this ratio is defined as percentage of debt-service payments (principal and interest), excluding interest on non-resident deposits, to exports earnings of goods and invisible earnings net of official transfer receipts.

❑ Our debt-service ratio crossed the prudent limit of 20% in 1986-87 and peaked to 25% in 1988-89. This was mainly on account of increased repayments and interest against past borrowings including the IMF. The subsequent decline in the ratio likewise reflects the substantial rise in export earnings coupled with the termination of liabilities towards the IMF on EFF loan.

❑ According to the latest RBI reports, the annual average debt service ratio during the Seventh Plan period worked out to 20.3% (22% according to table above) which was substantially higher than the average of 17.6% assumed in the Plan document.

❑ In the context of this ratio it may be noted that our surplus on current account due to export receipts and invisibles are often not adequate to meet the service obligations, and further debts are incurred to avert default.